# ROUTLEDGE LIBRARY EDITIONS: SAUDI ARABIA

Volume 7

# WESTERN STRATEGIC INTERESTS IN SAUDI ARABIA

# WESTERN STRATEGIC INTERESTS IN SAUDI ARABIA

ANTHONY H. CORDESMAN

LONDON AND NEW YORK

First published in 1987

This edition first published in 2015
by Routledge
2 Park Square, Milton Park, Abingdon, Oxon, OX14 4RN

and by Routledge
711 Third Avenue, New York, NY 10017

*Routledge is an imprint of the Taylor & Francis Group, an informa business*

© 1987 Anthony H. Cordesman

All rights reserved. No part of this book may be reprinted or reproduced or utilised in any form or by any electronic, mechanical, or other means, now known or hereafter invented, including photocopying and recording, or in any information storage or retrieval system, without permission in writing from the publishers.

*Trademark notice*: Product or corporate names may be trademarks or registered trademarks, and are used only for identification and explanation without intent to infringe.

*British Library Cataloguing in Publication Data*
A catalogue record for this book is available from the British Library

ISBN: 978-1-138-82515-4 (Set)
ISBN: 978-1-138-84639-5 (Volume 7)
Pb ISBN: 978-1-138-84676-0 (Volume 7)

**Publisher's Note**
The publisher has gone to great lengths to ensure the quality of this reprint but points out that some imperfections in the original copies may be apparent.

**Disclaimer**
The publisher has made every effort to trace copyright holders and would welcome correspondence from those they have been unable to trace.

# WESTERN STRATEGIC INTERESTS IN SAUDI ARABIA

ANTHONY H. CORDESMAN

**CROOM HELM**
London • Sydney • Wolfeboro, New Hampshire

© 1987 Anthony H. Cordesman
Croom Helm Ltd, Provident House, Burrell Row,
Beckenham, Kent, BR3 1AT

Croom Helm Australia, 44-50 Waterloo Road,
North Ryde, 2113, New South Wales

British Library Cataloguing in Publication Data

Cordesman, Anthony H.
    Western strategic interests in Saudi Arabia.
    1. World politics — 1985-1995  2. Saudi
    Arabia — Foreign relations
    I. Title
    327'.09171'3    DS227

ISBN 0-7099-4823-9

Croom Helm, 27 South Main Street,
Wolfeboro, New Hampshire 03894-2069, USA

Library of Congress Cataloging in Publication Data
applied for:

---

## To Bridget and Francis

---

Printed and bound in Great Britain by
Biddles Ltd, Guildford and King's Lynn

CONTENTS

List of Tables

I. OVERVIEW

    The Pivotal Role of Saudi Arabia ................................13
    The West and Problem of U.S. Domestic Politics ..............15
    The Saudi Arms Requests of 1985 and 1986 ....................15
    The Cost of "Taking Sides" ........................................17
    The Importance of Close Strategic Relations ....................19
    The Cost of "Taking Sides" to Israel ...........................20
    Impact on Western Power Projection
    Capabilities in the Gulf .............................................21
    Preserving the Proper Balance in Western
        Strategic Relations ..............................................23

II. WESTERN STRATEGIC INTERESTS IN SAUDI ARABIA

    The Historical Background ........................................25
    The Changing Forces Shaping Saudi
        Relations With the West .......................................27
    The Impact of Saudi Oil ............................................29
    The Impact of Western and Saudi Trade Relations .............37
    The Impact of Saudi Aid and Capital ............................39
    The Role of Saudi Arabia in the Gulf Cooperation
        Council ............................................................40
    The Broader Role of Saudi Arabia in Regional Affairs .........41
    The Arab-Israeli Peace Issue ......................................42

III. SAUDI ARABIA AND WESTERN POWER PROJECTION CAPABILITIES

Turkey ................................................................. 50
France ................................................................. 51
United Kingdom ................................................... 56
United States ...................................................... 61
The Impact of Saudi Bases .................................. 66

IV. REGIONAL THREATS AND THE MILITARY BUILD-UP IN THE GULF

Broad Patterns in the Regional Arms Race ...................... 74
The Impact of Technology Transfer ............................... 85
    The Problem of Conventional Proliferation ................. 85
    The Impact of New Soviet Systems ........................... 87
The Soviet Military Threat ........................................... 91
Soviet Arms Sales and Advisory Efforts ......................... 95
The Northern Gulf Threat ............................................ 98
The Red Sea Threat ................................................... 103
    The YAR and PDRY ................................................ 103
    Ethiopia ................................................................. 107
    The Sudan .............................................................. 108
    The Military Trends in the Red Sea Area ..................... 108
Instability in Saudi Arabia's Western Border Area ............ 109
    Egypt and Jordan ................................................... 109
    Syria ...................................................................... 110
    Libya and Radical Threats ........................................ 112
The Vulnerability of the Gulf Cooperation States ............. 112
    Bahrain .................................................................. 114
    Kuwait ................................................................... 115
    Oman ..................................................................... 117
    Qatar ..................................................................... 119
    The United Arab Emirates ....................................... 120
    The Impact of Cumulative Instability Within the GCC .... 121
The 360° Threat ....................................................... 122

V. THE DEVELOPMENT OF SAUDI FORCES

Saudi Defense Expenditures ....................................... 126
Saudi Military Manpower ............................................ 132
The Impact of Foreign Manpower ................................. 133
Military Industry and Offsets ....................................... 141

Near Term Force Trends ........................................142
The Development of Saudi Ground Forces and
Air Defense Corps ...............................................147
    The Problems of Equipment Diversification ...............149
    The M-1 Tank Issue ..........................................150
    Other Modernization Issues ..................................152
The Impact of the Saudi National Guard .......................153
The Saudi Navy ....................................................157
The Saudi Air Force ..............................................161

## VI. THE PIVOTAL ROLE OF THE SAUDI AIR FORCE

Saudi Arabia's Need For Air Defense .........................169
The Impact of Saudi Vulnerability on Saudi
    Military Modernization ......................................177
The Need for the Air Defense Enhancement
    Package ........................................................179
    Selecting the E-3A ...........................................184
    The Issue of Technology Transfer ..........................185
    The Impact of the AIM-9L Missile .........................187
    Providing Enhanced Range and Refueling Capability .....187
The Need for a Full $C^3I$/BM System: The Genesis
    of "Peace Shield" .............................................188
The Advantages to the West ....................................191
Setting the Stage for the Arms Sale
    Crisis of 1985-1986 .........................................193

## VII. THE SAUDI ARMS SALE CRISIS OF 1985-1986

The Original Saudi Arms Request: The "F-15 Package" .....196
The Strategic Rationale for the New F-15 Package ..........199
The Major Technical Issues .....................................200
    The Upgrading of Saudi Arabia's
        Existing 60 F-15C/Ds.....................................200
    The Purchase of 40 More F-15C/D MSIP ..................202
    The Purchase of Additional AIM-9L/P Missiles ...........202
    The Request for 800 Stinger Missiles .......................203
    The Sale of 12 UH-60 Blackhawk Helicopters ............204
    The Sale of 100 Harpoon Air-to-Ship Missiles ............204
The Missing Link: Dual Capability for the Saudi F-15 .......205
Impact on Western Contingency Capabilities and Needs .....207
Why the U.S. Denied the Sale ..................................210
The Saudi Decision to Buy From Britain ......................214
U.S. Efforts to Maintain Strategic Relations ..................217

The Strategic Impact of the Arms Sale
    Crisis of 1985-1986 ............................................... 220
    Impact on Britain .................................................. 220
    Impact on Saudi Arabia ....................................... 220
    Impact on the U.S. ............................................... 225
    Impact on Israel .................................................... 226
Broader Impact on Western Strategic
    Relations with the Gulf ......................................... 227
Lessons of the Arms Sale Crisis .................................. 229

## VIII. KEY ISSUES AFFECTING WESTERN AND SAUDI RELATIONS

The Problem of Saudi Stability ................................... 234
    The "Stability" of "Instability" ................................. 234
    External Forces for Internal Stability ....................... 238
    The Key Variables ................................................. 239
Informal Relations Versus In-Country Bases ................. 239
The Impact of Saudi Arms Needs on Israel's Security ....... 240
    Limitations on the Saudi Threat to Israel ................. 240
The Combined Impact of Current and Near
    Term U.S. Arms Sales ........................................... 247
    The Impact of the E-3A and Peace Shield ................ 247
    Upgrading Saudi Arabia's Existing 60 F-15C/Ds ......... 251
The Tornado Purchase and Future
    Saudi Air Modernization ....................................... 252
Minimizing The Risk to Israel of an
    Advanced Saudi Air Force .................................... 255
Improvements to the Saudi Army and National Guard ....... 258
Planning for the Absence of Peace ............................... 259

## IX. THE FUTURE OF WESTERN AND SAUDI STRATEGIC RELATIONS

Creating a Regional Strategic Partnership ..................... 261
    Better Cooperation in Arms Sales .......................... 262
    Dependence on U.S. Power Projection Capabilities ...... 263
    A Better Basis for Western Arms Transfers ............... 263
Balance Instead of Taking Sides ................................. 265
Maintaining the Search for Peace ................................ 265

BIBLIOGRAPHY ...................................................... 267

INDEX ................................................................... 291

TABLES

## Tables

| | | |
|---|---|---|
| 2.1 | OPEC Revenues and Oil Exports: 1973-1986 | 30 |
| 2.2 | Recent Patterns in Western Dependence on Gulf Oil | 32 |
| 2.3 | World Oil Reserves | 35 |
| 2.4 | The Impact of Saudi Arabia on GCC Defense Efforts in 1985/1986 | 41 |
| 3.1 | French Contingency Capabilities in the Middle East: 1985-1986 | 55 |
| 3.2 | British Contingency Capabilities in the Middle East: 1985-1986 | 60 |
| 3.3 | Strength of Typical U.S. Navy and Marine Air Wings | 62 |
| 3.4 | USCENTCOM Forces in FY 1986 | 65 |
| 3.5 | U.S. Military Contingency Facilities in the Near East | 68 |
| 4.1 | Major Weapons in Middle Eastern Forces Directly or Indirectly Affecting Saudi Arabia | 76 |
| 4.2 | Near Term Annual Trends in Arms Imports Impacting on the Gulf and Near East | 77 |
| 4.3 | Middle Eastern Arms Imports by Importing Country: 1979-83 | 80 |
| 4.4 | Trends in Western Market Share of Arms Sales to the Middle East--New Agreements | 84 |
| 4.5 | Key Near Term Trends in the Technology of Arms Sales to the Middle East During 1985-1995 | 86 |

| | | |
|---|---|---|
| 4.6 | New Soviet Systems Affecting the Gulf and Red Sea Threat. | 88 |
| 4.7 | The Soviet Threat to Western Oil | 92 |
| 4.8 | Major Arms Sales to the Near East and South Asia by Major Supplier. | 96 |
| 4.9 | Soviet Bloc Military Advisors and "Technicians" in the Middle East, The Gulf, and Africa. | 98 |
| 4.10 | The Trends in Iranian and Iraqi Military Forces: 1980-1985. | 100 |
| 4.11 | Comparative Military Effort of Red Sea and Key States Affecting Red Sea Security. | 109 |
| 4.12 | The Military Build-up to the West of Saudi Arabia | 111 |
| 5.1 | Saudi Military Imports and Spending | 127 |
| 5.2 | Recent Sources of Saudi Arms Imports 1979-1983 | 128 |
| 5.3 | Saudi Arabia's Main Source of Western Military Support: U.S. Military Assistance and Foreign Military Sales. | 130 |
| 5.4 | U.S. Personnel Supporting FMS Purchases in Saudi Arabia. | 135 |
| 5.5 | Trends in the Modernization of Saudi Forces: 1985-1995. | 143 |
| 5.6 | The Current Structure of the Saudi Army | 148 |
| 5.7 | The Current Structure of the Saudi National Guard | 155 |
| 5.8 | The Current Structure of the Saudi Navy | 158 |
| 5.9 | The Current Structure of the Saudi Air Force | 163 |
| 6.1 | The Saudi Air Defense Enhancement Package | 180 |
| 6.2 | The Military Tasks Necessary for Effective Saudi Air Defense. | 182 |
| 6.3 | The Advantages to the U.S. of the Saudi Air Defense Enhancement Package of 1982. | 191 |
| 7.1 | The Saudi Arms Request of 1985 | 198 |
| 7.2 | Multi-Stage Improvement Program (MSIP) for the Saudi F-15C/Ds. | 200 |
| 7.3 | Features of the F-15E Which Would *Not* have been on the Saudi F-15C/D MSIP. | 207 |
| 7.4 | Comparison of U.S. and Soviet Forces Available for A Gulf Contingency: 1986-1987. | 209 |
| 7.5 | Comparative Performance Characteristics of Key Fighter Aircraft Affecting the Saudi Air Force Modernization Program. | 223 |

| | | |
|---|---|---|
| 7.6 | The Lack of Standardization in the Air Forces of the GCC States | 228 |
| 8.1 | Comparative Middle Eastern Electronic Orders of Battle | 246 |
| 8.2 | The Mission Capabilities of the Saudi E-3A and Peace Shield | 249 |
| 8.3 | Comparative Air to Ground Performance of Key Western Fighter Types | 255 |
| 8.4 | Key Restricted U.S. Technologies Affecting the Saudi-Israeli Balance | 257 |

I. OVERVIEW

Ever since the Arab oil embargo of 1974, the West has sought to find alternatives to its dependence on imported oil. At the same time, the shock of that oil crisis has triggered reported Western efforts to secure its access to Gulf oil. These efforts were greatly accelerated in 1979 and 1980 by the fall of the Shah of Iran, the Soviet invasion of Afghanistan, and the beginning of the Iran-Iraq War, but they at best have had mixed success.

While the West has made progress in conservation and in reducing its need for energy as a percentage of GNP, it has fallen far short of its goals in finding new sources of energy. Key energy sources like coal and nuclear power have proved to present far more problems than the West estimated when it began its search for alternative fuels. Synthetic fuels, and energy sources like wind and geothermal energy have proved technically difficult and too costly for commercial scale production. While a major global recession and financial crisis in the Third World have created a temporary "oil glut", the West's long term dependence on oil imports is now projected to be even worse than any experts projected in the early 1970s.

The West has experienced similar problems in creating an effective capability to secure its oil imports. Western power projection forces and capabilities have declined steadily for the last two decades. Western Europe now has almost no capability to intervene in the Gulf and France is the only European nation that could deploy even one light attack carrier to the region.

U.S. efforts to build-up Iran's military capabilities as a pillar of regional security collapsed completely with the Shah's fall and the Iranian hostage crisis. The U.S. has since made major improvements in its regional power projection capabilities, but its U.S. Central Command (USCENTCOM) forces have limited land force strength, major shortfalls in strategic lift, and are totally dependent on friendly forward bases for effective military action.

Overview

This has left the West dependent on the political, military, and economic stability of the the Gulf. Roughly half the world's proven oil reserves are located in the Gulf region, and in the territory of eight nations: Iran, Iraq, Kuwait, Saudi Arabia, Bahrain, Qatar, the United Arab Emirates, and Oman. In spite of a decade of intense exploration in other areas, the Gulf is also the region with the highest potential for major new discoveries and the only area in the world where the discovery of new reserves is outpacing oil production.

This virtually forces the west to try to build sound strategic relations with the Gulf states. The west also has limited time to do so. The present "oil glut" will end by the early to mid-1990s. The West will then face growing competition from the Soviet bloc, and see the exports of Asian and African oil exporting nations drop steadily as their oil reserves are depleted. The current pause in the strategic competition for oil resources is only a lull in a steadily gathering storm.

THE PIVOTAL ROLE OF SAUDI ARABIA

The West, however, has few options for creating such strategic relations. Iran is in the midst of a hostile religious revolution and a war with Iraq whose outcome is exceedingly uncertain. No one can predict whether Iran will tilt back towards the West, tilt toward the USSR, or be a chronic source of regional instability. The only thing that seems certain is that Iran will not be a support to Western security, and that it may well be a serious threat.

Iraq has become steadily more moderate since the mid-1970s. It is, however, engaged in a brutal and uncertain war with Iran. It is unclear that Iraq's present regime will survive, or that Iraq will preserve its moderate course once it has to come to grips with the cost of the Iran-Iraq War and with the problem of financing its war debts and economic recovery. While it now seems most likely that Iraq will remain relatively moderate, and concentrate on economic development and its trade ties with the West, the West can scarcely count on such a future. Further, there are no serious prospects for any direct military or strategic alliance between Iraq and the West that would give the West significant contingency capabilities in the Gulf area.

This leaves the West dependent on the six southern Gulf countries: Saudi Arabia, Bahrain, Qatar, the United Arab Emirates, and Oman. All are moderate, all have shown a good ability to cope with the past tensions and problems in the region, and all have strong trade ties with the West. Further, all six states are united in the Gulf Cooperation Council (GCC), which is making slow but steady process towards creating a collective regional security structure.

The six Southern Gulf states, however, are not by any means equal. Five of the states are very small, and some are deeply divided. Only Saudi

Overview

Arabia has the combination of population, wealth, stability, and geography necessary to build-up a reasonable national deterrent, and to give the Gulf Cooperation Council real meaning.

Sheer geography also makes Saudi Arabia an essential security partner in any Western effort to create stable security relations with the West. Its borders and coastline dominate the Southern Gulf, Arabian Peninsula, and the northern coast of the Red Sea. While the West has contingency bases in states like Egypt, Oman, and Turkey that can be of great value, the West must have access to Saudi Arabia to deal with any serious Iranian or Soviet threat to the region.

In theory, it should be relatively easy for the West to create a sound strategic relationship with Saudi Arabia. Saudi Arabia and the West have clear and direct common interests. While they have different cultures and political systems, they share common strategic interests in the Gulf area and throughout the Near East. While they differ in terms of their trade and oil prices, they share a common commitment to private enterprise and to maintaining a stable balance of world trade.

This common interest has been demonstrated by Saudi Arabia's words and actions. Saudi Arabia often differs with given Western states in terms of specific policy issues and tactics, but these differences are rarely significant enough to prevent close cooperation. Even the differences over the Arab-Israeli peace issue are largely ones of timing and tactics. While Saudi Arabia has differed with the U.S. over the specific approach that should be taken to achieving an Arab-Israeli peace settlement, so have many of America's NATO allies. For the last decade, Saudi Arabia has consistently supported an Arab effort to reach peace settlement with Israel based on Palestinian rights and the return of the occupied territories.

Saudi Arabia has backed the West in key policy thrusts like its peace keeping effort in Lebanon in 1982. Saudi Arabia has also joined the West in its support of the Afghan freedom fighters, in efforts to stabilize world oil supplies and prices, and in efforts to check the expansion of radical and Soviet influence in the Near East and Southwest Asia.

If there is any major difference between Saudi Arabia and the West, it has been in Saudi Arabia's support of Syria, and in Saudi funding of Syria's military build-up. Such Saudi support of Syria has, however, been more the result of Saudi weakness, and need for outside military support, than the result of any political agreement with Syria's political aims and military ambitions. The Saudis have provided such aid as the price of eliminating a Syrian threat to Saudi Arabia's military and political security. It is important to note that Saudi Arabia has been Jordan's chief source of financial support within the Arab world in spite of the fact that Jordan has directly opposed Syrian efforts to block an Arab-Israeli peace agreement.

It is also notable that Saudi Arabia's strategic cooperation with the West has expanded steadily since the Shah's fall and the beginning of the Iran-Iraq

Overview

War. Saudi Arabia has openly turned to the West for arms and military advice and support, and has quietly turned to the West for security in the event of a major military threat or attack by Iran or South Yemen.

## THE WEST AND PROBLEM OF U.S. DOMESTIC POLITICS

Saudi and Western strategic relations are constantly threatened, however, by factors which have little to do with Western strategic interests, and which involve a clear split between the U.S. and Europe. The pressures of U.S. domestic politics threaten to divide Saudi Arabia from the West and to block any effective relationship between the Gulf states and the one Western state with the power projection forces to provide significant "over-the-horizon" reinforcements.

The U.S. has increasingly failed to balance its security ties to Israel with its ties to Saudi Arabia. Largely artificial fears regarding Israel's security have led to bitter and divisive Congressional and media debates over every major U.S. arms sale to Saudi Arabia. While each debate has touched upon the strategic and technical merits of the particular sale in question, the main focus of these debates has been the very different issue of the threat that U.S. sales to Saudi Arabia could pose to Israel, and the fear that close U.S. military relations with Saudi Arabia may somehow undermine U.S. support of Israel.

Saudi Arabia has responded by turning to other Western nations like France and Britain. The most dramatic of these shifts was the Kingdom's decision in late 1985 to turn to Britain for the sale of 72 Tornado aircraft, Hawk trainers, and the other equipment necessary to modernize its air force. This decision may mark a pivotal shift in Saudi relations with the West. Saudi Arabia had already turned to France and other states for much of the equipment and advice necessary to modernize its army and navy. Although Saudi Arabia's defense minister, Prince Sultan, has stated Saudi Arabia still wishes to purchase additional F-15s from the U.S., the fact remains that the Kingdom's decision to turn to Britain for its new combat aircraft threatens to sever Saudi Arabia's main remaining tie to the U.S.

## THE SAUDI ARMS REQUESTS OF 1985 AND 1986

In fact these debates have now reached the point where they have undermined U.S. and Saudi relations to the point where they threaten Western security. They have blocked U.S. capability to help Saudi Arabia modernize its military forces, and have made it steadily more difficult for the West to cooperate with the Southern Gulf states and other moderate Arab countries.

The key step in this crisis has been the recent debate in the U.S. over Saudi Arabia's request for additional U.S. fighters and the further modernization of its Air Force. In late 1984, Saudi Arabia requested U.S. help in modernizing its existing inventory of 60 F-15C/Ds to reflect the

Overview

changes being made in U.S. Air Force F-15C/D aircraft. It also requested the sale of 980 more AIM-9L and 630 more AIM-9P4 air-to-air missiles, the sale of the remaining 800 Stinger surface-to-air missiles which were part of a 1983 request for 1,200, and the sale of 100 Harpoon air-to-ship missiles to give the Saudi Air Force a defense capability against threat such as that from the Iranian Navy and the growing naval forces of radical Red Sea states. Saudi Arabia also sought the sale of 40 additional improved F-15C/D aircraft, plus eight attrition reserves to be kept in the U.S., and of 12 Blackhawk UH-60 unarmed helicopters to provide its army with a limited heliborne lift capability.

These sales were largely defensive in character, but they were also intended to lay the ground work for giving Saudi Arabia's F-15s full capability in the attack mission in addition to their primary air defense role. The ability to fly such attack missions is the only way Saudi Arabia can compensate for the acute weaknesses of its Army. The Saudi Army will not be able to bring its current seven brigades to full strength before the early 1990s, and must disperse its forces along the borders of a country roughly the size of the European Central Region or the U.S. east of the Mississippi. Saudi Arabia must also be prepared to aid its smaller fellow members of the Gulf Cooperation Council.

In fact, air power is the only way Saudi Arabia can build up its deterrent and defense capability in the face of the massive ground forces of Iran and Iraq, and the fact that the combined ground forces of the Yemens are already stronger than the entire Saudi Army. It is the only way in which the GCC can hope to offset its weaknesses, preserve its independence of action, and develop a capability to deal with low and medium level threats.

These new Saudi arms requests, however, provoked the same kind of "taking sides" within the U.S. that affected previous debates over Saudi purchase of U.S. M-60 tanks, the F-15C/D, the E-3A airborne warning and air control system (AWACS), and the AIM-9L. Although the Reagan Administration initially felt it could defend such sales on the grounds they were clearly intended to defend the Gulf and the West's key source of future oil imports, the requests triggered a bitter new domestic debate in which the Congress was put in the position of having to vote over whether the U.S. should maintain strategic ties to Israel or Saudi Arabia, should increase the Saudi "threat" to Israel, and over the precise nature of the Saudi role in helping to reach a peace settlement in the Middle East.

In early 1985, at virtually the same time as President Reagan was promising King Fahd he would support the Saudi request, the sale was already polarizing opinion in the U.S. Congress around issues which had nothing to do with the extent to which selling Saudi Arabia the arms it was requesting would serve Western strategic interests. Pro-Israel lobbying groups made blocking the Saudi sale one of their key political objectives for 1985, and forced every member of the Congress to "take sides" between

Overview

U.S. relations with Saudi Arabia and domestic political support from those who backed Israel.

## THE COST OF "TAKING SIDES"

This "taking sides" ignored the true nature of the strategic relationship between Saudi Arabia and the United States. More importantly, it ignored the true nature of Western strategic interests in the Near East and Southwest Asia. It made an arms sale important to the security of Western states into a domestic political issue that threatened the campaign financing and political base of any Congressman who supported the sale. It also eventually succeeded in forcing the Reagan Administration to tell Saudi Arabia that the Administration had no chance of obtaining Congressional support for the sale of additional F-15s or any other major new equipment and munitions. By mid-1985, President Reagan was forced to write a letter to King Fahd to this effect, and Saudi Arabia turned to Europe for its aircraft.

Saudi Arabia had already planned for this contingency. It had quietly been negotiating possible fighter purchases with both Britain and France, and Britain offered the most advanced aircraft and technology. By September, 1985, Saudi Arabia had bought 132 military aircraft from Britain. These included a total of 72 Panavia Tornados, consisting of 48 IDS attack variants and 24 Tornado F.3 air defense variants. They included 30 British Aerospace Hawk trainers to replace the existing British BAC-167 Strikemasters used in this role, and 30 Swiss Pilatus PC-9 turboprop trainers which British Aerospace was to reconfigure to meet Saudi requirements. The sale also included all the air munitions "normally" carried on the Tornado, including Skyflash air to air missiles, Dynamics Alarm anti-radiation missiles, Sea Eagle anti-ship missiles, and Hunting JP233 airfield attack systems.

The total value of the new arms package was over five million pounds, with at least 35% of the cost to be offset through European investment in Saudi Arabia. The sale also included British training and operational support services that would replace similar U.S. services.

The sale represented a radical shift in technology transfer from Saudi Air Force dependence on the U.S. to a British-led European effort, with 40% of the Tornado being made in the UK, 40% in the Federal Republic of Germany, and 20% in Italy. The timing of the sale also ensured that the Saudi shift to European aircraft would come quickly. The initial 20 IDS versions of the Tornado were delivered in 1986, and all 48 were scheduled to be delivered by 1988. The first delivery of the Tornado F.3 was not scheduled until 1988, but delivery was scheduled to be complete within sixteen months.

This weakening of the ties between the U.S. and Saudi Arabia still continues. It became clear during the course of the rest of 1985 and 1986 that Reagan Administration could not obtain solid political support for any

Overview

major new arms sale to Saudi Arabia, including the modernization of Saudi Arabia's existing 60 F-15C/Ds. The Administration was forced to let a similar major arms sale to Jordan die without full Congressional debate or action.

The best the Reagan Administration could do was to send forward a token arms package of missile systems. This new arms package included 995 AIM-9L air-to-air missiles, 671 AIM-9P4 air-to-air missiles, 100 Harpoon air-to-sea missiles, and 200 Stinger man-portable surface-to-air missiles, and its total value was $354 million. The Reagan Administration defended the package on the basis that Saudi Arabia already had all these weapons systems in inventory, and had demonstrated its ability to provide security from espionage and terrorists. It also claimed that the Iranian victory in Faw in early 1986 had led Saudi Arabia to urgently request additional missiles to improve its defenses against Iran.

Yet, the Administration still met so much Congressional resistance in an election year that it was forced to drop the Stinger man-portable surface-to-air missile from the package in spite of the fact the Saudis already had the Stinger and had proved they could preserve its security. The Reagan Administration also had to adopt a strategy based on a very low profile lobbying effort for the sale, and a tacit bargain with pro-Israeli lobbying groups to support a high level of aid for Israel and strengthen U.S. and Israeli strategic relations. Even then the Administration was constantly surprised by Congressional opponents of the sale.

The Administration was also forced to recognize that it could not get the support of the House of Representatives, and that the President could not get a majority of the Senate. Under U.S. law, his only way of making the sale was to accept the fact the Senate would pass a resolution against the sale, but use his influence to prevent the Senate from overriding a Presidential veto of the Senate bill. This meant the President would only need the support of one-third of the Senate.

When the first test vote came in May, 1986, four-fifths of the Senate voted for a bill opposing the sale. After weeks of political arm twisting, President Reagan finally won enough support to sustain his veto in June, 1986. He only won by a single vote, however, and this victory was so minor and so uncertain that it did almost as much to undermine U.S. and Saudi relations as to strengthen them.

The only positive event in two years of U.S. and Saudi strategic relations was that pro-Israel lobbyists chose to give priority to increased U.S. aid to Israel over yet another battle over the AWACS. As a result, the President was able to transfer the first of the five E-3A AWACS that Saudi Arabia had bought three years earlier with a simple letter of certification in June, 1986. The U.S. had clearly reached the point where it was unable to maintain full scale strategic relations with Saudi Arabia, and with any other moderate Arab state in the region other than Egypt.

Overview

## THE IMPORTANCE OF CLOSE STRATEGIC RELATIONS

Unfortunately for the West, these problems cannot be solved simply by dividing Western responsibility for the Middle East. Saudi Arabia and the Gulf are too pivotal to Western strategic interests, and the West cannot afford a strategy where Europe maintains close relations with friendly Arab states and the U.S. serves as the military sponsor and protector of Israel.

The basic problem is that Europe can meet the Arab world's needs for military equipment and advice, but it cannot provide the power projection forces needed to defend the Gulf. Only the U.S. can now deploy the sea, air, and land power necessary to check a major radical threat to a key Arab state and to ensure that the USSR cannot put military or political pressure on the region.

The U.S. cannot take sides against Saudi Arabia without critically weakening the West's overall capability to secure its supplies of imported energy. Such "taking sides" is also unnecessary. As this study shows, the U.S. and Europe can meet Saudi Arabia's military needs, and secure Western strategic interests in the Gulf and Red Sea, without creating any incremental threat to Israel. This does not mean Western arms sales can be made to Saudi Arabia without *any* risk to Israel. There is no doubt that the Tornado sale and meeting the Saudi request to upgrade its F-15s will significantly improve the overall capability of the Saudi Air Force. Saudi Arabia, however, does not present a meaningful military threat to Israel. It does not border on Israel, and the Kingdom faces serious threats on its Gulf and Red Sea coasts and borders to which it must give all its attention.

Saudi Arabia can at best build a limited regional military deterrent, and enough defensive capability to deal with low and medium level threats. Even then, it will be hard pressed to use the improvements in its air force to offset the continuing weaknesses in its ground and naval forces. It will encounter even more problems in trying to offset the weaknesses in the small military forces of the other members of the Gulf Cooperation Council.

Saudi ground forces have no meaningful capability to engage Israeli forces, and they will not acquire this capability in the foreseeable future. The Saudi Air Force cannot obtain delivery of, and absorb, the advanced combat aircraft it has ordered until the early 1990s. By that time, improvements to the Israeli Air Force will have outpaced the improvements in the Saudi Air Force. This Israeli technical edge is ensured by U.S. ability to transfer newer and far more lethal technologies to Israel.

While Israel and its supporters sometimes lump every Arab state together in the threat that Israel must face, the Camp David agreement and the Iran-Iraq War have left Israel with only one real military opponent. This opponent is Syria, and Syria is unlikely to obtain significant military forces from any moderate Arab state in a future conflict against Israel.

Overview

Saudi Arabia could commit a limited force of 40-60 aircraft to the total Arab forces that could engage the Israeli Defense Forces (IDF) in intensive combat. And, to do this, Saudi Arabia would have to restructure its air basing and support structure--which would provide ample warning of its intentions--and the resulting combat losses would almost certainly cripple the Saudi Air Force for years to come. Thus, the most that the West is likely to do by meeting the Saudi arms request is to reduce Israel's freedom of action in overflying Saudi territory.

Equally importantly, if the West does not meet Saudi Arabia's military needs it not only will cripple the Kingdom's national defense capability efforts to build up the military capabilities of the Gulf Cooperation Council. This seems likely to have drastic consequences, given the Soviet presence in the People's Democratic Republic of Yemen (PDRY) and Ethiopia, the massive Soviet arms transfer effort in the Yemeni Arab Republic (YAR), the uncertainties surrounding the Iran-Iraq War and the Iranian revolution, and the instability of key Red Sea states like the Sudan. The West also cannot afford to ignore the long term implications of a Soviet victory in Afghanistan or the growing economic problems the Soviet bloc is experiencing because of its lack of a secure future source of oil.

## THE COST OF "TAKING SIDES" TO ISRAEL

It is also difficult to see how dividing the U.S. from Saudi Arabia can serve Israel's interests. Where close ties between the Saudi and U.S. Air Force created the kind of political and military relations that reinforced Saudi Arabia's already strong reluctance to become involved in any military engagement with Israel, the undermining of U.S. and Saudi military relations has created growing Saudi hostility towards Israel. It also is leading to the creation of British equipped air units which theoretically can attack Israel without regard to U.S. support and future replacement. Further, it is giving Saudi Arabia advanced attack capability much more quickly than if the Kingdom bought aircraft from the U.S.

The underlying irony behind the growing split between the U.S. and Saudi Arabia is that Britain has salvaged the West's ties to Saudi Arabia, but it has done so in ways which will create a larger potential threat to Israel than ever would have existed if the U.S. had fully met Saudi arms requests.

If the U.S. had met Saudi Arabia's arms request, the new and upgraded F-15s would have been based on U.S. supported facilities in the Gulf and lower Red Sea, rather than on bases near Israel. The conversion of the existing Saudi F-15C/Ds to the improved "MSIP" version to be used in the USAF would have taken place in separate batches of 3 aircraft each. They would not have begun in less than 46 months (6 months contracting time and 40 month lead time) after a letter of offer (LOA) was signed and could not have been completed in less than three years. Even assuming that a letter of offer had been signed on 1 January, 1985, the conversions would not have been completed until 1992.

The Saudi purchases of 40 more F-15C/D MSIP fighters would have involved the same lead times for contracting and production. The earliest deliveries could not have taken place before early 1989 and could not be completed before 1990. Even if full operational training had begun in the summer of 1990, it could not have been completed before 1991-1992.

Whereas the British deliveries of the 48 Tornado IDS attack aircraft will be completed in 1988, and the remaining 24 F.3 air superiority fighters will be delivered by 1990. In contrast the U.S. sale would have had a much slower pace. It would have been at least 1992 before the Saudi Air Force would have been fully able to operate its new force of 102 upgraded F-15C/Ds. By then, many of Saudi Arabia's F-5s would be twenty-one years old (many are already thirteen years old), and at least half would be converted to the trainer and light support role. Saudi Arabia would also have had to withdraw all its existing 23 Lightning and 37 BAC-167 aircraft from service.

Equally importantly, any follow-on upgrading of the Saudi F-15s to give them full dual capability in the air-to-ground role would not have taken place before the early 1990s. The Kingdom would have been limited to upgrading from the F-5E/F bomb racks that the Saudi Air Force has modified for use on its F-15 to the use of multiple ejection racks (MER) like the MER-200, tangential fuel tanks which carry air-to-ground munitions, and the ability to deliver Maverick.

Saudi Arabia will now acquire Tornado fighters designed primarily for the attack mission and replace its F-5s much more quickly. Given its basing and support structure, it is almost certain to eventually base at least some of its initial deliveries of European fighters at its facilities in Tabuk--the only Saudi main base which does not have major U.S. support facilities and the only Saudi main operating base near Israel.

## IMPACT ON WESTERN POWER PROJECTION CAPABILITIES IN THE GULF

All of this would be comparatively unimportant if arms sales were the only issue. The problem for the west is that recent trends have undermined a strategic relationship with Saudi Arabia which is critical to the West. Only three NATO European states can still project any significant amount of power in the Gulf: Britain, France, and Turkey.

Britain can still deploy several RAF squadrons, and a significant number of frigates and escorts. Britain cannot, however, deploy a full brigade to the region, and could only deploy one light carrier at a time with a maximum of eight short range Harrier VSTOL fighters. Britain is rapidly losing amphibious ship strength, and will steadily reduce its power projection capabilities during the next decade.

## Overview

France could deploy several air force squadrons, and as many as two brigades, if it could obtain U.S. air and sealift support. France could also deploy a small carrier task force with one 22,000 ton Clemenceau-class carrier equipped with 30 fixed wing aircraft. This, however, compares with U.S. carriers displacing more than 70,000 tons and with 86 combat aircraft each. Further, because the U.S. has a serious shortfall of strategic lift, any French force deployed to the Gulf would have to come at the direct expense of U.S. deployment of forces with better equipment.

Turkey can only play a role in its border areas near Iraq and Iran. Its Third Army has considerable land and air forces in Eastern Turkey, but these forces are not equipped for operations far from Turkey's borders. Turkey also would have to strip its eastern defenses against the USSR.

The practical reality is that the United States is the only Western state which retains significant power projection forces that can help defend the Gulf. The U.S., however, has no full time bases in the region. Its only contingency facilities in the Gulf are in Oman, and these are suitable only for a defense of the Straits of Hormuz, and not the Gulf as a whole. The closest facility where the U.S. can station aircraft and troops in peacetime is at Diego Garcia, which is nearly as far away from Kuwait City as Dublin, Ireland.

The U.S. has previously compensated for this weakness by establishing the kind of military relations with Saudi Arabia that would give the U.S. suitable basing facilities in the Kingdom in a major crisis, and which created Saudi air and air defense forces standardized and interoperable with the U.S. forces in USCENTCOM. This has made U.S. military relations with Saudi Arabia a critical part of U.S. efforts to create an effective "over-the-horizon" deterrent in the Gulf.

Saudi Arabia never formally agreed to provide the U.S. with contingency bases, but it often requested U.S. reinforcements. Saudi officials and officers have conducted extensive talks with the commander of USCENTCOM and other senior U.S. officials. Like Oman, Saudi Arabia has played a strong role in forging the Gulf Cooperation Council, and would almost certainly cooperate with U.S. forces in the face of any threat to the Gulf or Red Sea area.

The Saudi Air Force operates U.S.-made F-15C/D, and F-5E/F fighters, and many Saudi squadrons now approach U.S. Air Force proficiency and qualification levels. Saudi Arabia also has the largest and most modern air bases in the Middle East. These bases could house up to two wings of U.S. Air Force fighters, and give them full munitions and service support. The U.S. has large numbers of contract personnel serving Saudi equipment in the Kingdom's Air Force, Army, National Guard, Navy, and large numbers of Saudi military and civilian personnel have had U.S. training and can operate with, or support and service, U.S. military equipment.

Saudi Arabia has equally modern naval facilities and ground bases. These now use only moderate amounts of major combat equipment which is standard in USCENTCOM forces, but they have extensive stocks of parts and munitions, and service and support equipment which can be used by U.S. units. The Saudi base at Hafr al-Batin (which is located in the critical border area near Kuwait and Iraq) will also have two mechanized brigades equipped with U.S. armor.

In fact, USCENTCOM may not be able to function in its most critical contingency roles without Saudi cooperation and wartime access to Saudi bases and facilities. While Oman, Turkey, and Egypt provide useful contingency facilities on the periphery of the Gulf and lower Red Sea, they cannot make up for the range and reinforcement problems USCENTCOM would face in defending the critical oil facilities in the Upper and central Gulf.

## PRESERVING THE PROPER BALANCE IN WESTERN STRATEGIC RELATIONS

The practical problem for both the West and Saudi Arabia is how to deal with this situation. Britain and France can replace the U.S. in the role of providing arms and military advice, but not in terms of the power projection capability needed to help deter the threats to the GCC or deal with a real military crisis. The combined carrier forces of Britain and France carry fewer combat aircraft than one full U.S. nuclear carrier. Britain and France can project demonstrative naval forces to the Gulf, but not major independent task forces. Their land and air power projection capabilities are measured in light infantry battalions and squadrons, not in full divisions and wings.

Geography and politics make Saudi Arabia pivotal to the defense of the Gulf, the Red Sea, the other moderate Gulf oil exporters, and most of the free world's oil supplies. The issue is not simply one of the fact that the Gulf has 50% of the world's proven oil reserves. The Kingdom alone has nearly 25% of the world's proven reserves, and Saudi Arabia and the other moderate Gulf states in the Gulf Cooperation Council have a total of 35%. Western strategic planning cannot afford to ignore the linkage between U.S. power projection capabilities and the fact that Saudi Arabia is the only Southern Gulf state large and strong enough to catalyze the other GCC states into military cooperation with the U.S.

Unless the West can find a more stable solution to this problem, the resulting split between the U.S. and Saudi Arabia will also undercut any moves towards linking the Kingdom to new peace initiatives. While Saudi Arabia can be legitimately criticized for its caution in joining the peace process, and for placing its own security above the need to move the peace process forward, it is directly exposed to a major threat from Iran, and to political pressure from radical states like the PDRY and Libya.

Overview

Saudi Arabia is equally exposed to pressure from Syria, Palestinian radicals, and religious fundamentalists and extremists like the Shi'ite movements in Iran and Lebanon. These movements have been the source of many assassination attempts and terrorist incidents throughout the Arab world, and many Arab moderates have paid with their lives for their moderation. These threats are also gaining in strength. The near collapse of peace initiatives and a widespread recession caused by the radical drop in oil prices is certain to increase these threats to the moderate Arab states.

Saudi Arabia must be able to demonstrate that its "linkage" to the U.S. and Europe will provide it with the security it needs. This does not require a change in European policy but it does require the U.S. to maintain a proper balance in its strategic ties with Israel and friendly Arab states. There is no doubt that an Arab-Israeli peace settlement is the most urgent Western strategic priority in the Middle East, but there can be no peace if moderate Arab states are left weak and isolated in the face of massive regional military build-ups in states like Iran. An Arab-Israeli peace will also not ensure peace in the Gulf. The price of peace is the same for Arab states as it is for the West, and that price is security.

## II. WESTERN STRATEGIC INTERESTS IN SAUDI ARABIA

Western strategic relations with Saudi Arabia are necessarily divided and complex. The West is often divided over the details of its policy towards the Arab world and the Gulf. The Arab-Israeli conflict constantly complicates the problem of establishing close relations, and often leads to serious day-to-day differences in policy. Nevertheless, the West and Saudi Arabia share far more strategic interests than divide them, and the overall pattern of military relations has been closer than each sides political statements would indicate.

### THE HISTORICAL BACKGROUND

The West has maintained friendly strategic relations with Saudi Arabia since its emergence as a modern state, and Britain and the U.S. have helped shape Saudi Arabia's military forces for more than half a century. Britain provided its first military advisers to the Saud family in 1914, long before Saudi Arabia became a Kingdom. The Kingdom granted the U.S. oil concessions in 1933, and gave the U.S. basing rights in Dhahran during World War II which the U.S. eventually transformed into its largest facility in the region. The U.S. sent its first military aid to Saudi Arabia in April, 1943, and laid the cornerstone of a U.S. military advisory role which has helped shape the development of Saudi military forces ever since.

These strategic relationships have had their ups and downs. Debates over the future of Palestine, and border conflicts between Saudi Arabia and the Trucial states, led to a break in military relations between Saudi Arabia and Britain that lasted from 1946 to the mid-1950s. The struggle between Saudi Arabia, Abu Dhabi and Oman over the control of the Buraimi Oasis even reached the point of military confrontation. British forces helped expel Saudi forces from the Oasis in October, 1955, and helped the Sultan of Oman expel the Saudis and Egyptian backed rebels from Nizwa in December of the same year.

While the Kingdom remained dependent on U.S. military assistance and advice throughout the late 1940s and mid-1950s, it did attempt to reach a modus vivendi with the new revolutionary regime in Egypt in the mid-

1950s, and even established a major Egyptian advisory presence. Nevertheless, it was the U.S. that developed the first major Saudi military modernization plan in 1952, and military relations continued in spite of complex struggles within the Royal Family and shifts in Saudi Arabia's relations with the West. The U.S. gave Saudi Arabia its first modern armor during this period, and a small air force of 9 B-26 bombers, 12 F-86 jet fighters, T-33A trainers, and C-123 transports.

As tensions increased between Saudi Arabia and Egypt, the Kingdom increased its military dependence on the U.S. A new security agreement was reached in April, 1957, and the U.S. began an effort to create a modern manpower base and military infrastructure that has continued ever since. The bloody overthrow of the Hashemite rulers in Iraq in 1958, and the beginning of the Yemeni civil war in 1962, helped further catalyze this Saudi shift towards the West. When Egypt began to bomb Saudi towns near the border with Yemen in November, 1962, Faisal turned to the United States and Britain for help in developing modern Saudi military forces.

Britain assumed a key role in advising the Saudi National Guard, and in 1963, the U.S. and Britain sold Saudi Arabia an air defense system consisting of 40 Lightning and Hunter fighters, 25 BAC-167 Strikemasters, and a medium to high altitude air defense and warning system, plus nearly 1,000 support personnel. The U.S. sold Saudi Arabia Hawk surface-to-air missiles and modern military communications. Both countries also helped Saudi Arabia modernize its Army. The U.S. provided 58 M-41 tanks, 55 M-47 tanks, and 15 light M-24 tanks, and Britain 30 M-6 and M-8 armored cars. This remained the core of Saudi armor until France began major arms sales to the Kingdom in 1970.

King Faisal's reign from 1964 to 1975 consolidated Saudi strategic relations with Britain and the U.S., and led to the first major Saudi purchases from France. The U.S. Corps of Engineers began a massive military building program in 1965 which eventually gave Saudi Arabia major military bases or cities on all of its critical borders and some of the most advanced air bases in the world. Britain rushed the deployment of aircraft and missiles to help defend the Kingdom against Egyptian and PDRY forces in 1966, and British Lightning F-53 pilots played a critical role in helping Saudi forces to drive South Yemeni troops out of Wadiah in November, 1969.

The 1967 Arab-Israeli conflict created new tensions between Saudi Arabia and the U.S., and Saudi Arabia turned to France for much of its armor. It bought 220 AML-90 Panhard armored cars in 1970 and 200 AMX-30 medium tanks, 250 armored personnel carriers, and large amounts of self propelled artillery in 1973. This marked the beginning of a Saudi policy of finding several sources of arms and military support that the Kingdom has continued to the present day. Saudi Arabia did not, however, break its ties to the U.S. Once the immediate tensions of the 1967 war faded, the Kingdom turned back to the U.S. It asked the U.S. for a new comprehensive military modernization plan in 1970, and for a National Guard modernization plan in 1971. It signed a naval modernization agreement with the U.S. in 1972, although it also bought eight hovercraft and 22 patrol boats from Britain.

Saudi Arabia's close strategic relations with the West survived the crisis surrounding the 1973 Arab-Israeli conflict and the oil embargo that followed. Saudi Arabia signed a new agreement for major U.S. support of the National Guard in April 1974, and a full scale military and economic cooperation agreement in June, 1974. It bought 250 M-60 medium tanks, 250 M-113 armored personnel carriers (APCs), over 300 artillery weapons and more Hawk surface-to-air missiles from the U.S. It also bought 250 armored fighting vehicles (AFVs) and light tanks from Britain, over 500 new armored vehicles and armored cars from both France and Britain, 34 French Alouette II helicopters, and 11 C-130 transports.

In January 1975, Saudi Arabia announced it had bought 60 F-5E/F fighters to complete the modernization of its air force, and in February, that it had hired the Vinnel Corporation of the United States to supply its National Guard modern mechanized brigades. That same year it bought 300 more AMX-30 medium tanks and 250 AMX-10 APCs from France, and 18 more C-130 tankers and transports from the U.S., together with 15 patrol boats and minesweepers, and 100 U.S. Harpoon missiles.

By the mid to late 1970s, therefore, Saudi Arabia had established a relatively stable pattern of military relations with Britain, France, and the U.S. that continued until the U.S. refusal to sell Saudi Arabia more F-15s in mid-1985. The U.S. Corps of Engineers and various U.S. companies provided Saudi Arabia with modern military infrastructure and $C^3I$ assets (command, control, communications and intelligence). The Saudi National Guard depended largely on U.S. assistance together with limited British aid, and Britain and France provided aid to the other Saudi internal security forces. The Saudi Army depended almost equally on French and U.S. assistance, the Saudi Navy was gradually shifting from U.S. to French support, and the Saudi Air Force depended primarily on U.S. aircraft and support for its first line force, but on Britain for support of the Lightning and a great deal of its training.

## THE CHANGING FORCES SHAPING SAUDI RELATIONS WITH THE WEST

Four series of events acted to consolidate Saudi strategic relations with the West during this period, and steadily increased the role and importance of Saudi Arabia in the region:
- o The first series of events was Britain's withdrawal from the Gulf, which led to a massive arms race between Iran and Iraq which destablized the entire region. Saudi Arabia was forced into a major military build-up, and to compete with regional powers armed

with weapons and technology roughly equivalent to those deployed in first line NATO and Warsaw Pact forces.
- o The second series was the death of Nasser and the decay of the radical forces within the Arab world to the point where they no longer retained their grasp on the popular imagination. This allowed the Kingdom and other conservative and moderate Arab states to deal openly with the threat from the remaining radical states with far less fear of popular unrest.
- o The third series of events was the October, 1973 war between Israel and its Arab neighbors and the resulting oil crisis. The initial Arab oil embargo exposed the vulnerability of Western energy supplies, and OPEC capitalized on this situation to make a tenfold increase in world oil prices. The resulting rise in oil revenues suddenly made Saudi Arabia one of the wealthiest states in the world. It also made it one of America's leading trading partners.
- o The fourth series of events included the Soviet invasion of Afghanistan, the fall of the Shah of Iran, and the outbreak of the Iran-Iraq War. These events forced the U.S. to replace its reliance on Iran's military forces with U.S. rapid deployment forces. It thus made the U.S. dependent on friendly contingency bases in the Gulf, and it thrust Saudi Arabia into the position of trying to build a regional deterrent and defense for the moderate and pro-Western Gulf states.

The net effect of all these events was to create a *de facto* strategic partnership between Saudi Arabia and the West. Saudi Arabia depends on Western military equipment and advice for the modernization of its forces and to help deter any attack by one of its more radical neighbors. Saudi Arabia also must depend on the U.S. for over the horizon reinforcements in the event of an all out attack by Iran or Iraq or in the face of any direct or indirect Soviet threat.

The West, in turn, depends on Saudi Arabia to lead the moderate Gulf States toward political and military cooperation, towards effective internal security efforts, and towards joint defense against low level threats. The U.S., in particular, needs Saudi military facilities and support to assist it in any major military intervention in the Gulf. The lack of such facilities would drastically undercut--if not cripple--any effort to defend the Gulf by USCENTCOM or the U.S. Navy.

This same series of events shifted Saudi strategic relations with the West from one of clear Saudi dependence to one in which Saudi Arabia was much more of a partner. While the West remains the senior partner, Saudi Arabia is not only a key source of oil, but an essential military and political catalyst of Gulf security. No improvement in Western military forces can substitute for Saudi Arabia's willingness to work with the West in bringing strategic stability to the region, for the role it can play in unifying the moderate Gulf states in the Gulf Cooperation Council, and for the broader role that Saudi Arabia can play in its relations with other Arab states and in the Red Sea area.

## THE IMPACT OF SAUDI OIL

The West and Saudi Arabia will always be "competitors" in the sense that the West will seek the lowest possible oil price and the lowest possible level of dependence on imports, while Saudi Arabia will seek to maximize its oil revenues and market share. Both will continue to compete over issues like price, Saudi Arabia's volume of production, increases in Saudi production of oil "products" versus Western. Protection of its refineries, and a host of other issues. No arrangements between the West and Saudi Arabia can eliminate the normal frictions of international trade--nor should they. The free market is ultimately the best way of minimizing energy costs and stabilizing the balance of trade.

Nevertheless, Saudi Arabia and the West share important common strategic interests in regard to oil. These include avoiding artificially high or low oil prices, and unstable swings in Western and Saudi trade and the world economy. This common interest has led Saudi Arabia to cooperate with the West in recycling "petrodollars", and in trying to smooth out the effects of the kind of the "boom and bust" cycle reflected in Table 2.1, and which will be even sharper in the late 1980s and early 1990s as the world shifts from the "oil glut" of 1986 to a new hardening of world energy prices.

Table 2.1: OPEC Revenues and Oil Exports: 1973-1986

| Country | Oil Revenues ($Billions Per Year) | | | | Oil Production (MMBD) | | | |
|---|---|---|---|---|---|---|---|---|
| | 73 | 80 | 84 | 86 | 73 | 80 | 84 | 86 |
| Saudi Arabia | 4.3 | 102.2 | 43.7 | 28.5 | 7.4 | 10.0 | 4.7 | 4.6 |
| Kuwait | 1.8 | 17.9 | 10.8 | 9.2 | 3.0 | 1.4 | 1.0 | 1.4 |
| Iraq | 1.8 | 26.1 | 10.4 | 9.9 | 2.0 | 2.6 | 1.2 | 1.7 |
| Iran | 4.4 | 13.5 | 16.7 | 10.4 | 5.9 | 1.5 | 2.2 | 1.9 |
| Libya | 2.2 | 22.6 | 10.9 | 6.2 | 2.2 | 1.8 | 1.1 | 0.9 |
| Qatar | 0.3 | 5.4 | 4.4 | 1.9 | 0.3 | 0.3 | 0.3 | 0.3 |
| UAE | 0.9 | 19.5 | 13.0 | 10.5 | 1.5 | 1.7 | 1.2 | 1.7 |
| Algeria | 1.0 | 12.5 | 9.7 | 3.9 | 1.1 | 1.1 | 1.0 | 0.6 |
| Ecuador | 0.2 | 1.4 | 1.6 | 1.8 | 0.2 | 0.2 | 0.3 | 0.3 |
| Gabon | 0.2 | 1.8 | 1.4 | 1.1 | 0.1 | 0.2 | 0.2 | 0.2 |
| Nigeria | 2.1 | 25.6 | 12.4 | 9.9 | 2.0 | 2.1 | 1.4 | 1.5 |
| Indonesia | 0.2 | 12.9 | 11.2 | 8.5 | 1.3 | 1.6 | 1.4 | 1.3 |
| Venezuela | 3.0 | 17.6 | 13.7 | 9.7 | 3.5 | 2.2 | 1.9 | 1.7 |
| Other | 0.6 | 8.0 | 5.7 | 4.4 | 0.9 | 0.8 | 0.8 | 0.7 |
| OPEC Total | 22.5 | 278.8 | 159.4 | 112.0 | 30.8 | 26.9 | 17.9 | 17.5 |
| Mexico | - | - | - | - | 0.6 | 2.2 | 3.0 | 2.6 |

Sources: The data for 1973-1984 are actual data based on reporting in the Petroleum Economist, July, 1985; Worldwatch Institute, Worldwatch Paper 66, Petroleum Institute Weekly, and BP Statistical Review of Energy. The data for 1986 are preliminary estimates based on the trends for the first half of 1986 as reported in William L. Randol and Ellen Macready, Petroleum Monitor, First Boston Corporation, New York, May, 1986.

A good example of such cooperation between Saudi Arabia and the West took place following the Shah's fall and the Iran-Iraq War. During 1980 and 1981, Saudi Arabia increased its oil production to 10 million barrels per day to reduce the pressure of near panic demand for oil and did so at the request of the United States and Europe. Saudi Arabia obviously benefitted from this increase in terms of revenues, but it also made a concerted effort to reduce the impact of the resulting oil crisis. When oil prices rose to $35 per barrel, and Saudi Arabia had to dispose of excess oil income equal to roughly $20 billion a year. The Kingdom cooperated closely with key European states and the U.S. Treasury in "recycling" these oil revenues and in finding patterns of investment that would not disturb Western economies. Saudi Arabia also cooperated with Western governments in efforts to stabilize the oil market, to aid oil importing developing states, and to create a stable pattern of investment in the West.

This cooperation has continued even though this rise in oil prices triggered a global recession and mass conservation, and decreased demand and forced oil prices down to well under $20 a barrel. This has reduced the demand for Saudi oil to monthly average levels as low as 2.3 MMBD in 1985, and cut Saudi oil revenues dropped from a peak of $102 billion a year in 1980, to around $30 billion in 1986. Even so, Saudi Arabia has cooperated with the West on payment scheduling and investment flows to minimize the impact of the shift in revenues during a time when it has faced a budget deficit of nearly $1 billion a month.[1] Further, it is Saudi Arabia which led the break-up of OPEC efforts to maintain prices by cutting world oil production. Saudi Arabia instead chose a strategy of increasing production that ensured a massive drop in prices. It did so, at least in part, to keep prices at levels that would ensure high long term Western demand.[2]

These price issues are marginal, however, compared to the common strategic interest the West and Saudi Arabia share in securing the Kingdom's ability to freely export oil. Wide swings take place in the West's dependence on Gulf oil from year to year, depending upon the health of the world's economy. Table 2.2 shows these swings in terms of the imports of key OECD countries from the Gulf area, during a period ranging from peak demand to a record low, and provides a good picture of the dependence of individual Western countries on oil imports. Table 2.2 also shows just how low Western dependence on the Gulf states can be, and the data for the record low in Gulf exports in the Third Quarter of 1985.

These swings take place in the West's oil demand, however, largely because of global economic conditions and they are extremely dependent on the ability of states outside the Gulf area to export large amounts of oil. These non-Gulf oil exporting states have only a limited portion of the world's oil reserves, and will inevitably drop sharply in export capacity over the next ten years.

## Table 2.2: Recent Patterns in Western Dependence on Gulf Oil
### (Million of Barrels Per Day)

**OECD Imports By Country** [a]

| | 1982 Total | 1982 Gulf | 1983 Total | 1983 Gulf | 1984 Total | 1984 Gulf | 1985 Total | 1985 Gulf |
|---|---|---|---|---|---|---|---|---|
| Total OECD | 17.9 | 8.1 | 16.6 | 6.6 | 17.0 | 6.5 | 15.9 | 5.6 |
| U.S. | 4.3 | .7 | 4.3 | .4 | 4.7 | .5 | 4.3 | .3 |
| Canada | -.1 | .7 | -.3 | .1 | -.3 | - | -.4 | - |
| Main Europe | 8.7 | 4.4 | 7.9 | 3.2 | 7.7 | 3.0 | 7.4 | 2.6 |
| France | 1.8 | .9 | 1.7 | .6 | 1.7 | .5 | 1.7 | .5 |
| Germany | 2.1 | .5 | 2.1 | .3 | 2.1 | .2 | 2.2 | .2 |
| Italy | 1.8 | .9 | 1.6 | .8 | 1.6 | .7 | 1.6 | .6 |
| Netherlands | .6 | .3 | .5 | .3 | .5 | .3 | .5 | .3 |
| Spain | 1.0 | .5 | 1.0 | .4 | .9 | .4 | .8 | .3 |
| **European Exporters** | | | | | | | | |
| Norway | -.3 | - | -.5 | - | -.5 | - | -.6 | - |
| U.K. | -.6 | .3 | -.9 | .2 | -.8 | .1 | -1.0 | .1 |
| **Smaller Europe** | | | | | | | | |
| Austria | .2 | .1 | .2 | - | .2 | - | .2 | - |
| Belgium | .4 | .2 | .4 | .1 | .4 | .1 | .4 | .1 |
| Denmark | .2 | - | .2 | - | .2 | - | .2 | - |
| Ireland | .1 | - | .1 | - | .1 | - | .1 | - |
| Finland | .2 | - | .2 | - | .2 | - | .2 | - |
| Greece | .2 | .2 | .2 | .1 | .2 | .1 | .2 | .1 |
| Portugal | .2 | .1 | .2 | .1 | .2 | .1 | .2 | .1 |
| Sweden | .4 | .1 | .4 | - | .3 | - | .3 | - |
| Switzerland | .2 | - | .3 | - | .2 | - | .3 | - |
| Turkey | .3 | .2 | .3 | .2 | .3 | .3 | .3 | .3 |
| Japan | 4.5 | 2.7 | 4.4 | 2.6 | 4.5 | 2.8 | 4.3 | 2.6 |
| Other OECD | .5 | .3 | .3 | .2 | .3 | .2 | .3 | .2 |

**Lowest Recent Imports From Given Gulf Countries** (3rd Quarter 1985)

| | Total | Bahrain | Iran | Iraq | Kuwait | UAE | Qatar | Saudi Arabia [b] |
|---|---|---|---|---|---|---|---|---|
| Total OECD | 5.14 | .03 | 1.12 | .87 | .52 | 1.06 | .31 | 1.2 |
| Total Europe | 2.49 | .0 | .82 | .74 | .32 | .11 | .03 | .47 |
| U.K. | .10 | .0 | .01 | .07 | .01 | .01 | .0 | .01 |
| France | .47 | - | .13 | .17 | .02 | .05 | .03 | .07 |
| FRG | .167 | .0 | .09 | .01 | .02 | .01 | - | .04 |
| Italy | .50 | .0 | .16 | .11 | .13 | .02 | .0 | .74 |
| Other | 1.26 | - | .43 | .39 | .14 | .03 | .01 | .271 |
| U.S. | .21 | - | .06 | .08 | .01 | .03 | .0 | .04 |
| Canada | .02 | - | .02 | - | - | - | - | - |
| Japan | 2.21 | .03 | .18 | .05 | .15 | .89 | .27 | .65 |
| Other | .22 | .01 | .08 | .01 | .04 | .03 | .01 | .05 |

Source: OECD computer data base, *International Petroleum Statistics Report*, 7/25/86.
a. Total includes oil imports regardless of source. Gulf includes all imports from the Gulf states.
b. U.S. imports from Saudi Arabia fluctuated from 0.04 to 0.55 MMBD during 1982-1985, Japanese imports fluctuated from 0.70 to 1.54 MMBD, OECD Europe fluctuated

from 0.47 to 2.40 MMBD, France fluctuated from 0.7 to 0.56 MMBD, West Germany fluctuated from 0.04 to 0.35 MMBD; and Italy fluctuated from .07 to .39 MMBD.

Table 2.3 shows Saudi Arabia has proven oil reserves of over 170 billion barrels. This is nearly 25% of the world's proven oil reserves and 28% of the Free World's reserves. Even these percentages are artificially low because Saudi Arabia has had little incentive to prove more reserves over the last five years. Saudi Arabia almost certainly can continue to prove more reserves than it consumes and exports for at least the next half-decade and may well be able to do so for the next decade.

This mix of Saudi production capability and reserves will be of steadily greater importance as time goes by. The expansion of alternative fuel supplies--such as nuclear power and synthetic fuels--and new discoveries has fallen far below the levels predicted in the 1970s and early 1980s. Even the most conservative estimates of oil demand, indicate that oil will provide at least 30% of the energy for OECD countries through the end of the 1990s.[3]

After a decade of intense Western effort to find alternative energy supplies and oil outside the Middle East, the U.S. Geological Survey shows virtually no increase in either the proven oil reserves or the estimated undiscovered oil reserves outside the Gulf. Further, the ratio of reserves to consumption had increased in the Gulf, and decreased virtually everywhere else. A 1983 study by the USGS concluded that,

"Demonstrated reserves of crude oil has declined over the past 10 years...discoveries have lagged over the same period...Rates of discovery have continued to decline over the past 20 years even though exploratory activity has increased..." [4]

A 1985 report by the USGS on efforts to discover new oil reserve outside the Gulf is even more discouraging.

"Clearly discoveries are on a downward trend from a high in the 1950s of some 35 billion barrels per year to a present day total of 10-15 billion barrels of new oil per year. Production of about 20 billion barrels per day has now outpaced discovery by a factor of two. The reality is... that the Middle East increasingly will monopolize world petroleum supplies...most of the world's conventional oil resources lie within the narrow confines of the Middle East and so does the production capacity. The economies of the western world rest on the daily production from the Middle East and indeed even the amount of oil transiting the Straits of Hormuz daily, some 7 to 8 million barrels is about two times the surplus producing capacity found outside the Middle East." [5]

The USGS cut its estimate of U.S. offshore oil reserves by 55% in 1985. Europe has no prospects of further major discoveries and North Sea oil production will decline steadily in the 1990s. The USSR is experiencing major problems in exploiting its proven reserves. Expected major discoveries in the PRC have not occurred, and increases in Mexican consumption are now expected to consume the increase in production.

In spite of the fact major oil exploration activities began in 30 new countries between 1979 and 1984, the total increase in all world reserves during that period was less than 1% and most occurred in the Gulf area. Further, several key OPEC countries outside the Gulf are now rapidly consuming their reserves: these include Algeria, Ecuador, Gabon, Indonesia, and Nigeria. None are likely to be oil exporters by the mid-1990s.[6]

## Table 2.3: World Oil Reserves

| Region and Country | Estimated Proved Reserves | |
|---|---|---|
| | Billions of Barrels | Percent of World Total |
| Gulf [a] | 396.18 | 24.6 |
| Bahrain | .17 | .02 |
| Neutral Zone | (5.4) | .8 |
| Iran | 48.5 | 6.9 |
| Iraq | 44.5 (65.0) [b] | 6.4 |
| Kuwait [c] | 92.7 | 13.3 |
| Oman | 3.5 | .5 |
| Qatar | 3.35 | .5 |
| UAE | 32.49 | 4.6 |
|   Abu Dahbi | (30.5) | - |
|   Dubai | (1.44) | - |
|   Ras al Khaimah | (0.1) | - |
|   Sharjah | (.45) | - |
| Saudi Arabia [d] | 171.7 | 24.6 |
| Other Middle East | 2.2 | .3 |
| Israel | .75 | .1 |
| Syria | 1.45 | .2 |
| Total Middle East | 398.38 | 57.0 |
| Africa [a] | 55.54 | 7.9 |
| Algeria | 9.0 | 1.3 |
| Angola | 1.8 | .3 |
| Egypt | 3.2 | .5 |
| Libya | 21.1 | 3.0 |
| Nigeria | 16.65 | 2.4 |
| Western Hemisphere [a] | 117.69 | 16.8 |
| U.S. | 27.3 | 3.9 |
| Mexico | 48.6 | 7.0 |
| Canada | 7.075 | 1.0 |
| Venezuela | 25.845 | 3.7 |
| Western Europe [a] | 24.425 | 3.5 |
| Britain | 13.59 | 1.9 |
| Norway | 8.3 | 1.2 |
| Asia-Pacific [a] | 18.5299 | 2.7 |
| Australia | 1.5 | .2 |
| Brunei | 1.4 | .2 |
| India | 3.0 | .42 |
| Indonesia | 8.65 | 1.2 |
| Malaysia | 3.5 | .5 |
| Total Non-Communist | 614.567 | 88.0 |
| Communist | 84.1 | 12.0 |
| USSR | 63.0 | 9.0 |
| China | 19.1 | 2.7 |
| Other | 2.0 | .2 |
| TOTAL WORLD | 698.667 | 100.0 |

a. Breakdown by individual countries includes only major exporting or reserve holding countries
b. The current official estimate is 44.1 billion, which has not been revised because of the Iran-Iraq War but most U.S. officials now estimate Iraqi proved reserves at 65 billion or more.
c. Kuwait's reserves are probably in excess of 100 billion and Saudi Arabia is near 200 billion. The reserves for Kuwait and Saudi Arabia include half of the Neutral Zone.
d. Neither Kuwait or Saudi Arabia provide up to date estimates of proven reserves.
Source: Adapted from Oil and Gas Journal, December 1984 and December 1985. U.S. Department of Energy show a slightly higher percentage of total reserves in the Middle East. See DOE/EIA-0219(84), pp. 79-81.

The West and Saudi Arabia have a further common interest in ensuring that the five smaller conservative Gulf states remain independent, and can freely export their oil. Kuwait, Qatar, Bahrain, the UAE, and Oman are now linked together with Saudi Arabia in the Gulf Cooperation Council (GCC), and they have a total of 130 billion barrels worth of proved reserves. As Table 2.3 shows, these five smaller Gulf states have a total of 19% of the world's proven oil reserves and 21% of the free world's oil reserves. In fact, these five small Gulf states have 10% more proven oil reserves than the entire Western Hemisphere, including Canada, Mexico, Venezuela, and the United States.[7]

Equally importantly, the GCC states have a total maximum sustainable oil production capacity of 15.8 million barrels a day. This compares with a total Gulf production capacity of about 20-25 million barrels per day, and is equivalent to roughly 50% of all OPEC production capacity. Saudi Arabia alone can produce up to 10.2 million barrels per day, or more than 40% of all the oil production capacity of all the Gulf states.[8]

The total oil import needs of the West and the Free World will fluctuate with political and economic conditions, but today's "oil glut" is almost certain to disappear by the early 1990s as the result of world economic recovery and economic growth. In fact, the "oil glut" could disappear overnight if the moderate Gulf states could not export freely, and the Iran-Iraq War made a major cut in Gulf exports a constant possibility.

A recent report by the U.S. Secretary of Energy indicates that even with today's supply and demand conditions, a cut off of Gulf oil could cause world oil exports to fall to as much as 3 to 4 million barrels below world demand. This would have an immediate impact on Europe and Japan, which get much of their oil from the Middle East, but it would also affect the U.S. The U.S. now gets only about 3% of its oil from the Gulf, but this low percentage of U.S. imports disguises the true nature of U.S. vulnerability. The U.S. now buys its oil from nations closer to the U.S.--largely because of lower transportation costs. In the event of a reduction in Gulf oil exports, however, the U.S. would have to compete with other importing nations on the world market. Even if it used its Strategic Petroleum Reserves, the U.S. might still face another massive oil price crisis.[9]

By 1990, the impact of any interruption could be much worse. Even before the 1986 drop in oil prices, the U.S. Department of Energy projected that Western and other importing nation demand for OPEC oil would recover from about 17 million barrels per day in early 1985, to 24-26 million barrels in 1990, as alternative sources like North Sea oil are depleted. These same projections indicated that world demand would rise to the point where real prices would begin to rise in real terms by 1992-95, and slowly increase to levels of at least $36 a barrel in 1985 dollars by 2000, and $55 by 2010. The most likely rise was projected to be $57 a barrel by 2000, and $84 by 2010. The study also projected that if the West continued to develop alternative energy supplies like nuclear power, synthetic fuels, and coal at the rate these supplies increased in the early and mid-1980, oil prices could rise to $80 a barrel by 2000 and $110 by 2010.[10]

The rapid drop in oil prices in 1985 and 1986 has made this situation much worse. It has forced producers to permanently close many low production and high cost stripper wells. It has also triggered a major race among the oil producing nations to produce as much oil as possible to try to compensate for the nearly 50% drop in oil prices between mid-1985 and mid-1986. This is good news for the West in the short run, but bad news in the long run. It means that Western alternative energy and conservation projects are now falling even further behind past goals and that exporting nations outside the Gulf are depleting their reserves 30-50% more quickly than past projections had indicated.[11]

Under these conditions, any sustained cut in the flow of oil from the Gulf could be expected to trigger a massive recession, or full scale depression, in the OECD countries. It could also be expected to trigger a crisis in the less developed countries that could lead to large scale famine or the collapse of their economies. The U.S. Department of Energy projects that the LDCs will double their demand for OPEC oil by 1995, and triple it by 2010.[12] If the control of Gulf oil should fall into radical or pro-Soviet hands, it would give a hostile power major leverage over every aspect of free world economic activity.

THE IMPACT OF WESTERN AND SAUDI TRADE RELATIONS

Saudi Arabia is an important trading partner of the West, and plays a significant role in shaping world monetary policy and foreign aid activities. In 1984, Italy, France, West Germany, Britain, Holland, and the other West European states all had a favorable trade balance with Saudi Arabia. Italy exported about $2.2 billion worth of goods and imported about $1.75 billion. France exported about $2.1 billion and imported $2 billion. West Germany exported about $2. billion and imported $0.8 billion. Britain exported about $1.9 billion and imported $0.7 billion. The Netherlands exported about $0.7 billion and imported $0.4 billion. The rest of Europe exported about $1.1 billion and imported $1.0 billion. [13]

Western Strategic Interests in Saudi Arabia

In 1985, the European Economic Community (EEC) exported about $10 billion worth of goods to Saudi Arabia in spite of the fact the Kingdom's imports fell 15% and oil production had hit a ten year low, and an annual average production level well below its 4.353 million barrel a day OPEC quota. The volume of trade is likely to continue to decline in 1986 and 1987, but should exceed $8 billion annually and favor Europe until oil prices begin to rise again in the early 1990s.[14]

Ironically, Saudi trade has been especially intense with the U.S., although the U.S. has recently imported comparatively little Saudi oil.[15] There are now about 271 U.S.-Saudi joint ventures in Saudi Arabia worth about $3.7 billion. U.S. contractors won about 25% of all Saudi government contracts in 1983, worth about $ 4 billion. More broadly, U.S. exports to Saudi Arabia grew at an average annual rate of 35% before the recent decline in oil prices and rise in the value of the dollar. Even today, Saudi Arabia is the sixth largest importer of U.S. goods, and U.S. exports take up roughly 20% of the Saudi market.

Since the early 1980s, the balance of U.S.-Saudi trade has followed the same pattern as European-Saudi trade, and has shifted decisively in favor of the U.S.. The U.S. imported about $73 billion worth of oil from Saudi Arabia between 1974 and 1984, and exported $48 billion worth of goods and services to Saudi Arabia. In 1982, however, Saudi Arabia imported $39 billion worth of goods, and exported $50 billion. In 1983, Saudi Arabia imported $ 7.9 billion worth of goods from the U.S., and exported $3.8 billion. This left Saudi Arabia with a trade deficit of $4.1 billion.

Preliminary U.S. Department of Commerce estimates indicate that Saudi Arabia imported $39.5 billion worth of goods in 1984, and exported $51.7 billion. It exported $4.7 billion worth of goods to the U.S. and imported $ 7 billion. This created a $2.3 billion trade advantage for the U.S. in a year when the high value of the dollar was otherwise creating a massive U.S. trade deficit. The GCC countries as a whole account for over 60% of all U.S. exports to the Arab countries in the Middle East and Africa, and U.S. trade with Saudi Arabia accounts for the bulk of U.S. trade with the GCC countries.[16]

The cut in oil prices will reduce the size of the West's trade surplus with Saudi Arabia, but is unlikely to alter the basic patterns in the flow of trade established in the mid-1980s until oil prices again rise in real terms in the early to mid 1990s. Trade will probably then resemble to the period where Saudi Arabia and the other GCC states had a favorable balance of trade with the West. This will further increase the importance of sound strategic relations to the West.[17]

## THE IMPACT OF SAUDI AID AND CAPITAL

There is no question that the drop in oil revenues has affected the Kingdom's wealth. It devalued the Riyal against the U.S. dollar in June 1986, and had a $24 billion deficit on current account in 1984, and may have had a $30 billion deficit in 1985. It faces at least a $20 billion deficit in 1986, and had to sell holdings in U.S. treasury bills to keep its liquid international reserves of $25-27 billion.[18] Saudi Arabia still has over $85 billion in foreign investments in the West, roughly 70% of which has been invested in the U.S., much of it in U.S. government securities. This investment ties much of Saudi Arabia's non-oil income to the performance of Western economies. In fact, these ties are part of a broad link between the investment policies of the GCC and the West.[19]

The GCC governments invested about $9 billion per year in the U.S. alone during 1980-1984, and private investment totaled billions more. Although U.S. Treasury figures are uncertain, GCC government investment in the U.S. was reported to have reached $82 billion in early 1983, with $46 billion in U.S. government securities. Other sources report that Kuwait alone had over $100 billion invested in Europe and the United States. While this GCC investment declined in 1984 through 1986, as the result of the fall in oil revenues, and is likely to decline further until the late 1980s, it will probably recover by 1990-1991. It represents a major source of foreign investment in the West, and is far larger than all other Middle Eastern and African investment combined.[20]

Saudi foreign aid has also been of value to the West. Saudi Arabia contributed some $48 billion in official foreign aid between 1970 and 1984, or roughly 5.8% of its GNP. This compares with an average of 0.3% of GNP for the industrialized countries, and neither the U.S. nor any other OECD nation currently gives significantly more than 1% of its GNP in foreign aid. Saudi Arabia provided $3.3 billion in foreign aid in 1984, or 3.2% of its GNP, in spite of the fall in its oil revenues, and the fact that the OPEC countries as a whole cut their aid by nearly $1 billion. This meant Saudi Arabia remained the fourth largest source of economic aid to developing countries after the the U.S. ($8.7 billion), Japan ($4.3 billion), and France ($3.8 billion).

Saudi aid has gone to 70 different countries: 25 in Asia, 38 in Africa, and 7 in the Middle East, although over 80% has gone to other Arab and Islamic states.[21] With the exception of aid to Syria, virtually all Saudi aid has gone to recipient nations where such aid has been of strategic value to the West. Saudi Arabia has raised its IMF quota from 90 million SDR in 1974 to $3.2 billion SDR in 1984. This is 10 times the rate of increase of the other six nations that sit on the IMF's Executive Board of Directors. [22]

Saudi Arabia has also been a primary source of Special Drawing Rights, or the equivalent of balance of payments loans, for the IMF's various aid funds. For example, Saudi Arabia has provided 2.3 billion SDRs--about 1/3 of the total--to the IMF's Special Oil Facility. Over 50 countries have used the facility--including six Western industrialized states. It has provided about two billion SDRs to the Supplementary Financing Facility, 8 billion SDRs to the IMF's Enlarged Access Program, and 1.5 billion SDRs to the General Agreement to Borrow. This had the net effect of providing over $10 billion worth of additional aid. Virtually all of this IMF aid activity went to nations where it directly served U.S. strategic interests as well as those of Saudi Arabia.[23]

Like Saudi trade, the volume of such aid will drop significantly along with the Kingdom's oil income, until oil prices recover. Saudi aid will still, however, play an important role in the Arab world, the Horn, North Africa, and Afghanistan. This aid is also almost certain to increase again in the early 1990s, as Saudi oil revenues rise along with world oil prices.

## THE ROLE OF SAUDI ARABIA IN THE GULF COOPERATION COUNCIL

The broad strategic importance of the Gulf Cooperation Council states has already been discussed, and Saudi Arabia plays the pivotal role in the GCC's efforts to create a regional deterrent and develop collective security arrangements.

Saudi forces must form the core of any regional efforts to create a stable pattern of deterrence. The other members of Gulf Cooperation Council cannot develop major military forces over the next decade. Bahrain, Kuwait, Oman, Qatar and the UAE lack the present and future manpower and financial resources to compete with most threat powers in the region. Further, in spite of the various public announcements of GCC exercises, the geography of the Gulf means that military cooperation between Gulf forces must ultimately consist of bilateral ties between Saudi Arabia and the smaller GCC states.

Oman is the only other GCC state with effective military forces, and its forces are still trained and equipped for infantry combat. There is little prospect that Oman will acquire more than a minimal modern air or armored component for its forces by 1995, although Oman's navy, air mobile, and artillery units should reach a relatively high level of proficiency by local standards. However, Oman also faces major funding limitations on its ability to acquire and operate modern weapons.

Table 2.4 provides a tangible illustration of Saudi Arabia's importance to the development of GCC military forces. The data on defense expenditures, military manpower, tank strength, and combat aircraft strength clearly show that Saudi Arabia is the only Gulf Cooperation Council nation that can adequately fund, arm, and equip modern high technology forces.

Table 2.4: The Impact of Saudi Arabia on GCC Defense Efforts in 1985/1986

|  | Defense Expenditure [a] | Military Manpower [b] | Tanks | Combat Aircraft |
|---|---|---|---|---|
| Bahrain [c] | 0.4 | 2,800 | 0 | 7 |
| Kuwait [c] | 1.8 | 12,000 | 240 | 76 |
| Qatar [c] | 2.0 | 6,000 | 24 | 17 |
| Oman | 2.1 | 21,500 | 33 | 52 |
| UAE [c] | 2.0 | 43,000 | 136 | 42 |
| Sub-Total | 8.3 | 147,800 | 433 | 194 |
| Saudi Arabia | 17.8 | 62,500 | 450 | 205 |
| Total | 26.1 | 210,300 | 883 | 399 |
| Saudi Arabia as a % of Total | 68 | 30 | 51 | 51 |

a. In current $ billions.
b. Total Active uniformed regular military and Saudi National Guard.
c. More than 50% of military manpower is expatriate. Large amounts of armor cannot be operated with existing forces.

Source: IISS, The Military Balance, 1985-1986.

## THE BROADER ROLE OF SAUDI ARABIA IN REGIONAL AFFAIRS

Saudi Arabia's political objectives differ from those of the U.S. in several important ways--most notably in regard to the Palestinian movement and Israel. At the same time, the Kingdom's politics and culture create a core of common interest that reinforces its strategic value to the West.

Saudi Arabia is the center of the conservative and moderate Islamic forces that offer the Arab world the option of modernization without radicalization. This position has led the Saudi government to take a pro-Western and anti-communist stand, and to systematically oppose Soviet efforts to expand its influence in the Gulf area and the rest of the Arab world. Saudi Arabia has consistently supported a policy of political and religious moderation in the Arab world, and the Kingdom has been one of the forces that has consistently attempted to move the Palestinian movement away from a posture of terrorism and armed struggle.

Saudi Arabia provided Oman with substantial aid in ending the radical and Soviet-backed Dhofar rebellion. It helped prevent a Nasserite and radical takeover in North Yemen. Its efforts to displace the USSR from South Yemen came close to success in 1978, helped push South Yemen into a peace with Oman in 1982, and are still the primary hope the West has of reducing Soviet influence in the PDRY. Though only partially successful, Saudi aid to North Yemen has been the main factor checking the growth of Soviet influence in that state.

Saudi Arabia has informally cooperated with the U.S. in aid to Jordan, Pakistan, the Sudan, and Somalia. In 1984 and 1985, it provided $550 million in aid to the Afghan freedom fighters, and exactly matched the U.S. aid program.[24]

The Kingdom played an important role in the 1981 negotiations of Special Ambassador Philip Habib, who was then attempting to remove all foreign forces from Lebanon. The Saudis worked actively and publicly to try to reach a solution in Lebanon after Israel's 1982 invasion, and for the September, 1983, ceasefire in the Shuf mountains. They helped secure Syrian agreement to several Lebanese attempts at peace negotiations.

The Kingdom has provided aid to friendly Sub-Saharan African states, and has made increases in its aid to states like Somalia and the Sudan, at the request of the U.S. Saudi Arabia has consistently encouraged Iraq and Syria to reduce their dependence on the USSR and is the only major pro-Western state with significant influence in both countries.

Saudi Arabia has not reestablished formal diplomatic ties with Egypt, but it never reduced trade or its numbers of Egyptian workers after the Camp David accords. It has tacitly supported the reintegration of Egypt into the Arab world, and has steadily increased low level contacts. The Saudis quietly aided Egypt in gaining readmission to the Islamic conference, and publicly supported Jordan when it resumed relations with Egypt, and made it clear that its aid to Jordan would continue.[25]

While Saudi aid to Syria has been an important factor in the Syrian arms build-up, Saudi Arabia has consistently used its oil wealth to moderate Syrian actions in Lebanon and to try to work out a solution to the continuing civil war in Lebanon. Saudi diplomacy has helped reduce the risk of conflicts between Syria and Jordan, and the tensions between Jordan and the Palestinians that grew out of the conflict of September 1970. In 1985, for example, Saudi Arabia tacitly supported King Hussein's efforts to persuade the PLO to reject armed struggle, supported the easing of tensions between Syria and Jordan, and supported efforts to bring Syria and Iraq together to help end the Iran-Iraq War.

THE ARAB-ISRAELI PEACE ISSUE

The differences between the West and Saudi Arabia over the PLO and the Arab-Israeli peace issue have stemmed largely from two causes. First, from Saudi Arabia's vulnerability and need to maintain relations with radical Arab states, and second, from serious differences in terms of attitudes toward tactics and Palestinian rights. Nevertheless, Saudi leaders have sought peace on terms that would recognize Israel's right to exist since at least the mid-1970s.

Saudi Arabia has long tried to compensate for its limited population and relatively small armed forces by maintaining friendly relations with radical political movements and states. Saudi Arabia must also constantly balance the conflicting demands of its ties to the West, its role in the Arab world, and its need to preserve its role in Islam. As a result, the Kingdom has adopted a quiet and "behind the scenes" style of diplomacy that avoids open confrontation, and has often used economic aid to build ties with states like Syria to minimize any political threat to the Kingdom.

While the Saudi regime has long been privately hostile to Qaddafi, it has never ceased to try to maintain correct relations, and has often sent Qaddafi pro forma messages of support as a means of reducing his hostility.[26] The Kingdom has also been extremely cautious about linking itself to U.S. peace initiatives because this makes it a target for Arab radicals and hostile states like Iran, can be used to challenge its legitimacy as the guardian of Islam's holy places, and risks alienating Syria and creating a new threat on its western border.

This cautious Saudi diplomacy, mixed with careful regard for all the rhetorical courtesies of Arab unity, has led to a great deal of misunderstanding in the West, and particularly in the U.S. This misunderstanding has been compounded by differences over tactics and attitudes towards the Palestinian movement. The fact remains, however, that both Saudi Arabia and the West have generally moved towards a common goal.

For all its differences with the U.S. over U.S. support of Israel, and with some other Western states over the proper tactics to use in the Arab-Israeli peace process, Saudi Arabia played a key role in persuading President Sadat to make his initial break with the USSR and in giving Egypt the financial and military support it needed to reach the initial Sinai accords. In 1975, Saudi Arabia helped persuade Syria to accept Egypt's second disengagement agreement with Israel by trading Saudi aid to Syria and recognition of its right to head an Arab Deterrent Force in Lebanon for Syrian support of the Egyptian position and a ceasefire between Syria and the Lebanese Christians.

Saudi Arabia opposed the Camp David accords on the grounds that they made no provision for Palestinian sovereignty on the West Bank and Gaza, or the creation of a peace settlement that would support Jordanian, Syrian, and Lebanese stability. Saudi Arabia had little choice other than to reject the Camp David accords. Like Jordan, it could not accept the vague language regarding the settlement of the issues of the West Bank and Palestinian rights. This was not only a matter of principle, any other position would have severely threatened the Kingdom's internal stability and popular support for the Saudi government. Unlike Egypt--which could afford to make such concessions because its primary interests lay in reducing its defense burden, expanding its economic ties with the West, and obtaining the return of the Sinai--Saudi Arabia could not turn a blind eye to these aspects of the Camp David accords.

Even if Saudi Arabia had been willing to ignore the West Bank issue, in spite of 30 years of commitment to the Palestinian cause, it could not sacrifice its legitimacy as the custodian of the Islamic holy places and weaken the basic underpinning of the Saudi regime. Saudi religious legitimacy is not only a factor that increases Saudi Arabia's strategic importance to the West, it is a key factor in the Kingdom's regional and internal security. Saudi support of Camp David would have cost it the support of many of its citizens, many of its foreign workers, and most of the smaller Gulf states.

This Saudi commitment to the Palestinian cause did not, however, preclude a willingness to recognize Israel.[27] As early as May 11, 1977, Crown Prince Fahd talked of "complete, permanent peace" and a normalization of relations with Israel, stating that "all Arabs, including the Palestinians," were ready to negotiate a Middle East settlement with Israel if Israel recognized the full rights of the Palestinian people. Prince Fahd asked President Carter to urge the Israelis to keep an open mind on a settlement that would be "just and lasting" and expressed "his strong hope that Israel would be reassured about the inclinations of his country toward the protection of Israel's security".

While upheaval in the Arab world following the Camp David accords led Saudi Arabia to step back from the peace issue, Prince Fahd reiterated these ideas once political tensions eased. In August 1981 he presented a formal eight point peace plan that closely followed the UN resolutions supported by the United States. The Fahd plan called for:

o Israeli withdrawal from all territory occupied in the 1967 war;
o Recognition of the Palestinian refugees' right to return to their homeland, or to compensation if they did not wish to return;
o Establishment of an independent Palestinian state in the West Bank and Gaza Strip, with East Jerusalem, which had been annexed by Israel, as its capital;
o A U.S. trusteeship of the occupied territories that would last only for a transitional period of a few months;
o Removal of all Israeli settlements from the occupied territories;
o Guarantees of freedom of worship in the Holy Land for all religions;
o Guarantees of the right of all states in the area to live in peace; and,
o Guarantees of such an agreement by the United Nations or "some of its members," presumably the United States and the Soviet Union.

The first five points in the Saudi plan, and possibly the last three, were unacceptable to the Begin government in the precise form presented by Prince Fahd. Nevertheless, advancing the Fahd plan constituted tacit recognition of Israel's right to exist. Further, Saudi Arabia spent nearly two years quietly advancing these proposals to the Arab world, and made them the cornerstone of its diplomacy at the Arab summit at Fez, Morocco, in 1982.

Saudi Arabia has consistently pursued its own peace strategy ever since. It took a leading role in trying to bring peace to Lebanon after the Israeli invasion of June, 1982, and worked closely with the U.S. when it was trying to reach a joint arrangement with Israel and Syria. It supported the agreement that the U.S. worked out between Israel and Lebanon in the spring of 1983 and the U.S. efforts to persuade Syria to accept some modus vivendi with Israel after the agreement failed to bring peace to Lebanon. It has since made major diplomatic efforts to limit the conflict in Lebanon.

Saudi Arabia has responded favorably to most European peace initiatives, and initially supported President Reagan's September 1982 peace proposal. It backed the call for peace negotiations at the subsequent Arab summit meeting at Fez. There is no question that Saudi Arabia still disagrees with aspects of the U.S. position towards a peace settlement with Israel. It could not formally link itself to King Hussein's new peace initiative in 1985 because of the risk of alienating Syria and triggering new radical pressure from Syria, and radical Palestinian elements in the Gulf. It did, however, strongly back the holding of the Palestinian National Council meeting in Amman which was the critical step in making this peace initiative possible.

Saudi Arabia has, however, supported the UN resolutions that tacitly recognize Israel's right to exist and the need for Arab peace negotiations with Israel. Its only objections to UN Resolution 242 have dealt with its treatment of the Palestinians solely as a "refugee problem" and not to its call for peace for all nations in the area. Its differences with the West now stem largely from the political requirement to pay careful attention to the views of Syria and various Palestinian factions, and to the timing and nature of U.S. recognition of the PLO, and not over the need for a peace that recognizes Israel and its need for secure borders.

---

[1] For a good summary discussion of the trends involved see the 1984 and 1985 annual reports of the Saudi Arabian Monetary Agency; David Fairlamb, "Why the Saudis Are Switching Investments", Dun's Business Month, May, 1985, pp. 56-60; "Saudi Arabia, Foreign Economic Trends and Their Implications for the United States", Department of Commerce, FET-85-79, September, 1985: and the "The Gulf Cooperation Countries: A Survey", Economist, February, 1986, pp. 29-48.

While the statistics involved are uncertain. Saudi Arabia seems to have averaged about 2.2 MMBD in 1985, with monthly production falling as low as 1.6 MMBD. The net Saudi revenue from crude oil and refined product in 1985/86 may have fallen as low as SR 90 billion ($24.61 billion). This forced Saudi Arabia to cut its budget target from SR 200 billion to SR 130 Million. Saudi Arabia responded by raising its production level and triggering a major oil price war in late 1985. As a result, Saudi oil production rose to about 4.5 MMBD.

## Western Strategic Interests in Saudi Arabia

Saudi Arabia then set a 1986/87 budget target of SR 170 billion. The basic trends in the Saudi budget during the period between oil scarcity and oil glut are shown below. Defense amounted for roughly 25% of the Saudi budget, with manpower, operations and maintenance costs rising to a level of $10 billion annually in 1986/1987. It should be noted, however, that these projections predate the drop in the spot market to less than $15 a barrel and further Saudi budget cuts are likely.

Saudi Arabian Public Expenditure: 1982-83 to 1986-87
(In Current Billions of SR with 1SR=$3.6507

|             | 82/83 | 83/84 | 84/85 | 85/86      | 86/87      |
|-------------|-------|-------|-------|------------|------------|
| Expenditure | 244.9 | 230.2 | 214.8 | 150/180    | 170/180    |
| Revenue     | 246.2 | 206.4 | 169.6 | 130.0      | 150.0      |
| Balance     | +1.3  | -23.8 | -45.2 | -20 to -50 | -20 to -50 |

Source: SAMA, MEED, 1 March, 1986, p. 24, and Wall Street Journal, March 22, 1985, p. 28. Data for 85/86 and 86/87 are estimates.

[2] For typical reporting on the Saudi role in OPEC's 1986 price war see the Economist, February 8, 1986, p. 61 and April 26, 1986, p. 70.

[3] The details of oil exploration in Saudi Arabia are summarized in the ARAMCO Yearbook and Facts and Figures. For a good discussion of overall world reserves, see the International Energy Annual of the U.S. Energy Information Adminstration, Washington, D.C., DOE/EIA-02(84), pp. 79-81, and "Worldwide Report", The Oil and Gas Journal, December 31, 1984, p. 71. This latter report shows total world proved oil reserves as totaling 699 billion barrels, with 84 billion in Communist countries (63 billion in the USSR and 2 billion in Eastern Europe), 118 billion in the West Hemisphere (27 billion in the U.S.), 55.5 billion barrels in Africa, 19 billion in Asia, 24 billion in Western Europe, and 398 billion in the entire Middle East.

[4] Charles D. Masters, David H. Root, and William D. Dietzman, "Distribution and Quantitative Assessment of World Crude-Oil Reserves and Resources", USGS, Washington unpublished, 1983.

[5] Charles D. Masters, "World Petroleum Resources--A Perspective", USGS Open File Report 85-248. It is interesting to note that for all the talk of major discoveries, no major oil reserves have been discovered outside the Gulf in the last half decade, and such promising areas as China and Mexico have not proved to ease the world oil supply situation. The PRC now has only 19 billion barrels of proved reserves--well below the reserves required for its own demand levels in the year 2000--and Mexico has 49 billion.

[6] See Charles D. Masters, "World Petroleum Resources--A Perspective", USGS Open File Report 85-248, 1985, and Christopher Flavin, World Oil: Coping With the Dangers of Success, Worldwatch Paper 66, Washington D.C., Worldwatch Institute, 1985.

[7] These estimates are confirmed by the U.S. Department of Energy. The DOE estimates that Kuwait has 92.7 billion in reserves, Bahrain has 170 million, Oman has 3.5 billion, Qatar has 3.4 billion, and the UAE has 32.5 billion (Abu Dhabi 30.5 billion, Dubai 1.44 billion, Ras al Khaimah 100 million, and Sharjah 450 million).

8 The estimation of both reserves and production capacity is now very complex because the data on Iran and Iraq have not been updated since 1980. The figures quoted here also count only production that can be sustained over a prolonged period. Installed capacity is significantly higher. See Anthony H. Cordesman, The Gulf and the Search for Strategic Stability, Westview, Boulder, 1984, pp. 16-18.

9 For a good projection of overall energy trends, and the impact of cuts in the flow of Gulf oil, see Energy Information Administration, Impacts of World Oil Market Shocks on the U.S. Economy, DOE/EIA-0411, July, 1983; Department of Energy, Energy Projections to the Year 2000, DOE/PE-0029/2, October, 1983, pp. 1-16 and Chapter II; and Secretary of Energy, Annual Report to the Congress, DOE-S-0010(84), September, 1984, pp. 1-12. For a more recent and more pessimistic projection, see CONOCO, World Energy Outlook Through 2000, April, 1985. Also see Richard B. Schmitt, "U.S. Dependence on Oil, Gas Imports May Grow", Wall Street Journal, April 23, 1985. For the details of European dependence on Gulf oil see OECD/IEA, Oil and Gas Statistics, 1985, No. 4, Paris, 1986.

10 DOE, World Energy Outlook Through 2000, April, 1985, p. 5 and Chapter 5. The estimate of U.S. reserves has been cut significantly since this report was issued, and the "oil glut" is having the side effect of leading to overproduction or shutting in of marginal wells much sooner than had been previously estimated. Current projections for North Sea oil show a steady and sharp decline in production after 1986-87, depending on oil prices. See the Wall Street Journal, March 17, 1986, p. 2, Washington Post, March 9, 1986, p. K, and New York Times, March 18, 1986, p. D-7

11 For a good summary of the impact on oil production and oil exporting states, see "Oil Turns Manic Depressive", Economist, February 15, 1986, pp. 61-62

12 Energy Information Administration, Impacts of World Oil Market Shocks on the U.S. Economy, DOE/EIA-0411, July, 1983; Department of Energy, Energy Projections to the Year 2000, DOE/PE-0029/2, October, 1983, pp. 1-16 and Chapter II; and Secretary of Energy, Annual Report to the Congress, DOE-S-0010(84), September, 1984, pp. 1-12.

13 Economist, January 18, 1986, p. 59, and April 26, 1986, pp. 70-71. For detailed historical breakouts, see Saudi Arabia, Foreign Trade Statistics, 1984 AD.

14 See the Economist Intelligence Unit, Regional Review: The Middle East and North Africa, 1986, London, Economic Publications, 1986, pp. 210-214, and Economist, January 18, 1986, p. 59.

15 According to the Department of Energy publication, Petroleum Supply Monthly, Saudi Arabia provided the U.S. with less than 450,000 barrels per day of crude oil and product during 1984-1985 out of average monthly import levels ranging from 3.9 to 6.2 million barrels per day. Indonesia, Nigeria, Venezuela, Canada, and Mexico all provided equal or greater imports.

16 The previous statistics are taken from the U.S. Department of Commerce, "Saudi Arabia", Foreign Economic Trends and Their Implications for the U.S., FET 84-80, July, 1984. For other recent trend data see the summary in Appendix A of Saudi Arabia, A Country Study, Department of the Army, DA Pam 550-51, Washington, D.C., 1985, pp 32-322.

17 The drop in oil prices affected Saudi Arabia the most before it led the cut in oil prices in 1986. Its average production dropped from 10 million to as low as 2.5 million barrels

per day, and its current account swung from a surplus of almost $40 billion in 1981 to a deficit of nearly $25 billion in CY1985. This was equivalent to 30% of Saudi Arabia's GNP.

In the first quarter of 1986, however, the Kingdom ended its role as OPEC swing producer and increased oil output to 4.5 MMBD. This triggered a massive drop in oil prices and the fall in income per barrel offset the increase total production. This forced the Kingdom to defer issuing its 1986/87 budget. This makes it almost impossible to estimate future trade patterns.

Similar problems affect all the other GCC and Gulf oil states except Kuwait. Kuwait's $85 billion in savings nearly equal those of Saudi Arabia, and it had a current account surplus of $5 billion in 1985. Kuwait may just be able to maintain a current account surplus in 1986, although it predicts $4 billion less in government revenues in 1986 than in 1985. Economist, April 26, 1986, pp. 71-72.

[18] EIU, Annual Regional Review: Middle East and North Africa, 1986, p. 210.

[19] The most negative recent estimate of Saudi wealth is by Eilyahu Kanovsky, an economist at Bar-Ilan University in Israel. He estimates that The Saudi budget surplus has dropped from $36 billion in 1980-81 to a $17 billion deficit in 1985-86. He estimates that Saudi monetary reserves have dropped from a peak of $150 billion to about $70 billion because $30 billion of the $100 billion reported to the IMF consists of uncollectable loans to states like Iraq. He also estimates Saudi defense expenditures for 1986-87 as being below $16 billion, but his estimate ignores oil barter and exchange agreements. See Hobart Rowen, "Reassessesing Saudi Arabia's Economic Viability", Washington Post, July 20, 1986.

[20] David Fairlamb, op cit., pp. 56-60; Osama Faquih, "Similarities in Economic Outlook Between the U.S. and Saudi Arabia", February 22, 1985; and Yusuf Nimatallah, "Arab Banking and Investment in the U.S.", IMF, February 22, 1985; and "The Economic and Fiscal Strategy of Saudi Arabia", Center for Strategic and International Studies, Georgetown University, Middle East Conference, March 20-21, 1985.

[21] For detailed breakouts of the distribution of Saudi aid, see The Kingdom of Saudi Arabia: Relief Efforts, Ministry of Finance and National Economy, Saudi Arabia, 1985, and Annual Report of the Saudi Fund for Development, 1984-1985, Saudi Arabia, 1985.

[22] It is almost impossible to estimate the flow of aid to Syria with any precision. U.S. government officials feel the largest component of Saudi Aid to Syria is an annual $529 million payment made under the terms of the 1978 Bagdhad summit. An Israeli source, Shemuel Meir, estimates total OAPEC aid to Syria and Jordan as follows:

|        | 1979  | 1980  | 1981  | 1982  | 1983  | % Change 1981-1983 |
|--------|-------|-------|-------|-------|-------|--------------------|
| Jordan | 1,008 | 1,212 | 1,172 | 948   | 691   | -41                |
| Syria  | 1,651 | 1,484 | 1,792 | 1,376 | 1,245 | -30.5              |

Strategic Implications of the New Oil Reality, Westview Press, Boulder, 1986, p.55.

[23] Op cit.

[24] Washington Post, June 20, 1986, p. A-30.

25 See U.S. Department of Defense, Saudi Arms Sale Questions and Answers, February 24, 1986, informal briefing paper for the U.S. Congress, p. X .17.

26 The U.S. government stated that it had no evidence of Saudi aid to Libya in any aspect of its military development or terrorist activities in its background briefing papers for the Congress in justifying its 1986 arms sales to Saudi Arabia. See Saudi Arms Sale Questions and Answers, February 24, 1986, p. X.56.

27 The U.S. government officially rejected Israeli charges that the Saudis had provided significant arms to the PLO in its background papers defending its 1986 arms sales to Saudi Arabia. The only Israeli evidence of such transfers was an unattached shipping label it claimed had been found on a Palestinian arms cache near Damour. This label proved to be from a 1977 shipment to Saudi Arabia of .22 caliber long rifle and .30 caliber linked ball and tracer ammunition. No such ammunition has been found in captured PLO stores and Israel refused to reply to repeated U.S. requests for further ammunition and has never claimed to have found such ammunition in Palestinian hands. As for charges that Saudi Arabia provided M-16 rifles to the PLO, the U.S. never sold M-16 rifles to Saudi Arabia, and the serial numbers on arms captured by Israeli turned out to be from M-16s sold to the Lebanese Army.

## III. SAUDI ARABIA AND WESTERN POWER PROJECTION CAPABILITIES

The political and economic factors that create strategic ties between the West and Saudi Arabia are only part of the story. One of the most critical factors shaping strategic relations is the fact that close military relations with Saudi Arabia are critical to the success of any large scale Western military action in defense of the Gulf. Further, this requires a special relationship between Saudi Arabia and the United States. While a close relationship between Europe and Saudi Arabia is adequate to serve the West's interests in many areas, any significant Western military action in the Gulf region must be led by the United States and will be dominated by U.S. forces.

The West's ability to play a military role outside Europe, the Mediterranean, and the Atlantic has changed radically since the early 1960s. The steady elimination of the last vestige of colonialism have led most Western states to create forces with sharply limited range and support capability. Only four Western countries are still capable of playing any significant power projection role in the Gulf: Turkey, France, Britain, and the United States. All of these states face major limitations on the power they can project. Turkey can only project power near its borders, and France and Britain no longer have major power projection forces. The U.S. must project its power nearly half way around the world and faces major limitations in terms of strategic lift and forward basing and facilities.

### TURKEY

Turkey has common borders with Iran, Iraq, Syria, and the Southwestern USSR. Up to half of its armed forces could play an out of area role in defending eastern and southern Turkey. Turkey has 45,000 men in Eastern Turkey, and its Third Army has more than six bases around Erzerum, with six more strung out along the 160 mile highway towards Agri. It is conducting active operations against the Kurds in the area around Hakkair and Chirze. In the spring of 1985, it sent some 30,000 men to reinforce units on the Syrian and Iraqi borders, and it has steadily built up the capability of the Third Army over the last year.[1] Turkey is expanding its strategic road net near both the Syrian and Iraqi borders, and is steadily increasing its ties to the Northern Gulf states. It has developed steadily stronger trade relations with the Middle East, and with Iraq and Iran in particular. It deployed forces equivalent to two divisions in Iraq in 1983, with Iraq's consent, in a military operation against the Kurds.

While Turkey would normally have to deploy most of its forces to meet the threat of Soviet or Greek action, Turkey could use at least six mechanized and/or armored divisions in operations near its borders with Iraq and Iran or Syria (up to 500 tanks, 800 AFV/APCs, and 400 artillery weapons). It also has one commando and one parachute brigade it could commit, and could deploy at least one mobile Gendarmerie Brigade with V-150 and UR-416 APCs suitable for light paramilitary action. The Turkish Air Force could deploy up to five fighter squadrons, and one recce squadron, and 2-4 Rapier/Redeye units (24 fire units), and is improving its $C^3I$ net, military facilities and air bases in Eastern Turkey.[2]

It is important to note, however, that Turkey is severely short of mobile combat and service support assets. It has a very poor communications net, lacks the logistics and infrastructure for extended power projection much beyond its border areas, and badly needs modern anti-tank weapons, portable artillery and other combat gear for mountain and urban warfare. Turkey would experience severe operational problems the moment it shifted from border or territorial defense to operations beyond its border. It has no real power projection capabilities and would require full scale external support for any operation outside its border areas.[3]

Turkey has also carefully avoided taking any political or military action implying that its forces could play any regional role other than self-defense. It is still deeply committed in Cyprus, and faces a massive Soviet and Bulgarian threat on its northern borders. It would probably avoid taking any contingency action that did not directly threaten its territory, and would almost certainly avoid playing any role in an Arab-Israeli contingency even if it involved a substantial Soviet presence in Syria. Turkey's willingness to intervene in the event of the collapse of Iraq or a Soviet move into Iran is unclear. It has publicly declared its facilities in Eastern Turkey are not U.S. or NATO contingency facilities for action in the Gulf, although such declarations are deliberately ambiguous.

FRANCE

Britain and France are the only Western European nations that still deploy substantial out of area forces in the Gulf, Red Sea, and Indian Ocean. It is important to note, however, that these British and French forces in the region are relatively small, and will normally be limited to roles in very low level conflicts. They do not have the strength or sustaining power to engage in armored, air, or naval combat in the Gulf, except against low level threats like the Dhofar rebel units in the PDRY or as part of a regional or U.S. led force. They have limited surface-to-air (SAM), electronic warfare (EW), and recce aircraft capabilities, but lack advanced sensor and intelligence systems other than maritime patrol aircraft, photo recce, and land/air/ship borne electronic support measures (ESSM).

Current French capabilities and trends are summarized in Table 3.1. France's main contingency forces now in the region consist of its forces in Djibouti, its Indian Ocean Command (ALINDIEN), and its South Indian Ocean Command. France could also deploy substantial land and air forces, including elements of the FAR ( Forces d'Action Rapide), and up to a two carrier task force to the Gulf in an emergency. France has some particularly well trained elite units for such operations, including the Foreign Legion.

The FAR, which was organized in its current form in June, 1983, has a nominal strength of 47,000 men, the majority of which are professionals. Its main combat units include the 6th Light Armored Division (Nimes), the 4th Air Mobile Division (Nancy), the 9th Marine Infantry Division (Nantes), the 11th Paratroop Division (Toulouse), and the 27th Alpine Division (Grenoble).

Two of these divisions have a new structure. The 6th Light Armored Division is a 7,400 man unit with two infantry regiments with armored vehicles, and two armored regiments with 36 AMX-10 reconnaissance vehicles and Milan anti-tank guided missiles. It has a command and support regiment, a 155 mm artillery regiment with 24 TR-155 mm towed guns, and an engineer regiment. Its total equipment includes 340 VAB armored personnel carriers, 24 VAB/Mephistos, 72 AMX-10RCs, 48 Milans, and 48 Mistral anti-aircraft missiles. The 4th Air Mobile Division has 250 helicopters, of which half are combat helicopters. It is organized into four combat helicopter regiments, two infantry regiments with anti-tank guided missiles, two engineering companies, and a command and support regiment.[4]

The FAR is not, however, dedicated solely or even principally to out of area missions. It has both a role in European combat and a potential role in out of area contingencies. Further, some elements are clearly organized for combat in the center region. The 4th Air Mobile Division, for example, is organized to halt Soviet armored penetrations at ranges up to 250 kilometers from its main position. The 27th Alpine Division is also best suited to a particular defense mission in Europe. Only the 6th Light Armored Division is specially configured for overseas deployment. The other two main out of area units would be the 9th Marine Infantry and 11th Paratroop Divisions. The 9th Marine Infantry Division has four infantry, one armored cavalry, one combat engineer, and one headquarters and support regiment. It is being equipped with the Panhard Sagaie armored car with a 90 mm gun to give it airportable anti-armor capability. The 11th Paratroop Division has six parachute, one parachute combat engineer, and one HQ and support regiments.[5]

In practice, most FAR units must be kept in Europe unless some other nation provides strategic lift, support, and sustaining capability. This is particularly true of any combat involving armored forces, or substantial enemy air power, since most FAR units have only limited air defense capability and are only equipped to fight against heavy armor in a defensive role. It seems unlikely that France could deploy more than one light division to any area in the Middle East, except Djibouti, without several months of build-up unless the U.S. provided most of the support and sustaining capability--both of which are areas where USCENTCOM already faces serious shortages.[6] In practice, France would probably be limited to a maximum of about three squadrons for any short term deployment, although it could certainly build-up much more substantial deployment and support capabilities over a period of three to six months. France would also need U.S. strategic lift to rapidly move air basing and air defense assets. [7]

France can deploy considerable air and naval power as well, but would again face the problem of strategic lift, support, and sustaining capability. France has never been able to buy the C-141 Starlifters it has sought from the U.S., cannot afford the C-5A, and has had to rely on limited numbers of DC-8F jet freighters, C-160 Transall twin turboprops, and old piston engine Noratlases. It is badly short of tankers for refueling and now is limited to a maximum of one regiment worth of long range airlift. Its tank landing ships are obsolete and most have been withdrawn from services, and funds are not available for the three 10,000 ton amphibious combat ships that France has sought since the early 1980s.[8]

The French Navy has redeployed most of its major surface forces to the Mediterranean since 1976, including its two carriers, the Foch and Clemenceau and many of its best ASW and air defense cruisers and destroyers like the Colbert, Suffren and Duquesne. The French carriers have a 22,000 ton standard displacement and 32,780 ton full load. Each normally carries 16 Super Etendards, 3 Etendard IVPs, 10 F-8E Crusaders, 7 Alize, and 2 Alouette helicopters. Unlike Britain and Italy, therefore, France retains true carriers, although French carriers scarcely compare with the full fleet carriers of the U.S., which can displace up to 85,000 tons.[9]

This gives France the ability to conduct naval operations the size of a carrier task force, although French carriers and ships lack the air defenses and anti-missile capabilities for operations against threats with modern missile equipped strike aircraft unless they can receive support from ground based fighters. France also would find it very difficult to sustain air operations from its carriers for any length of time because of its carriers small complement of aircraft and supply, and lack of air defense aircraft. Further, it lacks the replenishment capability to operate more than one carrier group in the Indian Ocean.

France spent some 2.5 billion French francs on out of area operations in 1985, of which 555 million francs was spent overseas. This included costs for the French forces that were in Lebanon, the protection of the Embassy in Beirut, the French presence in Chad, French operations in New Caledonia, and the creation of a new base there. France has also shown on many occasions that it can project small forces effectively--although it has generally needed U.S. assistance in strategic lift for significant long range troop movements.[10] For example, the U.S. provided a C-5A for the recent operations in Chad because French C-160 Transalls could not carry large weapons systems such as the Hawk missiles France used for air base protection.[11]

France also showed it could quietly provide significant internal security assistance to Saudi Arabia when it had to suppress radicals that seized the Grand Mosque in Mecca in 1982. France has, however, faced increasing political problems in sustaining out of area operations in cases like Chad. It is increasingly doubtful that the French public would support any intervention that produced significant casualties or required a sustained military presence in the face of hostile forces.

Any significant out of area deployments would also mean cutting France's capability to support the defense of the Atlantic and Mediterranean, although SACEUR and SACLANT have already declared that NATO has major deficiencies in ship strength to meet critical defense missions. The U.S. would have to provide substantial airlift and resupply for combat operations, and would have to provide intelligence support and air cover in the face of a Soviet or well equipped Third World air threat with long range air or ship to ship missiles.[12]

France is also experiencing steadily greater budget problems in out of area operations. While France now seems likely to remain in the Indian Ocean and Djibouti through 1995, it may well have to phase out one of its three carriers and/or delay construction and production of new carrier aircraft. Since the Super Etendards, Etendards, and F-8Es on French carriers, and much of the $C^3I$ and air/missile defense gear on French ships, are already obsolete or obsolescent, French carrier task force contingency capability is likely to drop to a one carrier demonstrative deployment only capability sometime between 1990 and 1995.[13]

France should, however, still be able to fund the deployment of more advanced maritime patrol aircraft, modern fighter-recce aircraft, and better ESSM systems. It plans to upgrade the surface-to-air missile defenses on many of its ships, including better close in protection. It will deploy improved SHORADs, although it has no heavier land-based SAMs it could deploy to the Gulf. French carriers are nuclear armed, and both French Mirage 2000s and Mirage IVs could provide theater nuclear support.

Saudi Arabia and Western Power Projection Capabilities

Table 3.1: French Contingency Capabilities in the Middle East: 1985-1986

Forces Normally Deployed In the Area:

Mediterranean Fleet:
  Two SSNs
  Nine Submarines
  Two carriers
  14 Destroyers/frigates/escorts.
  5 mine countermeasure ships
  5 amphibious ships

Peacekeeping:
  Lebanon (Unifil): 1,380: 1 infantry and 1 logistic battalion
  Sinai MFO: 40: 2 Twin Otter and 1 C-160 aircraft

Djibouti:
  Total manpower: 3,800 men
  Permanent and Prepositioned Forces:
    o 10th BCS (Command and Services Battalion)
    o 5th RIAOM (Overseas Regiment)
    o 13th DBLE (Demi-Brigade of the Foreign Legion,
      --ALAT (Army Light Aviation Unit) with 5 attack
      and 5 medium transport helicopters.
      --CDMB (Engineering Company)
    o One motorized company
    o Army Equipment includes AMX 13 light tanks, AMX with SS-11,
    AFVs, 105 mm battery, 1 AA artillery battery
    o One Mirage IIIC squadron with 10 fighters, and air elements
    with 1 C-160 transport, and two Allouette helicopters.
    o Naval elements with 1 Atlantic MPA.
  Rotated Units (every four months): One motorized company

ALINDIEN: Indian Ocean Inter-Service Overseas Command
  Total Manpower: 1,400
  Five Frigates, 3 minor combatants, 1 amphibious, and one support ship
  South Indian Ocean Joint Service Command: La Reunion and Mayotte:
  Total manpower: 2,200 men
  Permanent and Propositioned Forces
    o 53rd BCS
    o 2nd RPIMA (Marine Parachute Regiment)
  Rotated Units: One parachute company

Probable Maximum Out of Area Contingency Forces in France

Rapid Action Force
  1 Parachute Division (13,500)
  1 Air Portable Marine Division (8,500)
  1 Light Armored Division (7,400)
  1 Air Mobile Division (5,100)
  1 Signals Regiment
  Foreign Legion Force (8,500) 1 armored, 1 parachute, 4
  infantry, and 2 engineer regiments
  Independent Army Elements 1 Support Brigade and Two Mixed

## Saudi Arabia and Western Power Projection Capabilities

    Regiments

Naval Forces
    2 Carriers with 20 Super Etendard, 4 Etendard IV or 7 F-8E
    5 ASW and 2 AA Destroyers with Exocet, Crotale, and Malafon
    8 Frigates with Exocet.
    2 Amphibious Assault Ships with 9 LCM or 2 LST
    2-5 Diesel or Nuclear Submarines
    11 Support Ships
    5 Maritime Patrol Aircraft

Air Forces
    3 Mirage and 3 Jaguar Squadrons
    1 Mirage III Recce Squadron
    6 Crotale Batteries (8 fire/4 radar units)
    1 DC-8 and 2 C-160 transport squadrons
    60-80 armed Alouette II, Puma, and Gazelle army helicopters,
    some with HOT ATGM.
    2-5 transport Helicopter squadrons

Source: Adapted from the IISS, Military Balance, 1985-1986, and John Chipman, French Military Policy and African Security, Adelphi Papers, 201, IISS, London, 1985, p. 20.

## UNITED KINGDOM

    British military intervention capability in the Gulf is more difficult to estimate. Britain can still deploy a large portion of its forces for the Atlantic to the Mediterranean. Although it officially is no longer "East of Suez". It still provides a major advisory presence to many of its former Trucial states including Kuwait, and provides contract naval and air officers to Oman, as well as small SAS units. Britain also has increased its naval deployments in the Mediterranean, and has played an active role in patrolling the Gulf and Straits of Hormuz since the beginning of the Iran-Iraq War.

    This British role in the Gulf is particularly interesting because Britain is the only European power to have actively cooperated with the U.S. in out of area operations in the Gulf. While France also has maintained a naval presence in the area, it has refused to coordinate even at an informal command level and to join the U.S. and U.K. in convoying ships through the Gulf, just as it refused to coordinate closely with the U.S. and other European states in the 1982 peace keeping effort in Lebanon and in the 1984 effort to clear the Red Sea of mines.[14]

    The U.K. began joint action with the U.S. in the Gulf area with a demonstrative exercise in the Indian Ocean in October, 1980, which was clearly designed to demonstrate Western determination to keep the Gulf open in spite of the war. Britain maintained this presence at a demonstrative level until early 1984, when Britain publicly agreed to join the U.S. in convoying ships through the Straits of Hormuz after renewed threats by Iran. Britain then moved the frigate Brazen and destroyer Glamorgan to the Straits. By July, 1984, Britain had deployed the Glasgow, a Type 42 destroyer, and the

Charybdis, a Leander class frigate, plus the Royal Fleet Auxiliary ship Appleleaf in demonstrative sailings through the Gulf of Oman, the Straits of Hormuz, and into the Gulf. It also sent the Air Defense Troop of the 3rd Commando Brigade of the Royal Marines to the Gulf to provide air defense for British ships with shoulder-launched Shorts Javelin surface-to-air missiles. Since that time, Britain has fully coordinated plans for both convoying and mine clearing with the U.S.[15]

British Conservative politicians have often suggested that Britain should strengthen its out of area role, and Britain has regularly deployed ships in cooperation with the U.S. in the Gulf during the Iran-Iraq War. Britain also demonstrated excellent out of area contingency capabilities during the Falklands conflict. In practice, however, Britain has never obtained the defense budgets necessary to maintain or expand its out of area contingency forces. Both its presence in the Gulf and total power projection capabilities have declined steadily since 1968, and are likely to continue to decline further.[16]

An estimate of British contingency capabilities is provided in Table 3.2. Both Britain's 5th Airborne Brigade (2nd and 3rd Battalions) and the Royal Marines 3rd Commando Brigade (40, 42, and 45 battalions) are now specifically earmarked for out of area operations, and the Parachute regiment and a Gurkha battalion have out of area experience. The 5th Brigade has been specially equipped for such missions, and has been converted from an infantry to an airborne unit during the last two years. It has a special leading battalion group with artillery and combat engineer support designed for very rapid long distance deployment. Nevertheless, all such British forces have been affected by Britain's defense budget problems and are short of the air defense, armor, artillery, and lift required for operations against armored or mechanized Middle Eastern forces.[17]

Britain now has very limited carrier power, and would find it difficult to project more than one light carrier to the Gulf. Further, Britain would then be dependent on small numbers of comparatively short legged Harrier and Sea Harrier aircraft. The latest British carrier, the Ark Royal, was commissioned in 1985. It is only 680 feet long, however, and displaces only 20,000 tons. This makes it far closer to a U.S. LPH-class assault ship than a U.S. fleet carrier, which is more than 1,000 feet long and displaces over 65,000 tons. The Ark Royal also falls far short of a French carrier in terms of on board aircraft. The deck has a ski jump for VSTOL aircraft and it cannot operate with modern fixed wing naval fighters. The Ark Royal normally carries only 14 aircraft: five Sea Harrier fighters, three airborne early warning Sea King Helicopters, and six ASW Sea King Helicopters.

Even the coming refit of the Invincible will mean that Britain's largest "carrier" can only deploy a total of eight Harrier VSTOL fighters and twelve Sea King AEW and ASW helicopters. The Invincible is being expanded to allow the storage of missiles for more extended operations and is being given a new 12 degree ski jump to extend Harrier range, a modern Type 996 three dimensional radar, and three Goalkeeper 30 mm guns for terminal missile defense. Nevertheless, a British carrier task force would require U.S. air/missile defense coverage against a Soviet or sophisticated Third World threat, although the Sea Harrier now has improved air defense avionics and BVR air-to-air combat capability.

Britain probably would also require U.S. logistic and fuel support for any extended naval operations outside the Mediterranean and probably emergency supply of munitions and critical contingency specific parts and equipment. This U.S. supply was vital to British operations in the Falklands, and Britain has not been able to fund most of the post-Falklands improvements it originally sought in its power projection capabilities.

British amphibious capability is especially tenuous. The Atlantic Causeway, the sister ship to the Atlantic Conveyor which was sunk in the Falklands, was converted to an amphibious helicopter ship capable of carrying several hundred Royal Marines and heavy lift helicopters. It now, however, is laid up along with the Hermes, Britain's only dedicated commando carrier. This leaves Britain with a brigade sized amphibious lift capability which is dependent on two amphibious assault ships, five Sir Bedivere class logistic land ships (LSLs), two chartered merchant ships performed the same role, a series of flat bottomed landing craft, self-propelled pontoons, and Wessex and Sea King helicopters. These would be supported by requisitioned Ships Taken Up From Trade (STUFT) which include RO-RO ships, troop carrying ferries and liners, tankers, and break bulk and cargo ships. [18]

It is increasingly doubtful that Britain will replace its two aging amphibious assault ships or landing platform docks (LPDs), the Fearless and Intrepid, although both are already obsolescent. These were designed in the late 1950s, were laid down in 1962, and were commissioned in 1965 and 1967. These two ship are now twenty years old and at least need the equivalent of a service life extension program (SLEP) which would fully rebuild and modernize both vessels. They are, however, critical to British operations. They are the only ships with the command and control, helicopter landing, and amphibious craft loading capability to support the rapid assault operations essential to successful amphibious actions.

In fact, Britain lacks both modern amphibious dock ships (LPDs) and landing ships (LSLs). These create serious problems since Britain experienced major difficulties in trying to land in bad weather in the Falklands and could not conduct amphibious landings off the Danish coast in a 1984 Bold Gannet exercise because of bad weather. The LSLs are critical to any rapid landing of armor and heavy equipment across beaches. They too, however, need modernization including some added form of air defense.[19]

More broadly, Britain would now experience significant problems in conducting even brigade-sized operations against an opponent with extensive heavy armor and air power. British out of area forces are relatively lightly equipped and do not have main battle tanks or long range surface-to-air missile defenses. Britain would take at least two to three weeks to assemble the sea lift and forces to deploy a mechanized brigade, and could only use strategic airlift for such an operation if it were made available from the U.S.

Britain is not organized or equipped to conduct major land operations East of Suez, and lacks the ability to rapidly deploy more than light armor in Gulf contingencies, and this situation is unlikely to change. Even high speed movement of a reinforced battalion of British mechanized forces would now require supporting U.S. airlift or sea lift. British land forces will, however, steadily improve their AFVs, holdings of Milan and Improved TOW ATGMs, and modern SHORADs like the Improved Blowpipe, and Improved Rapier.

Saudi Arabia and Western Power Projection Capabilities

Table 3.2: British Contingency Capabilities in the Middle East: 1985-1986

Forces Normally Deployed in the Area

INDIAN OCEAN SQUADRON
2 destroyers/frigates
1 support ship

OMAN
SAS detachment
RAF contract pilots
RN seconded and contract officers

DIEGO GARCIA
1 Naval detachment
1 Marine detachment

CYPRUS
UNFICYP: 750 men
 Army: (3,250)
  o 1 Infantry battalion less 2 Companies
  o 1 Infantry battalion plus 2 Companies
  o 2 Armored recce squadrons
  o 2 Engineer and 1 logistic support squadrons
  o 1 Helicopter flight
 RAF: (1,347)
  o 1 Helicopter squadron

Probable Maximum Out of Area Contingency Forces in the U.K.

LAND FORCES
2 Armored recce regiments
10 Infantry battalions
2 Paratroop battalions
1 SAS regiment
 o Scimitar, Ferret and Fox AFVs
 o FV-432, Saracen, MCV-80, Spartan APCs
2-4 artillery regiments with 105 mm guns on AFVs or towed
155 mm howitzers.
1 SAM regiment with Rapier
2 SAM batteries with Blowpipe and Rapier
30-40 Helicopters: Gazelle AH-1 and Lynx AH-1, some with TOW

NAVAL FORCES
1 Commando brigade, 2 SBS assault squadrons with Blowpipe,
105 mm guns, Milan ATGMs.
2 Carriers with 10-15 Sea Harrier and Harriers, 9 Sea King
5 Destroyers with Sea Slug, Sea Cat, and Sea Dart SAMs
8-10 frigates with Exocet, Sea Wolf, Sea Cat
4-6 Nuclear and diesel submarines
2 Assault ships with 4 LCM and 4 LCVP, and Seacat SAMs.
4 Landing ships
15 Tankers, 6 store and 1 helicopter support ships.
5 Nimrod maritime patrol aircraft; AEW-2 Sea Kings
14 Commando and 20 ASW Sea King, 20 Lynx and Wasp helicopters

AIR FORCES
2-5 Tornado, Jaguar, and Buccaneer squadrons
1-2 Tornado and Jaguar recce squadrons.
1 Nimrod ECM aircraft.
1 VC-10 and 2-4 C-130 transport squadrons
20-30 Wessex, Chinook, and Puma helicopters.

Source: IISS, Military Balance, 1985-1986, pp. 41-43 and Peter Foot, Beyond The North Atlantic: The European Contribution, ASIDES, No. 21, Spring 1982, p. 28

## UNITED STATES

Given this background, it is clear that the United States is the only Western power that can intervene in the Gulf in a moderate to high level conflict. The U.S., however, will be critically limited by the availability of bases and facilities in the area. In fact, the size of the forces it can commit to the region are determined more by the limitations on its strategic air and sea lift, forward basing and support facilities, and the risks inherent in redeploying U.S. forces from other regions, than by the total combat forces available from the U.S. order of battle. The U.S. has steadily improved the forces it can commit to the Middle East which are tailored to regional needs and contingencies since the fall of the Shah of Iran, but the U.S. must rely heavily on prepositioned equipment and stocks in the Gulf to minimize the strain on its strategic lift, and on access to friendly bases so that it can allocate its lift resources to moving U.S. combat forces, rather than creating bases and support facilities.

The U.S. can draw on two groups of forces: the forces already in the Mediterranean area and those in the U.S. The U.S. forces already in the Mediterranean normally include 470 army personnel in Greece, 3,950 in Italy, and 1,250 in Turkey. These are largely support personnel, but many could support out of area operations. The U.S. Air Force has 5,300 men in Spain, and a tactical wing with three squadrons of 72 F-16A/B. One tactical fighter wing with F-4E fighters is deployed in the U.S. on an "on call" rotational basis. The Air Force has 5,800 men and two air base groups plus one Ground Launched Cruise Missile (GLCM) unit in Italy; 2,700 men and two air base groups in Greece, and 3,800 men and two air base groups in Turkey.

The U.S. Sixth (Mediterranean) Fleet has a nominal strength of 27,000 men. It typically has two nuclear attack submarines (SSNs), two full fleet carriers, twelve major surface combatants, eleven support ships, one Amphibious Ready Group (3-5 ships and a battalion-sized landing team or Marine Amphibious Unit), and three stores ships with prepositioned combat equipment. It has major base facilities at Rota, Spain (3,600) and at Gaeta, Naples, Sigonella, and La Maddalena in Italy (5,250). The U.S. Marine forces afloat normally total 1,900 men or one Marine Amphibious Unit

(MAU). An MAU has a reinforced infantry battalion group, including tank and artillery elements, and composite air group with AV-8B fighters and helicopters, and an additional logistics unit. [20]

What is especially important to note about such a force is that it is not just an assembly of ships but includes fully ready and functional carrier task groups. It also involves more airpower than the far smaller carriers deployed by other NATO countries. The size of a typical air wing in a carrier task group is shown in Table 3.3. Not only is one U.S. carrier task group considerably stronger than the total naval forces of any other NATO nation, it is capable of self defense, major air operations, and limited forced entry through amphibious or helicopter assault.

The other Western forces available for a Gulf contingency do not meet this test. No other NATO nation has a single carrier task group capable of self-defense against a modern air force, and no allied carrier group is normally equipped to support land or air operations against an enemy equipped with modern combat aircraft and tanks.

Table 3.3: Strength of Typical U.S. Navy and Marine Air Wings

| Aircraft Type | Function | Squadrons | Aircraft |
|---|---|---|---|
| **A. Carrier Air Wing** | | | |
| F-4, F-14 (TARPS) | Fighter (Reconnaissance) | 2 | 24 |
| A-7, F/A-18 | Light Attack | 2 | 24 |
| A-6, KA-6D | Medium Attack (Tanker) | 1 | 14 |
| S-3A | ASW (Fixed Wing) | 1 | 10 |
| SH-3 | ASW (Rotary Wing) | 1 | 6 |
| EA-6B | Electronic Warfare | 1 | 4 |
| E-2C | Airborne Early Warning | 1 | 4 |
| | | 9 | 86 |
| **B. Marine Corps Air Wing** | | | |
| F-4, F-18 | Fighter | 4 | 48 |
| A-4, A-18, AV-8A | Light Attack | 2-3 | 38-57 |
| A-6 | Medium Attack | 1-2 | 10-20 |
| KC-130 | Tanker/Transport | 1 | 12 |
| EA-6B | Electronic Warfare | 1 | 4 |
| RF-4 | Reconnaissance | 1 | 7 |
| OV-10 | Observation | 1 | 12 |
| AH-1 | Attack Helicopters | 1 | 24 |
| CH-53, CH-46 | Transport/Utility Helicopters | 6-7 | 131 |
| UH-1 | Helicopters | 9 | 120 |
| | | 27-30 | 403-432 |

Source: DoD, Annual Report, FY1984, p. 163

The second part of U.S. regional contingency capabilities is easier to define: it includes the forces allocated to USCENTCOM. These forces are shown in Table 3.4., and once again it is important to contrast them with the other forces NATO can deploy. Britain, France, and Turkey can play an important role in Indian Ocean-Red Sea-Gulf scenarios, but their forces combined lack the muscle to sustain even moderate level military operations.

This does not, however, mean that USCENTCOM would find it easy to operate in the region, or is without flaws. Over 40% of USCENTCOM's combat support units are not combat ready. Current plans to improve U.S. strategic airlift will only provide about 50 million-ton miles per day worth of capacity in FY1990, versus the 66 million ton miles per day that is USCENTCOM's requirement, and it is unlikely USCENTCOM will get the airlift it needs before the year 2000--if ever. The Navy is closer to meeting its goal of 4.6 million dead weight tons worth of capacity, and should meet this goal by FY1990.[21]

Nevertheless, USCENTCOM is far short of its total goals for shore-based prepositioning. It now has a goal of 300,000 short tons worth of prepositioned supplies and equipment and only 20% of this is available afloat and another 13% ashore. It has only 77% of its goal of 150,000 tons worth of prepositioned ammunition, all of it afloat. It has 41% of its goal of 12 million barrels worth of prepositioned petroleum, oil, and lubricants (POL), with 5% prepositioned on shore in the area, 8% afloat, and 28% stored out of the USCENTCOM area.[22]

USCENTCOM would also face major sustainability problems. If one considers its total theater requirements for both prepositioned and rear deployed sustainability, it has only 43% of its one million short ton requirement of supplies and equipment (10% prepositioned), only 31% of its 16 million barrel requirement of POL (all 31% prepositioned), 71% of its 495,000 tons worth of munitions (24% prepositioned), and 51% of its threat oriented items (4% prepositioned). It will not meet its goals for water distribution capability until FY1991, will have only 6.4 million barrels of POL storage capability in FY1991, and will only rise from 52% of its medical bed capacity in FY1986 to 73% in FY1991. It has serious shortages in tactical communications, particularly in the major facilities or nodes needed for intensive combat. It now has only 64% of its equipment and will only have 78% in FY1992.

Even when all currently programmed steps are completed in the early 1990s, it will still take several weeks for the U.S. to deploy the equivalent of a two division force, and a month to six weeks to deploy three full divisions. These forces will still be light on armor compared to the major powers in the Northern Gulf.[23] The U.S. also faces the practical reality that carriers are vulnerable in Gulf waters, or anywhere else where they cannot operate a long range air and missile defense screen and enemy operations can strike from nearby air bases or the terrain masking provided by land.

Further, the U.S. Navy will be badly short of mine clearing capability. The U.S. has four mine clearing vessels in the regular U.S. Navy and 52 in the reserve fleet, but none are in Southwest Asia, and they would take so long to mobilize and deploy that it is unlikely they would arrive in a contingency where time was critical. The U.S. Navy also has three mine clearing helicopter squadrons, but they also take several weeks to deploy and would compete with other U.S. forces for available strategic airlift.[24]

The U.S. Air Force will be almost totally dependent on access to friendly air bases. Its effectiveness will also be heavily dependent on having sheltered, defended, well stocked, and interoperable facilities with suitable $C^3I/BM$ capabilities. Such bases now exist only in Spain, Morocco, Italy, Greece, Israel, Egypt, Turkey, Oman, and Saudi Arabia, and contingency access is uncertain and scenario dependent.

Major land force operations will be heavily dependent on friendly locals and good staging facilities. Strategic sea and air lift will be critical. This means free access to critical NATO and Middle Eastern staging facilities such as those in the Azores, Morocco, Egypt, and Oman. The struggle to conduct successful operations half a world away from the U.S. will be difficult at best.

## Table 3.4: USCENTCOM Forces in FY 1986

| Force and Element | Manpower |
|---|---|
| U.S. Central Command Headquarters | 1,100 |
| U.S. Army-Central Forces Command | 131,000 |
|     Headquarters U.S. Army Central Command (Third U.S. Army) | |
|     XVIII Airborne Corps Headquarters | |
|     82nd Airborne Division | |
|     101st Airborne Division (Air Assault) | |
|     24th Infantry Division (Mechanized) | |
|     6th Armored Cavalry Brigade (Air Combat) | |
|     1st Corps Support Command | |
| U.S. Navy Forces-Central Command | 123,000 |
|     Headquarters, U.S. Naval Forces Central Command | |
|     3 Aircraft Carrier Battle Groups [a] | |
|     1 Surface Action Group | |
|     3 Amphibious Groups | |
|     5 Maritime Patrol Squadrons | |
|     U.S. Middle East Task Force (Bahrain) | |
| U.S. Marine Corps Forces | 70,000 |
|     1 Marine Amphibious Force (MAF), including | |
|         1 Marine Division | |
|         1 Marine Aircraft Wing [b] | |
|         1 Force Service Action Group | |
|     1 Marine Amphibious Brigade (MAB), including (16,000) [c] | |
|         1 Marine Regiment (reinforced) | |
|         1 Marine Air Group (composite) | |
|         1 Brigade Service Support Group | |
| U.S. Air Force, Central Command Air Forces (9th Air Force) | 33,000 |
|     7 Tactical Fighter Wings [d] | |
|     3 1/3 Tactical Fighter Wings (available as attrition fillers) | |
|     2 Strategic Bomber Squadrons [e] | |
|     1 Airborne Warning and Control Wing | |
|     1 Tactical Reconnaissance Group | |
|     1 Electronic Combat Group | |
|     1 Special Operations Wing | |
| Unconventional and Special Operations Forces | 3,500 |
| TOTAL | 291,600 |

Source: Data furnished by USCENTCOM, and in the Department of Defense, Annual Report, FY1986, p. 212

a) A typical active Navy carrier wing consists of nine squadrons (approximately 86 aircraft): two fighter squadrons, two light attack squadrons, one medium attack squadron, plus supporting elements for airborne warning, antisubmarine and electronic warfare, reconnaissance, and aerial refueling operations.

## Saudi Arabia and Western Power Projection Capabilities

b) An active Marine Corps air wing typically consists of 23-25 squadrons (338-370 aircraft) with: four fighter attack squadrons, two or three light attack squadrons, one or two medium attack squadrons, plus supporting elements for electronic warfare, reconnaissance, aerial refueling, transport, airborne assault, observation, and tactical air control.

c) The MAB is currently the only element of the MAF which has prepositioned equipment. By FY1987-1988, the full MAF will have prepositioned equipment on ships although the other two sets will be located for missions in NATO and Asia.

d) Each Air Force Wing typically contains three squadrons of 24 aircraft each. (Combat support units, such as those composed of EF-111 electronic warfare aircraft, are generally organized into squadrons of 18 to 24 aircraft ) By the end of FY1989, the U.S. will have the equivalent of 40 tactical fighter wings--27 active and 13 Air National Guard and Reserve).

e) There are a total of 7 B-52G squadrons assigned to general purpose as well as nuclear missions. These have a strategic reconnaissance and anti-shipping mission as well as a conventional land bombing role.

## THE IMPACT OF SAUDI BASES

These limitations on U.S. capabilities help explain why Western access to Saudi bases and facilities could be so critical in a conflict, and why the quality of U.S. military relations with Saudi Arabia is so important to protecting the Gulf's oil supplies.

Saudi Arabia has never formally agreed to provide the U.S. with contingency bases. The politics of the Gulf preclude Saudi Arabia from overtly granting base facilities without a clear and immediate threat. It would be accused of neocolonialism, of supporting an ally of Israel, and of having brought superpower confrontation into the region. Saudi Arabia has, however, quietly consulted U.S. defense planners and senior USCENTCOM officers regarding U.S. use of Saudi facilities in an emergency, and it has made USCENTCOM "over the horizon" reinforcement capabilities one of the mainstays of its defense planning.

Saudi Arabia has often sought U.S. deployments in past contingencies, and these have recently included detachments of U.S. minesweeping forces, USAF F-15s, and USAF E-3A AWACS aircraft. Saudi Arabia still has U.S. E-3A AWACS aircraft deployed on its soil which were first requested during the Iran-Iraq War, and a small USAF detachment which operates in a joint headquarters at Dhahran, and shares data on the Iran-Iraq War and other developments in the Gulf.

The Saudi Air Force's past reliance on U.S. equipment has also given it the capability to conduct joint operations with U.S. forces, to support USAF reinforcements, and to provide $C^3I$ and support facilities. The Saudi Air Force now operates 60 F-15C/Ds, and nearly 100 F-5E/Fs. It uses U.S. training and maintenance standards, and many Saudi squadrons now approach USAF proficiency and qualification levels. Saudi Arabia also has the largest and most modern air bases in the Middle East. These air bases have extensive shelter facilities, and those in the Gulf and lower Red Sea areas are equipped to support U.S.-made F-15 and F-5 aircraft. They are also defended with Hawk missiles, and will soon have the new Peace Shield command, control, communications, and intelligence ($C^3I$), and air control

## Saudi Arabia and Western Power Projection Capabilities

and warning (AC&W) system using U.S. E-3A AWACS aircraft and advanced ground radars and electronics.

Such Saudi air facilities could base up to two wings of USAF fighters, and give them full munitions and service support. The U.S. has large numbers of contract personnel servicing Saudi equipment in the Air Force, Army, National Guard, and Navy, and large numbers of Saudi military and civilian personnel have had U.S. training and can operate with, or support and service, U.S. military equipment.

If Saudi Arabia had been successful in obtaining the additional 40 improved F-15C/Ds and modern U.S. attack munitions to supplement its air-to-air weapons that it requested in 1985, it would have further developed and equipped a network of bases in the Gulf (Riyadh, Dhahran, and dispersal facilities at Hafr al-Batin), and in the Red Sea Area (Taif, Khamis Mushayt, Sharurah, Jiddah, and Tabuk), that could have allowed large amounts of U.S. air power to deploy in 48 to 72 hours to the most threatened areas in the Gulf.[25]

Further, Saudi bases are located in areas where U.S. carriers cannot operate their aircraft effectively without moving into the Gulf. The Gulf is a highly vulnerable area for such operations. Hostile states like Iran have anti-ship Harpoon missiles and can launch suicide air attacks with only limited warning, and Soviet attack fighters and bombers can launch air-to-ship missiles after taking advantage of the terrain masking provided by the mountains in Iran and with far less chance of detection than in the open sea.

Saudi Arabia has equally modern naval facilities and ground bases. These bases have extensive stocks of parts and munitions, and service and support equipment, which can be used by USCENTCOM forces. The Saudi base at Hafr al-Batin (which is located in the critical border area near Kuwait and Iraq) will also have two full brigades equipped with U.S. armor.[26] Saudi army and naval bases have some of the most sophisticated infrastructure and service facilities in the world, and can both speed the deployment of U.S. forces and make them more effective once they arrive.

These bases take on special importance because geography and politics make Saudi Arabia pivotal to the defense of the Gulf, the Red Sea, the other moderate Gulf oil exporters, and most of the free world's oil supplies. Table 3.5 shows the full range of U.S. contingency bases in the region. Yet, for all the bases listed in Table 3.5, the U.S. only has four sets of bases or basing facilities it can use to defend the Gulf and must rely on bases in Oman and Saudi Arabia. The only other Western bases in the entire region are the French facilities in Djibouti in the Red Sea, and the British advisory presence in Oman.

Saudi Arabia and Western Power Projection Capabilities

Table 3.5: U.S. Military Contingency Facilities in the Near East

| Base | Status |
|---|---|

**NORTH AFRICA AND STAGING POINTS**

Morocco

| | |
|---|---|
| Slimane | Agreement signed in May, 1983. A former B-47 base closed in 1963 which is now being modernized to support C-141 and C-5 operations. |
| Navasseur | This base or Rabat may be given similar modernization later. |

Liberia

| | |
|---|---|
| Monrovia | Agreement signed in February, 1983, to allow U.S. to make contingency use of international airport for stage air operations. U.S. will fund expansion of airport to allow use of C-5s, C-17s, and C-141s. |

Portugal

| | |
|---|---|
| Lajes | Negotiations were completed in 1983-84 to keep Lajes as a major air staging point for U.S. air movements. The fuel, runway, and other facilities at this base in the Azores are being upgraded. |

**EASTERN MEDITERRANEAN AND RED SEA AREA**

Egypt

| | |
|---|---|
| Suez Canal | U.S. has been granted tacit permission to move warships through the Canal. |
| Cairo West | The U.S. shares an un-named air base with Egypt, and normally deploys about 100 men on the base. It has been used for joint F-15 and E-3A AWACS operations. |
| Ras Banas | Still under negotiation. Ras Banas would provide basing capabilities for C-5 aircraft, and for unloading and transit of SL-7 and other fast sea lift ships. |

| | |
|---|---|
| Djibouti | Access agreement and arrangements with French allow port calls and access to maritime patrol aircraft. |

Turkey

| | |
|---|---|
| Mus<br>Batman<br>Erzurum | The U.S. has informal arrangements to use three Turkish air bases near the Soviet border, Iran, and Iraq. These bases are NATO bases and are being funded to allow the deployment of U.S. heavy lift aircraft and fighters. |

**GULF AND RED SEA**

## Saudi Arabia and Western Power Projection Capabilities

| | |
|---|---|
| Diego Garcia | Used through a long term lease with the U.K. signed in the mid-1960s. The base provides 12,000 foot runways and facilities suitable for B-52 and heavy airlift facilities, and is where seven U.S. prepositioning ships in the Gulf are now deployed. |
| Seychelles | Satellite tracking and communications base with NASA and Air Force personnel. |
| **Kenya** | |
| Mombassa<br>Moi Airport<br>Kenya Naval base | Provides a potential staging point, maintenance facilities, and port call. Access agreement signed in mid 1970s. Facility expansion program completed in 1983. |
| **Somalia** | |
| Mogadishu Airport<br>Berbera | Staging facilities for U.S. air and sea movements. Limited repair capability. Expansion completed in 1983. |
| **Oman** | |
| Al Khasab | Small air base in the Musandem Peninsula near Goat Island and Straits of Hormuz. Limited contingency capability. Largely suited for small maritime patrol aircraft. |
| Masira | Island being expanded to a major $170 air and naval staging point, with limited deployment of prepositioning ships. |
| Thumrait & Seeb Air bases | Contingency air base facilities. Now used by U.S. maritime patrol aircraft. |
| Saudi Arabia | No formal basing agreements, but the U.S. has deployed F-15s, KC-10 and KC-135 tankers, and E-3As to Saudi air bases in emergencies, and operates E-3As from Riyadh. All Saudi major air bases have the sheltering and facilities to accept extensive U.S. air reinforcements and/or support U.S. deployment of heavy lift aircraft. |
| Bahrain | U.S. Middle East Force deploys in Bahrain, although formal agreement has lapsed. A 65 man U.S. support unit is present |

Adapted from material provided by USCENTCOM, and from Barry M. Blechman and Edward N. Luttwak, International Security Yearbook, 1983/84, St. Martin's Press, New York, 1984, pp. 154-159.

The only permanent fully active Western base in the Indian Ocean and Gulf area is on the British island of Diego Garcia in the Southern Indian Ocean--where the U.S. now prepositions much of USCENTCOM's equipment. This base is so far to the South, however, that it is nearly as far away from the key strategic areas in the Upper Gulf as is Dublin, Ireland. The U.S. is also helping Turkey strengthen its bases in Eastern Turkey, but

Turkey has firmly stated that it will not provide contingency bases for USCENTCOM, and that it must make defense of its territory against the USSR its primary concern. The bases in Turkey are also useful primarily for contingencies involving a Soviet invasion of Northern Iran.

The U.S. has contingency bases in Oman--the one Gulf state whose internal and external politics allow it to grant such facilities with minimal risk to its security. Oman provides important staging facilities on the island of Masirah, allows the U.S. to fly maritime patrol aircraft from its soil, and has supported contingency arrangements to allow U.S. tankers to stage out of Omani air fields and refuel U.S. carrier aircraft flying from the Indian Ocean. Oman, however, is too far east to allow U.S. forces to efficiently defend most of the Gulf oil fields and key oil nations like Kuwait.

All of these factors make Western access to Saudi bases like the ones at Dhahran and Hafr al-Batin critical in any major defense of the Gulf against a threat from Iran, Iraq, or the USSR. In fact, USCENTCOM probably cannot function in its most critical contingency roles without Saudi cooperation and wartime access to Saudi bases and facilities. While Diego Garcia, Djibouti, Turkey, and Egypt provide useful contingency facilities on the periphery of the Gulf and lower Red Sea, they cannot make up for the range and reinforcement problems the West would face in defending its critical oil facilities in the Upper and central Gulf.

The problem the West now faces is that Britain can help Saudi Arabia modernize its forces, but it cannot help Saudi Arabia or the U.S. compensate for the failure to standardize on the key aircraft and munitions used by USCENTCOM. Further, the fact that Britain and France help maintain close military relations between Saudi Arabia and the West is not an effective substitute for the kind of U.S.-Saudi relations that would increase Saudi willingness to provide the U.S. with forward basing facilities or develop informal links between USCENTCOM and Saudi and other GCC military forces.

---

[1] "Guarding Turkey's Eastern Flank", The Middle East, April, 1986, pp. 9-10.

[2] This estimate is based on working data from Defense Marketing Services, various editions of Jane's Defense Weekly, and the International Institute for Strategic Studies, Military Balance, 1985-1986.

[3] Andrew Borowiec, "Turks Seek Aid To Upgrade Army", Washington Times, May 16, 1986, p. 7.

[4] Jonathan Marcus and Bruce George, "French Rapid Deployment Force", Jane's Defense Weekly, 28 April 1984, pp. 649-650; Giovanni de Briganti, "Forces d'Action Rapide", Armed Forces Journal, October, 1984, pp. 46-47. Note of General Fricaud-Chagnaud, "La Force d'Action Rapide", July 2, 1986.

5 Ibid.

6 Ibid

7 It should be noted that any discussion of French and British deployment capabilities is necessarily time sensitive. Both nations could build-up a major out of area presence over a period of months using sealift and by drawing down on support equipment and assets normally reserved for European defense. Provided that sufficient domestic political support could be sustained, both nations could also reconfigure existing units and forces or simply assemble new units out of the force elements of other major combat units. The tacit assumption made here is that most out of area action will require very rapid reaction, involve serious political and financial constraints, and occur in a climate where the defense of Europe must still be given clear priority.

8 Giovanni de Briganti, "Forces d'Action Rapide", Armed Forces Journal, October, 1984, pp. 46-47; and "France's Special Operations Forces", Defense and Foreign Affairs, June 1985, pp. 32-33.

9 John Jordan, Modern Naval Aviation and Aircraft Carriers, New York, Arco, 1983, pp. 22-25, and Defense News, June 26, 1986, p. 7.

10 When France conducted Operation Mantua in Chad in 1984, it had to lease 24 Boeing 747s for 22 days. It chartered C-5As for the operations in Chad in 1986. Jane's Defense Weekly, March 15, 1986, p. 454.

11 The Crotale is only effective to about 12,000 feet versus up to 52,000 feet for Hawk. As a result, the SAMs transportable on French lift aircraft cannot reach medium and heavy bombers. Although France deployed only 900 men, it also had to move its 24 armored vehicles by land from the Cameroons since it lacked airlift for such vehicles. Jane's Defense Weekly, 15 March, 1986, p. 454.

12 For a good recent description of the goals of the French Navy, see Pierre Lachamade, "The French Navy in the Year 2000", Jane's Naval Review, London, 1985, Jane's, pp. 79-90. This precludes recent budget cuts but still indicates the probable future strengths and weaknesses of French naval out of area capabilities.

13 Jean de Galard, "French Overseas Action: Supplementary Budget", Jane's Defense Weekly, 14 December, 1985, p. 1281

14 French warships have cruised the Gulf of Oman since October, 1980, but have conspicuously avoided any joint action. Jane's Defense Weekly, 11 February, 1984, p. 181.

15 Ibid and Jane's Defense Weekly, 28 July 1984, p. 93.

16 For illustrative British views see Lt. General Sir Geoffrey Howlett, "NATO European Interests Worldwide-Britain's Military Contribution, RUSI Journal, Vol. 130, No. 3, September, 1985, pp. 3-10; Simon O Dwyer-Russel, "Beyond the Falklands-The Role of Britain's Out of Area Joint Forces", Jane's Defense Weekly, 11 January, 1986, pp. 26-27; "Battle Continues to Preserve British Amphibious Warfare Capability", Jane's Defense Weekly, 8 February, 1986, p. 185; "UK's Amphibious Dilemma", Jane's Defense Weekly, 12 April 1986, pp. 661-662; Professor Neville Brown, "An Out of Area Strategy?", Navy

International, October, 1982, pp. 1371-1373, and Keith Hartley, "Can Britain Afford a Rapid Deployment Force?", RUSI Journal, Volume 127, No. 1, March, 1982, pp. 18-22.

[17] See Simon O'Dwyer-Russel, "Marines Fear Loss of Capability", Defense Attache, No. 3, 1984, pp. 60-68; and "Beyond the Falklands-The Role of Britain's Out of Area Joint Forces", Jane's Defense Weekly, 11 January, 1986, pp. 26-27.

[18] RUSI News Brief, May, 1986, pp. 5-6.

[19] It should be noted that the Dutch Royal Marines no longer have amphibious lift of their own and use British amphibious ships as part of the UK-NL Amphibious Force.

[20] Estimate based on IISS, Military Balance, 1985-1986, and data furnished by DoD Public Affairs, January, 1986.

[21] The seventeen prepositioning ships now deployed carry some 165,000 short tons of ammunition and supplies. To put this into perspective, this is equivalent to more than 6,100 C-141 sorties.

[22] These and the following shortfall statistics are taken from the FY1987 USCENTCOM command briefing as provided by USCENTCOM.

[23] For an excellent recent treatment of U.S. build-up capabilities in the region, see Thomas McNaugher, Arms and Oil, Washington, Brookings, 1985, pp. 53-89.

[24] David M. Ransom, Lt. Colonel Lawrence J. MacDonald, and W. Nathaniel Howell, "Atlantic Cooperation for Persian Gulf Security", Essays on Strategy, Washington, D.C., National Defense University, 1986, p. 102.

[25] Saudi Arabia originally planned a base at Al Kharj, near Riyadh, for its E-3As. This base expansion has been cancelled due to funding reasons, but may be reinstated because of the problem of securing Riyadh airport against terrorism.

[26] This base was originally designed for three brigades, and has considerably better equipment storage and support facilities than its normal deployment strength of two brigades indicates. Saudi Arabia has also discussed the possibility of converting one brigade to a "Gulf brigade" which would include forces from other GCC countries.

# IV. REGIONAL THREATS AND THE MILITARY BUILD-UP IN THE GULF

Saudi Arabia can only play a significant strategic role in the Gulf, Red Sea, and Near East, if it has the strength to deter or defend itself against possible threats. The Gulf and Red Sea areas are not only one of the world's most tempting strategic targets, they are one of the world's most unstable regions. These threats are not simply potential threats. The Iran-Iraq War and the Iranian revolution present a constant risk of escalation that will involve the Southern Gulf states. The Saudi Air Force has already fought one major engagement with the Iranian Air Force to keep the Gulf's tanker routes open, and it faces the risk of further Iranian attacks at any time.

While Iraq has become steadily more friendly to the conservative Gulf states since 1978--a trend reinforced by its dependence on aid from the GCC states as the result of the Iran-Iraq War--it is also becoming a massive military power. No one can guarantee that this power can continue to defend against Iran, that its present regime will remain in power, or that Iraq will be friendly once the war is over. The only thing that can be guaranteed is that Iraq will retain thousands of main battle tanks and hundreds of combat aircraft.

A still unidentified power mined the Red Sea near Saudi Arabia and Egypt in 1984.[1] The U.S.S.R. is steadily expanding its presence in the PDRY, YAR, and Ethiopia, and operates reconnaissance and intelligence aircraft from airfields in both the PDRY and Ethiopia. After several years of relative quiet, the PDRY is again becoming internally unstable, and is slowly building up its military forces.

Current threats, however, are only part of the problem. Saudi Arabia cannot measure its military forces or arms purchases against today's threat. It will not be able to make any major new equipment purchases fully operational and effective until the early to mid-1990s, and it must then be able to employ its "first line" weapons systems for a useful life of at least ten years. Saudi Arabia is not buying or updating its aircraft to meet today's threat: it must buy aircraft which have a credible "life cycle" for at least the period of 1991-2001, and ideally for a life cycle of 1991-2015.

No one can predict the exact rate at which particular potentially hostile nations will build-up their forces and technology, or the extent to which currently friendly or neutral states will shift their attitudes. No one can predict just how much the Soviet bloc will need oil, or the extent of Soviet ambitions. At the same time, some aspects of the future threats to the Gulf and the free world's sources of imported oil are clear:

- o A massive regional arms build-up is taking place on all of Saudi Arabia's borders. The size of current and potential hostile forces and the weapons strength of current and potential threats, are increasing far more quickly than Saudi Arabia can hope to increase its own forces;
- o There is a need to extend Saudi Arabia's limited deterrence and defense capabilities to cover five smaller, and often unstable, conservative Gulf states;
- o There is a growing Soviet capability to intervene directly in the region which will take a far more tangible form if the USSR can fully suppress the Afghan freedom fighters.
- o The massive Soviet arms transfer and military advisory effort virtually surrounds the Kingdom;
- o The threat from the Iran-Iraq War is almost certain to lead to continuing political tension and military build-ups through the end of this century;
- o There is a threat of radical hostility and growing Soviet penetration in the Yemens;
- o There is a threat of radical pressure from Ethiopia and possibly the Sudan;
- o A massive military build-up in Syria may become as much a threat to Saudi Arabia and Jordan as to Israel;
- o Inevitable shifts in the technology of the weapons deployed in the region will give hostile states technology roughly equivalent to the E-3A, Tornado, and F-15C/D by the mid-1990s.

## BROAD PATTERNS IN THE REGIONAL ARMS RACE

The sheer rate of military build-up in the region presents a major challenge to Saudi Arabia. The Kingdom is a nation of only 6-8 million, with armed forces of only 51,000-75,000 men (depending on whether the National Guard and security forces are counted). It must compete with neighboring nations with far larger manpower pools, and seek stability in a region characterized by an arms race that has now lasted for two decades.

Tables 4.1 and 4.2 illustrate this point. These tables provide a rough estimate of the force trends in the region through 1990--the last date at which even rough regional estimates are possible. At the same time, they illustrate the rate of total force build-up in recent years, and the competition between major arms exporters and importers.

There is no rigid correlation between expanding military forces and arms imports and a conflict, or between the growth of neighboring military forces and the threat to Saudi Arabia. Nevertheless, Saudi Arabia's wealth and strategic position make it an obvious target for any state or combination of states that feels it can bring sufficient pressure to bear.

This "logic of arms" has long shaped Saudi perceptions of the strategic threats in the region--just as the U.S. must base the size of its forces against the potential threat posed by the USSR, and not on its current forces or political intentions--and seems certain to do so in the future. Saudi Arabia must also take full account of the volatile nature of many neighboring regimes.

Egypt, for example, was once the strongest Arab radical state. It is now the strongest moderate. Libya has shifted from a conservative kingdom to a radical threat to every moderate and conservative Arab state. Syria has grown from a minor military power, whose internal political turmoil had little impact on the Gulf, to a military power whose forces numerically exceed those of Israel and whose current political stability depends on the life of one man and rule by a small religious minority.

Lebanon's stability has been transformed into a constant state of civil war, and Lebanon is now the scene of an emerging Shi'ite radicalism that has joined with Iran in becoming a growing threat to every moderate Arab state. The Sudan seems to be drifting into chaos, and the Yemens and Ethiopia have been the scene of political turmoil and military build-up for more than a decade.

Regional Threats and the Military Build-Up in the Gulf

### Table 4.1: Major Weapons in Middle Eastern Forces Directly or Indirectly Affecting Saudi Arabia

| Country | Main Battle Tanks | | | | | Combat Aircraft | | | | |
|---|---|---|---|---|---|---|---|---|---|---|
| | 73 | 79 | 82 | 84 | 90 | 73 | 79 | 82 | 84 | 90 |
| Egypt | 1880 | 1600 | 2100 | 1750 | 1950 | 620 | 563 | 429 | 504 | 550 |
| Jordan | 420 | 500 | 569 | 750 | 800 | 52 | 73 | 94 | 103 | 136 |
| Israel | 1700 | 3050 | 3600 | 3600 | 4000 | 488 | 576 | 634 | 555 | 530 |
| Lebanon | 60 | 0 | 0 | 142 | 200 | 18 | 16 | 8 | 3 | 21 |
| Syria | 1170 | 2600 | 3990 | 4100 | 4400 | 326 | 389 | 450 | 503 | 600 |
| Sub-Total | 5230 | 7750 | 10259 | 10342 | 11350 | 1504 | 1617 | 1615 | 1668 | 1837 |
| Bahrain | 0 | 0 | 0 | 0 | 36 | 0 | 0 | 0 | 0 | 16 |
| Iran | 920 | 1735 | 1110 | 1000 | 1500 | 159 | 447 | 90 | 95 | 200 |
| Iraq | 990 | 1800 | 2300 | 4820 | 5000 | 224 | 339 | 330 | 580 | 600 |
| Kuwait | 100 | 280 | 240 | 240 | 300 | 34 | 50 | 49 | 49 | 60 |
| Oman | 0 | 0 | 18 | 18 | 40 | 12 | 35 | 37 | 52 | 70 |
| Qatar | 0 | 12 | 24 | 24 | 40 | 4 | 4 | 9 | 11 | 27 |
| Saudi Arabia | 85 | 350 | 450 | 450 | 700 | 70 | 178 | 191 | 203 | 239 |
| UAE | 0 | 0 | 118 | 118 | 160 | 12 | 52 | 52 | 43 | 70 |
| North Yemen | 30 | 232 | 714 | 664 | 700 | 28 | 11 | 75 | 76 | 90 |
| South Yemen | 50 | 260 | 470 | 450 | 550 | 20 | 109 | 114 | 103 | 120 |
| Sub-total | 2175 | 4669 | 5444 | 7784 | 9026 | 563 | 1225 | 947 | 1212 | 1492 |
| Algeria | 400 | 500 | 630 | 700 | 800 | 206 | 260 | 306 | 330 | 330 |
| Libya | 221 | 2000 | 2900 | 2800 | 3300 | 44 | 201 | 555 | 535 | 600 |
| Morocco | 120 | 140 | 135 | 120 | 228 | 48 | 72 | 97 | 106 | 130 |
| Tunisia | 0 | 0 | 14 | 14 | 68 | 12 | 14 | 8 | 8 | 24 |
| Sub-total | 741 | 2640 | 3679 | 3634 | 4396 | 310 | 547 | 966 | 979 | 1084 |
| TOTAL NEAR EAST | 8146 | 15059 | 19382 | 21760 | 24772 | 2377 | 3389 | 3528 | 3859 | 4413 |
| Ethiopia | 50 | 624 | 790 | 1020 | 1200 | 37 | 100 | 113 | 160 | 180 |
| Sudan | 130 | 150 | 190 | 73 | 130 | 50 | 36 | 30 | 34 | 57 |
| Somalia | 150 | 80 | 140 | 240 | 300 | 100 | 25 | 55 | 64 | 72 |
| Turkey | 1400 | 3500 | 3550 | 3532 | 3700 | 288 | 303 | 402 | 458 | 560 |
| TOTAL OTHER | 1730 | 4354 | 4670 | 4865 | 5330 | 475 | 464 | 600 | 716 | 869 |

(1) Numbers are generally taken from the IISS Military Balance and SIPRI Year Book data for the appropriate year. All estimates for 1990 are made by the author.

Regional Threats and the Military Build-Up in the Gulf

Table 4.2: Near Term Annual Trends in Arms Imports Impacting on the Gulf and Near East (In current $ millions)

|  | 72 | 74 | 76 | 78 | 80 | 82 | 84 | 86 | 88 | 90 |
|---|---|---|---|---|---|---|---|---|---|---|
| **North Africa** | | | | | | | | | | |
| Mauritania | - | - | 20 | 30 | - | 10 | 12 | 15 | 15 | 18 |
| Morocco | - | 20 | 210 | 440 | 350 | 260 | 250 | 250 | 220 | 250 |
| Algeria | 10 | 20 | 320 | 725 | 525 | 1,100 | 850 | 800 | 750 | 775 |
| Libya | 160 | 330 | 1,000 | 2,000 | 2,200 | 2,400 | 1,800 | 1,800 | 2,000 | 2,000 |
| Chad | - | - | 10 | 5 | 1 | 5 | 5 | 5 | 5 | 6 |
| Tunisia | 10 | 10 | 10 | 35 | 140 | 60 | 115 | 120 | 140 | 15 |
| Egypt | 550 | 230 | 150 | 400 | 550 | 2,100 | 1,500 | 1,700 | 1,600 | 1,800 |
| Sub-Total | 730 | 610 | 1,720 | 3,639 | 3,766 | 5,935 | 4,532 | 4,690 | 4,730 | 4,999 |
| **Levant** | | | | | | | | | | |
| Israel | 300 | 950 | 975 | 900 | 825 | 1,000 | 1,350 | 1,600 | 1,700 | 1,800 |
| Syria | 280 | 825 | 625 | 900 | 2,700 | 2,300 | 1,800 | 1,700 | 2,000 | 2,000 |
| Jordan | 30 | 70 | 140 | 170 | 260 | 825 | 650 | 800 | 750 | 800 |
| Lebanon | 20 | 10 | 10 | 20 | 40 | 40 | 65 | 65 | 45 | 50 |
| Sub-Total | 630 | 1,855 | 1,750 | 1,990 | 3,825 | 4,165 | 3,065 | 4,165 | 4,495 | 4,650 |
| **Red Sea** | | | | | | | | | | |
| Sudan | 20 | 30 | 50 | 120 | 100 | 170 | 200 | 200 | 180 | 200 |
| Ethiopia | 10 | 10 | 50 | 1,100 | 575 | 290 | 300 | 280 | 280 | 300 |
| Somalia | 20 | 90 | 100 | 240 | 190 | 70 | 110 | 120 | 135 | 140 |
| North Yemen | 10 | 10 | 20 | 90 | 550 | 240 | 200 | 230 | 280 | 290 |
| South Yemen | 20 | 40 | 40 | 140 | 240 | 50 | 90 | 110 | 150 | 165 |
| Sub-Total | 80 | 180 | 260 | 1,690 | 1,655 | 820 | 900 | 940 | 1,025 | 1,095 |
| **Gulf** | | | | | | | | | | |
| Iran | 525 | 1,000 | 2,000 | 2,200 | 400 | 1,300 | 1,600 | 1,800 | 1,900 | 2,300 |
| Iraq | 140 | 625 | 1,000 | 1,600 | 1,600 | 4,300 | 3,800 | 3,800 | 3,300 | 3,000 |
| Iran-Iraq Total | 665 | 1,625 | 3,000 | 3,800 | 2,000 | 5,600 | 5,400 | 5,600 | 5,200 | 5,300 |
| Saudi Arabia | 100 | 340 | 440 | 1,300 | 1,800 | 2,600 | 2,700 | 2,400 | 2,800 | 2,900 |
| Kuwait | 5 | 10 | 80 | 300 | 40 | 130 | 100 | 300 | 200 | 250 |
| Bahrain | - | - | - | - | 80 | 40 | 80 | 90 | 90 | 110 |
| Qatar | - | - | 5 | 20 | 90 | 250 | 200 | 220 | 220 | 240 |
| UAE | 10 | 50 | 100 | 50 | 170 | 40 | 220 | 240 | 260 | 280 |
| Oman | 5 | 10 | 10 | 270 | 100 | 100 | 120 | 125 | 140 | 155 |
| GCC Total | 120 | 410 | 635 | 1,940 | 2,280 | 3,160 | 3,420 | 3,375 | 3,710 | 3,935 |
| Sub-Total | 780 | 2,035 | 3,635 | 5,740 | 4,280 | 8,760 | 8,820 | 8,975 | 8,910 | 9,225 |
| **Other** | | | | | | | | | | |
| Turkey | 150 | 150 | 320 | 220 | 290 | 420 | 400 | 450 | 500 | 520 |
| India | 210 | 190 | 490 | 290 | 700 | 1,200 | 1,400 | 1,500 | 1,600 | 1,750 |
| Pakistan | 110 | 100 | 190 | 210 | 380 | 440 | 570 | 620 | 680 | 720 |
| Afghanistan | 20 | 80 | 50 | 90 | 10 | 160 | 180 | 200 | 220 | 230 |
| Sub-Total | 490 | 520 | 1,050 | 810 | 1,380 | 2,220 | 2,550 | 2,770 | 3,000 | 3,220 |
| Total Region | 2,715 | 5,200 | 8,415 | 13,869 | 14,906 | 21,900 | 19,861 | 21,540 | 22,160 | 23,199 |

Source: Author's estimate based on computer data provided by the U.S. Arms Control and Disarmament Agency.

## Regional Threats and the Military Build-Up in the Gulf

While the detailed statistics in Tables 4.1 and 4.2 may be confusing to anyone other than an area expert, the broad trends are clear. Even if one makes the assumption that the current fall in oil revenues will reduce the past rate of arms imports--and that Iran will only be beginning to rebuild the military strength it had under the Shah by 1990--the land and air threat to Saudi Arabia and the conservative Gulf states will increase far more quickly than the GCC states can hope to increase their forces. This is not simply a matter of tanks and aircraft, it is also a matter of increases in the capability of nations like Iran, Syria, and Iraq to project land and air forces outside their own territory:

o Syria will become a major regional power as well as an Arab-Israeli confrontation state. It will increase its tank and aircraft strength while vastly increasing force quality. It will acquire the ability to strike deep into Iraq, Jordan, and Western Saudi Arabia, and to threaten the road and air routes to the Gulf from Jordan and Turkey.

o Iran will rebuild its forces. It will increase its present tank strength by at least 50%, and its air strength by well over 100% and possibly over 200%. It will strengthen its navy and improve its battle readiness. By the early 1990s, its mix of new European and Communist-bloc made equipment is likely to roughly equal the quality of the equipment in NATO and Warsaw Pact forces, and Iran's forces will be supported by greatly improved $C^3I$ and electronic warfare equipment.

o The Yemens will expand their forces, but more importantly, will greatly improve in force quality. They will pose a significantly greater threat to Oman and Saudi Arabia.

o Libya will continue to expand its capability to arm and finance radical threats to the Gulf states.

o Ethiopia will begin to emerge as a significant regional military power, with the ability to fly and fight its own aircraft, and threaten traffic through the Red Sea as well as the Asir and the Southeastern regions of Saudi Arabia.

o The Sudan may significantly increase the strength of its air and naval forces, and could become a significant threat in the Red Sea.

The air build-up reflected in Table 4.1 will be particularly important. The bulk of the Soviet made aircraft now in the Gulf, Levant, and Red Sea areas will be replaced during 1988-1995, and the USSR has already begun to transfer extremely advanced fighters like the MiG-29 to the Third World. Given the probable pattern in Soviet arms exports, the existing fighters in nations like the PDRY and Ethiopia will be replaced with fighter types with roughly three times the range, and five times the attack payload and lethality of the existing fighters. Even the Soviet export versions of the MiG-21 and

## Regional Threats and the Military Build-Up in the Gulf

MiG-23 now in Iraq and Syria will be replaced by fighters with twice their range and three times their current attack payload and lethality.

By the early 1990s, Saudi Arabia will confront Soviet fighter types with air to air combat capabilities roughly equivalent to the Saudi Air Force's F-15 C/Ds and Tornados, and probably forces with Soviet-made AWACS and electronic warfare aircraft. The threat Saudi Arabia must plan for goes far beyond the issue of the growth in threat numbers. It includes the growth in threat capabilities and aircraft quality.

These arms trends reinforce the need for an effective Western arms transfer policy towards Saudi Arabia, and Table 4.3 adds additional data on the trend in arms sales by seller nation. It shows that the world arms market has become steadily more oriented towards sales to the Near East and Southwest Asia. It also shows that Soviet and other Communist sales are steadily increasing relative to those of the West, and often in states which are serious potential threats to Saudi Arabia and the other Gulf oil exporters.

Table 4.3: Middle Eastern Arms Imports by Importing Country: 1979-83
(Current $ millions)

| Importer | Total | USSR | US | FR | UK | FRG | IT | CZ | PRC | RO | PO | Others |
|---|---|---|---|---|---|---|---|---|---|---|---|---|
| **North Africa** | | | | | | | | | | | | |
| Mauritania | 20 | - | - | 10 | - | - | - | - | - | - | - | 10 |
| Morocco | 1,785 | - | 430 | 950 | - | 5 | - | - | 50 | - | 50 | 300 |
| Algeria | 3,660 | 3,200 | - | 30 | 50 | 300 | - | - | - | - | - | 80 |
| Libya | 12,095 | 5,800 | - | 850 | 40 | 380 | 700 | 575 | 310 | 310 | 230 | 2,900 |
| Chad | 15 | - | - | 10 | - | - | - | - | - | - | - | 5 |
| Tunisia | 385 | - | 110 | 130 | 5 | 20 | 70 | - | 10 | - | - | 40 |
| Egypt | 5,645 | 40 | 2,400 | 1,200 | 570 | 210 | 320 | - | 300 | - | 50 | 550 |
| Sub-Tot. | 23,605 | 9,040 | 2,940 | 3,180 | 665 | 915 | 1,090 | 575 | 670 | 310 | 330 | 3,885 |
| **Levant** | | | | | | | | | | | | |
| Israel | 3,805 | - | 3,800 | - | - | - | - | - | - | - | - | 5 |
| Syria | 10,530 | 9,200 | - | 200 | 180 | 40 | - | 470 | 90 | 20 | 30 | 300 |
| Jordan | 3,430 | 230 | 970 | 1,000 | 1,100 | 5 | - | - | 10 | - | - | 110 |
| Lebanon | 395 | - | 250 | 90 | 10 | - | 10 | - | - | - | 5 | 30 |
| Sub-Tot. | 18,160 | 9,430 | 5,020 | 1,290 | 1,290 | 45 | 10 | 470 | 100 | 20 | 35 | 445 |
| **Red Sea** | | | | | | | | | | | | |
| Sudan | 640 | - | 110 | 10 | 10 | 270 | 10 | - | 70 | - | 60 | 100 |
| Ethiopia | 1,900 | 1,800 | - | - | - | - | 20 | 10 | - | - | - | 70 |
| Somalia | 580 | - | 30 | 5 | 5 | - | 410 | - | 50 | - | 10 | 70 |
| YAR | 2,355 | 1,200 | 200 | 30 | - | 10 | 5 | - | - | 250 | 10 | 650 |
| PDRY | 1,510 | 1,500 | - | - | - | - | - | - | - | - | - | 10 |
| Sub-Total | 6,985 | 4,500 | 340 | 45 | 15 | 280 | 445 | 10 | 120 | 250 | 80 | 900 |
| **Gulf** | | | | | | | | | | | | |
| Iran | 5,365 | 40 | 2,400 | 1,200 | 575 | 210 | 320 | - | 300 | - | 50 | 550 |
| Iraq | 17,620 | 7,200 | - | 3,800 | 280 | 140 | 410 | 40 | 1,500 | 400 | 850 | 3,000 |
| Sub-Tot. | 22,985 | 7,240 | 2,400 | 5,000 | 855 | 350 | 730 | 40 | 1,800 | 400 | 900 | 3,550 |
| Saudi Arabia | 12,125 | - | 5,100 | 2,500 | 1,900 | 525 | 200 | - | - | - | - | 1,900 |
| Kuwait | 450 | 30 | 180 | - | 50 | 70 | 110 | - | - | - | - | 10 |
| Bahrain | 120 | - | 10 | 40 | - | 40 | 10 | - | - | - | - | 20 |
| Qatar | 765 | - | 10 | 440 | 310 | - | - | - | - | - | - | 5 |
| UAE | 620 | - | 20 | 350 | 90 | 110 | 30 | - | - | - | - | 20 |
| Oman | 565 | - | 80 | 20 | 430 | - | 10 | - | 5 | - | - | 5 |
| GCC | 14,645 | 30 | 5,400 | 3,350 | 2,780 | 745 | 350 | - | 5 | - | - | 1,960 |
| Sub-Tot. | 37,630 | 7,270 | 7,800 | 8,350 | 3,635 | 1,095 | 1,895 | 1,235 | 1,805 | 400 | 900 | 5,510 |
| **Other** | | | | | | | | | | | | |
| Turkey | 1,865 | - | 750 | 10 | 5 | 850 | 150 | - | - | - | - | 100 |
| India | 4,695 | 3,400 | 40 | 80 | 875 | 5 | 50 | 120 | - | 5 | - | 120 |
| Pakistan | 1,830 | 20 | 550 | 550 | 10 | 190 | 40 | - | 390 | - | - | 80 |
| Afghan. | 1,830 | 1,800 | - | - | - | - | - | 20 | - | - | - | 10 |
| Sub-Tot. | 10,220 | 5,220 | 1,340 | 640 | 890 | 1,045 | 240 | 140 | 390 | 5 | - | 310 |
| Region | 96,600 | 35,460 | 17,440 | 13,505 | 6,495 | 3,380 | 3,680 | 2,430 | 3,085 | 985 | 1,345 | 11,050 |
| World | 169,530 | 56,540 | 40,375 | 16,710 | 9,465 | 6,630 | 4,650 | 3,935 | 3,455 | 3,100 | 1,990 | 22,680 |

Source: ACDA, World Military Expenditures and Arms Transfers, 1985, Washington, GPO, 1985.

This conclusion is reinforced by Table 4.4, which examines the trend in new arms agreements in the Middle East and the relative trends in total market share. The key shifts in Table 4.4 clearly reflect the growth of Communist arms transfer relative to the West. It is interesting to consider these data in the light of the full range of information released by the United States Government on world arms sales:[2]

o The growth of Middle Eastern arms imports is part of a general global shift towards arms sales to Third World states. Sales to the Third World accounted for roughly 85% of all world arms imports in 1985, versus 78% in 1983 and 75% in 1973.

o Similar shifts are taking place in Third World defense expenditures. These have risen from 17% of the world total in 1973 to 21% in 1983 and 25% in 1985.

o Arms sales in North Africa, the Near East, and Southwest Asia in current dollars totaled nearly 42% of all world arms transfers, even though these nations accounted for only 8% of total world defense expenditures.

- o Arms transfers to the Middle East from past sales almost totally dominated the arms transfers of developed states to developing countries. During 1980-1983, they represented 59% of U.S. transfers, 62% of major West European transfers, 40% of Soviet transfers, and 58% of other Communist transfers.
- o Defense expenditures in North Africa, the Near East, and Southwest Asia in current dollars were only about 8% of the world total in 1983, the last year for which ACDA and the Central Intelligence Agency have hard data, but they were growing at a rate of over 11%. The defense expenditures of the OPEC states were growing even faster--at a rate of 13.3%.
- o Arms sales to the Middle East during 1981-1983 increased at an annual rate of roughly 11.5%. This compares with a rate of about 1.1% for the developed world and 7.7% for the developing world, and 3% for NATO.
- o This high rate of growth in arms sales to the Middle East compares with 2% for NATO, 2.1% for all OECD countries, 2.6% for the Warsaw Pact, 1.9% for all of North America, 2.5% for East Asia, 2.5% for all of Europe, 4.6% for South Asia, 5.0% for Latin America, and 8% for Africa.
- o The expenditures of the OPEC states alone totaled 36% of all world arms imports. This compares with 11.4% of all world arms imports for NATO, 15.7% for all OECD countries, 6.1% for the Warsaw Pact, 1.9% for all of North America, 9.8% for East Asia, 18.3% for all of Europe, 5% for South Asia, 7.6% for Latin America, and 15% for Africa.

- o The rate of increase in arms imports in the Middle East was faster than in any other region except Latin America, which imports only about 1/6th as many arms. The other two high growth regions were Africa (9%) and South Asia (9%).
- o The total volume of arms imports by Middle Eastern and Gulf states rose from $29.0 billion in 1974-1978 to $65.4 billion in 1979-1983.
- o Communist arms transfers to Middle Eastern and Gulf states rose from $24.5 billion to $44.4 billion. Soviet sales rose from $7.5 to $20.4 billion, and other Communist states including the PRC and Vietnam rose from $0.5 to $4.3 billion.
- o European arms sales to Middle Eastern and Gulf states rose from $5.5 billion in 1974-1978 to over $16 billion in 1980-1983. French arms sales led the increase, and rose from $1.8 billion to $9.7 billion. German sales rose from $1.0 to $1.2 billion. Italian arms sales rose from $0.6 to $1.3 billion. Britain's sales rose from $2.1 to $5.1 billion.
- o Growing competition from Asia, Latin America, and other European states increased the size of sales to Middle Eastern and Gulf states from $1.9 to $2.3 billion.
- o More recent U.S. reporting includes South Asia and North African states with Middle Eastern and Gulf states. These reports show, however, that the Near East and Southeast Asia accounted for 75% of all new Third World arms agreements in 1982-1985, and 73% of all deliveries.
- o The U.S. and Soviet Union now have a virtually equal share of sales to Near East and Southeast Asia. The U.S. has 26% and the USSR has 25.7%. West Europe has 27.3%. The USSR leads, however, in actual arms deliveries with 27.5% to 26.3% for the U.S. and 21.9% for West Europe.
- o The U.K. has experienced the largest recent growth in market share, thanks to the Tornado sale. The British share rose from 1.6% in 1984 to 21.8% in 1985. The U.S. increased its sales to the Middle East, but lost market share. U.S. arms sales rose from $28.5 billion in 1976-79 to $30.5 billion in 1980-83. This was the worst performance of any major exporter except West Germany, which could not complete several key contracts because of political constraints on arms exports.
- o Because of the high unit cost of Western arms, particularly those of the U.S., the Western share of actual weapons transfers is far lower than the share of arms sales measured in dollar terms. From 1978-1985, the USSR has led in the delivery of tanks, self propelled guns, artillery, APCs and AFVs, supersonic combat aircraft, subsonic combat aircraft, other aircraft, surface-to-air

missiles, helicopters, major surface combatants, and submarines. West Europe has led in minor surface combatants, and guided missile patrol boats. The U.S. has not led in any category.

The latest data on total sales to the Middle East released by the U.S. Arms Control and Disarmament Agency also reflect the growth of Soviet influence. These data are shown in Table 4.4 If one compares the four year period of 1977-1980 with the four year period of 1981-1984, Soviet arms sales to the Middle East rose from $9.2 billion to $15.9 billion, and from 18% to 23% of all sales. Total communist arms sales to the Middle East rose from $10.4 billion to $19.6 billion, and from 21% to 28% of all new sales agreements.

The U.S., in contrast, suffered sharply from its inability to make new arms agreements in the face of pro-Israel lobbying groups and pressure on the Congress. New U.S. arms agreements dropped in value, even in current dollars, from $15.6 billion in 1973-1976, to $14.6 billion in 1977-1980, and $11.9 billion in 1981-1984. In contrast, new Soviet arms agreements rose in value, in current dollars, from $9.2 billion in 1977-1980 to $15.9 billion in 1981-1984. The U.S. lost about 8-10% of its market share in the Middle Eastern arms sales--or nearly $10 billion dollars--during 1981-1984, and this drop preceded the virtual collapse of U.S. arms sales efforts that begun in 1985. While West European sales helped offset the decline in U.S. influence, they did not rise enough to prevent a major growth in Soviet arms sales and military influence.

Table 4.4: Trends in Western Market Share of Arms Sales to The Middle East--New Agreements (In Billions of Current U.S. Dollars)

| Exporter | 1977-1980 | | | 1981-1984 | | |
|---|---|---|---|---|---|---|
| | $Millions | % of All Sales in Middle East | % of Total World Wide Sales of Seller | $Millions | % of Total Sales in Middle East | % of Total World Wide Sales of Seller |
| **Non-Communist** | | | | | | |
| U.S. | 14.6 | 29 | 38 | 11.9 | 17 | 22 |
| France | 12.0 | 24 | 68 | 13.9 | 20 | 65 |
| U.K. | 4.7 | 9 | 52 | 2.0 | 3 | 40 |
| FRG | 1.5 | 3 | 22 | 1.0 | 1 | 14 |
| Italy | 3.1 | 6 | 51 | 1.8 | 3 | 43 |
| Other NATO | 0.6 | 1 | 14 | 1.8 | 3 | 45 |
| Other Non-Communist | 1.5 | 3 | 25 | 8.0 | 12 | 44 |
| **Communist** | | | | | | |
| USSR | 9.2 | 18 | 20 | 15.9 | 23 | 38 |
| Other Warsaw Pact | 1.2 | 2 | 17 | 3.7 | 5 | 35 |
| Sub-Total | 10.4 | 21 | 19 | 19.6 | 28 | 37 |
| Other Communist | 1.4 | 3 | 63 | 7.3 | 11 | 74 |
| **Grand Total** | 49.8 | 100 | 34 | 68.3 | 100 | 25.7 |

Source: Adapted from Arms Control and Disarmament Agency, World Military Expenditures and Arms Transfers, 1985, Washington, GPO, 1986, pp. 42-47

The U.S. share of the regional arms sales market has dropped for several reasons, but all of these reasons have the net impact of increasing the relative influence of the Soviet Union throughout the region. The U.S. is not a major supplier to Iran or Iraq. Many Arab states are turning to other arms sellers because they feel the U.S. has failed to move Israel towards a peace settlement. The Southern Gulf countries and most Arab states no longer perceive the U.S. as a reliable arms supplier because of Congressional refusal to support the export of advanced arms. The Soviet Union and other Communist states have made arms sales a critical part of their hard currency exports and do not have to sell their arms at market prices.

Fortunately for the West, Western European and other Non-Communist arms exporters have expanded their sales. They have done so for several reasons. One is price, the strong dollar has raised U.S. costs, and American arms prices have also risen more quickly in real terms than those of France, and Italy, and most Asian, Latin American, and other suppliers. Further, nations with state owned and state supported arms industries often can undersell the U.S. because of subsidies and more favorable credit terms. Nevertheless, the main reason is political: No other Non-Communist arms exporter now has significant military ties to Israel.

## Regional Threats and the Military Build-Up in the Gulf

The relative position of specific Western states in selling military and defense related services and construction is more complex, but again Europe is increasing Europe's importance relative to the U.S. The U.S. is steadily losing its share of military related construction because many competing local and Asian companies can offer these services more cheaply. The U.S. share of the service and maintenance market has grown because of the added complexity of U.S. weapons systems, but European nations have positioned themselves to compete in much of this market. The expansion of British and French sales to both Saudi Arabia and the other Gulf countries will inevitably expand Europe's share of sales of military services, and Singapore, South Korea, and Taiwan are beginning to offer service and support for U.S. combat aircraft.

The positive side of these trends is that many of the cuts in the U.S. role in providing military goods and services to Saudi Arabia and other friendly nations in the Middle East have been offset by West European sales. At the same time, the relative impact of Soviet arms sales is increasing and with it the vulnerability of Saudi Arabia, the GCC, and other moderate Arab states.

This growth in Soviet military influence in the region is likely to continue through the next decade because of (a) U.S. inability to become a reliable source of arms and military assistance to any Arab state not formally at peace with Israel, (b) growing pressure on the USSR to sell arms as a main source of hard currency, and (c) advances in technology which will lead to major new arms exports, many of which the U.S. may be unable to provide for domestic political reasons.

### THE IMPACT OF TECHNOLOGY TRANSFER

The rate of technology transfer to the Near East and Southwest Asia has increased to the point where it is becoming a major problem. A decade ago, there was usually a 5-10 year lag between the initial deployment of major new weapons systems in U.S., NATO, Soviet, and Warsaw Pact forces, and any large scale sale of such arms to the developing world. That lag is now being eliminated. Western Europe is selling aircraft, armor, and ships to developing nations at the same time it introduces such systems to its own armed forces. The USSR is not only selling its new MiG-29 fighters to India, it is selling coproduction rights. Soviet SS-21 missiles appeared in Syrian forces almost at the same time they became fully operational in Soviet forces in East Germany.

### THE PROBLEM OF CONVENTIONAL PROLIFERATION

Saudi Arabia, its conservative and moderate neighbors, and the West face a massive problem in terms of "conventional proliferation". By the time that all the new Tornados become fully operational in Saudi forces, a wide range of new weapons technologies will be present in the forces of potentially hostile nations. These technologies are summarized in Table 4.5.

## Table 4.5: Key Near Term Trends in the Technology of Arms Sales to the Middle East During 1985-1995

| Weapon/Technology | Impact |
| --- | --- |
| Challenger, AMX-40, M-1, T-80, Merkava II | Advanced tanks with 3rd and 4th generation fire control systems, spaced and other advanced armor, and advanced 120 mm guns. Will be matched by advanced types of other armored fighting vehicles. |
| ITOW, HOT, AT-6, AT-7, and AT-8, Hellfire, | Advanced anti-tank missiles with full automatic tracking or fire forget capability. |
| MRLS, BM-24, BM-25, ASTROS | Western and Soviet multiple rocket launchers capable of firing advanced submunitions and "smart" minelets at ranges beyond 30 Km. |
| Night vision devices | Widespread use of night vision devices. "24 hour" infantry, helicopter, and armored combat. |
| Secure, switched, advanced communications | Conversion to advanced secure communications with automated tactical message traffic and battle management capabilities. |
| SA-10, Patriot, Improved Hawk, SA-12 | Advanced surface to air missiles which cannot easily be suppressed with current weapons and electronic warfare means. Many will be netted with advanced sensor and battle management systems and linked to advanced short range systems. |
| SHORADS: SA-14, Stinger-POST, etc. | Next generation short range crew and man portable surface-to-air missiles and radar guided AA guns with far better tracking and kill capability and greater ranges. Many will be "netted" into an integrated battlefield and point defense system. |
| E-3A (Imp), E-2C (I), IL-76, SUAWACS | Airborne warning and control aircraft capable of managing large scale air wars using radar and electronic support measures (ESM) equivalent to NATO-level capabilities. |
| F-15E, MiG-29, SU-27, Lavi, F-16C, F-20A, Mirage 2000, Tornado | Next generation air combat and attack fighters with far more accuracy and up to twice the range payload of existing fighters. |
| Aim 9L/M, Phoenix, Mica, AA-8, AA-X10, AA-X-P2, Super 530, Python III | Advanced short and long range multi-aspect air-to-air missiles which greatly improve the air to air combat capability of all modern fighters. |
| Durandal, Paveway ERAM, ACM, SUU-65 WASP, J-233 | Advanced air-to-surface munitions including runway suppression, anti-armor, anti-hardpoint, anti-personnel, anti-radar, and other special mission point and area weapons with far more lethality than current systems. Many will use stand off weapons like glide bombs or advanced dispensers for low altitude single pass penetrations under radar. |
| RPVs, IMowhawk, MiG-25 (I) | Improved air borne sensor and reconnaissance platforms which can provide advanced targeting, intelligence, and battle management data. |

| | |
|---|---|
| PAH-2, AH-64, Mi-24 | Next generation attack helicopters with much longer ranges, improved air-to-air missiles, 3rd or 4th generation launch and leave anti-tank guided missiles, and air defense countermeasures. Will be supported by steadily improved troop lift helicopters with improved protection and firepower. |
| Peace Shield, Project Lambda, Lion's Dawn and $C^3I$/BM Systems | Air sensor and battle management systems equivalent to NATO NADGE level systems for integrating fighter and SAM defenses. Many with advanced attack mission control capabilities. |
| Maritime Patrol Aircraft | More advanced versions of E-2C-type aircraft armed with ASW weapons and air-to-surface missiles. |
| FAC(M), Missile Saar 5, Lupo, F-2000, etc. | Next generation missile patrol boats and corvettes with Frigates: Improved Harpoon and other moderate range advanced ship-to-ship missiles. |
| Sea Skua, Harpoon II, Exocet II, Gabriel III/IV, AS-4, AS-6, AS-7 | Advanced ship, shore, and air launched anti-ship missiles with advanced sensors and electronics, and far more lethal payloads. Can kill war ships and tankers far more effectively than today. |
| Coastal Submarines | Advanced diesel submarines with excellent silencing, moderate cruise ranges, and smart torpedoes. |
| SS-22/SS-23 | Advanced surface-to-surface missiles with ranges up to 900 miles. |
| Nerve gas | Widespread stocking of single or binary nerve gas agents and limited CBW defense capabilities. |

Western arms sales to Saudi Arabia can only have a limited effect in helping Saudi forces cope with these trends. Saudi Arabia will almost certainly be unable to use technology to compensate for its limited ground and naval strength. While it may maintain some technical "edge" over the equipment in neighboring forces, this edge is unlikely to compensate for their superior mass. The only force where Saudi Arabia can hope to use technology to compensate for its weakness in aircraft numbers is the Air Force, and there are risks even here.

## THE IMPACT OF NEW SOVIET SYSTEMS

It is also important to note that the Tornados, and the 60 F-15C/Ds already in Saudi Air Force inventory, will not face a MiG-21, F-4, F-5, or MiG-23 threat in the late 1980s and 1990s. They will face a threat equipped with first line French fighters like the Mirage 2000, and a wide range of new Soviet systems. Table 4.6 provides a brief technical summary of some of the new Soviet systems that will enter hostile air and air defense forces in the late 1980s and 1990s, and provides a clear indication of why Saudi Arabia is seeking to modernize its air forces:

Regional Threats and the Military Build-Up in the Gulf

## Table 4.6: New Soviet Systems Affecting the Gulf and Red Sea Threat

### Airborne Warning and Air Control Systems

- Il-76 Mainstay: An E-3A like aircraft which entered developmental production in 1984, and which has a rotating radome saucer and refueling probe. Likely to enter Gulf and Red Sea threat forces in the early 1990s.

### Fighters and Fighter Bombers

- MiG-23MF Export II: An improved version of the MiG-23 Flogger E with the full High Lark radar. This expands radar coverage of the export version with the Jay Bird radar from a search range of 18 miles to 53 miles and tracking range from 12 to 34 miles. Unlike the previous export MiG-23, this fighter has good look up capability and a limited look down capability. It has much more sophisticated avionics, built-in ECM, and possibly an optional IR pod. Unlike previous export versions, it can use advanced Soviet air-to-air missiles like the AA-7 (an IR/SARH missile with a 20 mile range) and AA-8 (a multi-aspect missile similar to the AIM-9J with a range of 3.5-4 miles). This aircraft may enter service in Syria and Iraq during 1985 or 1986.
- MiG-29 Fulcrum: First of a completely new generation of Soviet fighters which is roughly equivalent to the F-16. Entered service in 1984, and has a large pulse-doppler with moderate look down/shoot down radar with day/night and all weather combat capability. Maximum speed is Mach 2.2, and combat radius is 500 miles. Primarily an air defense aircraft, but is equipped for dual-role attack mission. Carries six AA-10 missiles (similar to the AIM-9L and AIM-9M), and has wing and fuselage racks for bombs and rockets. To be coproduced in India. Likely to enter Iraqi, Syrian, and Ethiopian forces in the late 1980s.
- SU-27 Flanker: Similar to the MiG-29 in air defense and dual role capability, but somewhat slower and with much longer range. Maximum speed is Mach 2.35 and combat radius is 715 miles. Carries eight radar homing AA-8 missiles and up to 13,000 pounds of attack munitions. May enter Gulf threat forces in the late 1980s, but the early 1990s is more likely.
- MiG-31 Foxhound: The first Soviet long range fighter with an advanced look-down, shoot down capability. A two seat air defense oriented fighter with a superior pulse doppler radar and avionics display and the ability to carry eight air-to-air missiles. Maximum speed is Mach 2.4 and combat radius is 930 miles. Carries a new radar homing version of the AA-9. Likely to enter Gulf threat forces in the early 1990s.
- SU-22 Fitter: An improved version of the Fitter J attack aircraft. This aircraft has been supplied to Libya and may enter Gulf threat forces during the next three years. Performance data are uncertain.
- SU-24 Fencer: An advanced long range attack fighter which entered service in 1984. It has advanced attack avionics and a weapons officer who sits next to the pilot. It has an advanced variable wing system and roughly five times the range and payload of any previous Soviet attack fighter. Maximum speed is Mach 2.18. Combat radius in LO-LO-LO) missions is over 200 miles. HI-LO-HI radius with 4,000

pounds of munitions is 1,100 miles. Unlikely to enter Gulf threat forces until the early 1990s. Maximum payload is 17,635 lbs of attack munitions.
- o SU-25 Frogfoot: A new Soviet close support attack fighter which has demonstrated excellent performance in Afghanistan. Somewhat lighter and slower than the U.S. A-10, but more maneuverable. Carries a heavy caliber tank killing gun, rockets, and bombs. Maximum speed is 546 Mph, combat radius is 345 miles.

Surface to Air Missile Systems
- o SA-5 Gammon: Long range high altitude radar guided SAM defense system with speed above Mach 3.5, a slant range of 185 miles, and a ceiling of 95,000 feet. Already deployed in Syria.
- o SA-8 Gecko: A mobile six launcher vehicle mounted SAM system with a range of 6-8 miles and a ceiling of 20,000 feet. Now being deployed in Jordan and Syria, and may be entering the Yemens and Ethiopia during the next year.
- o SA-10: A single state advanced SAM system which became operational in the Spring of 1984. The SA-10 can accelerate up to 100 "G" to a cruising speed of Mach 6, and a range of 60 miles with an advanced radar and multiple target engagement capability. Will probable replace the SA-6 and SA-3 in the Near East and Gulf.
- o SA-11: An advanced new short range system now deployed alongside the SA-6 in Soviet forces with radar guidance and speeds in excess of Mach 3. Range is 18.5 miles. The four rail launcher is vehicle mounted and can be netted into an air defense system along with the SA-6. This system is likely to deploy to the Gulf area in the late 1980s.
- o SA-12: A dual mode anti-aircraft and anti-cruise missile system just entering production. The dual launcher system has an estimate range of 60 miles. This advanced system is unlikely to deploy to the Gulf before the early 1990s.
- o SA-13: A tracked vehicle mounted missile which replaces the SA-9, and is netted with the ZSU-23-4 tracked radar guided AA gun. It has a range of 5 miles and can hit targets at altitudes between 165 and 16,000 feet. It has far superior low altitude tracking capability to previous light Soviet SAMs and very fast reload capability. Already deployed in Syria.

Source : Aviation Week, Jane's, Air Force Magazine, Jane's Defense Weekly.

The U.S.S.R. is making much more rapid progress in fighter design than many experts have previously predicted. The MiG-23 in service with Warsaw Pact forces marked the first major departure in twenty-five years from the relatively simple and mass produced MiG-15, 19, 17, and 21 and the Sukhoi Su-7 through Su-22. Its Tumansky R-27 engine was the first Soviet afterburning turbofan and its Highlark doppler air intercept radar and laser range finder made it roughly comparable to the F-4J.

The Su-24, which appeared in 1974, was the first Soviet fighter optimized for the attack role, and seemed a close copy of many features on the F-111. Its new features included a swing wing design, separate weapons control officer, and an all-weather and terrain-following capability, plus extensive internal fuel space and external munitions carrying capability.

While the Fencer has not yet been deployed outside the Warsaw Pact, it seems likely that the Su-24C will appear in the forces of potential threats by the early 1990s. The Su-24C has a modern pulse doppler radar and advanced attack avionics, and a new inertial navigation systems (INS) and electronic countermeasure (ECM) suite roughly comparable to NATO avionics. It can deliver 2,000 Kg of payload at a combat radius of up to 1,800 Km, and has a combat radius of 322 Km (LO-LO-LO)-950 Km (LO-LO-HI) with 2,500 kilograms of payload. Its terrain-following capability means that only a fighter with advanced look-down/ shoot-down capability like the F-15C/D MSIP can successfully defend against it.

The USSR's new first line fighters continue this trend. The MiG-31 is an upgraded MiG-25 with an advanced "semi-look down" radar, an additional crew member, 6 advanced AA-9 Acrid air-to-air missiles with limited anti cruise missile capability, a new engine with better subsonic performance, and considerable additional engine and air frame refinements over the MiG-25. It is specifically designed to work with the USSR's new Mainstay AWACS.

It is the Su-27 and MiG-29, however, that are most comparable to advanced Western fighters like the F-15, which are designed for high performance at subsonic speeds, and which Saudi Arabia must plan to face no later than the early 1990s. These two aircraft both have heads-up displays (HUDs), advanced infrared search/track sensors, full all weather mission capability, digital data links, and true look-down/shoot-down capability. They have hard points and connections for sophisticated attack mission avionics, and can fire air-to-air missiles beyond visual range.

While the F-16, F-15, and Tornado are often treated as fighters which have no equal in the forces of potential threat nations, it is important to note that both the Su-27 and MiG-29 can outmaneuver the F-15C/D, F-16A/B, and Tornado F.3 in a number of ways in a substantial part of their flight envelope. Both Soviet fighters have a nominal maximum speed of Mach 2.3, and the MiG-29 seems to have a higher thrust to weight ratio than the F-16A/B while the Su-27 is both slightly larger than the F-15C/D and Tornado and has a Tumansky R-31 engine with a 13,600 Kg thrust which is 25% higher than that of the F-15C/D.[3]

Equally impressively, the USSR is matching or surpassing the former U.S. advantage in fighter radar range and avionics sophistication. While the exact radar range of the Su-27 and MiG-29 is not yet public, various U.S. government sources have made it clear that the Foxfire radar on the MiG-25 can detect fighter sized targets at ranges of 60 nautical miles, which is beyond the detection range of Saudi Arabia's current APG-63 radar. They have also noted that the MiG-23's Highlark radar exceeds the detection range of the F-16A/B--which lacks the MiG-23s look down and shoot down capability. The long range track-while-scan pulse Doppler radars of the MiG-29 and Su-27 match or outperform the radars on the F-15C/D and Tornado F.3. [4]

## THE SOVIET MILITARY THREAT

The Soviet Union is also steadily improving the strength readiness of the forces it can deploy in the Gulf area, and particularly the strength of the air units it deploys along its southern border. These forces are shown in Table 3.7, and recent reports indicate a build-up in the 34th Tactical Aviation Army (TVA) from 400 active and 175 reserve aircraft in June 1979 to 900 active and 350 reserve aircraft in April 1985. A similar build-up is reported in the 6th TVA from 175 active and 75 reserve aircraft to 400 active and 100 reserve aircraft.

The totals in Table 4.7 do not include over 115,000 men and massive new air facilities in Afghanistan. While experts differ over the details of this Soviet force expansion in Afghanistan, most agree that there are now 9,000-10,000 Frontal Aviation personnel in the country, some 650 helicopters (including 2 attack helicopter regiments and 124 Mi-24 attack helicopters), 30 Su-25s, 30-45 MiG-23s, 75-90 MiG-21s, 6-12 MiG-25s, and 75-90 Su-17s. The Soviets have built or improved major air facilities at Baghram, Kabul, Mazer-E-Sharif, and Jalalabad and have military air facilities at Herat, Shindand, Farah, Lashkar Gah, Serden Band, Askargh, and Qandahar.[5]

# Regional Threats and the Military Build-Up in the Gulf

Table 4.7: The Soviet Threat to Western Oil

| Service | Forces | Personnel & Equipment |
|---|---|---|
| Army | 1 Tank Division | 11,000 |
| | 21-22 Motorized Rifle Divisions | 152,000 |
| | 2 Airborne divisions | 15,000-18,000 |
| Naval Infantry | 2 Regiments | 5,000 |
| Frontal Aviation | 2 Tactical Air Armies | 6 Fighter Regiments |
| | | 6 Fighter-Bomber Regiments |
| | 34th TAA in Transcaucasus MD | 900 MiG-21, 23, 27; Su-24,25,27 |
| | 6th TAA in Turkestan MD | 400 MiG-21, 23, 21R, Mi-8 |
| Naval Aviation | Long range bombers and anti-ship air-to-surface missile carriers | Over 100 on short notice |
| Navy | 1 Small ASW Carrier Task Group | Would depend on contingency |
| | Several Guided Missile Task Groups | |
| | Nuclear and conventional submarines with long range missiles | |
| | Landing Port Dock (550 man lift) and maximum of 8 Alligator-class LSTs (325 men/26 tanks each) | |

[a] Recent reports indicate a build-up in the 34th TVA from 400 active and 175 reserve aircraft in June 1979 to 900 active and 350 reserve aircraft in April 1985. A similar build-up is reported in the 6th TVA from 175 active and 75 reserve aircraft to 400 active and 100 reserve aircraft.

Source: Anthony H. Cordesman, The Gulf and the Search for Strategic Stability, Westview, Boulder, 1984, p. 818 and the IISS, Military Balance, 1985-1986.

## Regional Threats and the Military Build-Up in the Gulf

It seems unlikely that the USSR will take the risk of directly challenging the U.S. in the Gulf in the near future. The Soviet Union seems likely to remain bogged down in Afghanistan for at least several more years, and seems unlikely to risk any adventures in Iran until friendly political elements gain far more strength. The fact remains, however, that it does have an immense military presence on the edge of the Gulf, and this gives it immense political and strategic leverage.

As will be described shortly, the USSR is also creating a major presence in the Red Sea area. It is building major naval facilities in Ethiopia and has significant naval and air facilities in both Ethiopia and South Yemen. It already has immense strategic lift capability and its advantage in proximity means that it can move forces and heavy equipment into the Gulf and Red Sea areas more quickly than the U.S. This Soviet strategic lift will expand in the late 1980s as the USSR deploys its new Condor military transport. The Condor will have about 125 metric tons lift capability compared to 92 metric tons for the U.S. C-5A, and will be the largest air transport in the world.[6]

The USSR maintains a significant Indian Ocean and Red Sea Fleet, and the Soviet Navy will be able to deploy a true carrier task force into the area by the early 1990s with a new class of 65,000 ton carriers. The Soviet fleet in the area now averages 20-25 ships, and normally includes nuclear submarines, destroyers, frigates, mine vessels, intelligence ships, support vessels and transport ships.[7]

This naval presence is linked to the Soviet Union's military advisory and basing presence in the region. The USSR has long had anchorages and access to facilities in the PDRY, and used them during part of its intervention during the Yemeni civil war in 1986. It is establishing a major naval base at Dahlak off the coast of Ethiopia with a drydock, MCMV, naval infantry detachment, and staging facilities for IL-38 maritime reconnaissance aircraft. The USSR is the Seychelles' largest arms supplier and has delivered some $18 million in arms. It keeps up a steady pattern of ship visits, regularly transits military transports through the main airport of Mahe, and has sent naval vessels to help prop up the regime.[8]

These developments mean the USSR will steadily expand its strategic leverage in the Gulf and Red Sea areas. While USCENTCOM and the U.S. Navy will remain the primary deterrent to any Soviet attempt to use such forces for overt aggression, the Gulf states must still develop their own forces to provide some level of deterrence and self-defense capability, and to avoid a situation where they are so weak that the Soviet Union, or some Soviet-backed state, could intervene before USCENTCOM or other Western forces could arrive.

There are five additional variables which could radically increase the Soviet threat to Saudi Arabia and the Gulf during the next decade. These include:

- **Oil:** It is likely that the USSR will become radically more dependent on oil imports during the next decade. The USSR presents extraordinary problems in estimating proven reserves in terms of economically producable oil, and some experts now feel its undiscovered oil reserves may ultimately prove as large as its proven reserves. Nevertheless, Soviet production fell from 616 million metric tons in 1983 to 612 million metric tons in 1984, and 595 million metric tons in 1985.[9] This was the first drop in production since World War II, and occurred in spite of massive infusions of capital and the priority given a resource that accounts for two-thirds of Soviet foreign exchange earnings, and the USSR now maintains an extremely high ratio of production to proven reserve. (The ratio is 10-14 versus over 100 for Saudi Arabia and Iraq and 250 for Kuwait.)

  Many of the USSR's reserves are also in the Volga-Urals and Tyumen oil fields--both of which have high lifting costs and low recovery from conventional extraction methods. There are growing reports of overproduction of Soviet wells, and some estimates indicate that as many as 20% of the wells in the Tyumen field (which produces half of all Soviet output) are now shut down due to lack of spares. The USSR has experienced growing problems in meeting its oil production quotas, and is virtually certain to fall short again in 1986. Soviet oil production is now at about 11.9 MMBD when Soviet plans call for production of well over 12.5 MMBD. It would be extremely dangerous to assume that the USSR will be able to maintain its past levels of production and exports--much less increase production--and its development of alternative energy resources now lags far behind Soviet goals. These trends could greatly increase the pressure on the USSR to find some means of dominating a Gulf oil nation.[10]

- **Afghanistan:** A Soviet victory in Afghanistan may well be possible if the USSR is ruthless enough to continue its tactic of striking at the Afghan population as a substitute for its inability to locate and suppress the Afghan freedom fighters. Such a victory would not only give the USSR vastly increased military credibility and strategic leverage in the Gulf area, it would give it greatly enhanced capability to threaten Iran and Pakistan.

- **Iran:** There does not seem to be any immediate prospect that Khomeini's death, or the other currents of Iranian politics, will bring a pro-Soviet or Marxist movement to power. The Iranian revolution is, however, building up a deadly legacy of alienation in terms of economic mismanagement, the murder and suppression of minorities, and losses from the Iran-Iraq War. It is impossible to rule out the possibility that some Marxist element will come to power during the next 10 years or that some faction or strong element in Iran will seek Soviet aid and intervention to give it internal power. Such Soviet intervention could radically change the entire defense structure of the Gulf almost over night.

o <u>The Yemens:</u> As will be discussed later, there is a possibility that the tensions in North Yemen (YAR) and South Yemen (PDRY) could explode into another civil war and result in a united Yemen. Such unity could only be achieved with Soviet arms and backing, and could transform the Soviet advisory and basing presence in the Yemens into a major military capability. The USSR has already demonstrated that it can conduct massive military airlifts to the PDRY in a matter of days, and is helping both the PDRY and YAR expand their current air and naval bases and forces.

o <u>The Soviet Threat to Africa:</u> The USSR has steadily expanded its efforts to win power and influence in the Horn of Africa, and this region seems likely to be convulsed by economic and political crises throughout the next decade. There is at least some possibility that the USSR could expand its presence in Ethiopia to include Soviet backed regimes and basing facilities in the Sudan and Somalia.

SOVIET ARMS SALES AND ADVISORY EFFORTS

Even if none of these forces affect Soviet behavior--and the cumulative probability of some impact is significant--the USSR is certain to aggressively expand its arms sales and military advisory efforts in every nation that poses a current or potential threat to the Gulf and Saudi Arabia. The threat posed by such arms sales is much more serious than the dollar data which are issued by CIA and ACDA, and which are used in most press and academic reporting, implies.

The dollar trends shown in Tables 4.2 and 4.3 do not portray the volume of arms involved. They disguise the fact that the USSR provides far more weapons per dollar than the U.S., and that states like Saudi Arabia must make a massive investment in munitions and military support equipment that generally is not included in the cost estimates made for Soviet client states.

Unfortunately, no unclassified data are available on the specific dollar cost to weapons delivered ratios for particular nations in the region. These ratios are reflected, however, in the broad regional patterns shown in Table 4.8.

Table 4.8: Major Arms Sales to the Near East and South Asia by Major Supplier

| Weapons Type | USSR | U.S. | Major West European [a] |
|---|---|---|---|
| **1978-1981** | | | |
| Tanks and Self Propelled Guns | 4,210 | 1,402 | 405 |
| Artillery | 4,090 | 493 | 675 |
| APCs and Armored Cars | 5,150 | 4,495 | 1,970 |
| Major Surface Combatants | 16 | 3 | 7 |
| Minor Surface Combatants | 10 | 5 | 55 |
| Submarines | 3 | 1 | 2 |
| Supersonic Combat Aircraft | 1,180 | 182 | 195 |
| Subsonic Combat Aircraft | 85 | 18 | 30 |
| Other Aircraft | 95 | 111 | 170 |
| Helicopters | 630 | 7 | 235 |
| Guided Missile Patrol Boats | 23 | 0 | 19 |
| Surface-to-Air Missiles | 11,475 | 2,634 | 1,095 |
| **1981-1985** | | | |
| Tanks and Self Propelled Guns | 1,835 | 1,820 | 420 |
| Artillery | 2,295 | 684 | 420 |
| APCs and Armored Cars | 4,320 | 3,397 | 1,010 |
| Major Surface Combatants | 4 | 17 | 17 |
| Minor Surface Combatants | 19 | 12 | 25 |
| Submarines | 6 | 0 | 0 |
| Supersonic Combat Aircraft | 710 | 209 | 205 |
| Subsonic Combat Aircraft | 85 | 6 | 40 |
| Other Aircraft | 175 | 18 | 55 |
| Helicopters | 405 | 4 | 115 |
| Guided Missile Patrol Boats | 9 | 0 | 18 |
| Surface-to-Air Missiles | 7,630 | 1,768 | 460 |
| **1977-1984** | | | |
| Tanks and Self Propelled Guns | 6,045 | 3,222 | 825 |
| Artillery | 6,385 | 1,177 | 1,040 |
| APCs and Armored Cars | 9,470 | 7,862 | 2,980 |
| Major Surface Combatants | 33 | 7 | 24 |
| Minor Surface Combatants | 29 | 17 | 80 |
| Submarines | 9 | 1 | 2 |
| Supersonic Combat Aircraft | 1,890 | 391 | 400 |
| Subsonic Combat Aircraft | 170 | 24 | 70 |
| Other Aircraft | 270 | 129 | 225 |
| Helicopters | 1,035 | 11 | 350 |
| Guided Missile Patrol Boats | 32 | 0 | 37 |
| Surface-to-Air Missiles | 19,105 | 4,402 | 1,155 |

a. Major West European includes France, U.K., FRG, and Italy.
Source: Adapted from Richard F. Grimmett, Trends in Conventional Arms Transfers to The Third World by Major Supplier, 1978-1985, U.S. Congressional Research Service, Report 86-99F, May 9, 1986.

While the data in Table 4.8 exclude major arms transfers from East Europe, the PRC, North Korea, and Vietnam, they still show that the USSR has exported over 6,000 tanks and self-propelled guns to the Middle East since 1978. This compares with a little over 4,000 for the U.S. and Western Europe. Similarly, the USSR has exported 1,890 supersonic jet combat aircraft to the Middle East versus 791 for the U.S. and Western Europe. Although the U.S. and Europe have sold about twice as many arms to the Middle East as the USSR over the last decade, *when such transfers are measured in dollar terms*, they have sold substantially less than half the number of major weapons.

A detailed analysis of recent trends indicates that the number of Soviet Bloc weapons transfers to the Middle East has increased sharply relative to those of the West since 1982, and that European weapons transfers are increasing faster than those of the U.S. This reflects the impact of massive arms purchases by Iraq, Syria, Algeria, Libya, and North Yemen; increasing European efforts to capture the Western share of the arms markets, and rising U.S. unit costs coupled with political problems in selling to the Arab world.[11]

Equally significantly, the USSR has a massive military advisory presence in the region. This presence is shown in Table 4.9, and it is important to note that the USSR backs its direct military advisory effort to the nations which surround Saudi Arabia with efforts to infiltrate host nation communications, educational, police, intelligence, and internal security forces.

Regional Threats and the Military Build-Up in the Gulf

Table 4.9: Soviet Bloc Military Advisors and "Technicians" in the Middle East, The Gulf, and Africa

|  | Advisors: DoD Estimate as of 1985 | | | Advisors | Native |
|---|---|---|---|---|---|
|  | Soviet | East | Cuban | CIA '84 | Military Trained In Soviet Bloc |
| Algeria | 850 | 250 | 15-170 | 790 | 250 |
| Iran | - | - | - | 50 | - |
| Iraq | 450 | - | - | 1,300 | - |
| Kuwait | 5 | - | - | - | - |
| Libya | 1,820-2,300 | ? | (3000?) | 2,800 | 200 |
| Morocco | - | - | - | - | - |
| Syria | 2,480-4,000 | 210 | - | 5,300 | - |
| North Yemen | 500 | - | - | 510 | - |
| South Yemen | 1,100-1,500 | ? | 1,200 | 1,100 | 150 |
| Ethiopia | 1,250-3,000 | 700 | 13,000 | 2,600 | 350 |
| Other | - | - | - | 50 | - |
| Afghanistan | 4,000 | - | - | 2,025 | 500 |
| India | 150 | - | - | 500 | 250 |
| Angola | 1,000-1,400 | 500 | 19,000-20,000 | 1,700 | 300 |
| Benin | 80 | - | 50 | - | - |
| Burundi | 35 | - | - | - | - |
| Cape Verde | 25 | - | 20 | - | - |
| Congo | 300 | 15 | 3,000 | - | 50 |
| Equatorial Guinea | 40-50 | 200 | 25 | - | - |
| Guinea | 85-150 | - | 50 | 60 | 140 |
| Guinea Bissau | 200 | - | 40-50 | 55 | 30 |
| Mali | 180 | - | - | 50 | 25 |
| Malagasy Republic | 400 | - | 55 | - | - |
| Mozambique | 500-525 | 100 | 100-215 | 1,300 | 1,200 |
| Nigeria | 50 | - | - | 10 | 400 |
| Rwanda | 15 | - | - | - | - |
| Sao Tome | - | - | 100 | 170 | - |
| Sierra Leone | - | - | 90 | - | - |
| Sudan | - | - | - | 55 | - |
| Tanzania | 60 | 15 | 100 | 65 | - |
| Zambia | 150 | - | - | 50 | - |
| Other | - | - | - | 400 | - |

Sources differ significantly. The first three columns are taken from Soviet Military Power and other Department of Defense sources. The other columns are taken from CIA, Handbook of Economic Statistics, 1985, September, 1985, CPAS 85-10001, pp. 120-128

## THE NORTHERN GULF THREAT

The Soviet threat is only part of the problem that Saudi Arabia faces. Iran and Iraq have the wealth to build up massive air and ground forces, are politically unstable, have a history of aggressive ambitions in the region, and now have military machines with a half decade of military experience.

In fact, the Iran-Iraq War is the most immediate military threat the Saudis face. The Saudi Air Force already clashed with the Iranian Air Force in June, 1984, The victory of Saudi F-15s, backed by the E-3A AWACS, over Iranian F-4s is probably a critical factor explaining why Iran has limited its attacks on shipping in the Gulf and has never attempted to use the kinds of raids it conducted on Kuwait to put pressure on the Southern Gulf states within range of the Saudi Air Force. Iran has certainly been careful to limit its attacks to areas significantly east of Qatar where it can take advantage of the present range, strength, and $C^3I$ limits in Saudi air defenses.

While Table 4.10 shows that Iran's lack of a major source of military equipment since the Shah's fall has given Iraq a major edge in terms of equipment and technology it can import, Iran can still launch major spoiler attacks at Saudi Arabia and the other GCC countries, as well as encourage Shi'ite separatism and religious tension, and there is still some risk that Iran can use its air or naval power to threaten Gulf shipping, or achieve a coup d'etat in Bahrain. Further, any Iranian victory over Iraq would not only make Iran the Gulf's dominant military power, it would pose a direct threat to Kuwait which no combination of current or projected GCC forces can deal with.

There is no way to predict the outcome of the fighting or how long Iran's clerical regime can rule with or without victory and/or without Khomeini. While Iraq has won the latest rounds of fighting, as it did during most of 1984, it also made serious mistakes in responding to Iran's February, 1985, and February, 1986, offensives and suffered a serious defeat when Iran successfully invaded the Iraqi city of Faw, just opposite to Kuwait. Iran achieved significant initial successes in both sets of offensives, and Iraq suffered high casualties. Iraq does have superior equipment strength and technology, and the advantage of excellent defensive positions, but any major tactical mistakes could still cost it the war.

Iran, in turn, continues to experience considerable turmoil within the Majlis and Cabinet, and the war does seem to be producing a rising social and political backlash. Iran has also run down much of its military inventory to the point where it will be virtually forced to rearm once the war is over. The PRC cannot provide Iran with competitive arms and technology. While Western Europe may be willing to sell Iran the arms it will need, Iran might also turn to the U.S.S.R. The ambitions of its new class of military leaders remain obscure (as is the case with Iraq's new class of generals). While a clerical regime seems most likely over the next five years, it is impossible to rule out some form of "man on horseback" once Khomeini is gone, and it is impossible to predict his ambitions and politics.

Regional Threats and the Military Build-Up in the Gulf

Table 4.10: The Trends in Iranian and Iraqi Military Forces: 1980-1985

| Force Category | 1980 Iran | 1980 Iraq | 1985 Iran | 1985 Iraq |
|---|---|---|---|---|
| **TOTAL MILITARY MANPOWER** | 240,000 | 242,250 | 805,000 | 642,000 |
| **LAND FORCES** | | | | |
| Regular Army Manpower | | | | |
| Active | 150,000 | 200,000 | 250,000 | 600,000 |
| Reserve | 400,000+ | 256,000 | 350,000 | 75,000 |
| Revolutionary Guards/ People's Militia | | | 250,000 | 650,000 |
| Hezbollahi (Home Guard) | | | 2,500,000 | |
| Arab Volunteers | | | | 10,000 |
| Division Equivalents | | | | |
| Armored (Divisions/Brigades) | 6+4 | 12+3 | ? | 6+3 |
| Mechanized | 3 | 4 | 3 | 5 |
| Infantry and Mountain | 0 | 4 | 7/2 +1. (a) | 5+4.(b) |
| Major Combat Equipment | | | | |
| Main Battle Tanks | 1,740 | 2,750 | 1,000 | 4,820 |
| Other Armored Fighting Vehicles | 1,075 | 2,500 | 1,190 | 4,000 |
| Major Artillery | 1,000+ | 1,040 | 1,030 | 3,500 |
| **AIR FORCES** | | | | |
| Air Force Manpower | 70,000 | 38,000 | 35,000 | 38,100 |
| Combat Aircraft | 445 | 332 | 50-95.(c) | 580.(d) |
| Combat Helicopters | 500 | 41 | 50? | 171 |
| Total Helicopters | 750 | 260 | 150-370 | 391 |
| **NAVY** | | | | |
| Navy Manpower | 26,000 | 4,250 | 20,000 | 4,500 |
| Destroyers | 3 (e) | 0 | 3(e) | 0 |
| Frigates | 4 (f) | 1 (g) | 4(f) | 1. (g) |
| Corvettes | 4 | 0 | 2 | (h) |
| Missile Patrol Craft | 9 (i) | 12(j) | 7-10.(i) | 10.(j) |
| Hovercraft | 14 | 0 | 10 | 0 |
| Maritime Patrol Aircraft | 6 P-3F | 0 | 2 P-3F | 0 |

a. 7 Mechanized divisions with 3 brigades each and a total of 9 armored and 18 mechanized battalions. Also 2 special forces divisions, 1 airborne brigade, and eight division sized Revolutionary Guard formations organized in battalions.
b. Includes 5 Infantry divisions and 4 mountain divisions. There are also 3 independent special forces brigades, 9 reserve brigades, and 15 People's Volunteer Infantry Brigades.
c. Includes 35 F-4D/E, 50 F-5E/F, 10 F-14A, and 3 RF-4E. Large numbers of additional combat aircraft are in storage due to lack of parts.
d. Includes 7 Tu-22, 8 Tu-16; 4 FGA squadrons with 100 MiG 23-BM, 6 with 95 Su-7 and 80 Su-20, 1 with 12 Hunter FB-59/FR-10, and 5 Super Etendard with Exocet being replaced with

## Regional Threats and the Military Build-Up in the Gulf

18 Mirage F-1 with Exocet; 1 recce squadron with 5 MiG-25; and 5 interceptor squadrons with 25 MiG-25, 40 MiG-19, 150 MiG-21, 45 Mirage F-1EQ, and 4 Mirage F-1BQ.
e. 3 equipped with Standard Arm SSMs.
f. Equipped with Sea Killer SSM
g. 4 Lupo frigates on order
h. 6 Italian 650 ton corvettes on order.
i. Equipped with Harpoon surface to surface missiles.
j. Equipped with Styx missiles.

Adapted from various editions of the IISS Military Balance and work by Drew Middleton for the New York Times

Saudi Arabia not only faces these uncertainties regarding an Iranian victory and Iran's future politics, it must cope with similar uncertainties regarding Iraq. Saudi Arabia is all too conscious that Iraq is becoming a massive military power, and that any peace or cease fire between Iran and Iraq will leave many critical problems unresolved regarding both Iranian and Iraqi attitudes and actions:

- o Iran will probably face a decade of political turmoil and further religious conflict. There is no way to predict how, and how fast, it will rearm, but it may well have to turn to the USSR as its only source of arms. It is important to note that Iran successfully operated about 450 modern combat aircraft at the time of the Shah's fall and retains the basing and infrastructure to support a first line fighter force roughly twice the size that Saudi Arabia can hope to field.
- o Iranian acquisition of several hundred modern Soviet fighters, or Mirage F-1/Mirage 2000 equivalents, would allow it to challenge Saudi Arabia even if it were fully equipped with the F-15 C/D MSIP and F-15Es it is now requesting, particularly because of Saudi Arabia's inability to cover the Eastern or lower Gulf. Iran has also operated a force of about 1,700 main battle tanks, or four times the present strength of Saudi forces. Its current Army manning is close to 20 times that of Saudi Arabia, and its navy represent a continuing threat. The Iranian Navy has 3 modern missile equipped destroyers, 4 modern missiles equipped frigates, and large numbers of Hovercraft and landing ships.[12]
- o Iraq's trend towards political maturity, and friendship towards Saudi Arabia began in the mid 1970s, and before the Iran-Iraq War. This position has been reinforced by the painful lessons of that conflict, but there is no guarantee that the present Baath regime will remain in power. There is a good chance that Iraq's considerable military forces could come under hostile or radical control during the late 1980s to mid 1990s.
- o Iraq already has about 1.3 million men under arms, and some 3,700 tanks, 532 combat aircraft, and 409 helicopters. It has 60 Mirage F-1s and 165 MiG-23, MiG-25, and SU-20 fighters. It

will replace at least 200 of its current fighters with advanced types such as the Mirage 2000 and MiG-29 by the early 1990s. This will not only give it massive land superiority over Saudi Arabia, but air superiority--unless Saudi Arabia can obtain the F-15C/D MSIP and F-15Es it is now requesting. Iraq also has ordered a significant number of new naval vessels, including four Italian missile equipped *Lupo* frigates and six 650 ton corvettes.[13]
o Iraq and Iran are likely to emerge into a world "oil glut" with a massive need for revenue and substantial surplus oil export capacity--both can probably export at around 4 MMBD within a year to two years after the war versus current exports of under 2 MMBD. This raises the specter of major pressure on Saudi Arabia to cut its own production or of a massive new production/price war in OPEC at a time when oil prices might otherwise begin to rise. While "oil wars" are not a direct military threat, they certainly are viewed as one of the most serious strategic threats the Kingdom faces.
o Iran must eventually find some massive new source of arms, and this may mean it will eventually turn to the USSR for arms which are competitive in technology and performance to those Iraq is obtaining from Western Europe.
o Iraq already has a major capability to strike at tankers and targets in the Gulf. By the late 1980s, it will have modern strike fighters equivalent to those in the French and Soviet air forces with a range of up to 800 miles and much heavier and more lethal air-to-ship and air-to-surface missiles. Iraq also has vast supplies of modern land force armor, advanced munitions, and $C^3I$ equipment on order. Like Iran, it is certain to steadily expand its land and air strike capability against the Gulf and GCC nations throughout the next decade.[14]

No currently foreseeable outcome of the Iran-Iraq war can free Saudi Arabia, the other GCC states, or the U.S. from the realities of the threat from the Northern Gulf states. The basic numbers in terms of key measures and military forces reflect realities that no strategist can ignore.

Saudi Arabia and the GCC have only one conceivable advantage over Iran and Iraq that allows them to create a significant deterrent: this advantage is the ability to use their oil wealth to buy superior technology and to take advantage of the geography of the Gulf to use air power and advanced technology to compensate for their weakness in land forces and air strength. The comparative figures on manpower, tank numbers, and aircraft numbers reveal inherent weaknesses which grow out of the size of GCC forces, and which the Southern Gulf states simply cannot overcome.

Regional Threats and the Military Build-Up in the Gulf

THE RED SEA THREAT

Saudi Arabia already faces serious potential threats from a number of Red Sea states. These threats take on special meaning because of Saudi Arabia's geography. Oman is the only GCC state that could aid Saudi Arabia in dealing with a Red Sea threat and it could only provide support in dealing with the PDRY. Saudi Arabia is also far too large to use most of its bases and forces to support or cross reinforce those on other fronts. Saudi air forces cannot operate against the Red Sea from bases in Hafr al-Batin, Dhahran, or Riyadh. Forces at Tabuk cannot support forces at Sharurah or Khamis Mushayt.

Saudi Arabia must disperse its limited ground forces to forward bases throughout the country, and this has left it with an exceptionally poor force density on any given front. Its growing naval forces are limited in readiness and capability and will remain so for the next decade, while Northern Gulf and Red Sea naval threats can be expected to grow steadily thoughout this period. This, in turn, has made air power Saudi Arabia's only means of compensating for the weakness and dispersal of its land and naval forces.

Saudi Arabia can only use air power in such a role, however, if (a) its limited first line fighter strength has the range and refueling capability to mass quickly, (b) its air units can maintain a decisive technical and performance edge over threat forces, (c) it can provide sufficient air defense capability to provide air cover for Saudi ground forces, naval forces, and key targets, (d) it can provide sufficient dual capability in the attack mission to offset its limited ground strength and give it time to reinforce its army units, and (e) its air units are cumulatively strong enough to provide at least limited coverage of the Northern Gulf or Red Sea front while facing an active threat on the other front.

THE YAR AND PDRY

The virtual economic collapse of the PDRY, accompanied by a continuing internal struggle for power following Ismail's replacement by Ali Nasr, allowed Kuwait, Saudi Arabia, and the UAE to "buy off" the threat from South Yemen in the early 1980s. The PDRY exchanged ambassadors with Saudi Arabia and the U.K. in 1983, agreed to accredit a non-resident ambassador from Oman, condemned the mining of the Red Sea in 1984, and played a relatively moderate role in trying to heal the splits in the PLO.

It is far from clear, however, how long the PDRY will stay bought. Saudi and other Gulf money has been very limited since 1982, with Abu Dhabi providing the bulk of external aid from GCC states (About $30 million annually). This, coupled to a disastrous set of floods in the Spring of 1982, has meant that the PDRY has lacked the external funding (70%) it needed for its 1981-1984 five year plan.

Debt service has risen from $3.4 million annually in 1980 to $252 million in 1986, and South Yemen owes almost $1 billion, nearly half of which is owed to the USSR and Soviet bloc states. The PDRY has also seen its annual balance of payments deficit grow from $39 million in 1978, to $368 million in 1984. This was formerly offset in part by worker remittances, but these have dropped significantly in 1984 and 1985.[15]

Equally importantly, the long standing rivalry between Ali Nasr Muhammad and his more radical deputy, Brigadier General Ali Antar, led to civil war in 1986 and forced most of the PDRY's "moderate" radicals to leave the country. The new ruler of the PDRY is a pro Moscow hardliner--as are his other colleagues and rivals. The factions favoring unification with the YAR--by force if necessary--and a harder line towards Saudi Arabia and Oman now seem firmly in power.[16]

South Yemen also remains a fairly large military power by Arabian and Red Sea standards. Its desertion rate is high, and its overall military proficiency is low--especially in operating aircraft, armor, and military electronics. Nevertheless it does have sufficient ground forces to pose a threat to Oman, Saudi Arabia, and North Yemen although there are no signs that it is improving its training and organization at the same rate as Saudi, YAR, and Omani forces.

The PDRY already has about 27,500 men under arms plus about 15,000 militia and paramilitary forces. It has over 700 tanks, and FROG-7 and SCUD-B missiles. It has 135 combat aircraft, including 20 MiG-23/27 and 30 Su-20/22s, one Soviet corvette, and six missile equipped patrol boats. This force strength compares with a total of 38,000 regular military for Saudi Arabia, 450 medium tanks, and 205 combat aircraft. Even a relatively small state like the PDRY has much larger heavy armored forces than Saudi Arabia, and the PDRY can concentrate all of its strength on a single front.

The PDRY will have to replace most of its 45 MiG-21s and SU-20/22s, most of its 30 light fighter trainers, and all 10 of its IL-28 bombers by the early 1990s. The recent history of Soviet force modernization support indicates that it will get first line Soviet export fighters as replacements.[17] It is likely to build up to a total strength of about 1,200 tanks and 150-170 combat aircraft by the early 1990s.

The PDRY also has a significant Soviet military presence which seems to have been reinforced since the civil war in January, 1986. There is a large Soviet military advisory effort supported by at least some security advisors in the police, internal security, and intelligence branches. The Soviet Naval squadron in the Indian Ocean and Red Sea area now totals 20-25 units, including surface ships and cruise missile and attack submarines, and often uses Socotra and Aden as a port or anchorage. Recent Pacific Fleet developments indicate that true Soviet carrier task forces may begin to visit the Indian Ocean by the late 1980s, and the PDRY is the most logical center for such operations. The USSR maintains extensive intelligence and communications facilities in the PDRY, and Soviet IL-38 May maritime patrol aircraft fly regularly from Al-Anad airfield. The USSR has delivered more than $2 billion worth of military equipment since 1968.[18]

There also is still at least some possibility that North and South Yemen will be combined under a single radical regime. The situation in North Yemen remains as unstable as ever. President Saleh does not seem to be immediately threatened with political upheaval or outside subversion, and recent unification negotiations seem to have helped stabilize relations with the PDRY. Ali Nasr visited North Yemen for relatively cordial talks before his overthrow, and a Supreme Yemen Council was set up in 1983 that provides a Joint Ministerial Committee (JMC) chaired alternatively by both Presidents, and which has met sporadically in their alternative capitals--most recently in Sanaa in December, 1985.[19] Some experts believe that the existence of the JMC, coupled to agreements on reduced trade barriers, joint development projects, and the joint manning of border posts, may meet the ideological demand for "unity" without the kind of political union that could weaken the YAR, but others see it as creating an ideological push towards unification which could lead to the merger of the two countries through some future coup.

There were reports of such a coup attempt in the YAR in late September, 1984, just before President Saleh left to sign a 20 year treaty of friendship with the USSR. They have surfaced again since a series of Cabinet reshuffles began in December, 1984, and the civil war in the PDRY in January, 1986. These reports are somewhat dubious, but are valid indicators of the continuing tension in the country.

North Yemen's economic development has never recovered from the effects of a December, 1982, earthquake, and even though it introduced major austerity measures in 1983, its economy has weakened to the point where there are few near term prospects of development other than the possibility of oil. While some discoveries in the YAR have been promising, the results are uncertain. South Korean reports of commercially viable production levels of 100,000-200,000 BPD have officially been denied by the Yemen Hunt Oil Company and national oil company (Yominco). At the same time, President Saleh announced in September, 1985, that the Alif oil field in the Marrib-Jawf area had estimated reserves of 300 million barrels.[20]

The YAR's massive trade deficit is still growing, its external debt has risen at a rate of over 30% annually, and remittances from workers in other nations have steadily diminished since 1980. While Saudi Arabia has deliberately subsidized labor from the YAR to help maintain North Yemen's stability, and remittances approached $1.3 billion in 1985, they are almost certain to drop in 1986-1990. This is critical because the exporting of labor has been the YAR's main industry.

Industrial and mercantile development remains low, and efforts to cut the growing dominance of Qat in agriculture since 1972 have fallen far short of the nation's goals. Economic growth has been only about half the 7%

called for in the 1982-1986 development plan, and the YAR has not approached its investment goal of $6.4 billion. The YAR has been heavily dependent in recent years on aid from Saudi Arabia and Abu Dhabi, but the cuts in GCC oil revenues are reducing such aid.

While the central government is improving its control over the country, it still does not fully control the countryside outside the major cities and key lines of communication, and desertion rates to the Saudi Armed forces remain high.[21]

The YAR still, however, is building a major military force by local standards. It has 37,000 men in its armed forces--or roughly the total strength of the regular Saudi forces. It has 850 main battle tanks. This is roughly twice the heavy armor strength of Saudi Arabia, although the overall readiness and maintenance of most YAR army equipment is poor. The YAR now has 92 combat aircraft, although some of these aircraft are now relatively old and poorly maintained. The YAR plans to expand its force to 130-150 by 1990. At least 42 of its existing fighters will have to be replaced with new aircraft by the early 1990s, and the YAR will probably receive 70-100 modern Soviet fighter types over the next decade.[22]

While the YAR can scarcely be called pro-Soviet, the USSR plays a steadily increasing role as an advisor and supplier of its military forces. The YAR signed a 20 year friendship treaty with the USSR on October 9, 1984, and the USSR has provided the YAR with roughly one-third of the foreign loans it has needed to survive in recent years. The USSR has a 500 man advisory group, which is far larger than the U.S.-Saudi groups, and Soviet technicians now maintain most of North Yemen's complex military equipment. The initial Soviet-YAR arms agreement of 1979 has expanded from an initial level of $1 billion to over $2 billion, with $1.4 billion worth of actual deliveries. These include new major deliveries of armor, including T-62 tanks, which began in mid-1985. The USSR signed a new friendship treaty with North Yemen in 1984, and while President Saleh continues to support economic alignment with the GCC states and the West, U.S. military aid plays a token role at best.[23]

Saudi influence in North Yemen has slowly diminished during the last five years and seems likely to continue to do so. Saudi Arabia has also slowly lost influence over the Northern tribes, just as their conservative leaders have lost influence over an increasingly expatriate work force.

Neither the PDRY nor the YAR are particularly stable regimes and both states still suffer from deep internal divisions and are economic basket cases. Both have a major economic motive to put pressure on Saudi Arabia, although recent oil exploration activity in both countries indicates that oil exports may eventually slightly ease this situation.

It is likely, therefore, that Saudi Arabia will have to continue to plan its military and political strategy to cope with a threat from either or both Yemens, and do so in spite of the obvious basing and deployment problems it faces in dividing its forces between coverage of the Gulf, Red Sea, and the Southeast. This need to divide Saudi forces is already reflected in the fact that the forces at Sharurah and Khamis Mushayt are being given a considerably higher readiness and force improvement priority than those at Tabuk, and that the military cities (Army, Air Force, and Air Defense) at Khamis Mushayt have been steadily expanded.

## ETHIOPIA

The Ethiopian regime is hostile to the Saudi regime, and harbors deep seated resentment of Saudi Arabia because of Saudi financing of the Eritrean rebels, and support of hostile regimes in the Sudan and Somalia. As the previous tables have shown, Ethiopia has become a major military power in the Red Sea area. It has received more than $4 billion in Soviet arms since 1975, and signed agreements for $1 billion more.

The extent of Soviet involvement in Ethiopia is indicated by the fact the USSR made new major arms deliveries to the port of Aseb to help Ethiopia in its 1985 campaign against the Eritrean rebels, including T-55 tanks, APCs and AFVs, and more MiG-23 fighter bombers. Direct Soviet logistic and advisory support was the only reason that Ethiopia was able to deploy some 50,000 troops in less than three weeks in August, 1985, and capture the key town of Barentu in spite of the fact it was the rainy season.[24]

Ethiopia has at least 300,000 men in uniform, and another 170,000 men in paramilitary units. Although its terrain is often unsuited to armored warfare, it has some 1,010 main battle tanks. It now has only about 160 combat aircraft, but the USSR is conducting extensive MiG-21 and MiG-23 training, and Ethiopia is likely to build up to 230-270 combat aircraft by the early 1990s. Most of these fighters will be MiG-23 or follow-on fighters.

Ethiopia already has 24 armed helicopters and is steadily increasing its overall helicopter strength. While the Mi-24 only has a range of 99 miles, and the new Mi-28 has a range of 150 miles and could not operate against Saudi Arabia from across the Red Sea, these helicopters could rapidly deploy and operate out of the Yemens. The new Soviet Mi-26 heavy transport aircraft can carry up to 100 troops, or even armored vehicles, for ranges of 497 miles and is well equipped for night operations. Ethiopia also has a Soviet supplied navy of two frigates, seven missile-equipped patrol boats, and 14 other patrol craft and landing craft.[25]

Ethiopia also now provides the only true Soviet naval base in the area, on the island of Dahlak. The USSR has an 8,500 ton floating dry dock, floating piers, helipads, fuel and water storage, a submarine tender, and other repair ships. Guided missile cruisers, and nuclear submarines routinely call at Dahlak for service, and Soviet IL-38 May aircraft operated from Dahlak until they were destroyed by Eritrean rebels in May, 1984.[26]

While Ethiopia has previously been "pinned down" by its civil war with various rebel groups, these have been hit hard by the current famine and massive new Soviet support, and Ethiopia may well emerge as a major radical threat. Ethiopia also has political and strategic links to the PDRY and Syria, and may now be selling its stocks of U.S. arms to Iran. Ethiopia is a member of a Tripartite Alliance with the PDRY and Libya which was signed in 1981, although this alliance has not been particularly active in recent years, and Libya withdrew its People's Bureau (embassy) from the PDRY on September 25, 1984.[27]

While most such radical alliances remain of peripheral importance, Saudi Arabia may be faced not only with a much more active and hostile Ethiopia but much stronger linkages between its radical neighbors. Given Ethiopia's large military forces, and the ability of the PDRY and Ethiopia to control the lower Red Sea, this could become a major strategic threat at almost any time from the late 1980s on.

## THE SUDAN

The Sudan also may become a radical and hostile regime during the next decade, although it is far too soon to predict this as a trend. Nimeiri's fall does not seem to have ended the growing civil war in the Sudan, and it is unclear whether the current military government can consolidate power in the North, much less over the entire country.

The Sudan has been able to hold popular elections and a moderate conservative has come to office. Nevertheless, the nation's economic development has virtually halted, it faces a crushing debt burden, it suffers from a continuing drought and famine in much of the country, and it has not been able to make major progress in dealing with a civil war and revolt in the South.

Libya has actively courted the new military government since Nimeiri's fall, and the U.S. is experiencing growing problems in dealing with the Sudan's new officials. If the Sudan does become hostile, the combination of the threats in the Red Sea and in related areas in Africa could become far more serious.

## THE MILITARY TRENDS IN THE RED SEA AREA

The military efforts of the states in the Red Sea area are summarized in Table 4.11, and any major new radical combination of these states could greatly increase the threat to Saudi Arabia's oil shipments from the area, the movement of pilgrims, and ability to ship oil and gas directly to the Red Sea.

Table 4.11: Comparative Military Effort of Red Sea and Key African States Affecting Red Sea Security

|  | Defense Expenditure ($Millions) | Arms Imports ($Millions) | Military Manpower | Battle Tanks | Combat Aircraft |
|---|---|---|---|---|---|
| Sudan | 269 | 76 | 56,600 | 170 | 45 |
| Egypt | 4,143 | 1,700 | 460,000 | 1,750 | 427 |
| Libya | 3,800 | 1,900 | 73,000 | 2,800 | 535 |
| Ethiopia | 450 | 503 | 306,000 | 1,020 | 160 |
| Somalia | 148 | 60 | 62,550 | 230 | 64 |
| Chad | 52 | 7 | 4,200 | (10) | (2) |
| CAR | 35 | 5 | 2,300 | 4 | (10) |
| Zaire | 170 | 30 | 26,000 | (60) | 39 |
| Uganda | 90 | 30 | 18,000 | 17 | (6) |
| Kenya | 240 | 50 | 13,650 | 76 | 28 |
| Saudi Arabia | 17,700 | 3,300 | 62,500 | 450 | 205 |
| North Yemen | 579 | 260 | 36,550 | 664 | 76 |
| South Yemen | 227 | 310 | 27,500 | 550 | 120 |

Source: Adapted from the IISS, Military Balance, 1985/1986; ACDA computer data base for World Arms Transfers and Military Expenditures. Military data differ from text which is adapted to include information from other sources.

## INSTABILITY IN SAUDI ARABIA'S WESTERN BORDER AREA

Saudi Arabia also must measure its forces to take account of possible threats from its western borders. While direct military threats are now unlikely, Syria has long put political pressure on Saudi Arabia and Kuwait. No one familiar with the Near East is likely to place much faith in "intentions" as a test of force requirements. Saudi Arabia is forced to take account of "capability" as well as "probability".

### EGYPT AND JORDAN

Neither Egypt nor Jordan seem likely to become a significant threat to Saudi Arabia during the next decade, but both are affected by the same general forces of instability as Saudi Arabia, and both are more vulnerable in terms of religion and economics and possibly in terms of internal politics.

Egypt remains the largest Arab state, and controls the key strategic life line through the Suez Canal. Although its military forces have declined sharply in total strength since its break with the USSR, it remains far more powerful than Saudi Arabia, and a radical or hostile Egypt would be a major threat. Similarly, Jordan has long stabilized Saudi Arabia's western flank and limited the political and military leverage Syria could exert on the Kingdom. Its forces have not modernized at the same rate as those of other Arab states, but they remain the most professional of all Arab armies and any coup in Jordan could change the Kingdom's security position overnight.

## SYRIA

Syria has never been a direct threat to Saudi Arabia and some Saudi leaders, such as Crown Prince Abdullah, have close ties to Syria. Nevertheless, Saudi Arabia has paid dearly in economic and military aid to ensure that Syria's political radicalism has never been translated into hostile political action against it, and the future attitudes of a post-Assad Syria are unclear.

While it seems likely that any successor regime will be more concerned with Israel and internal conflicts than with any political ambitions in the Gulf, the fact remains that Syria's pressure on Iraq has gravely increased the risks created by the Iran-Iraq War, and that the Kingdom cannot rely on Syrian stability or friendship. Once President Assad is gone, and his hold on the country seems to be weakening, Syria may well come under more radical rule or be destabilized by the tensions between its Sunni majority and ruling Alawite minority.

Further, the growth of Syrian military forces has given it ample capability to threaten Saudi Arabia as well as Jordan. Syria has ordered over $19 billion worth of arms from the USSR, and there are nearly 4,000 Soviet advisors in country--more than in any other Third World nation. There are an additional 1,000 Soviet economic technicians, and Syria is now heavily dependent on Soviet economic credits as well as Arab aid.

Syria has more than 402,500 men in uniform, 4,200 main battle tanks, and 500 combat aircraft. About 400 of these aircraft are medium to high performance types. As Table 4.12 shows, Syria's forces match or exceed those of Israel, approach those of Iraq, and vastly exceed the forces of any combination of the GCC states. Syria seems to have been the first Arab country to get the advanced version of the MiG-23 discussed earlier, and will probably get the MiG-29 within the next three years. It has recently received SA-13 surface-to-air missiles and was the first country outside the Warsaw Pact to get the SA-5 and SS-21 missiles. It will be able to pose a major threat to Saudi Arabia and Kuwait for the foreseeable future.[28]

Regional Threats and the Military Build-Up in the Gulf

Table 4.12: The Military Build-Up to The West of Saudi Arabia

| Category | Israel 1982 | Israel 1986 | Syria 1982 | Syria 1986 | Jordan 1982 | Jordan 1986 | Egypt 1982 | Egypt 1986 |
|---|---|---|---|---|---|---|---|---|
| **Total** | | | | | | | | |
| Defense Spending ($billions) | 6.1 | 3.6 | 2.4 | 3.3 | 0.4 | 0.5 | 2.1 | 4.1 |
| Manpower (1,000s) | | | | | | | | |
| Active | 174.0 | 142.0 | 222.5 | 402.5 | 72.8 | 70.3 | 452.0 | 445.0 |
| Conscript | 120.3 | - | 120.0 | - | - | - | 255.0 | 250.0 |
| Mobilizable | 500.0 | 512.0 | 345.0 | 673.0 | 107.8 | 105.3 | 787.0 | 825.0 |
| **Army** | | | | | | | | |
| Manpower (1,000s) | | | | | | | | |
| Active | 135.0 | 104.0 | 170.0 | 210.0 | 65.0 | 62.8 | 320.0 | 320.0 |
| Conscript | 110.0 | 88.0 | 120.0 | 135.0 | - | - | 180.0 | 180.0 |
| Moblizable | 450.0 | 400.0 | 270.0 | 55.0 | - | - | 620.0 | 643.0 |
| Tanks | 3,600 | 3,650 | 3,990 | 4,200 | 569 | 795 | 2,100 | 2,159 |
| APCs | 8,000 | 8,000 | 1,600 | 3,000 | 1,022 | 882 | 3,030 | 2,750 |
| Artillery/MRLs | 960 | 1,000 | 2,100 | 2,300 | 274 | 239 | 2,000 | 2,100 |
| **Air Force and Air Defense Forces** | | | | | | | | |
| Manpower (1,000s) | | | | | | | | |
| Active | 30.0 | 28.0 | 50.0 | 130.0 | 7.5 | 7.2 | 113.0 | 105.0 |
| Conscript | 7.0 | 2.0 | - | - | - | - | 60.0 | 60.0 |
| Mobilizable | 35.0 | 65.0 | - | - | - | - | 133.0 | 117.0 |
| Total Combat Aircraft | 634 | 684 | 450 | 583 | 94 | 121 | 429 | 427 |
| Bombers | 0 | 0 | 0 | 0 | 0 | 0 | 14 | 13 |
| Attack/Int. | 432 | 402 | 0 | 0 | 0 | 0 | 0 | 103 |
| Attack | 174 | 130 | 205 | 193 | 29 | 68 | 218 | 73 |
| Interceptor | 28 | 0 | 244 | 280 | 45 | 35 | 152 | 164 |
| Recce/EW | 28 | 25 | 0 | 10 | 0 | 0 | 45 | 36 |
| OCU | 0 | 0 | 0 | 0 | 20 | 15 | 0 | 0 |
| Armed Helicopter | 42 | 90 | 16 | 100 | 0 | 8 | 24 | 48 |
| Major SAM Bns/ Bty/Sites | 15 | 15 | 75 | 126 | 5 | 5 | 151 | 100 |
| **Navy** | | | | | | | | |
| Active Manpower | 9.0 | 10.0 | 2.5 | 2.5 | 0.3 | 0.3 | 20.0 | 25.0 |
| Conscripts | 3.3 | 3.3 | - | - | - | - | 15.0 | 10.0 |
| Mobilizable | 10.0 | 10.0 | 5.0 | 5.0 | - | - | 35.0 | 40.0 |
| Submarines | 3 | 3 | 0 | 0 | 0 | 0 | 12 | 14 |
| Guided Missile Destroyer/Escort/ | 27 | 24 | 18 | 22 | 0 | 0 | 19 | 30 |
| Frigate/Corvette | 2 | 6 | 2 | 2 | 0 | 0 | 8 | 10 |
| Small Combat | 44 | 45 | 12 | 19 | 9 | 9 | 56 | 104 |
| Amphibious | 7 | 12 | ? | 2 | 0 | 0 | 20 | 21 |

Source: Adapted from various editions of the IISS Military Balance and the JCCS Middle East Military Balance. Note that these figures do not show equipment in storage, use estimates which often do not reflect actual readiness of manpower and equipment, and use dated material. For example, the IISS data for Israel reflect virtually no updating between 1982 and 1986, and grossly exaggerate the size of Egypt's operational forces and equipment holdings in both 1982 and 1985. In fact, virtually no Soviet supplied equipment in Egyptian forces is combat operational and the true strength of Egyptian forces is less than one-third the totals shown. These figures are deliberately presented as a contrast to the trend curves shown earlier which reflect more substantial adjustments by the author.

## LIBYA AND RADICAL THREATS

The problem of Libya and radical threats is more complex. There is little question that Libya's rhetoric about Israel disguises the fact that it is far more of a threat to moderate Arab regimes than it will ever be to Israel. Libya has sponsored virtually every radical opposition movement in the Gulf area; it has attempted to subvert the Saudi armed forces and sponsored assassination attempts; it has supported Iran, the PDRY, and Ethiopia in hardline or radical actions and in their military build-up. It is supporting extremist left wing Islamic elements in the Sudan, Lebanon, and possibly in Syria.

Libya has sponsored subversive movements in Saudi Arabia and the other Gulf states for years, and has sponsored several assassination attempts against members of the Royal family and efforts to get members of the armed forces or internal security forces to back a coup. Libya probably supported or carried out the mining of the Red Sea in 1984. Libya also supplied approximately 72 Scud B missiles to Iran for use against Iraq.

Over half of Libya's massive inventories of armor and combat aircraft are now in storage and could be used to rapidly supply a hostile Gulf or Red Sea state. This now includes nearly half of the $10 billion worth of arms that Libya has received from the USSR. While Libya is not a Soviet satellite, it does have about 2,000 Soviet military advisors, and 1,200 East European advisors and technicians, in Libya. Libya is, therefore, a powerful catalytic threat to Saudi Arabia and every other moderate Arab state.[29] It lacks serious military forces, but it acts as a constant pressure increasing the risk of political instability and the emergence of hostile radical regimes.

## THE VULNERABILITY OF THE GULF COOPERATION STATES

The problems Saudi Arabia faces in dealing with these threats are compounded by the vulnerability of its conservative neighbors and by the small size of their military forces. These forces have no standardization and poor interoperability. While they are gradually improving, many are still show piece forces which cannot operate effectively except in carefully planned exercises, have few native combat troops, and have whole foreign manned combat units with little loyalty to the nation or regime.

The creation of the Gulf Cooperation Council (GCC) in February, 1981, may eventually help this situation. It already has led to improved internal security initiatives (1982) and improved efforts at defense cooperation (1983). It is still more political than military, and rhetoric is often substituted for serious planning, but the GCC did hold its first military exercises, Peninsular Shield I, in autumn 1983. The Peninsular Shield II exercises were held near Hafr al-Batin in October, 1984, and brought fairly large forces together for the first time (10,000 men, 3,200 armored and other

## Regional Threats and the Military Build-Up in the Gulf

vehicles, mobile artillery and tanks, and air units using F-5 and F-15 fighters and C-130 transports). Meetings in the summer and winter of 1984 strengthened air defense and maritime surveillance cooperation, and the GCC carried out a series of exercises in 1985.

The GCC has also taken some faltering initial steps towards common military planning and tentatively agreed to creating a 10,000 man joint strike or "intervention" force near Shuaib Al Batin. Some progress has occurred in actually organizing this force, although the GCC states have not been able to agree on its precise role and composition. Kuwait has improved its cooperation with the other states in internal security and intelligence since an Iranian assisted assassination attempt on the Emir of Kuwait in May, 1985, but it still refuse to sign the GCC multilateral security agreement because of disagreements on extradition and hot pursuit. Oman has also sought levels of aid for its contribution to the force which are unlikely to be forthcoming. Although progress has been slow in sharing intelligence data within the GCC, some progress has been made in sharing data on subversive and terrorist groups and the situation is now far better than in 1980.[30]

Nevertheless, the smaller GCC states now generally can contribute little more than symbolic military forces, and many would require protection from Saudi Arabia's already overstretched forces or the West in even a low level military contingency. Even the smaller conservative Gulf states can spend a great deal on defense, but no GCC states other than Saudi Arabia and Oman can hope to build a significant deterrent or defense capability, and Oman is acutely limited in the amount of modern heavy weaponry it can buy and operate effectively.

This may be of critical importance to both Western and Saudi interests since a hostile takeover of one of the other GCC states might cripple both Saudi defense efforts and those of USCENTCOM. The geography of the Gulf makes Kuwait a particularly vital buffer to the defense of Saudi Arabia, but this geography simultaneously exposes Kuwait to attacks from Iran and Iraq. Saudi Arabia cannot hope to secure traffic through the Gulf unless air cover can be provided to Bahrain, Qatar, the UAE and Oman, and any hostile regime in these countries could rapidly undermine the whole structure of Saudi Arabia's present defense efforts by bringing air and land forces to some of the most vulnerable areas on Saudi Arabia's borders. Saudi Arabia must base the size of its forces not only to support its smaller neighbors--something it can only do with airpower--but to help resist any outside pressure that might bring a radical regime to power.

Fortunately, most of the smaller Gulf states seem to be relatively secure against immediate threats to their political security of the kind that could overthrow their present regimes, or turn them into hostile radical states. All, however, are potentially vulnerable to outside pressure and threats unless they can count on strong outside assistance. These vulnerabilities that become clearer as each of the other GCC states is examined individually.[31]

Regional Threats and the Military Build-Up in the Gulf

## BAHRAIN

Bahrain has only token military forces and little prospect of building up a real military capability at any time in the future. It now has only 2,800 men in its armed forces, no tanks, no real navy, and acquired its first modern combat aircraft--six F-5Es--in 1986. Saudi Arabia has helped finance the construction of a military air base in Bahrain and the acquisition of Improved Hawk MIM-23B missiles and F-5 fighters. Bahrain will have acquired a total of 12 F-5s, and some Improved Hawk defenses, by the early 1990s, but it will still have to depend on Saudi Arabia for the financing of its armed forces, and for most of its air, naval, and land defense.[32]

Bahrain is also the weakest GCC state in terms of social coherence. Its Royal family has done a poor job of sharing the national budget, demonstrating its concern for the poor, and showing its respect for Islamic custom. Bahrain is also divided on religious grounds. The ruling Khalifa family is Sunni, although Bahrain has a 60% Shi'ite majority, and 37% of its population consists of expatriates from other countries, of which at least 8% is still Iranian.[33]

Bahrain has, however, significantly improved its internal security efforts since a Shi'ite-Iranian coup attempt in December, 1981. It has quietly consulted with both Britain and the United States regarding both internal security assistance and defense against Iran, and discussed contingency plans for Saudi military assistance. It has also improved its treatment of its Shi'ite majority, its controls over foreign labor, and its surveillance of the relatively limited PFLOAG elements in the country.

Unfortunately, the Khalifa family has also reacted to the 1981 coup attempt by increasing its centralization of power, and it does not rule or administer well. The regime is not popular, and the government's favoritism and corruption have produced some hostility. Two new arms caches were discovered in 1984, and as many as 30 people may have been arrested.

Bahrain also faces declining oil resources, and a sharp contraction of its offshore banking operations. This has created an unusual amount of unemployment among the native labor forces, particularly among the younger Shi'ites. Saudi Arabia does, however, seem likely to continue to subsidize Bahrain 250,000 BPD BAPCO refinery by providing 70% of its oil, and Bahrain is developing its own "tourist" industry and shipyards, and diversifying into industries using its still extensive stocks of gas feedstock.

The completion of the 25 Km causeway between Bahrain and Saudi Arabia in December, 1985, should aid Bahrain's "resort area" income as well as ease Saudi ability to reinforce Bahrain in an emergency. Nevertheless, Bahrain seems likely to be under considerable economic strain until there is some recovery of oil prices.

None of the pressures on Bahrain seem immediately threatening, but it is uncertain how long it can go on without an improvement in the leadership from the Khalifa family and some broadening of power. Saudi Arabia is now providing Bahrain with the economic support it needs, but it cannot provide it with political cohesion or leadership.

It is also a sign of the rather shallow concern for security in the GCC, that Bahrain and Qatar revived their absurd rivalry over the Hawar Islands and the coral reef of Fasht-e-Dibal, which divide the two countries. This rivalry is far more a matter of feuding between two royal families than any serious issue over oil wealth, and scarcely was of serious importance at a time when GCC solidarity was of particular importance because of the Iranian victory at Faw. After a minor clash in April, 1986, in which Qatari helicopters fired on construction crews working on Fasht e-Dibal. Both nations called military alerts, and deployed troops. Bahrain reinforced Hawar and Qatar reinforced Fasht e-Dibal. The countercharges included claims that Qatar might seek Iranian aid. While Saudi and GCC attempts at mediation finally succeeded, and a GCC observation team was sent to end the disagreement, the resulting message was scarcely one of Gulf unity and strength.[34]

### KUWAIT

Kuwait has stronger military forces than Bahrain, but is experiencing serious problems in military modernization and has no prospects of creating an independent deterrent or defense capability. Its 12,000 man military forces are largely expatriate, poorly trained, and erratically equipped. Its total army manpower is only about 10,000 men, and is equivalent to about one Western brigade slice. It has no real ability to deploy its strength of 260 main battle tanks (of which 160 are first line Chieftains). Further, most of its support personnel are foreign civilians, and Kuwait lacks the ability to sustain its forces in the field without such civilian support.

Kuwait has no real navy, although its forced involvement in Iran and Iraq's tanker war, which has led to damage to a number of ships going to Kuwait, has led it consider buying modern missile patrol boats, hovercraft, helicopters, and a variety of other naval weapons. At present, its only naval forces are part of the Ministry of the Interior, and include eight Lurssen patrol boats, six of which have Exocet MM-40 missiles, and some light coastal vessels and support craft.

Kuwait's air force is slowly improving in effectiveness, but now has only 76 combat aircraft and 23 helicopters. Its 4 Hawker T-67s are obsolete, and it has only 30 A-4KU/TA-4KU attack fighters in full combat ready service. It is experiencing severe problems in converting to the 34 Mirage F-1CK fighters it is now absorbing, even though it has evidently contracted for Pakistani service and support crews.

Kuwait badly needs Improved Hawk surface-to-air missiles and an air defense C³I system netted with that of Saudi Arabia. U.S. refusal to sell Kuwait Stinger missiles in June, 1984, however, led it to delay any action on such a purchase. Kuwait then responded by buying some $327 million worth of Soviet arms, none of which can be netted into an effective air defense system. While Kuwait is still oriented towards buying arms from the West, it now may not buy an air defense system which is fully compatible with that of Saudi Arabia.

Kuwait has, however, been scared into improving its internal security and protection against terrorists and infiltrators. An assassination attempt on the Emir on May 26, 1985, and a series of sea front bombings on July 11th, which killed 12 and injured 89, dramatized just how serious Kuwait's problems really were. So did the discovery of other bombs targeted against key oil facilities, members of the ruling elite, and the U.S. Embassy. This led to mass deportations--some 400 immediately after the bombings and up to 20,000 by early 1986. It also led to the organization of much stronger anti-terrorism forces and the procurement of a great deal of advanced security equipment. After the Iranian seizure of Faw in early 1986, Kuwait also began to actively procure sensors and weapons to guard against naval infiltration.

It is unclear, however, how well this will really work. Kuwait has long been caught between Iraq and Iran. Syria has backed anti-Iraqi groups operating in Kuwait, probably including those that have been responsible for much of the recent terrorism. Iraq has put pressure on Kuwait for war aid tantamount to blackmail, and has evidently resorted to threats against members of the Royal family. It also has recently revived its request to lease the island of Waribah. Iran has varied from direct and critical attacks on Kuwait's support of Iraq to attempts to calm the situation, but remains an obvious threat.

As for internal stability, Kuwait also faces growing uncertainties. Until recently, it did a good job of reacting to the shifting political currents and demands of its native Kuwaiti population, and controlling foreign labor. It maintained a relatively free press and lively public assembly until mid-1986, when the ruling emir, Sheik Jaber al-Ahmed Al Sabah, dissolved the 50 member National Assembly and clamped down on the press.

The Emir took this action because the election of a more radical parliament in October, 1985. This rapidly led to repeated speeches and articles attacking Iran and Syria, attacks on Government Ministers for being insufficiently Islamic, and criticism of the Royal family for failing to do enough to preserve Kuwait's security and for suppressing its involvement in Kuwait's long standing stock market scandal. What remains to be seen is whether Kuwait will be more stable without these relief valves.[35]

Kuwait does, however, a good job of distributing its oil wealth to Kuwaiti nationals, and the Al Sabah regime's conservation policies, conspicuous "non-alignment" between East and West, use of technocrats, and investment in a Fund for the Future have all helped to stabilize the political situation.

The main threat to Kuwaiti security is likely to be the fact that 70% of Kuwait's labor force, and 61% of the population is still foreign. Kuwait also has a high birth rate (6.2%), and its young population is becoming politicized more rapidly than the Al-Sabah family can coopt it or liberalize the government. The Al-Sabah family has lost popularity since the Suq al-Manakh collapse in 1982. It is coming under increasing attack both for failing to listen to the nation's younger technocrats and for being insufficiently Islamic. It did not prove as able to influence the outcome of the 1985 National Assembly elections as in the past, and it is experiencing growing problems with Sunni fundamentalists and the impact of declining trade and economic growth.

Kuwait also has a 20-30% Shi'ite population, if expatriate Iranians are included (4-6% of total), and it has not been able to develop consistent policies for dealing with either the Shi'ites or Palestinian expatriates which would enhance its internal stability. It has already suffered from at least 12 Shi'ite backed bombing incidents since December 1983, one major hijacking, and one assassination attempt against its ruler. It is unclear whether Kuwait can easily handle the unrest from its Shi'ites or the large number of illegal immigrants from Iran. It has already had to imprison over 60 extremists, and deport at least 253 more for "political opinions". Coupled to external pressure from Iran and/or Iraq, this creates at least some long term risk of political instability.

### OMAN

Oman has good military forces. It has about 21,500 regulars and 16,500 highly trained regulars in its Army. Omani soldiers and officers are respected throughout the Gulf and often form an important portion of the total military manpower of other GCC states, especially those of the UAE. These forces, however, are not highly sophisticated, and the Omani army consists largely of light mechanized infantry. Oman now has a token force of about 33 main battle tanks (27 Chieftains and 6 M-60A1) with more Chieftains on order. It has only about 120 armored vehicles in inventory, including the previous tanks.

Oman's air force has 52 combat aircraft, but its 15 Hunters and 12 BAC-167 Strikemasters are obsolete. Only its 20 Jaguars are modern combat aircraft, and they have limited air defense capability. Oman is also heavily dependent on British support, although it is training about 14 pilots a year and roughly 20% of its support personnel are now Omani. Oman has sought up to two squadrons of F-16 or Tornado fighters, an improved air defense system, and U.S. aid in mechanizing its army. It so far, however, has lacked the funds for such major procurement efforts in spite of the fact

Britain has offered preferential terms for a Tornado sale. It has, however, ordered eight Tornados on order as part of a $340 million arms package, and is expanding Thumrait air base into a fully modern facility.[36]

The Omani Navy is still a small 2,000 man force. Its major vessels are four patrol ships equipped with Exocet. It also has a converted royal yacht, four small coastal patrol ships, two logistic ships, five landing craft, and a training ship. This Navy has performed relatively well, but is far too small to help secure the Straits of Hormuz without extensive British and U.S. aid, and lacks the air and maritime reconnaissance support to operate effectively in the Indian Ocean.

Oman did, however, conduct impressive public military exercises in 1985. Its March, 1985, exercise was called Codename Thunder and involved roughly 10,000 men. It was the largest and most effective exercise that any GCC state has conducted, and Oman regularly plays an important role in GCC exercises.[37]

Its main military strengths are a good cadre of Omani personnel and excellent British advisors. It appointed an Omani officer to the post of Commander of the Army for the first time in 1984.[38] It is spending almost $2 billion annually (or 40% of its total budget) on defense, and the other GCC states pledged to provide $1.8 billion in aid over 12 years in September, 1983.[39] Nevertheless, Oman will be hard pressed to create even a minimal deterrent to the threat from Iran by the early 1990s and could have problems if it was attacked by South Yemen.

Fortunately, Oman has extensive U.S. contingency facilities and a strong presence of British advisors, officers, NCOs, and technicians. Both British and U.S. ships routinely support Oman in patrolling the approaches to the Straits of Hormuz, and the U.S. can rapidly supplement Omani forces with over-the-horizon reinforcements. The modernization of Omani forces should allow them to deal with low level contingencies and create some deterrent capability against medium level conflicts even without U.S. reinforcements.

Oman is one of the best managed states in the Near East and Southwest Asia. While its population is becoming increasingly politicized and less tolerant of Britain's role in Oman's government, the Sultan has coopted a large number of former rebels, modernized his government, and increased the rate of Omanization. Oman's second five year plan has been relatively successful, and the country has succeeded in increasing oil sales in spite of the decline in the world market. This has helped to offset the serious decline in its oil revenues, which have provided nearly 90% of government revenues.

While Oman will experience economic problems until the oil market recovers, it seems capable of sustaining its most critical development efforts without any political backlash. Oman's proven oil reserves have expanded from 2.5 billion barrels in 1983 to 4 billion barrels in 1985, and its agriculture, light industry, and infrastructure are capable of sustaining slow and steady growth in spite of sharply diminished funds for its new Third Five Year Plan. About 25% of Oman's population is expatriate, mostly Pakistani and Indian, but it is not politically active. Only the succession issue seems to present an immediate risk, and Sultan Qabus is young enough so that this is largely a risk of assassination.

As for foreign relations, Oman has increasingly tried to defuse some of the political costs of its ties to the U.K. and U.S. Oman established diplomatic relations with the USSR in 1986, and has made a point of trying to maintain good low level relations with Iraq without causing a confrontation with Iran. It has been involved in minor border squabbles with Sharjah, but its only serious problem remains the PDRY. In spite of the establishment of diplomatic relations with South Yemen, ambassadors were never exchanged because the PDRY refused to settle several border disputes, and the new regime in Aden may present Oman with serious problems.

## QATAR

Qatar lacks the native manpower to field significant military forces, although an increasing number of young Qataris are joining the armed forces and a steadily rising number of component young native officers is being trained. Qatar now has only 6,000-7,000 men in its armed forces, and its 24 AMX-30 main battle tanks and 17 combat aircraft (3 Hunter FGA-78/T-79, 1 T-79, 8 Alphajet, and 5 Mirage F-1C/B) are more symbolic than signs of serious combat capability. The bulk of its combat forces, and virtually all of its technical and maintenance personnel are still expatriate.

Qatar does have 6 more Mirage F-1E/B aircraft and Improved Hawk missiles on order, however, and is negotiating for a new major arms sale in reaction to the escalation of the Iran-Iraq War and the resulting tanker war in the Gulf. It is trying to expand its small 700 man Sea Arm into a real navy, and already has three French guided missile patrol boats with Exocet. Still it hopes to find the funds to finance a French constructed modern air base at Doha. Qatar is also negotiating to buy a squadron of modern fighters like the F-16 or Mirage 2000, but funding is now very uncertain. Qatar will have to rely on Saudi Arabia for most of its air and naval defense through the year 2000.

Qatar has improved the sharing of its oil wealth in recent years, and its society is gradually becoming politicized without becoming radicalized. The Al-Thani family has done a relatively good job of maintaining living standards and private sector opportunities in spite of declining oil revenues, and its recent cuts in government budgets and development activity have so far been healthy. While there were rumors of a Libyan and Iranian Shi'ite backed coup attempt in September, 1983, these have never been confirmed. What seems to be more serious are constant rumors of feuding within the ruling Al-Thani family, some of which surfaced again during Qatar's absurd 1986 border confrontation with Bahrain.

Qatar's main internal security problem, however, is the fact that 90% of its labor force is expatriate, and 46% of its total population is expatriate non-Arab--including 10% Iranian. This allows Qatar to absorb much of the shock of declining oil income simply by reducing foreign labor, but Qatar has experienced steadily growing problems and tensions with this portion of its work force and has had to greatly strengthen its security controls--particularly of Iranians and Shi'ites. The large expatriate population is likely to present problems during the next decade, but does not seem likely to threaten Saudi security.

## THE UNITED ARAB EMIRATES

The United Arab Emirates is a somewhat different problem. It remains deeply divided, and most of its 43,000 man military forces are expatriate and under the de facto command of individual Sheiks. Like Qatar and Kuwait, its 40,000 man army cannot really operate its 136 main battle tanks (100 AMX-30 and 36 OF-40 Lion), other armor, and artillery effectively in combat. Its army is divided into separate forces for each of the major sheikdoms, is poorly organized, and equipped with far too many diverse equipment types for effective combined arms operations.

The UAE now has 42 combat aircraft and seven armed helicopters, but its Hunter FGA-76/T-77s are obsolete and it is experiencing severe problems in operating its 30 Mirage 5ADs, 3 Alphajets, and 10 MB-236KD/LD counter-insurgency aircraft effectively, in spite of the fact that virtually all maintenance and support is performed by Jordanians, Moroccans, and Pakistanis. These problems in supporting advanced aircraft should increase sharply as it takes delivery of the 36-40 Mirage 2000s, 24 Hawk fighters, 3 Alphajets, and 34 combat helicopters it has on order, although Abu Dhabi is creating major modern air base at Suwaihan. The UAE has 42 Improved Hawk units (342 missiles) and Skyguard twin 35mm anti-aircraft guns on order, but will take at least three years to deploy these SAMs as fully effective forces.

The UAE's small 1,500 man navy is also divided by sheikdom. Its only major combat ships are 6 guided missile patrol boats with Exocet and nine coastal patrol boats. The force is almost totally dependent on foreign personnel and advisors. There are plans, however, to create a one billion dollar naval base at Tawila if funds become available.

The UAE's military efforts remain something of a farce and are likely to continue at the "glitter factor" level of military procurement and competence for the next decade. The UAE will be dependent on Saudi Arabia and/or U.S. rapid reinforcement forces, for its air and maritime defense in the face of any serious threat from Iran through the year 2000.

In regard to internal stability, the individual Sheiks that lead the UAE continue to struggle for power. Only Abu Dhabi's forces participate in GCC exercises. Dubai has resisted Abu Dhabi's support of Iraq, and pushed for relations with the USSR. The UAE's one strong leader--Sheik Zayid bin Sultan al Nuhayyan of Abu Dhabi--has no strong successor. The sons of his principal rival, Sheik Rashid of Dubai, are divided about the merits of increasing federalism within the UAE.

This rivalry between Abu Dhabi and Dubai reached the point in 1985 where Dubai created its own air line as a rival to Gulf air, and tensions with Sharjah and the smaller Emirates are growing as the decline in oil income forces more budget and project cutbacks. In a more serious arena, the sheiks have split over the UAE's attitudes towards the Iran-Iraq War with Abu Dhabi favoring Iraq and Dubai and Sharjah favoring their traditional trading partner, Iran.

There is no inherent reason that any of these political and economic problems should destabilize a nation with such wealth and strong strategic incentives to remain unified. Nevertheless, the overall level of economic management remains by far the worst in the Gulf and only Abu Dhabi and Dubai have done a reasonable job of sharing the nation's oil wealth. The UAE also has a problem with foreign labor. Only 19% of the UAE's population is now Emirian, and only 42% is Arab. Over 80% of the labor force is expatriate, and there is a significant Shi'ite minority. Abu Dhabi, Dubai, Sharjah, and the other states still do not coordinate adequately on internal security, much less on military affairs.

The visible divisions among the Sheiks have greatly weakened the UAE's efforts at economic development. This has led to a growing disenchantment among its technocrats, and to the politicization of the UAE's youth. The resulting resentments and tension now lack a clear political focus, but could become much more serious if the Sheiks should quarrel to the point where they return to the paralytic divisions of the 1970s, or fail to deal with the cut in oil revenues by spreading more widely their oil and gas income.

## THE IMPACT OF CUMULATIVE INSTABILITY WITHIN THE GCC

The GCC states are not particularly unstable by Third World standards, but there are serious pressures within them. They all face a long and uncertain period of transition from family rule to some form of more modern state with broader public participation. They all must deal with serious problems in terms of religious tensions, problems in modernization, and problems in dealing with a young and politically awakening population.

No one can predict which of these pressures within the GCC states will become most dangerous to Saudi Arabia and Western interests in the region. The problem that both Saudi Arabia and the West face is that there is at least a moderate *cumulative* probability that one of the more vulnerable conservative Gulf states will become radicalized over the next decade.

Saudi Arabia and the West will then be forced to act. The risk of such a shift is simply too great. If they fail, the geography of the Gulf would ensure that Saudi Arabia and remaining conservative GCC states would face a radically different land, air, and naval threat.

Any shift in Kuwait's position would remove the buffer between the Kingdom and Iraq and possibly Iran. A radical Bahrain could place hostile aircraft within less than five minutes flying time of key Saudi oil, power, and water facilities. The same would be true of Qatar. If any element of the UAE became hostile, Saudi Arabia's air force and navy would experience major problems in trying to operate in the Eastern Gulf, and any combination of such an element of the UAE with a hostile Iran would further undermine Saudi Arabia's political and military security structure. A hostile Oman would threaten all naval and shipping traffic through the Gulf, make a British military role in the Gulf far more difficult, and force a massive restructuring of USCENTCOM to deploy without the stocks and bases in that country.

## THE 360° THREAT

There is no easy way to summarize all these pressures on the Kingdom, and potential threats to the West's strategic interests in the Gulf. The problem is never one of a single threat from a single direction, or of a threat that can easily be defined in military and political terms. While the Northern Gulf states and the USSR obviously have the most forces, other states border directly on Saudi Arabia and can pose an equally great, if not greater, political threat.

The key point is, in fact, that the Kingdom faces a "360° Threat". Military forces cannot be shaped quickly. New combat units take a decade to mature, and new major military bases take up to five years to build. Governments and political attitudes can change overnight. Many of the surrounding governments are already hostile, and most of the remainder are at least partially unstable. The steady flood of arms into surrounding states is expanding the potential military threat on every border.

With luck, diplomacy and politics can contain this situation without conflict, but the chances of such luck continuing for the next decade, if Saudi Arabia does not build-up its own forces and have convincing strategic ties to the West, seem slim indeed. Luck is also scarcely a wise basis for securing access to half of the world's proven oil reserves.

---

[1] For an excellent analysis of the Red Sea mining incidents in 1984, see Dr. Scott C. Truver, "Mines of August: An International Whodunit", Proceedings of the U.S. Naval Institute, May 1985, Volume III/5/987, pp. 94-118.

[2] All of the following arms transfer data are based on the data base developed by the CIA, and reported by ACDA. The primary written sources are ACDA, World Military Expenditures and Arms Transfers, 1985, Washington, GPO, 1985, and Richard F. Grimmett, Trends in Conventional Arms Transfers to the Third World By Major Supplier, 1978-1985, Washington, CRS Report 86-99F, May 9, 1986. While the individual data

from SIPRI are sometimes useful, the data base is so uncertain and varying in quality as to be useless for reporting on regional trends.

[3] See Jim Bussert, "Can The USSR Build and Support High Technology Fighters?", Defense Electronics, April, 1985, pp. 121-130: Bill Sweetman, "New Soviet Combat Aircraft", International Defense Review, 1/1984, pp. 35-38; Bill Gunston, Modern Soviet Air Force, ARCO, New York, 1982, PP. 84-88 and 112-116; Martin Streetly, "Su-24 Fencer C; Major Equipment Change", Jane's Defense Weekly, June 22, 1985, pp. 1226-1227; James B. Schultz "New Strategies and Soviet Threats Spark EW Responses", Defense Electronics, February, 1985, pp. 17-21; Daniel P. Schrage, "Air Warfare: Helicopters and the Battlefield, Journal of Defense and Diplomacy, Vol. 3, No. 5, pp. 17-20; "Helicopter Special", Defense Update, Number 60, March 1985.

[4] Soviet MiG-29s have already been delivered to India, and may soon be delivered to Syria as part of a July, 1986, arms agreement that would provide such advanced technologies as the MiG-29, SA-8, SA-11, SA-13, SA-14, and SS-23. Washington Times, July 21, 1986, p. 3A, and Jane's Defense Weekly, July 26, 1986, p. 92.

[5] "Soviet Air Force in Afghanistan", Jane's Defense Weekly, July 7, 1984, pp. 1104-1105, and G. Jacobs. "Afghanistan Forces: How Many Soviets Are There?", Jane's Defense Weekly, 22 June, 1985, pp. 1228-1233; Department of Defense, Soviet Military Power, 1986, pp. 136-138.

[6] DoD, Soviet Military Power, 1985, pp. 83-84

[7] Ibid, pp. 126-125; IISS, Military Balance, 1985-1986, p. 30.

[8] DoD, Soviet Military Power, 1986, pp. 132 and 135-136.

[9] Chicago Tribune, July 3, 1986, p. 3-9, and July 20, 1986, p. 7-1; Economist, July 5, 1986, pp. 62-63;

[10] For a good summary of recent trends see Gary Lee, "Soviet Oil Output Shows a Decline", Washington Post, April 3, 1985. The broad trends in Soviet oil production are well summarized in William L. Randol's "Petroleum Monitor", First Boston Corporation, Vol. 4, No. 4, April, 1985. Also see Mikhail S. Bernstam, Soviet Oil Woes", Wall Street Journal, January 10, 1986, Ernest Conine, "Soviets Sit on Oil's Power Keg", Los Angeles Times, February 17, 1986, and "Mother Russia's $9 Billion Headache" Economist, July 5, 1986, pp. 62-63.

[11] Richard F. Grimmett, Trends in Conventional Arms Transfers To The Third World By Major Supplier, 1978-1985, U.S. Congressional Research Service, Report 86-99F, May 9, 1986, pp. CRS 26-27, and 44.

[12] See the IISS, Military Balance, 1980-81 and 1984-85 for details.

[13] See Mark Heller, Dov Tamari, and Zeev Eytan, The Middle East Military Balance, Jaffe Center for Strategic Studies, Tel Aviv University, 1985, and the IISS, Military Balance, 1985-1986, for details on Iraq's current force strength.

14 For an excellent analysis of the current threat to Gulf tankers, see Dr. Raphael Danziger, "The Persian Gulf Tanker War", Proceedings of the Naval Institute, May, 1985, 160-176

15 Economist Intelligence Unit, EIU Regional Review: The Middle East and North Africa, 1985, Economist Publications, New York, 1985, pp. 267-271. Ibid, 1986 edition, pp. 277-284.

16 Ibid

17 These force strength estimates, and those that follow throughout the rest of this chapter, are taken from Mark Heller, Dov Tamari, and Zeev Eytan, The Middle East Military Balance, Jaffe Center for Strategic Studies, Tel Aviv University, 1985, and the IISS, Military Balance, 1985-1986.

18 Department of Defense, Soviet Military Power, 1985, GPO, Washington, 1985, pp. 123 and 128; and Soviet Military Power, 1986, GPO, Washington, 1986, pp. 135-136.

19 Economist Intelligence Unit, EIU Regional Review: The Middle East and North Africa, 1986, Economist Publications, New York, 1986, p. 268.

20 Ibid, pp. , p. 267-275.

21 EIU, Regional Review: The Middle East and North Africa, 1985, pp. 257-265

22 Heller, Middle East Military Balance, pp. 226-230.

23 Department of Defense, Soviet Military Power, 1985, pp. 123-129; and Soviet Military Power, 1986, GPO, Washington, 1986, p. 136.

24 Soviet Military Power, 1986, GPO, Washington, 1986, p. 132.

25 IISS, Military Balance, 1985-86; Air Force Magazine, March 1985, p. 108.

26 Department of Defense, Soviet Military Power, 1985, pp. 123-129; and Soviet Military Power, 1986, GPO, Washington, 1986.

27 For good recent discussions of Soviet and Ethiopian strategy in the Horn see Lt. Colonel David R. Mets, "The Dilemmas of the Horn", Proceedings of the Naval Institute, April, 1985, pp. 49-57; and Samuel Makinda, "Shifting Alliances in the Horn of Africa", Survival, January/February, 1985, pp. 11-19.

28 Syria signed a preliminary July, 1986, arms agreement that would provide such advanced technologies as the MiG-29, SA-8, SA-11, SA-13, SA-14, and SS-23. Washington Times, July 21, 1986, p. 3A, and Jane's Defense Weekly, July 26, 1986, p. 92.

29 Department of Defense, Soviet Military Power, 1986, GPO, Washington, 1986, p. 134.

30 Economist Intelligence Unit, EIU Regional Review: The Middle East and North Africa, 1986, Economist Publications, New York, 1986, p. 16.

31 The military data used in this section are based on the IISS Military Balance, 1985-1986, Heller, The Middle East Military Balance, and the DMS data base on foreign military markets, Middle East and Africa. The data on ethnic and religious divisions are taken from Heller; the CIA, World Factbook, 1985; and Middle East Review, 1985 and 1986, World of Information, Saffron Walden, England, 1985. For additional background see the author's The Gulf and the Search for Strategic Stability, and Thomas L. McNaugher's "Arms and Allies on the Arabian Peninsula", Orbis, Volume 28, No. 3, Fall, 1984, pp. 486-526.

32 Saudi Arabia promised up to $700 million in military aid during GCC planning meetings in early 1984. It is unclear how much of this aid will be available in the near term, given the growing cash squeeze in Saudi Arabia.

33 All demographic statistics used for Bahrain and the rest of the GCC states are based on CIA estimates in the relevant country sections of The World Factbook, 1985, Washington, GPO, 1985.

34 Jane's Defense Weekly, 14 June, 1986, p. 1087, and Defense and Foreign Affairs Weekly, May 26, 1986, p. 4.

35 Wall Street Journal, July 7, 1986, p. 16. The 1982 collapse of Kuwait's highly speculative "camel market" left six of Kuwait's banks with $4.1 to $4.4 billion in bad loans.

36 Economist Intelligence Unit, EIU Regional Review: The Middle East and North Africa, 1986, Economist Publications, New York, 1986, p. 193.

37 Richard Green, Editor, Middle East Review, 1986, London, Middle East Review Company, 1986, pp. 168-167.

38 The new army commander, Major General Naseeb Bin Haman Bin Sultan Ruwaihi, is almost certainly qualified for the post. It is important to note, however, that he was appointed at the end of 1984 when General Sir Timothy Creasy was replaced as Chief of Defense Staff by Lt. General John Watts. There are rumors this replacement occurred partly because of his insistence on an exemplary jail sentence for Robin Walsh, a British MOD official accused of misappropriating $8,700 in MOD funds. Walsh died in an Omani jail in October, 1984. This was followed by broader accusations that up to $74 million annually was being wrongly appropriated by the Ministry of Defense, and that both British and Omani officials knew of the problem. EIU Regional Review, pp. 186-187.

39 Oman has refused to support the creation of a Gulf Defense Force at al-Batin. This is partly because it is under Saudi command, and partly because the force is primarily oriented towards the defense of Kuwait, and Kuwait has pressed for freer movement of Gulf labor than Oman prefers and refuses to sign intelligence agreements that would provide more data on the movement of politically sensitive individuals. This reflects a high level of vestigial rivalries and issues between the GCC countries. For example, Abu Dhabi and Dubai refused to fully cooperate during the initial Peninsular Shield exercises.

# V. THE DEVELOPMENT OF SAUDI FORCES

Saudi Arabia's military development clearly reflects the country's understanding of two key facts. The first is the scale and complexity of the threats described in Chapter IV. The second is the fact that it is dependent on Western military equipment, technology, and military advice. These facts help explain the central thrusts behind Saudi military modernization, behind its search for close strategic relations with the U.S., and behind its emphasis on the strength of its Air Force and the modernization of its air capabilities.

## SAUDI DEFENSE EXPENDITURES

Saudi Arabia's small manpower and technical base ensures that it cannot build up large ground forces to match those of its neighbors. It is forced to rely on technology as a substitute for manpower, and on Western support for its combat forces while it creates its own technicians and support manpower. This reliance on technology, however, has forced it to make extremely high levels of defense expenditure in a "brute force" effort to create the capability to support high technology forces. It has also forced it to give priority to its air force as a substitute for the slow pace of modernization in its Army, National Guard, and Navy. This is a driving factor behind the current Saudi requests for aircraft and munitions.

Few developing countries have spent as much on defense as Saudi Arabia, but few countries have had to begin with so limited a military and technical infrastructure, and faced so many challenges. Saudi Arabia's defense expenditures have had to respond to a massive regional arms build-up, and to rapidly expanding threats on all its borders. Saudi Arabia has had to buy advanced technology, and pay the extraordinarily high cost of creating high technology forces without a base of trained manpower and modern military infrastructure.

Since the late 1960s, this effort has been driven by the impact of Britain's withdrawal from the Gulf, the massive arms race between Iran and Iraq, and the arms race and fighting between the Red Sea states. Saudi Arabia had to begin this effort with only token military forces, and has had to conduct a "brute force" effort to use money to make up for constraints in manpower, facilities, and time.

## The Development of Saudi Forces

This "brute force" effort has concentrated on support and infrastructure, rather than combat forces. It has been shaped and driven by various U.S. plans and studies over a period of nearly two decades, and it has been relatively successful. Saudi Arabia has slowly built up division and brigade sized military cities to guard its borders. It has built up some of the most modern air bases in the world, created several new military ports, and established extensive training, logistics, and headquarters facilities. There is no easy way to cost this, but the bulk of the Saudi modernization effort has been planned and supervised by the U.S. Army Corps of Engineers, and much of it is reflected in the U.S. FMS budget. Tables 5.1 and 5.2 provide a picture of the overall trends in foreign military sales to Saudi Arabia, and how they relate to Saudi defense spending.

Table 5.1: Saudi Military Imports and Spending
(Millions of Constant 1982 U.S. Dollars)

| Year | Total Defense Spending | Defense Spending As a Percent of GNP | National | Total Arms Imports | Arms as A Percent of Total Imports |
|---|---|---|---|---|---|
| 1973 | 2,287 | 13.2 | 17.5 | 156 | 4 |
| 1974 | 4,729 | 10.9 | 34.7 | 613 | 11.8 |
| 1975 | 10,587 | 17.4 | 34.1 | 413 | 5.9 |
| 1976 | 14,483 | 19.1 | 35.5 | 688 | 5.0 |
| 1977 | 13,797 | 15.3 | 25.3 | 1,293 | 5.9 |
| 1978 | 14,523 | 15.9 | 29.0 | 1,789 | 6.3 |
| 1979 | 17,230 | 18.1 | 27.3 | 1,522 | 4.9 |
| 1980 | 19,140 | 14.4 | 26.7 | 2,096 | 5.9 |
| 1981 | 21,501 | 12.9 | 28.1 | 3,089 | 8.2 |
| 1982 | 24,159 | 15.7 | 27.7 | 3,100 | 7.6 |
| 1983 | 26,088 | 24.3 | 29.6 | 3,166 | 8.4 |

Source: Arms Control and Disarmament Agency, World Military Expenditures and Arms Transfers, 1985, Washington, GPO, 1986, pp. 79, 121, and 134.

The Development of Saudi Forces

Table 5.2: Recent Sources of Saudi Arms Imports 1979-1983

| Source | Total Value ($ Current Millions) | Percent of Total |
|---|---|---|
| **Major Western Countries** | | |
| France | 2,500 | 20.6 |
| FRG | 525 | 4.3 |
| Italy | 200 | 1.6 |
| U.K. | 1,900 | 15.7 |
| U.S. [a] | 5,100 | 42.1 |
| **Major Communist** | | |
| Czechoslovakia | 0 | 0 |
| Poland | 0 | 0 |
| PRC | 0 | 0 |
| Romania | 0 | 0 |
| USSR | 0 | 0 |
| All Other | 1,900 | 15.7 |
| Total | 12,125 | 100 |

a. Includes some U.S. Corps of Engineers construction equipment
Source: Arms Control and Disarmament Agency, World Military Expenditures and Arms Transfers, 1985, Washington, GPO, 1986, pp. 79, 121, and 134.

The trends in Tables 5.1 and 5.2 are complex, but a close examination reveals a consistent pattern: Saudi Arabia has bought remarkably few major arms in comparison with its total defense expenditures. It has spent its money on construction, operations and maintenance, and personnel.

This point becomes clearer in Table 5.3, which compares the patterns in U.S. FMS sales to Saudi Arabia from 1950 to 1984. It shows that the U.S. has sold Saudi Arabia nearly $20 billion worth of construction agreements, and delivered about $13 billion worth. This compares with about $28 billion in other FMS agreements, of which about $15 billion have been delivered.

Table 5.3 also shows just how important the U.S.-Saudi connection has been to the Kingdom's military development. U.S. sales of military construction services have approached the level of all other military sales, and they exceeded all Saudi arms imports well into the late 1970s. The construction totals in Table 5.3 also show that the West has done more than provide Saudi Arabia with arms and military advice: U.S. modernization plans and the construction activities of the U.S. Army Corps of Engineers have dominated development of Saudi military bases, facilities, and lines of communication.

## The Development of Saudi Forces

Even so, Table 5.3 understates the role the U.S. has played in shaping Saudi Arabia's military modernization since the mid-1970s. Many major Saudi military projects which have not been funded through FMS have been the result of U.S. plans or studies, and have been designed and/or supervised by the U.S. Army Corps of Engineers. The U.S. has been the principal architect behind most of Saudi Arabia's transition from a low level infantry force to a relatively modern military force which has gradually built up one of the most sophisticated basing and military infrastructure systems in the developing world.

Fortunately for the security of the Gulf, this "brute force" period in Saudi military development is now reaching its end. While nearly $10 billion worth of U.S. military construction services are still in the pipeline, many are now associated with the completion of the high technology aspects of Saudi Arabia's force structure like its air base sheltering program. Its key military "cities", ports, air bases, training and support facilities, and headquarters are nearing completion.

The Development of Saudi Forces

Table 5.3: Saudi Arabia's Main Source of Western Military Support: U.S. Military Assistance and Foreign Military Sales
($ Current Millions By U.S. Fiscal Year) [a]

| Year | Foreign Military Sales | | Military Construction | | Commercial |
| --- | --- | --- | --- | --- | --- |
| | Agreements | Deliveries | Agreements | Deliveries | Exports |
| 1950-1975 | 3,683.1 | 705.7 | 6,901.6 | 663.8 | 68.3 |
| 1976 | 1,826.6 | 461.4 | 5,451.5 | 465.5 | 92.7 |
| 1977 | 1,122.8 | 1,066.1 | 589.9 | 483.9 | 44.1 |
| 1978 | 1,312.2 | 1,129.2 | 647.0 | 1,193.3 | 166.3 |
| 1979 | 5,449.6 | 940.5 | 1,021.0 | 1,193.3 | 166.3 |
| 1980 | 2,954.2 | 1,124.2 | 1,590.8 | 1,457.9 | 29.0 |
| 1981 | 1,042.6 | 1,435.8 | 877.4 | 1,491.6 | 71.5 |
| 1982 | 5,347.3 | 2,072.8 | 1,888.2 | 1,775.6 | 50.0 |
| 1983 | 891.4 | 3,860.9 | 716.5 | 2,153.2 | 251.8 |
| 1984 | 2,840.3 | 1,950.0 | 263.0 | 1,470.8 | 359.5 |
| 1985 | 2,791.4 | 1,904.2 | 743.0 | 901.0 | 186.5 |
| 1950-1985 | 29,261.4 | 16,650.8 | 20,698.8 | 13,556.8 | 1,364.1 |

a. Unlike most states receiving U.S. foreign military sales, Saudi Arabia has paid for virtually all of its purchases from the U.S. It has never received MAP merger funds, and has not received any Military Assistance Program funds since 1976. Its total MAP funds from 1950 to 1975 totalled only $239 million. Saudi Arabia also received $1.8 million in excess defense articles during 1950-1975, and $12.5 million in International Military Education and Training (IMET) during 1950-1975. It received $234 million in financing before 1976, all of which it repaid.
Source: Department of Defense, Foreign Military Sales, Foreign Military Construction Sales, and Military Assistance Facts, Washington, D.C., DoD, September 30, 1985.

This completion of Saudi Arabia's basic military infrastructure will ease both the burden of Saudi defense expenditures and the Saudi transition to dependence on British, French, and other non-U.S. military equipment. Saudi defense expenditures must drop because of the major decline in oil revenues. At the same time, the completion of Saudi Arabia's military facilities should allow it to proceed with the key elements of its military modernization in spite of this decline.

Saudi Arabia has cut its total FY 1986 national budget by 6.1% relative to its FY 1985 budget. It plans to cut total FY 1986 expenditures to about $55.4 billion, and this will ease the Saudi deficit--although it may still experience a deficit of over $10 billion. The Kingdom already had to cut actual FY 1985 spending levels 18% below a planned level of $59 billion because revenue totaled only $46.3 billion, and was 22% short of the

## The Development of Saudi Forces

original FY 1985 budget projections. Saudi oil revenue is currently falling even further below the FY 1986 projections used in formulating the budget.

The FY 1986 Saudi defense budget is planned to be $17.7 billion (64.6 billion Riyals), or 32% of the total budget, although the oil revenue deficit may lead to some cuts. The $17.7 billion figure is 20% less than the defense budget in FY 1985, although the FY 1985 budget was a 5% increase over the previous year. This planned FY 1986 defense budget compares with a peak of almost $23 billion on defense in 1984-85, a year in which a combination of aid to Iraq and Syria also drove foreign aid expenditures up to $10.5 billion.[1]

At the same time, it is clear that FY 1986 defense expenditures of $17.7 billion still represent a high level of defense spending for a nation with Saudi Arabia's military forces, and it seems unlikely that Saudi defense spending will ever drop below $15 billion in CY 1985 dollars unless there is a massive further cut in Saudi oil revenues. It also seems likely that Saudi Arabia will continue high levels of indirect defense spending in the form of foreign aid. The mix of threats it faces seem likely to force it to continue its high level of defense effort regardless of the present decline in its oil revenues.

Even if Saudi defense budgets should drop below $15 billion, the Kingdom probably can sustain reduced levels for several years without harming its basic defense program because it has largely completed a $30 billion dollar investment in military facilities and infrastructure, and retains a relatively modern major weapons mix. Expensive as first line combat equipment now is, Saudi Arabia can buy its essential needs with a budget far lower than its peak past budgets ($22 billion in 1983/84, and $22.7 billion in 1984/85). The Kingdom can also draw on its extensive capital holdings or easily manipulate its delivery schedule on major weapons and projects so that the key cost component comes after 1988, when most energy experts predict oil prices will begin at least a limited recovery.

Nevertheless, defense will impose a strain on the Kingdom's resources in a period when its oil production has dipped to levels as low as 2 MMBD, or half what the OPEC used for planning its national budget, and other prices have dropped to the point where even major increases in Saudi production will now produce far more limited increases in revenue.[2]

Saudi Arabia has slowed down many of its payments for defense purchases and is seeking barter deals and a high level of offsets. This could gravely reduce the U.S. market share of defense sales to Saudi Arabia if the U.S. does not provide it with the equipment it is currently seeking. Revenue problems are also pushing Saudi Arabia to accept lowest bids on military maintenance--something that has already hurt its ground based air defenses-- and, again, a failure to meet Saudi arms needs could lead to more third country maintenance contracts. Given past precedents, this would reduce the capability of Saudi bases and facilities to accept USCENTCOM forces.

The Development of Saudi Forces

SAUDI MILITARY MANPOWER

The key military problem Saudi Arabia faces in meeting the threats outlined in Chapter IV is not money, but manpower. While Saudi Arabia often exaggerates its population and military manpower for political purposes, it seems fairly clear that Saudi Arabia now has a total native population of only 7-9 million and only about 82,000 men in its armed forces--27,000 of which are in its paramilitary Royal Guards and National Guard. This compares with an Iranian population of over 40 million and over one million men under arms, with an Iraqi population of over 14 million and over one million men under arms, with a Syrian population of over 9 million with more than 800,000 under arms, and with a total population in the Yemens of about 8 million with 77,000 under arms.[3]

Saudi Arabia's regular military forces now comprise about 52,000 men. By any comparative standard, it would take about 75,000-100,000 men to adequately man the Kingdom's current force structure. Even a full scale draft would probably fail to give the manpower to meet its limited force expansion plans. Saudi Arabia solves this problem by:

o A heavy dependence on foreign support and technicians (now over 10,000 personnel);

o Using small elements of Pakistani and possibly Turkish forces in key speciality and technical areas--such as combat engineers-- to "fill in" the gaps in Saudi land forces, and Pakistani forces to fill out one brigade (the 12 Armored Brigade) at Tabuk;

o Use of French and British internal security experts.

o Selective undermanning while it builds its training and manpower base;

o Concentrating on building a fully effective air force as a first line deterrent and defense; and,

o A *de facto* reliance on over the horizon reinforcement by the U.S., France, Pakistan, or some other power to deal with high level or enduring conflicts.

These are all intelligent methods of reducing the manpower problem, but they still leave many gaps and weaknesses in Saudi forces. The limitations in Saudi military manpower are also forced on Saudi planners by Saudi demographics, by civil competition for skilled manpower--which still makes it extremely hard to retain army personnel in spite of the contraction of the Saudi economy--and by the need to maintain a 25,000 man National Guard for internal political and security reasons.

None of these manpower constraints will change significantly during the next decade, and Saudi Arabia can only hope to reach and maintain a technical edge over regional threats by concentrating on the modernization and Saudisation of its combat arms while continuing to rely on foreign support. The Kingdom must allocate virtually all of its increasing output of

## The Development of Saudi Forces

skilled military manpower to operational forces and command roles, and it cannot hope to replace Western technical support.

At the same time, there is no way that the Kingdom can hope to compete with most of its larger neighbors in sheer manpower or land forces. While it has talked about conscription for more than a decade, this can only be a token solution and any full scale program would have unacceptable political and economic costs. Although Saudi Arabia's total population is uncertain, it is reasonably clear that the Kingdom now has a maximum of about 1.8 million males eligible for military service. Only 60,000-90,000 new males fit for military service reach draft age every year, and it is unlikely that this number will climb above 200,000 before the year 2000.[4]

The demand for these males in the civil economy will continue to exceed supply almost regardless of the shift in oil revenues, and most will strongly prefer civil careers. Coupled to the fact that it generally takes at least 24 months to turn a conscript into an effective soldier in most developing states, this scarcely implies a political and economic climate where the Kingdom could adopt more than the most limited conscription plan. While Saudi Arabia has recently indicated that it may introduce a draft during the next year, such a draft would also be politically unpopular and extremely difficult to enforce.[5] It can at best be a political incentive to increase active manning levels, rather than a broad popular draft that makes a major increase in Saudi total manning.

The National Guard adds to this Saudi manpower problem. The Kingdom's internal politics indicate that Crown Prince Abdullah will concentrate on seeking to convert the portion of the Guard that is actually fit for military service (about 8,000-10,000 men) into a fully mechanized force rather than allow its manpower to be absorbed into the regular military. This conversion of the Guard is likely to increase the strain on Saudi manpower rather than reduce it. It also is likely to raise the level of competition between the various services, particularly if the Ministry of Interior continues to build up its own internal security and counter terrorist forces. These Ministry of Interior forces now total about 8,500 men.

### THE IMPACT OF FOREIGN MANPOWER

These internal manpower problems are a key reason why Saudi Arabia must depend on substantial numbers of U.S., and Western European, and other advisors and technicians well into the late 1990s. It must continue to concentrate most of its own military personnel in combat arms and combat support, and must rely heavily on outside help even to create a purely defensive set of military capabilities.

As a result, Saudi Arabia will continue to need something approaching its current 2,000-3,000 European technicians and advisors, 5,000 U.S. technicians and experts, and 500 U.S. military advisors well into the 1990s.[6] The U.S. portion of this manpower is only part of the foreign

## The Development of Saudi Forces

advisory effort, and Saudi Arabia depends heavily on Britain for air training and support, and France for naval and army training and support. Nevertheless, the breakdown of U.S. military and contract personnel supporting FMS purchases in Saudi Arabia shown in Table 5.4 provides a good illustration of the wide mix of companies involved and of the kind of role Western states are likely to play in the future.

### Table 5.4: U.S. Personnel Supporting FMS Purchases in Saudi Arabia

| U.S. Government Civilian and Military Personnel Function | Personnel | U.S. Civilian Contract Personnel Function | Personnel |
|---|---|---|---|
| U.S. Military Training Mission | 187 | AEA Electromechanical Systems | 4 |
| APO | 13 | A.R. Ramlah Corp | 2 |
| MAC | 8 | Boeing | 16 |
| ACC | 36 | Demauro Shuwayer Co. Ltd. | 6 |
| Commissary | 4 | Ericsson | 1 |
| Medical Clinic | 4 | FMC | 7 |
| C-130 Crews | 19 | General Technical Services, Inc. | 1 |
| Technical Advisory Field Team (TAFT) | 103 | HCA | 312 |
| MTT | 16 | Al Henaki | 2 |
| OPM/SANG | 89 | Al-Husseini ADA | 1 |
| AFDC-LSG | 109 | Honeywell | 6 |
| Corps of Engineers | 519 | Hughes Aircraft | 4 |
| TDY (largely ELF-1 AWACS) | 530 | Hyundai Construction | 17 |
| | | ICCI/AI Muraibid Est | 1 |
| | | Johnson Brothers International | 2 |
| | | Landarun and Brown | 14 |
| | | Litton | 162 |
| | | Lockheed | 709 |
| | | McDonnell Douglas | 599 |
| | | Almusaadiah-Pepper | 2 |
| | | Northrop | 617 |
| | | Obeid and Al Mulla | 10 |
| | | OPS | 23 |
| | | Pacific Architects and Engineers | 41 |
| | | Prefab Eld Co. Ltd. | 4 |
| | | Rabya | 1 |
| | | Raytheon | 283 |
| | | Ret-Ser Engineering Agency | 1 |
| | | Samwhan Corp | 4 |
| | | Saudi Computer Service | 5 |
| | | Saudi Medical Service | 37 |
| | | SBT/Erectors | 1 |
| | | SHIN WHA | 1 |
| | | SIBIC BASIL | 661 |
| | | SIYANCO | 283 |
| | | Transworld Services | 20 |
| | | Vinnel Corporation | 404 |
| | | Wallace International Ltd. | 3 |
| | | Westinghouse | 2 |
| | | Weimer and Trachte | 1 |
| | | YOU ONE | 1 |
| | | BDM | 26 |
| | | Saudi Arabian International Stores | 1 |
| | | SOGREB/BELL/HAZAR | 3 |
| | | Computer Science Corporation | 45 |
| | | BASI | 2 |
| | | Day and Zimmerman | 9 |

Source: Response to Section 36(A)(7) of the Arms Control Act on U.S. Government and Civilian Personnel resident in Saudi Arabia on assignments relating to FMS as of May 4, 1985.

## The Development of Saudi Forces

It is important to note that the bulk of the U.S. personnel working on defense related contracts in Saudi Arabia are not working on weapons related projects, but on construction normally listed as civil personnel. Further, Table 5.4 shows a small--but growing--number of U.S. personnel are working for Saudi or Arab firms.

Nevertheless, Saudi Arabia must find U.S. or European technicians in order to ensure that it can get the maintenance and upgrade support it needs for its new weapons systems, and suitable military advice, and training. The new E-3A Peace Sentinel and Peace Shield programs will raise the total significantly. So will the nearly 2,000 British technicians and advisors needed to help Saudi Arabia convert to and operate its Tornados, Hawks, and Pucaras, although Britain already carries out much of the basic training for the Saudi Air Force and helps to support Saudi Arabia's remaining Lightning fighters.

This interdependence between Saudi Arabia and the West is deliberately given a low political profile. Like the role of U.S. plans and the U.S. Army Corps of Engineers in shaping Saudi military modernization, it is best left as a quiet reality, rather than given a high profile in a way that leads hostile local states, radical political movements, and the USSR to accuse Saudi Arabia of giving the U.S. "bases", or of betraying the Arab cause by close ties to Israel's principal ally. A shift to more reliance on Britain may also help defuse this issue, although it is too early to tell how various hostile Arab states and Arab radical groups will react.

It is also too early to tell just how much the Saudi shift to new British aircraft will affect the recent increasing visits of USCENTCOM personnel to Saudi Arabia, and the quiet upgrading of the personnel at the U.S. mission's headquarters in Dhahran and those supporting the joint Saudi-U.S. section at Riyadh. Further, while the shift to British support seems unlikely to present major problems, the Kingdom has had problems with its advisory groups in the past

Saudi Arabia, for example, turned to France for much of its naval equipment in part because of the inadequacies of the U.S. Navy advisory personnel sent to the Kingdom. The Saudi Air Force now is heavily dependent on USAF advisory teams at the Saudi Air Force headquarters, at Riyadh Air Base, King Abd al-Aziz Air Force Base at Dhahran (F-15 and F-5 support), and the King Faisal Air Academy, and at each Saudi air base.

Senior Saudi Air Force officers have been pleased with the quality of the U.S.A.F. "Elf-1" unit that is operating four E-3As, KC-10 and KC-135 tanker aircraft, and TPS-43 gap-filler radars in Saudi Arabia while the Saudi Air Force trains and prepares to operate its own E-3As and the new "Peace Shield" $C^3I$/BM system it is buying from the U.S.[7] The 500-plus man Elf-1 unit is based at Dhahran Air Force Base, and has already provided Saudi Arabia with key training in operating an air defense system and using the E-

3A AWACS. In addition, the Saudi Air Force has made increasing use of special U.S. task teams assigned for specific missions on a temporary duty basis.

Further, the Saudi Air Force has on the whole been pleased with its civilian contractor teams from Northrop, Boeing, and McDonnell Douglas. These are generally supported by contractor teams from each of the major U.S. aircraft manufacturers, and Northrop and McDonnell Douglas personnel have played a key role in training and supporting Saudi personnel as part of the Peace Hawk (F-5) and Peace Sun (F-15) programs, although Saudi Arabia is increasingly supporting its F-5s on its own and already maintains its own C-130s. The Kingdom has also made use of independent U.S. defense consulting firms like Braddock, Dunn, and McDonald (BDM). In 1983, BDM had at least $7.4 million worth of contracts with the Saudi Air Force, including a $3.9 million contract for operating Saudi Arabia's logistics-oriented reporting, analysis, and management information system (RAMIS) and a $3.5 million aeronautical engineering support contract.

Saudi Arabia will now have to add a major new British advisory presence, although it already has a 2,300 man British Aerospace team providing a wide range of training services in addition to supporting its remaining Lightnings. It will also have to adapt British training, support services, $C^3I$, and combat techniques and blend them with those it has learned from the U.S. This should not be prohibitively difficult, but it will certainly present more problems than added purchases of U.S. F-15s, particularly since the Kingdom will have to restructure its U.S. designed $C^2I$ system to support much more advanced air attack operations.

This Saudi dependence on Western aid offers broad advantages. It underpins virtually every aspect of Saudi Arabian modernization in a way most developing states lack. Its predominantly civilian character gives it a lower political profile than a military effort, and still allows Saudi Arabia to concentrate on the "Saudization" of its combat crews, maintenance crews, and intermediate service crews. While this does mean that the Saudi Air Force depends on Britain and the U.S. for service and resupply in any extended training or combat use of its forces, it allows Saudi Arabia to eliminate dependence on U.S. personnel in combat.

The Saudi army training and support effort draws less praise, both from the Saudis and from former U.S. and French personnel. There seems to be a general consensus that the Saudi Army is modernizing much more slowly than the Air Force, and has weaker teams and poorer contractor support. The French and U.S. advisory effort supporting Saudi Arabia's ground-based air defenses has also been less effective than the support for the Saudi Air Force. The quality of contractor advice seems to have been low to mediocre, and the French and U.S. Army advisory efforts often seem to have accepted problems rather than tried to solve them.

## The Development of Saudi Forces

The improved C³I system for Saudi Arabia's Hawk and fixed SHORAD defenses, that is part of the comprehensive U.S. Peace Shield C³I/Battle Management system, may improve Saudi ground based air defenses. This effort will be complicated, however, by the fact that Saudi Arabia's $4.5 billion deal with France to buy an extensive net of Shahine short range air defense missiles owed as much to politics--and to the need to give France guaranteed arms purchases that would ease the burden of refinancing Iraq's military debt--as to well planned requirements.

The land based air defenses operated by the Saudi Air Defense Corps are unlikely to approach the Air Force in providing the readiness and combat capability that Saudi Arabia needs. The Air Defense Corps has also experienced major problems in managing its procurements and maintenance contracts. This is a key factor explaining Saudi interest in the Stinger man portable surface-to-air missile--which does not need sophisticated C³I or battle management.

The U.S. Navy has advisors headquartered at Dhahran, and has training teams at the Saudi Navy bases at Jiddah and Jubail and at the main training base at Dammam. The U.S. has improved the quality of the personnel assigned to the Saudi Naval Expansion Program, but serious problems remain and France has taken over the bulk of the advisory role.

The problems in the U.S. Navy advisory effort have stemmed from several causes. The U.S. initially failed to select high quality personnel, but Saudi Arabia also advanced over-ambitious expansion plans. Further, the U.S. Navy did not operate or procure the kind of heavily armed and high technology small vessel Saudi Arabia sought. France has been in a position to provide such vessels, but has had major problems in providing training, maintenance, and follow-on technical support. The Saudis are now considering seeking additional aid in naval training and modernization from the U.K.

The U.S. Army Corps of Engineers generally draws praise from the Saudis, and helped to build-up the relationship between U.S. and Saudi forces. It has also generally been successful in creating effective military bases and facilities, although often at an extremely high cost. Unfortunately, neither the Corps nor any Saudi has had the authority to tightly manage construction efforts, and the Corps' role in the Kingdom is gradually coming to an end. The Saudi government has also resisted Corps' efforts to standardize designs and construction patterns--which might otherwise have significantly reduced the cost of major Saudi efforts.

The U.S. has tightened up the quality of the regular uniformed personnel assigned to advising the National Guard, and has improved the analytic and contracting support provided to the mission in both Saudi Arabia and the United States. Nevertheless, the National Guard remains a critical problem. The Guard's modernization continues to lag and much of the input of its foreign advisers is ignored. These problems have grown to the point where

## The Development of Saudi Forces

it has been necessary to the U.S. to impose strict security limits on any discussion of these problems by current or former advisors.

Prince Abdullah has made it clear that the official U.S. military role in advising the Guard must be kept more limited than for the regular services. There are only about 50 military and 100 civilian advisors to the Guard, and the 404 men in the Vinnell Corporation have a more independent role than that of other contract advisors. This limits the role the U.S. government can play in ensuring that the Guard gets the advice and support it needs. Prince Abdullah has also indicated his intention to seek non-U.S. advisors and training personnel, although it is unclear how far this effort will progress.

The Guard also has an acute shortage of educated and technically trained personnel, and this has hampered the U.S. advisory effort. It also seems to have delayed the Guard's effort to learn how to maintain its Cadillac Gage armored vehicles, and Saudi Arabia has evidently been slower in converting to self-maintenance of this equipment than any of the other 30-odd developing nations that have bought it.

The Kingdom's future need for the deployment of foreign military combat units is more uncertain, Saudi Arabia does allow the U.S. Air Force Elf-1 team to operate on Saudi territory pending the transfer of the new air defense system it is buying from the U.S. It also takes advantage of warning and intelligence data from U.S. vessels in the Gulf and has held several low level exercises with U.S. naval and air forces.

What is less clear is Saudi dependence on foreign security and land force units. Rumors that it has obtained the support of Thai and South Korean security forces cannot be confirmed. There is, however, considerable evidence that Saudi Arabia has sought contingency support from France and Pakistan, and that some French and Pakistani security forces are in the country.

There are also some reports that the French reinforcement role may be more significant than providing internal security advisors. Some sources have hinted that the equivalent of a French mechanized brigade set of equipment is prepositioned at Sharurah in special storage, and there are contingency plans for French forces to stage out of Djibouti or fly directly to Khamis Mushayt to reinforce Saudi Arabia in an emergency. These reports are very uncertain, but the French Navy seems to have conducted low level exercises with the Saudis, and could play a key role in areas like minesweeping--where neither the Saudis nor U.S. Navy have adequate capability.

Western officials have indicated in the past that a Pakistani training "brigade" is deployed at the Saudi army base at Tabuk. This "brigade" actually fills out most of the 12th Saudi Armored Brigade. There are around 11,000-15,000 Pakistani troops and advisors now in Saudi Arabia. While there has been some friction between the Saudis and Pakistanis, the Pakistani elements seem to function fairly well.[8]

## The Development of Saudi Forces

These forces--possibly with limited Turkish support contingents--provide a significant portion of Saudi Arabia's engineers and combat support personnel, and there are some reports they also provide the cadres necessary to allow Pakistan to rapidly deploy substantial combat forces in an emergency. Like the French advisory effort at Tabuk, they also serve as deterrent against Israeli attacks, although the French presence at Tabuk is now only 20-30 men, and the bulk of the French army effort in Saudi Arabia has shifted to Taif and Khamis Mushayt.

Such external forces would lack air power and armored strength, but would have the advantage of being Muslims and, in the case of Jordanians, of speaking Arabic. They also would ease the problems the West would face in committing ground and air troops to any complex contingency where the case for intervention was politically ambiguous.

A Jordanian role in Saudi Arabia seems more tenuous. U.S. efforts to help Jordan build up its contingency capabilities to intervene in the Gulf were leaked to the press in October 1983. These reports indicated that Jordan was developing a two brigade force of 8,500 men. The Jordanian forces were to receive training assistance from the U.S., to airlift from 8 C-130 transports, and to be armed with TOW antitank weapons, Stinger surface-to-air missiles, and $C^3I$ equipment. The U.S. was to sell Jordan three additional C-130s, to give it a total of eight, but this would only provide lift for 70 paratroops and 100 troops per aircraft. The U.S. was to provide large-scale lift in an emergency.

The initial cost of the program, which included the land force equipment, was $220-230 million. This was to come from U.S. foreign military sales loans, and Saudi Arabia was to provide Jordan with the money. Further sales of up to $470 million of FMS equipment were to include F-16 fighters and other major equipment necessary to allow Jordan to resist a major air or armored threat. This Jordanian force, however, seems to have been tailored largely to provide a rapid reaction force that could support the smaller GCC states. The U.S. air package also seems to have been tailored to help Jordan develop its own defense capabilities in the face of a massive Syrian military build-up.

In any case, the U.S. did not fund the package and told Jordan in January, 1986, that it would be unable to meet its request for modern fighters and other major combat equipment. While Europe will probably meet Jordan's needs for combat equipment in the same way it met those of Saudi Arabia, it seems doubtful that Jordan will now fund any rapid deployment force, and far more likely that it will concentrate on its own defense.

As for the internal effects of this Saudi dependence on foreign personnel, they seem unlikely to have any significant destablizing effects. The situation in Saudi Arabia differs radically from that in Iran under the Shah in that the foreign military advisors have a relatively low profile and are not dominated by one Western nation. Many such advisors are Muslim, and the living standards of most advisors do not contrast unfavorably with those of Saudis. Saudi Arabia also does not have large numbers of recently educated students or workers who feel displaced and discriminated against by the hiring of a foreign labor pool. In any case, this is not excessive or destabilizing, and much of the foreign manpower supporting Saudi forces will leave in the late 1980s as Saudi Arabia completes its massive military equipment construction program.

MILITARY INDUSTRY AND OFFSETS

Saudi Arabia is also taking several steps which should ease both its defense expenditure and foreign manpower problems. It has coupled most of its recent major arms sales to either arrangements that force the seller to buy Saudi oil, arrangements ranging from barter to market share agreements, or to offset arrangements that force the seller to buy Saudi goods and services from the Kingdom's civil sector or to help expand Saudi Arabia's small but growing military industries. These sales arrangements affect the Kingdom's recent aircraft purchases from Britain and the Peace Shield air defense $C^3I$ system it has bought from the U.S.

Saudi Arabia already assembles some of its small arms, including the Heckler and Koch G3 machine gun. It is expanding its industries to produce newer types of small arms, military spares, and electronic components, and has developed plans to produce naval equipment, and assemble light armor. One new major project may involve a deal worth up to $3 billion with a German consortium led by Rheinmetall G.m.b.H and Thysenn AG to create the plants necessary to produce most Saudi munitions and provide an export capability to sell to the rest of the Arab world.[9]

There are also reports that the Kingdom signed an agreement in October, 1984, with Brazil to train Saudi workers and help Saudi Arabia use the same manufacturing techniques that have proved successful in Brazil. Reports also surface in early 1986 that Saudi Arabia had signed an arms for oil and technical cooperation deal which would have included the Tucano T-27 trainer, 1,000 Osoro battle tanks, Urutu and Cascaval armored vehicles, and Avibas Astros II multiple rocket launchers. These reports have been denied, but Saudi Arabia continues to show an active interest in industrial cooperation with Brazil. [10]

Saudi Arabia's $5 billion Peace Shield air defense $C^3I$ system involves a contract calling for offset arrangements affecting $3.4 billion worth of the contract. These offsets called for each element of the Boeing-led consortium to invest in economically viable projects where Saudi firms will provide matching funds. The investments are to go into Saudi manufacturing industries, preferably in high technology areas. Projects include telecommunications, aircraft engine overhaul, and electrical equipment.

## The Development of Saudi Forces

Saudi Arabia is also attempting to get GCC support for the creation of a joint GCC arms industry, where Saudi Arabia would be a major producer.[11]

The five billion pound British aircraft sale of 1985 was renegotiated in mid-1986 to revise the repayments scheme to allow Saudi Arabia to pay the entire contract price in oil over an extended period of time. It was also agreed that Britain would invest up to 35% of the contract's technical element in Saudi Arabia under an offset arrangement similar to that used in the U.S. Peace Shield program.[12]

### NEAR TERM FORCE TRENDS

These factors help explain the force trends shown in Table 5.5 Saudi military modernization cannot be based on a conventional approach to military spending or the use of military manpower. It must be based on slowly evolving the ability to operate a limited number of high technology forces, on a high degree of dependence on other states, and on giving priority to the services and equipment which can most rapidly strengthen Saudi Arabia's deterrent and defense capabilities.

The Development of Saudi Forces

Table 5.5 Trends in the Modernization of Saudi Forces: 1985-1995

Army:

o Growth from about 35,000 to 45,000 men.

o Filling out a now skeleton structure of 4 mechanized brigades, two armored brigades, and one paratroop brigade.

o The airborne brigade will slowly expand from a strength of one battalion and several companies and become fully operational. The Royal Guard brigade will become a light mechanized unit.

o Armor will rise from 450 tanks to over 500, with Saudi Arabia concentrating on modernization rather than forced expansion. OAFVs will rise from 570 AFVs to about 700 and APCs will rise from about 800 to 900. Major artillery will rise from 180 to about 300.

o The army will acquire large numbers of modern anti-tank weapons and SHORADs.

o Some prepositioned unit equipment will exist for use by French and Pakistani forces.

o Improved deployment of the Improved Hawk missiles, acquisition of large numbers of Shahine mobile surface-to-air missiles (as part of a $4.5 billion deal in January, 1984) to provide oil field and ground installation protection, and integration into the Peace Shield $C^3I$/BM system will significantly improve the new Saudi Air Defense Corps and Saudi Arabia's ground based air defenses. The Air Defense Corps still will have readiness and proficiency problems in the early 1990s, however, and ground based air defense of maneuvering Army units will only be poor to fair.

o Major procurements will give Saudi Arabia relatively large numbers of top quality weapons but leave it with an extremely diverse mix of equipment to support, and make it even more heavily dependent on external technical and service support.

o The Kingdom will acquire 12 Blackhawk helicopters with an option to buy 12 more. It is studying plans to acquire a regiment equivalent strength in combat helicopters, with emphasis on attack helicopters, in the 1990s.

o Training and readiness will improve steadily, but not keep pace with the impact of the Iran-Iraq War in improving the quality of Iranian and Iraqi forces, or the impact of the Arab-Israeli war in improving Israeli and Syrian forces. Saudi Arabia will continue to rely on U.S., French, and Pakistani (Bangladesh) assistance in training.

o The Saudi Army was not impressed by its experience with the French AMX-30, with trials of the U.S. M-1 tank, or by the cost/performance of the M-1/M-2/M-3 combination. It is now examining the British Challenger, and is interested in the Leopard II, and coproduction arrangements with Turkey to build the tank and other German armored equipment including the Marder family of MICVs. This represents part of a growing link between the Turkish and Saudi armies. If it cannot standardize on the Leopard II, it is likely to buy

## The Development of Saudi Forces

the Challenger, French AMX-32 or AMX-34 tank. It is also examining a major buy of French OAFVs, and French artillery both for military reasons and because of the political problems in buying arms from the U.S. This will reduce U.S. military ties to Saudi Arabia and reduce interoperability and standardization with USCENTCOM as Saudi Arabia halts its procurement of major U.S. armor at a total of 250 M-60A3 tanks.

o The Saudi army will probably standardize on U.S. equipment at Hafr al-Batin and build-up to a two brigade level there. It will standardize on French equipment at Sharurah and Tabuk with a mix of equipment at Khamis Mushayt. It is unclear how Saudi Arabia will distribute any new purchases of German armor or its next generation of tanks, but it is most likely to deploy any new French armor at Tabuk. The same uncertainties exist regarding reports of a Saudi $1 billion arms deal with Brazil that would lead to substantially deliveries of Cascaval EE-9 armored personnel carriers.

o By the early 1990s, the end result will be that Saudi Arabia will have an army capable of fighting reasonably well in prepared defensive positions to the rear of Saudi Arabia's borders, and of dealing with a relatively low level threat like the PDRY, but lack offensive and maneuver warfare capability.

o The Army will be critically dependent on air cover and support and unable to defend or fight without it.

<ins>National Guard and Security Forces</ins>:

o The future of the National Guard will depend upon the political influence of Crown Prince Abdullah. He and several collateral princes would like to create an independent force of at least two fully armored brigades equipped with M-1, Leopard II or AMX-32/34 tanks, and suitable OAFVs and artillery, although the eventual upgrading of the Guard's present V-150s now seems more likely.

o The Guard has evolved from a light infantry force to a brigade headquarters with 4 mechanized, 16 infantry, and 24 irregular battalions. It now has only to upgrade two of its battalions to light mechanized forces with two more in process, regardless of the fact it formally inaugurated a full brigade early in 1985. It should, however, reach the strength of a full light mechanized brigade by the early 1990s.

o The Guard will acquire at least 500 more OAFVs to supplement its present 240 V-150s during the next 5 years. It will acquire substantial additional TOW and self-propelled ITOW weapons, some heavy artillery, and improved air defense.

o The Guard will also improve in readiness and proficiency, but will remain a highly politicized internal security force dependent on foreign technical and service support. It will not be able to operate effectively at a full brigade level until the early 1990s.

o The Ministry of the Interior anti-terrorist, Frontier Force, and Coastguard will expand from 8,500 men to about 11,000. They will acquire some highly trained and equipped cadre units supported by foreign technical advisors with combat capability. Overall internal security standards will, however, depend more on political activity than effective internal security forces.

# The Development of Saudi Forces

Navy:

o The navy will increase from a token strength of about 2,700-3,500 men to 4,500 by 1995. It will, however, be at less than half its minimum required strength, and will depend on foreign technical, service, and basing support.

o Both the Red Sea (Western) and Gulf (Eastern) flotilla headquarters are already fully operational. Major active force deployments to the Western Fleet should take place over the next two years.

o Both fleets will acquire significant combat strength by local standards as Saudi Arabia will finish taking delivery of a total of 4 F-2000 French frigates in the late 1980s, and at least 2-4 more major ships will be delivered by 1990.

o Guided missile patrol boat strength will increase from 14 to 17-21 vessels. The Kingdom will acquire Improved Harpoon for both its ships and aircraft.

o The Saudi air force will start extensive joint training with the navy in the late 1980s, using its E-3As in the maritime patrol mode. F-5E-IIs and later F-15s or Mirage 2000s will practice air support. The Navy would like to buy at least 2 MPAs of its own by 1990 and a total of 5 by 1995.

o The Navy will slowly build-up its helicopter strength (now 4 SAR and 20 ASM Dauphine 2) and transition from AS-15TT ASMs to a more advanced variant during the early 1990s.

o The Kingdom is seeking a more advanced mine warfare capability than its 4 MSC-322s now provide, and is studying purchase of minewarfare helicopters, but probably cannot develop a meaningful mine warfare capability against advanced mines until after the mid-1990s. It will remain heavily dependent on U.S. or French support.

o The Navy will acquire Otomat shore missile defenses for the point defense of key areas by the late 1980s.

o Amphibious capability is being built-up from 16 U.S. landing craft and vessels to include 8 hovercraft and 2 logistic support ships. At least 4 more large amphibious vessels may be purchased by 1993.

o Overall naval readiness and proficiency will remain low well into the early 1990s. The Kingdom will become steadily more dependent on French advice and service, and on other European suppliers, and U.S. influence and role will decline. The navy will not begin to emerge as a fully effective force even by regional standards until the mid-1990s.

## The Development of Saudi Forces

<u>Air Force</u>:

o Manpower will gradually increase from 14,000 to about 21,000 men.

o Combat aircraft strength will increase from about 203 aircraft to 240 .

o First line combat aircraft will increase from 60 F-15 C/D, optimized for the air defense mission, to 140 aircraft with dual capability in the air defense attack mission. By late 1989, Saudi Arabia will have 48 Tornado attack fighters, 24 Tornado air defense fighters, and 60 F-15C/Ds.

o Saudi Arabia will transition from advanced IR missiles to a full BVR capability by the late 1990s. It will transition from a reliance on Maverick and LGBs to extensive use of smart area and hard target submunitions during the early 1990s.

o All Lightnings will be phased out by the late 1986-1988, and Saudi Arabia will expand its second line combat strength from 62 F-5E IIs to a total of 100 aircraft including 40 of a new type by the early 1990s. It will then slowly shift its F-5Es to a third echelon role.

o The Kingdom will retain at least 20 of its F-5Fs into the early 1990s, but phase out its F-5Bs and most of its 38 BAC-167 trainers. It will deploy 36 new Hawk light attack trainers by 1988.

o Saudi Arabia has completed the initial deployment of its 8 RF-5E recce fighters, and will complete deployment of its 5 E-3A AWACS by the late 1980s. It may buy at least 3 additional E-3As, or other heavy recce/AC&W/MPA aircraft to give it a two front coverage, and a more advanced recce fighter during the early 1990s.

o The new ground based Peace Shield $C^3I$ system should start to become effective by the late 1990s and greatly improve land/air coordination and the Kingdom's air battle management capabilities.

o Saudi Arabia will expand its tanker force from 8 KC-130H to include 8 KE-3 heavy tankers by the late 1980s, and will buy additional tankers in the early 1990s. It will use refueling to increase effective sortie rates and deployment capability and as a substitute for aircraft numbers.

o The Saudi transport fleet may increase from 30 C-130E/Hs to include 40 more C-212-200s by the late 1980s, and then to include additional B-747 variants. Airlift will be used to redeploy Saudi ground forces and to provide a strategic lift capability for GCC use and to bring in ground forces from outside the area.

o Helicopter strength will rise from 36 (12 AB-206A, 14 AB-205, 10 AB-212) to add at least 22 more AB-212 and 8 KV-107 helicopters by 1990. Effective strength is likely to exceed 80 helicopters by the early 1990s, and the Air Force may acquire some combat helicopters by 1992.

o All of the main Saudi bases should be fully sheltered by 1990, and be able to take major reinforcements. The key combat bases will be at Dhahran, Taif, Khamis Mushayt, Riyadh, and Tabuk, although some discussion is being given to creating an advanced base at Hail rather than Tabuk. The air strips and facilities at Hafr al-Batin and Sharurah may be expanded to contingency bases with shelters and MOB support capabilities by the mid 1990s.

o The Saudi Air Force should have the most effective air force in the Gulf and Red Sea areas by the late 1990s, although it will not be able to compete with an air force like Israel's. It will remain fully dependent, however, on foreign technical and support services.

o The Saudi Air Force will seek interoperability or cooperability with the GCC air forces during the next decade, but the result will be little more than a facade. Although the SAF will provide advanced training facilities, the lack of standardization in combat aircraft and $C^3I$/BM capability will prevent full integration, and most other GCC air forces will buy "glitter factor" aircraft in larger numbers than they can support or make effective.

## THE DEVELOPMENT OF SAUDI GROUND FORCES AND THE AIR DEFENSE CORPS

The broad thrusts summarized in Table 5.5 help explain the emphasis Saudi Arabia now places on the development of its Air Force, its search for improved combat aircraft and dual capability in the attack role, and its emphasis on close military relations with the West. This emphasis on high technology in air power is reinforced by the problems Saudi Arabia faces in modernizing its Army, National Guard, and Navy, and by the limits it faces in expanding its air strength.

The current structure of the Saudi Army is shown in Table 5.6. This table shows that Saudi Arabia is now in a state of transition towards a mix of French and U.S. Army equipment, with a total of about 550 main battle tanks. The Saudi Army must now concentrate on filling in its present paper strength of two armored, four mechanized, and one air borne brigade. It would, however, like to build up substantially by the late 1990s or early 2000s.

In theory, this expansion would mean an expansion from a current paper strength of seven brigades to 11 brigades, but the Saudi Army is now undermanned by about 40-65%, and has significant problems in retaining skilled technicians and NCOs. Even by Gulf standards, an eleven brigade force would require a minimum of 150,000 men, and the Saudi Army will be hard pressed to build up above 45,000 before the mid 1990s.

The Development of Saudi Forces

## Table 5.6: The Current Structure of the Saudi Army

**Total Manning**
    Active: 34,000-38,000
    Conscript: 0
    Reserve: 0

**Major Formations**
    Armored Brigades (French equipped) 3
        (3 tank, 1 Mechanized Infantry Battalions) [a]
    Mechanized Brigades (U.S. equipped) 3
        (1 tank, 3 Mechanized Infantry Battalions) [b]
    Airborne Brigade 1
        (2 paratroop battalions,
        three special forces companies)
    Royal Guard Regiment 1
        (3 battalions)
    Artillery Battalions [b] 5
    Anti-Aircraft Battalions [b] 18
    Surface to Air Missile Batteries [b] 14
        (12 IHawk with 216 missiles, and 2 with 12
        Shahine launchers and 48 missiles and AMX-30SA
        30mm SP AA guns)

**Key Equipment**

- **Main Battle Tanks**: 450: 300 AMX-30, 150 M-60A1, with 150 M-60A3 and 150 M-60A3 conversion kits on order
- **OAFVs/APCs**: 1,880: 200 AML60/90, 350 AMX-10P (Some with HOT), 1,300 M-113, 30 EE-11, and some Panhard M-3 and Urutu. (20 VCC-1 with TOW, and 60 AMX-10P, , 180 VCC-1 with TOW, and Urutu APCs on order.)
- **Artillery**: 422: Model 56 105mm pack howitzers, 100 M-101/2 105mm howitzers, 29 FH-70 and 18 M-198 towed 155mm howitzers, 275 M-109 and GCT 155mm self-propelled howitzers, 81mm M-30 and 107mm mortars. (ASTROS MRLS, 24 M-198 and 43 FH-70 155mm howitzers on order.
- **Anti-Tank Weapons**: 2,000+ TOW, 4,292 Dragon, HOT (plus 2,000 obsolete SS-11 and 300 obsolete Vigilant) anti-tank guided missiles, 75, 90, and 106mm recoiless rocket launchers; and 5,548 (Improved TOW and 400 Jpz SK-105 mm anti-tank guns on order or in the process of delivery).
- **Surface-to-Air Missiles**: 12 Improved Hawk Batteries with 216 missiles, 2 Shahine batteries with 12 fire units and 48 missiles plus AMX-30SA 30mm self propelled AA guns. (100 Shahine II surface-to-air missiles on order.)
- **SHORADs**:M-163 Vulcan 20mm self-propelled weapons, AMX-30SA 30mm self propelled AA guns, 200 35mm AA guns, and M-42 self-propelled 40 mm AA guns. Redeye manportable and 200 Stinger surface-to-air missiles. (200 Stinger launchers and 600 reload missiles on order).

**Key Bases and Facilities**:
o Hafr al Batin (Now one brigade, building up to division size). Tabuk (Building to one division, plus one brigade). Khamis Mushayet (Building to one division). Sharurah (one brigade plus one brigade set of equipment prepositioned). Riyadh (Royal Guard Regiment plus some elements of Airborne Brigade).

a. Another unit is in the process of formation. Given the actual strength of these units, they are missing sufficient elements so that they are only equivalent to 3 brigades.

b. Some elements are significantly short of full complement of Saudi troops
Source: Adapted from IISS, JCSS, and DMS data bases by the author.

## THE PROBLEMS OF EQUIPMENT DIVERSIFICATION

The manpower problems in the Saudi Army will be compounded by its need to operate a complex mix of different equipment from many different nations shown in Table 5.6. The end result of the diversification of its sources of army equipment has been to effectively double its life cycle costs and training and support burden. These problems have been increased by a combination of politically oriented purchases from its major oil customers and the inability to obtain a consistent supply of equipment from the U.S. because of internal U.S. domestic politics.

Much of the equipment the Saudi Army has purchased has required modification or changes to its original technical and logistic support plan before it could be operated in large numbers, and some key items still present major servicing problems. These problems have been compounded by the need to disperse most of the Army's combat forces to three distant corners of the Kingdom, by the erratic quality of contractor support, and by an over ambitious effort to create a modern logistical system that has lacked proper Saudi and U.S. advisory management.

The Saudi Army's mix of different types of armor has been a particular cause of such problems. The U.S. M-60s have proved reasonably reliable and effective, but the crew compartment cannot be cooled effectively and the M-60 can develop internal temperatures of well over 120 degrees. Saudi Arabia's 300 French AMX-30s have presented more substantive problems. They lack the armor, firepower, and operational availability to be kept in service much past the 1980s.

The AMX-30 has relatively light armor and is not competitive with any of the newer Soviet and Western-made tanks now being deployed in the region (e.g. T-62/72/80, M-60, Khalid, Merkava, Chieftain, and Challenger). While the adoption of newer anti-armor round technology has made up for the lack of penetrating power in the Obus G rounds that France originally sold the Saudi Army, the AMX-30s fire control and range-finding capability is inadequate to help Saudi tank crews make up for their lack of experience, and the AMX-30 lacks the power, cooling, and filtration for desert combat.

This compounds Saudi Arabia's modernization problems, and has created a source of tension with the United States that serves as a good illustration of the need for a stable military relations between the two countries. The U.S. has a natural interest in testing its new M-1 tank and M-2 fighting vehicle in the Gulf, as well as in seeing Saudi Arabia buy heavy armor that would be directly compatible with the equipment used by USCENTCOM forces.

## THE M-1 TANK ISSUE

The U.S. began preliminary discussions of an M-1 tank test and evaluation effort in Saudi Arabia in 1982. By early 1983, these discussions produced a detailed test plan, and Saudi tank and maintenance crews had begun training on the M-1 tank at Fort Knox, Kentucky. The Saudi National Guard requested the sale of 57 M-1 tanks, and the Saudi Army made it clear that it was actively interested in procuring the M-1 and in standardizing on U.S. equipment.

These Saudi-U.S. discussions began at a time when shifts in the politics of the Arab-Israeli conflict and the impact of President Reagan's 1982 peace initiative made an M-1/M-2 sale seem possible without serious Israeli and Congressional opposition. It offered both the U.S. and Saudi Arabia major advantages. The net effect of such a Saudi purchase would be (a) to lower the unit cost of the M-1 and M-2 to both the U.S. and Saudi Arabia, and (b) allow both armies to standardize on a mix of armor that could be used by both Saudi forces and U.S. reinforcements.

Unfortunately, these discussions leaked to the press, and were published in the February 1983 issue of the International Defense Review. They received broader exposure in the New York Times on 4 March 1983, in an article by Richard Halloran, and in a form that stressed a goal of 1,200 tanks which neither the U.S. nor Saudi Arabia had ever seriously discussed.

The senior Pentagon official who had provided the data on a background basis had failed to consider Saudi, Israeli, or Congressional sensitivities. As a result, the story turned preliminary talks into a "plan" and triggered immediate U.S. domestic political opposition. Worse, the leak was accompanied by discussion of Saudi Arabia's problems with reduced oil revenues and with paying for M-1 tanks at a reported cost of nearly $2 million each. This immediately led to debates within Saudi Arabia regarding the "waste" of Saudi funds on a highly controversial tank that was still having teething problems in U.S. forces.

This embarrassment was compounded when the U.S. tried to issue a denial of the story. On 15 March, the Associated Press carried both a report on the sale and a categorical denial by Henry Catto, the Assistant Secretary of Defense (Public Affairs). When Halloran repeated the story with more details on 4 April, the Pentagon issued another denial, this time on a non attributable basis.

By then, however, a web of false rumors surrounded the Saudi-U.S. discussions, including reports that 800-1,000 of the tanks would be prepositioned solely for the use of USCENTCOM forces. By 26 March, the BBC was picking up major propaganda attacks on the sale from groups like the Soviet-backed Radio Peace and Progress, which attacked both the Saudi royal family and U.S. "imperialism." [13]

## The Development of Saudi Forces

The problems grew even more serious when the U.S. demonstration team sent to Saudi Arabia attempted to demonstrate the M-1. The team did not speak adequate Arabic, and during the resulting trials several problems occurred simply because the two sides could not communicate. While the M-1 tank did present some legitimate problems in terms of service and fuel needs, and interior heat and crew fatigue, the demonstrations and trials failed largely because of communication problems.

This mishandling of U.S. and Saudi military relations is all too typical of what has happened in a U.S. domestic political climate where there is little practical understanding of the strategic importance of U.S.-Saudi military relations, and where virtually every sale is debated almost solely in terms of its theoretical impact on the security of Israel. It also came during a period when the U.S. was actively trying to persuade Saudi Arabia to put pressure on King Hussein of Jordan to support President Reagan's peace initiative and on Syria and Lebanon. And, it came at a time when the U.S. was seeking Saudi support in persuading the other Gulf states to standardize on U.S. air defense systems. Needless to say, it did little to enhance the prospects for peace or to improve Saudi-U.S. military cooperation.

Saudi Arabia was virtually forced to respond by seeking other sources of supply, and renewed previous contacts with West Germany. In late May, Saudi Arabia announced the Prince Sultan would visit Germany for health reasons. In fact, he met with West German Chancellor Helmut Kohl at the latter's home in Ludwigshafen to discuss possible arms purchases. This was announced officially in Bonn on 13 June, and the announcement was followed by reports that Saudi Arabia might buy up to 800 Leopard II tanks, 800 Marder armored fighting vehicles, and 200 Gepard air defense vehicles.

Saudi Army experts have since again visited France to examine France's new AMX-32 and AMX-40 tanks. They also have examined the British Challenger, and General Dynamics even quietly sent another M-1 evaluation team into Saudi Arabia in 1985. It is unclear, therefore, where Saudi Arabia will buy its new armor, although this is now more likely to come from Europe than the U.S.

It is also difficult to know just how much the previous sequence of political events in the U.S. have acted to push the Saudi Army away from a major arms purchase in the U.S. and towards a buy from Western Europe. Trials of the U.S. M-1 tank eventually did take place near Sharurah. According to Saudi sources, they were not successful because of suspension problems, internal heat problems in the crew compartment, and an inability to provide proper engine filtration and cooling. The operating conditions in the Gulf proved considerably more demanding than in "textbook" exercises in Egypt. Saudi Arabia also retains some interest in a buy from the U.S. in spite of these problems, largely because of its ability to strengthen its de facto ties to the U.S. and USCENTCOM without creating the kind of political problems inherent in granting a formal base or prepositioning arrangements.

Nevertheless, the political embarrassment that occurred over the M-1 issue provides an important paradigm for the present Saudi arms request in several important respects. It exposed the kind of informal relations that can be of great strategic value to both the U.S. and Saudi Arabia. It made Saudi military ties to the U.S. an embarrassment, a source of weakness rather than of strength. It undercut relations at a time when the U.S. badly needed Saudi political and diplomatic support.

Like the F-15 sale, it did nothing to protect Israel since Saudi Arabia could immediately turn to Western Europe for equally effective arms. If anything, it weakened a Saudi dependence on U.S. arms and technical support that acts as a powerful factor to persuade Saudi Arabia to avoid any confrontation with Israel.

OTHER MODERNIZATION ISSUES

To return to the broader problems in Saudi Army and Air Defense Corps modernization, the Saudi Army also needs to improve its air defense, artillery, and helicopter strength. Unfortunately, an initial U.S. contractor effort to improve the integration of the Saudi Air Defense Corps' Improved Hawks, Shahines (Improved Crotale), anti-aircraft gun, and land-based radar and $C^3I$ systems has not been successful, and has tended to highlight the need to improve Saudi air capabilities.

Even if the Saudi Army and Air Defense Corps can develop the ability to use the air defense equipment it is buying, its ability to fight in defensive positions against superior forces will depend heavily on the quality of its air cover, the ability of the Saudi Air Force to link its operations with those of the Army, and its ability to provide close air and interdiction support.

It seems unlikely, however, that the Saudi Air Defense Corps can hope to do more than properly integrate its Hawk defenses before the mid-1990s, and create a few effective mobile Shahine units.[14] Saudi forces will have to be far more dependent on air power than the strength of their land based air defense forces indicates, and will need systems like Stinger which do not require sophisticated training or full integration into the new Saudi "Peace Shield" air defense system.

The Saudi Army also has serious problems in making its artillery properly effective. These problems include a lack of suitable numbers of modern types, and the need for better mobile fire-control and ammunition supply equipment. They may be solved in part by orders for the FH-70 155mm howitzer. It seems more likely, however, that Saudi Army artillery capabilities will suffer from major mobility, support, and sustained fire problems well into the 1990s, and again reinforce the need for enhanced air attack capability.

## The Development of Saudi Forces

The Saudi Army's search for helicopter forces raises different issues. The Saudi Army is now deployed nearly 600 miles from the Kingdom's main oil facilities in the Eastern Province, and even though the combat elements of a brigade are now deploying to the new Saudi Army base at King Khalid City near Hafr al-Batin in 1984, the Saudi Army will still be dispersed so that roughly one third of its strength is deployed at the ends of a triangle reaching to Saudi Arabia's borders with the angles located at Tabuk, Hafr al-Batin, and Sharurah-Khamis Mushayt.

Helicopters offer a limited solution to this problem. They can both provide rapid concentration of force and allow Saudi Arabia to make up for its lack of experience in large-scale maneuver. It is far from clear, however, how Saudi Arabia can absorb or support large numbers of attack and troop lift helicopters it needs, or the kind of advisory and technical support required. The Saudi Army is seeking to buy 12 Blackhawk helicopters, with an option to buy 12 more, from the U.S. It is also studying the long term option of developing a helicopter force using a total of 60-100 U.S. AH-64 attack, Blackhawk utility and support, and Chinook CH-47 transport helicopters by the mid 1990s.

The U.S. Army is probably the only force that could support such a purchase with the mix of conversion, training and service capabilities the Saudis need, but such a purchase again opens up the problem of military relations with the U.S. and U.S. domestic politics. If these political barriers again block such a sale, the U.S. Army could again lose precisely the kind of forward interoperable weapons and support capabilities it needs to make USCENTCOM effective, while Saudi Arabia will be forced to turn to France or the FRG for similar weapons.

Regardless of these future purchases, the Saudi Army will continue to lack a proper balance of modern equipment. It also will not be large enough to concentrate significant forces on a given front unless it can move forces from another major military city, and all the way across Saudi Arabia. This would take a minimum of a week to 10 days. Even then, Saudi Arabia will lack the massive armored forces of its stronger neighbors.

Training has been a problem in the past, and will continue to be so. Many of the Saudi Army's training plans have not been executed, and maneuver training has been poor. The army's mix of U.S., French, German, Spanish and British equipment presents major conversion problems, and the army had been much slower in providing the trained manpower necessary to absorb such equipment than the Air Force. Once again, this highlights the fact that the Saudi Army must depend on Air Force support to help make up for its own deficiencies.

### THE IMPACT OF THE SAUDI NATIONAL GUARD

All of these problems will be compounded by the fact that Saudi Arabia must divide its manpower between the Army and the National Guard.

## The Development of Saudi Forces

Although the National Guard's future may depend upon the complex politics within the Saudi royal family following King Khalid's death, the Saudi National Guard seems likely to remain a lightly armed internal security force whose main mission is to ensure the loyalty of Saudi Arabia's traditional tribes [15]. At the same time, the National Guard will use at least 25,000 men, or about 30-40% of the Kingdom's active trained military manpower, in a paramilitary force that is far more suited to internal political and security needs than to creating an effective deterrent or defense against outside threats.

The current force structure of the National Guard is shown in Table 5.7. While the National Guard's current purchases do not seem over ambitious, and the Guard is now better trained and deployed, it cannot absorb large numbers of heavy arms. Even if it is given them for political reasons, the National Guard will continue to have little value as a regular combat force. In fact, the greatest single uncertainty in the Saudi military modernization process is whether the National Guard can be effectively trained and equipped to deal with terrorism and paramilitary threats, and what role the Army, Air Force, and Navy should play in aiding it in this mission.

## The Development of Saudi Forces

Table 5.7: The Current Structure of the Saudi National Guard

**Total Manning**
    Active: 10,000
    Conscript: 0
    Reserve: (Part time or reserve 15,000
        by Western definition )

**Major Formations**

    Mechanized "Brigades" 2
    All Arms Battalions [a] 4-6
        (Are part of mechanized brigades)
    Regular Infantry Battalions 16
        (Closer to Companies by Western definition)
    Irregular Infantry Battalions 24
        (Largely part time tribal forces)
    Cavalry Squadron 1
        (Ceremonial)
    Support units (?)

**Key Equipment:**
- 240 V-150 Commando Cadillac Gage armored cars, with 206 equipped with British Racal communication systems.
- M-102 105mm towed howitzers
- TOW anti-tank guided missiles, and 106mm recoilless rifles
- 81 mm mortars
- 20mm Vulcan AA guns and towed 90 mm AA guns
- 489 additional Commando are on order, including V-300 APCs and V-150 AFVs with a mix of heavy machine guns turrets, TOW, 90mm guns, and 20mm AA guns.

**Key Bases and Facilities:** Eastern Province (Now one brigade). Riyadh (Gradually forming Brigade). Other tribal areas: Battalion sized elements are scattered throughout the country, and serve as a major source of subsidies to the traditional tribal leaders.

**Additional Internal Security Forces:**

- **Ministry of the Interior:** A counter terrorist unit equipped with helicopters, some guided missiles, and non-lethal gas. An 8,500 man Frontier Force and Coastguard with 8,500 men. The Coastguard has a large inventory of small craft with several hundred small ships, 16 SRN-6 hovercraft, and 8 BH-7 hovercraft on order. Readiness, training, and combat effectiveness is generally very low. Finally a General Civil Defense Administration unit with 10 Kawasaki helicopters.

- **European:** French: A small battalion size equivalent of advisors. Pakistani: Some. British: Ex-SAS provide security outside Saudi Arabia for the Royal Family and some other key officials.

a. Up to 8 units are shown in order of battle. Effective strength seems to be 4.
Source: Adapted by the author from IISS, DMS, and JCSS data bases.

The National Guard began to hold significant training exercises for its first 6,500 man Mechanized Brigade, the Imam bin Mohammed al-Saud Brigade, during the early 1980s. It has established a brigade sized presence, and a limited oil field security force in the Eastern Province. The Mohammed al-Saud brigade held a 10-day exercise in the desert about 250 miles west of Riyadh in early 1983. While it experienced its habitual problems in translating tribal into regular military discipline, and the force was well below its authorized manning level, the maneuvers were relatively successful. Units moved from as far away as the Eastern Province, and the key mechanized elements performed relatively well.

The National Guard formally inaugurated its second mechanized "brigade" in a ceremony on March 14, 1985. This new unit was called the King Abdul Aziz Brigade, and was formed after another relatively successful round of set piece exercises called "Al Areen" near Bisha. Prince Abdullah then spoke of expanding the Guard to 35,000 men, and of building up to three mechanized "brigades": by 1989. While each of the present Saudi "brigades" have a strength closer to two reinforced motorized infantry battalions by Western Standards, rather than the four shown in the Saudi order of battle, they would have modern infantry support and antitank weapons.

Nevertheless, the bulk of the Guard remains a traditional tribal force. It is dominated by the 11,000-15,000 men in its *Firqa* (full-time tribal) and *Liwa* (part-time irregular) units. Many of its "troops" are actually retired military, descendants of the troops that fought with King Abd al-Aziz, or the sons or relatives of tribal leaders.

The Guard's manpower still serves to the age of 60-65, much of it is directly recruited and paid by tribal or regional chiefs, and many positions have a quasi-hereditary status. It is heavily recruited from the Otaiba and Mutair tribes (of the areas between Makkah and Riyadh and the northeast). It has only gradually recruited new and educated personnel who are loyal to a service rather than a given leader or subleader.

The National Guard is also more a means through which the royal family allocates funds to tribal and Bedouin leaders than a modern combat or internal security force. The Guard helps key princes maintain close relations with the tribes in each region. It has not evolved into a force that can deal with urban disorder, oil field security problems, or border security problems, although it can do a good job of dealing with ethnic and tribal divisions.

This makes the Guard politically vital to ensuring the integration of Saudi Arabia's tribes into its society, but it does not mean the Guard has found a clear military mission. As Table 5.6 shows, the Guard's current force structure and equipment also fail to provide air mobility and the specialized units necessary to deal with urban warfare and terrorist activities. Such specialized forces might come from the army and air force, but there seem to be no clear plans for this. If anything, creating new internal security forces under the Ministry of Interior means that there is yet another force competing for a role and manpower--particularly since this force is under Prince Naif, who is King Fahd's full brother and a member of a competing branch of the royal family.

This lack of a clear thrust behind the Guard's modernization also means that Saudi Arabia is not doing an adequate job of preparing for the low-level military threats that it may be more dangerous on a day-to-day basis than the major military threats building up on its borders. French and Pakistani aid can help in the interim, as can the small security units being built up under the Ministry of the Interior, but the Guard does more to weaken the Army's manpower pool than provide an added source of military capability. This again increases the importance of the Air Force in providing the reach, reaction capability, and firepower missing in Saudi ground forces.

## THE SAUDI NAVY

The Saudi Navy also has limited capability to absorb its modern equipment, and must depend heavily on air support. The Saudi navy faces a decade of expansion before it can become a true "two sea" force capable of covering both Saudi Arabia's Gulf and Red Sea coasts. Even then, it will depend heavily on air support, and ultimately on reinforcement by USCENTCOM and the British, French, and U.S. navies.

The current size of the Saudi Navy is shown in Table 5.8. It is now completing the construction of two major, fully modern naval bases at Jiddah and Jubail. When it deploys fully to the Red Sea, it will be divided into a Western Fleet with its main facilities at Jiddah and an Eastern Fleet with its main facilities at Al Qatif/Jubail. The Navy will also have facilities at Ras Tanura, Dammam, Yanbu, and Ras al Mishab.

The Development of Saudi Forces

## Table 5.8: The Current Structure of the Saudi Navy

**Total Manning**
    Active: 3,500
    Conscript: 0
    Reserve: 0

**Major Formations**

    Western Flotilla      HQ Jiddah
    Eastern Flotilla      HQ Al Qatif/Jubail

**Major Ships and Equipment**

- 4 X F-2000 French-made frigates with 8 Otomat surface-to-surface missile launchers, 26 Crotale surface-to-air missiles, one 100 mm surface gun and 4 40 mm twin AA guns, 6 torpedo tubes (4 X F-17p and 2 X Mk 46), Sea Tiger fire control system, and 1 SA-365 missile equipped helicopters. Some are not yet commissioned or fully operational.
- 4 X 732 ton Tacoma Guided missile corvettes with two Harpoon RGM-84 launchers with four missiles each, 1 76mm L62 Oto Melara gun, one 20mm Phalanx, two 40mm grenade launchers and 2X3 Mark 32 torpedo launchers.
- 9 X 384 ton Peterson Guided missile patrol boats with two Harpoon RGM-84 missile launchers with two missiles each, one 76 mm Oto Melera L-62 gun, one 20mm Phalanx, two 20 mm guns, and six Mark 32 torpedo tubes.
- 1 X 100 ton large ex-U.S. coast guard cutter with a 40mm gun.
- 3 X 160 ton Lurssen Jaguar patrol boats with 2 40mm guns and 4 21"/53mm torpedo tubes.
- 4 X 320 ton MSC-322 coastal minesweepers.
- 45 light patrol craft: 8 X 90 tons, 12 X 26 tons, and 15 X 25 tons, many now with Coastguard.
- 16 landing craft: 4 LCU, 8 U.S. LCM-6, and 4 LCVP.
- 24 AS-365N (Dauphine II) helicopters. 4 for the sea air rescue mission and 20 equipped with AS-15TT air-to-surface missiles.

**Major Orders:** 2 Mod Durance 10,500 ton logistic support ships with 4 X 40mm guns and 2 Dauphine helicopters each, 8 BH-7 hovercraft, 200 AS 15TT missiles, Otomat coastal defense missiles, and possibly two Atlantic maritime patrol aircraft.

**Key Bases and Facilities:** Western Flotilla is Headquartered at Jubail. Eastern Flotilla is headquartered at Al Qatfi/ Jubail. Main command facility is at Riyadh. Other bases include Ras Tanura, Dammam, Yanbu, and Ras al Mishab.

Source: Adapted by the author from IISS, DMS, and JCSS data bases

Like most Saudi facilities, the Saudi Navy's bases are exceptionally capable and well stocked. The main bases will eventually have up to five years of stocks on hand, and will have initial deliveries of two years' worth of inventory. The Jubail base is now the second largest naval base in the Gulf and stretches nearly eight miles along the coast. It already has its own desalinization facility, and is designed to be expandable up to 100% above its present capacity.

The Saudi Navy is procuring an automated logistic system similar to that in the other services, and with extensive modern command and control facilities. It will have this system operational, and hardened command centers at Riyadh, Jubail, and Jiddah, by the end of 1985. It will also acquire automated data links to the E-3A, with the ability to obtain data from the E-3A AWACS as it operates in the ocean surveillance mode. Other U.S. designed facilities include a meteorology laboratory, a Harpoon missile and Mark 46 torpedo maintenance facility, an advanced technical training school, and a Royal Naval Academy.

By the end of 1986, the Saudi Navy will have taken delivery on the rest of its major frigates and support craft and will have a 34-ship force, plus 24 missile-equipped helicopters. It is also seeking to expand its manpower from 2,800-3,500 to 4,500, is examining the possible purchase of mine hunting helicopters, and is discussing the possibility of joint exercises with the U.S., French, and Omani fleets in the Indian Ocean.

The major deliveries under the U.S. phase of the Saudi naval expansion effort are nearing completion. They are part of a now completed U.S.-managed Saudi Naval Expansion Plan (SNEP) that experienced severe political and quality problems and led the Saudis to turn to France for naval aid and equipment. Nevertheless, the U.S. will continue to support the U.S. equipment in the Saudi Navy and has delivered nine patrol gunboat, missile (PGG) craft, and four patrol chaser missile (PCG) craft. The Saudi Navy has also procured four coastal minesweepers, two large harbor tugs, two utility landing craft, and eight LCM-6 mechanized landing craft.

All nine PCGs, built by Peterson Builders, were operational at Jubail by mid 1984. These PCGs have computerized fire-control with twin Harpoon surface-to-surface missiles. They have both gas turbine and diesel engines and can go from 16 to 30 knots. They displace 385 tons and are 190 feet long. Each is also armed with Oto Melera 76mm guns, Mark 67 20mm cannon, Mark 19 40mm grenade launchers, Mark 2 81mm mortars, and the Vulcan/Phalanx close-in defense system. They have Sperry Mark 92 fire-control systems and full communications, radar, navigation, and IFF equipment.

Four U.S. supplied PCGs constructed by Tacoma Boatbuilding, are in active service with the Saudi Navy. These ships displace 732 tons and are armed with two Harpoon launchers with four missiles, plus the Mark 309 antisubmarine warfare system, two triple Mark 32 torpedo launchers, a 76mm gun, one 20mm Phalanx air defense gun and two 40 mm grenade launchers.

The U.S. has already delivered 162 Harpoon missiles, 28 Mark 46 torpedos, and ammunition for the 76mm guns and other weapons. The U.S. Navy Expansion Program team in Saudi Arabia now has about 25 military and civilian employees. Saudi Arabia has regularly renewed its contracts for

U.S. naval support, although it has turned to France as the major source of its naval ships and weapons.

The Saudi Navy first turned to France in 1980, in an effort to accelerate its modernization, obtain better support, and obtain more advanced ships than it could get from the U.S. It signed a modernization package costing $3.4 billion, and then signed another contract that effectively made the French the primary future source of support and modernization for future Saudi orders. The basic details of the systems the Saudi Navy has ordered from France are shown in Table 5.8.

The follow-on French program which began in 1982 is called Sawari (Mast) I. It has reached a minimum value of 14 billion French francs, or $1.9 billion, and may have escalated in cost to over $3 billion. It will deliver 4 missile-equipped 2,000-ton frigates and 24 missile-equipped helicopters, 2 fuel supply vessels, Otomat missiles for the frigates, AS-15 missiles for the helicopters, and additional training services. Saudi crews are already training in France to operate the vessels.

The end result of both U.S. and French sales will be a very powerful force in terms of equipment. It will create a two fleet Saudi Navy with ocean surveillance, coastal defense, anti-air, anti-surface, and anti-submarine capabilities and some of the most modern equipment in the world. At the same time, this equipment mix would normally require a force of at least 8,000 men, and probably close to 15,000.

The Saudi Navy, however, is unlikely to meet its goal of 4,500 men by the mid 1990s. Even with automation and foreign support, it will not be able to operate much of its equipment effectively before the early 1990s. Further, Saudi Arabia is already examining options that would expand it still further. Prince Sultan met with France's President Francois Mitterrand and Defense Minister Charles Hernu in May 1983. Only Saudi Arabia's reduced oil revenues seem to have prevented agreement on a new program called Sawari II.

Although some problems have surfaced, Saudi Arabia has been happier with the support it has obtained from the French Navy than with the support it has received from the French Army. This is reflected in its plans for the new Sawari II program, which would cost an additional $1.6-2.12 billion. The program would provide at least two more 2,000-ton frigates and possibly 4,000-ton frigates as well. It also may include mine sweeping helicopters and two AMD-Breguet Atlantic Nouvelle Generation (ANG) maritime patrol aircraft as the first step in the procurement of a much larger force. Other equipment may include lift and troop-carrying helicopters, surveillance and intelligence equipment, and special warfare equipment.

Even without Sawari II, the Saudi Navy may be in for serious "indigestion" problems during 1985-1995. It should be able to use some of its major combat ships effectively, and counterbalance the limited surface capabilities of regional powers like Iran, Iraq, South Yemen, and Ethiopia---

## The Development of Saudi Forces

all of which have severe naval readiness and modernization problems of their own. At the same time, the Saudi Navy will not be able to absorb what it already has on hand or in delivery, and new orders will simply increase the overload.

The role of advisor to the Saudi Navy may also become more difficult. It is unclear that the French Navy is ready for this challenge. It will soon have to transition to the role of training and supporting a major naval force that uses equipment that is not standard in the French Navy. As for the U.S. Navy, its advisory role will continue at a low level. The Saudi Navy added $31 million more worth of technical services contracts with the U.S. to its previous total of $49 million on 1 March 1983. The U.S. once informally proposed the sale of FFG-7 class frigates, but it is more likely that the U.S. Navy will be limited to providing support and training for its past deliveries.

This may be just as well for the U.S. Both the Saudi Navy and its principal advisor are in for a troubled decade. Certainly, the Saudi Navy's credibility will be heavily dependent on the $C^3I/BM$ data it receives from the E-3A AWACS, and the degree of air cover and attack support it can get from the Air Force. This will be particularly true of any missions in support of other GCC states. The Navy is making progress, but not enough to operate as an independent force. It will be heavily dependent on support from the Saudi Air Force in low to medium level contingencies and require support from the U.S. Navy in any major conflict.

### THE SAUDI AIR FORCE

All of these trends in defense spending, manpower, and the development of Saudi Arabia's other services help explain why Saudi Arabia has put so much effort into the expansion of the Saudi Air Force. The Air Force offers the fastest increase in deterrent capability per dollar and unit of skilled manpower. It is the only service that can cover Saudi Arabia's 2.3 million square kilometers of territory. It represents the investment most capable of cross reinforcement of the other services. It also has the most impact in terms of regional prestige, and the most credibility in terms of being able to support other GCC states or to operate with USCENTCOM forces in a major crisis.

It is not surprising, therefore, that Saudi Arabia has achieved its greatest success in this aspect of its military modernization program. The Saudi Air Force's current strength is shown in Table 5.9, and it is backed by excellent foreign support. Saudi Arabia has been able to draw on U.S. Air Force and contractor support to create some of the most modern air facilities in the world. No U.S. or NATO base has sheltering or hardening equal to the Saudi bases at Dhahran and Khamis Mushayt, and similar facilities will be built at all of Saudi Arabia's main operating bases.

As has been mentioned earlier, Saudi Arabia now performs most of the support and service for its Lockheed C-130s and its F-5E/F units have also

## The Development of Saudi Forces

reached proficiency levels approaching those of many Western squadrons, and Saudi Arabia has so far been remarkably successful in converting to its new F-15C/Ds. In fact, the Saudi Air Force's transition to the F-5E and F-15 has been smooth enough to indicate that the Saudis can absorb its new Tornados and effectively operate a modern air force of 250 combat aircraft by the early 1990s.

## The Development of Saudi Forces

Table 5.9: The Current Structure of the Saudi Air Force

**Total Manning**
    Active: 14,000
    Conscript: 0
    Reserve: 0

**Major Formations** (Squadrons/Aircraft)
- Total Combat Aircraft — 211
- Fighter Ground Attack: 6 Tornado GR.1, 3/62 F-5E and 24 F-5F — 92
- Air Defense: 3/60 F-15 C/D [a] — 60
- Air Defense/Attack: 1/23 Lightning F-53/T-55 [b] — 23
- Reconnaissance: 8 RF-5E (2 more kept in U.S. as attrition reserve). — 8
- AWACS: 1 E-3A delivered, 3 in process of delivery — 4
- OCU: 13 F-5B — 13
- Training: 2/39 BAC-167 — 38
- Helicopter: 2 squadrons with mix of 28 AB-206, 24 AB-205, and 33 AB-212, 4 Augusta AS-61A/61A4 — 89
- Transport: 3 squadrons with mix of 49 C-130E/H, 8 KC-130H, and 2 Jetstar. — 59
- In Reserve: 17 Lightning F-53, T-55; 12 Reims F-172G/H/L — 29
- Air Defense Command: New element of RSAF to control missile, gun and radar elements

**Major Orders:**
24 Tornado ADV air defense fighters; 42 Tornado GR.1 ground attack fighters; 30 Pilatus PC-9 trainers; 30 BAe Hawk trainers; 5 F-5E and 1 F-5F fighter attack; 4 E-3A AWACS; 1 B-747, 4 CN-235, and 40 C-212-200 transports; 8 KE-3 tankers; 2 ECM aircraft; 22 AB-212 and 8 KV-107 helicopters; 101 shipsets of F-15 conformal fuel tanks; and 600 AIM-7F, 995 AIM-9P, 671 AIM-9P, 100 Harpoon ASM, and 1,600 Maverick missiles.

**Key Weapons and Munitions:**
- Firestreak, Magic-R-550, Redtop, 2,367 AIM-9L and 660 AIM-9P air-to-air missiles.
- 2,000+ Maverick AGM-65 air-to-surface missiles. Mark 83 laser guided bombs, Snakeye, CBU laser guided bombs.
- AN-TPS 43, 43E, and 63 radars. Ferranti surveillance radars.
- Chucker II and two other types of target drone aircraft.
- Dragon microlight surveillance aircraft.

**Key Bases and Facilities:**
Headquarters at Riyadh, plus transportation, training, and E-3A/K-7 base. Major operating bases at Dhahran, Taif, Khamis Mushayt, and Tabuk. Dispersal bases at Sharurah and Hafr al-Batin. Support base at Jiddah. Normal deployments are 36 F-5B/E/F, 24 F-15C/D, and 3 AB-212 at Dhahran; 22 F-5E/F 16 F-15C/D and 3 AB-212 at Khamis Mushayt; 36 F-5E/F, 20 F-15 C/D, 8 RF-5E, 20 AB-206, 18 AB-212, and 3 SH-3D at Taif; 38 BAC 167, 21 C-130, 13 Cessna 172, and 3 AB-212 at Riyadh; 23 C-130 at Jiddah, and 23 Lightning and 3 AB-212 at Tabuk.

a. effective strength may be less than 13.
b. 2 more in U.S. as attrition reserve.
Source: Adapted by the author from IISS, DMS, and JCSS data bases.

While the role of the Saudi Air Force will be discussed in depth in Chapter VI, it is important to note just how well Saudi Arabia has shown it can operate today's most advanced fighters. The first of its 60 F-15C/Ds were operational in Dhahran by early 1983. A second squadron was formed at Taif by the end of 1983, and a third became operational at Khamis Mushayt in July 1983. By late 1984 and early 1985, the Saudi Air Force was conducting major joint exercises in both the Gulf and Red Sea Areas, and conducting Red-Blue or aggressor exercises similar to those employed by the U.S. Air Force.

While Saudi Arabia lacked the $C^3I$/BM systems, advanced avionics and electronics, munitions, and attack capabilities to match U.S. Air Force proficiency levels, it had demonstrated a high level of squadron readiness, had begun to perform much of its own major support on the F-5, and was providing Saudi support of the F-15 at its bases in Dhahran and Khamis Mushayt.

This experience is important because the Saudi Air Force badly needs to replace many of its existing aircraft. Its 38 BAC-167 trainers are only armed with 7.62mm machine guns. They no longer can be used in any combat function and soon will be too old to use as trainers. It bought its now obsolete Lightning fighters from the U.K. under pressure from former Secretary of Defense Robert S. McNamara--as part of a then covert three cornered deal designed to allow the U.K. to buy the F-111.[16] The Lightning never had the range, dual capability, avionics, and performance Saudi Arabia needs. The remaining 23 Lightnings are now at the end of their useful life, and should phase out in 1986-87.

More generally, Saudi Arabia will also face problems in replacing the Lightning, because it has informally stated that it does not plan to base its F-15s and Tornados in Tabuk--the only active air base near Israel. This means the Saudi Air Force must rely on its F-5Es, or some successor fighter, once the Lightnings phase out at one of its most important main combat bases. While Tabuk is the one active Saudi base near Israel, it is also a key base in defending Saudi air space near the upper Red Sea and Syria.

The Saudi F-5E-IIs and F-5F are advanced models equipped with INS, refueling probes, and the ability to fire Maverick (the F-5F can also fire laser guided bombs). They have proved to be excellent fighter aircraft. The oldest, however, are now thirteen years old and nearing the end of their useful life, and the F-5 production line is closed. The F-5s also are too short ranged and too limited in avionics and payload to cope with the kind of advanced threat aircraft being introduced into the region, or to deploy from one air base in support of another. They will have to gradually be phased into a training and light support role, and 20-30% of Saudi Arabia's F-5 strength is already devoted to full time training missions.

It is also important to note that Saudi Arabia badly needs the attack capabilities of the Tornado. The Saudi F-15C/Ds do an excellent job of meeting Saudi air defense requirements--particularly since Saudi Arabia obtained the conformal fuel tanks necessary to extend their range, tankers for refueling, and advanced air-to-air missiles as part of the U.S. Air Defense Enhancement Package sold to Saudi Arabia in 1982.

The Saudi F-15C/Ds, however, are currently virtually one mission aircraft. The Saudi Air Force cannot use the F-15 effectively in the air to ground role, although the F-15C/D has the potential ability to carry up to 10,960 lbs of air-to-ground ordnance without reducing its ability to carry ECM gear and its normal load of Sidewinder and Sparrow air defense missiles if it is equipped with modern attack munitions racks and dispensers.[17] While Saudi Arabia has modified the bomb racks for its F-15s so that they can carry a five bomb rack under each wing pylon, they are very high drag system and force the F-15 to fly at subsonic speeds until it releases its bombs.

The Saudi F-15C/Ds also lack the radar and bomb delivery computers and software necessary to use the F-15 in low altitude penetrations and to continuously calculate weapon release and impact point. This means they cannot use the automatic air to ground, electro-optically (EO) guided missile, or continuously displayed impact point (CDIP) modes of their heads up displays, or fly the kind of attack sortie that minimize expose to SAMs and enemy fighters and have relatively poor accuracy.

The Saudi Air Force does not have the MER-200 racks necessary to carry air-to-ground ordnance efficiently under the wings of the F-15s (each MER can carry six 500 lbs bombs and one MERs can be carried under each wing and another under the body in addition to the conformal fuel tanks), or the tangential racks that allow each of the two conformal fuel tanks under the body of the F-15 to carry 4,400 lbs of air to ground ordnance even when the F-15 is maneuvering at 5.5 G.[18]

Although the U.S. Air Force recommended that the Saudi Air Force be given a dual capable advanced fighter back in 1977, when it conducted the original studies leading to the U.S. sale of the F-15, U.S. domestic politics have precluded any sale of the bomb racks and the attack systems necessary to make the F-15C/D effective in this role. This means that approximately half of Saudi Arabia's total first line fighter strength has been unable to perform effective attack missions, or provide attack support to Saudi land and naval forces. This problem is also compounded by the fact that Saudi Arabia will need most of the advanced avionics being developed for the U.S. Air Force F-15C/D MSIP program to allow it to provide optimal air cover at long ranges.

The success of Saudi Air Force modernization has, therefore, depended on the Saudi Air Force and on its eventually acquiring either a modern dual capable fighter or full dual capability for its F-15s. It is this requirement which has triggered Saudi Arabia's original arms request to the U.S., and which explains why it turned so quickly to Britain for Tornado attack fighters when the U.S. rejected the sale.

[1] Data are based on excerpts of the new Saudi national budget, and the Wall Street Journal, March 22, 1985.

[2] Washington Post, July 23, 1985

[3] Unless otherwise specified, the military data quoted here are taken from the relevant country sections of the IISS, Military Balance, 1984-1985; CIA, The World Factbook, 1983; and Mark Heller, Dov Tamari and Zeev Eytan, The Middle East Military Balance, 1984, Jaffe Center for Strategic Studies, Tel Aviv University, Tel Aviv, 1985.)

[4] Figures are based on estimates taken from the CIA, The World Factbook, 1984, pp. 199-200.

[5] Jane's Defense Weekly, May 15, 1985; New York Times, April 28, 1985.

[6] Does not include the 500+ men in the ELF-1 AWACS detachment.

[7] $C^3I/BM$ = command, control, communication, and intelligence/battle management system.

[8] The Economist, January 21, 1984, p. 34

[9] Wall Street Journal, October 8, 1985, p.35.

[10] Los Angeles Times, March 7, 1986, p. 2-14

[11] Economist, January 21, 1984, p. 34.

[12] Jane's Defense Weekly, 14 June, 1986, p. 1075.

[13] Ironically, the Congress was notified of an actual Saudi tank purchase on 2 August 1983. The purchase, however, was of 100 M-60A3 tanks and not 1,200 M-1s. The M-60A3 sale had long been in train, and had no significant impact on the regional balance in the Gulf, much less the Arab-Israeli conflict.

[14] The Saudi Air Defense Corps renewed its contract for technical assistance support from Raytheon for its IHawk surface-to-air missiles in May, 1986. This contract has been running since 1976, and was renewed for three years at a cost of $518 million. Jane's Defense Weekly, 7 June, 1986, p. 1019.

[15] For an interesting Israeli view of the role of the National Guard, see Mordechai Abir, "Saudi Security and Military Endeavor", The Jerusalem Quarterly, No. 33, Fall 1984, pp. 79-94

[16] See the author's, The Gulf and the Search for Strategic Stability, pp 122-126.

[17] R. D. M. Furlong, "Operational Aspects of the F-15 Eagle, International Defense Review, 3/1975, pp. 129-139

18 Ibid, and Aviation Week and Space Technology, April 26, 1982, p. 27

## VI. THE PIVOTAL ROLE OF THE SAUDI AIR FORCE

Saudi Arabia can afford delays in the modernization of its other services, but it cannot afford delays in the modernization of its Air Force. The Kingdom is forced to make air power the pivotal element of its efforts to create a national and regional deterrent. The Saudi Air Force is the only way Saudi Arabia can create a defense capability that can deter its larger neighbors, and make up for its limited supplies of skilled manpower.

At the same time, the Saudi Air Force must rely on small numbers of high performance aircraft. Saudi Arabia can at best support a first line combat force of about 200-220 aircraft. It has no hope of operating an Air Force with the air strength of its larger neighbors. Iraq, for example, has over 530 combat aircraft rather than any effort to match threat air strength. Syria has 650, and Iran had over 400 fighters--plus 150 combat helicopters--before the Shah's fall.

Saudi Arabia must use its Air Force to defend a large territory with widely scattered population centers and oil facilities. While the Kingdom is most vulnerable on its Gulf coast, it faces threats on all its borders. The Air Force is also the only Saudi military force that can rapidly deploy in support of its smaller neighbors, particularly the oil rich states of Kuwait and the UAE.

Saudi access to first line force structure aircraft, sensors, $C^3I$ assets, and air munitions is essential if the kingdom is to create a convincing deterrent to attacks on its own territory and the prestige and capability to build the military unity of the Gulf Cooperation Council. In fact, the real issue shaping Saudi Arabia's military modernization is not whether it needs advanced fighter aircraft, but whether it can obtain the right mix of fighter aircraft and foreign support to serve its own interests, those of regional stability, and indirectly those of the West.

The answer to these question is dependent on the extent to which the Saudi request is a proper extension of its new $C^3I/BM$ systems, of its existing force structure, and of its need to combine improved air defense coverage with an improved attack capability to compensate for Saudi and GCC weakness in land forces.

## SAUDI ARABIA'S NEED FOR AIR DEFENSE

In order to make this evaluation, it is necessary to understand that the current thrust of Saudi Air Force modernization is the product of joint Saudi and western planning that began shortly after the fall of the Shah of Iran, and which resulted in detailed force plans during the last days of the Carter Administration.

The Iran-Iraq War was the major catalyst affecting this joint planning process. The need to give Saudi Arabia effective air power took on new meaning when Iran retaliated against Iraq's invasion by launching its first major strikes against Iraqi oil facilities in December, 1980. These Iranian air and naval attacks demonstrated that a few sea and air strikes could destroy all of Iraq's oil-loading facilities in the Gulf and halt up to 3.2 MMBD of oil exports to the West. They transformed the climate of U.S. and Saudi planning from planning for worst case scenarios to one of dealing with immediate threats.

The Saudi Air Force and U.S. Air Force had already begun a joint feasibility study to examine the options for modernizing the Saudi fighter force and air defense system as the result of Saudi Arabia's desire for a new first line fighter and the fall of the Shah of Iran. The U.S. agreed to provide Saudi Arabia with a detailed plan for the modernization of its air force in April, 1980, although the study was given relatively low priority because of the fear of domestic political problems with the supporters of Israel in an election year. The study was initiated in September, 1980, in the midst of President Carter's campaign for re-election, and was completed in December 1980--after the Iran-Iraq War had begun, and Ronald Reagan had defeated President Carter.

The U.S. study was not formally released to the Saudis until March, 1981, in order to give the new Reagan Administration time to take a policy position on its recommendations. By this time, however, the Saudis had been fully aware of the study's contents for nearly four months, and both the Saudis and the USAF had already used it to plan a more comprehensive approach to Saudi air defense. This plan called for major improvements in Saudi Arabia's ability to use its F-15s for air defense, for a new Saudi air control and warning (AC&W) system, and for improved Saudi air attack capabilities.

The study focused on basic problems that still shape Saudi Arabian defense planning and are likely to do so for the foreseeable future. Saudi Arabia must concentrate on defending key population centers and economic facilities. Saudi territory too large for comprehensive air defense of all its air space or borders. Saudi Arabia's land borders are 4,537 Km long and it has an additional coastline of 2,510 Km. It's total territory is 2.3 million

## The Pivotal Role of the Saudi Air Force

square kilometers. To put this in perspective, Iraqi territory totals only 445,000 square kilometers, and Iranian territory totals only 1.6 million kilometers. The total air space of all the other GCC is only about 321,000 kilometers of air space, and both Yemens cover 518,000 square kilometers. To put it differently, Saudi Arabia must defend an air space roughly 110 times that of Israel.[1]

Saudi Arabia is also forced to disperse its air assets to a relatively few air bases, and these bases are too far apart to support each other without the use of long range fighters and refueling. Saudi Arabia only can afford to provide one major air base to cover each threatened area of the country. Saudi Arabia now bases its first line combat aircraft in four key air bases: in *Dharhan*--which covers its main oil facilities and key Gulf cities; in *Taif*--which covers Saudi Arabia's main port, its holy cities, and key agricultural and population areas in the lower Red Sea area, in *Khamis Mushayt*, which covers the Yemens and which can reinforce the air strip at Sharurah, and at *Tabuk*, which must cover the upper Red Sea, Jordan, Syria, and Israel, and potentially help reinforce the air field at *Hafr al Batin*--which is the Saudi Army's key defense point to meet any threat from the Northern Gulf.

These few bases can only provide limited cross reinforcement capability, even if they refuel and rearm at Riyadh, unless Saudi squadrons change their deployments from one base to another. It is 650 nautical miles (NM) from Khamis Mushayt to Dhahran. It is 443 NM from Khamis Mushayt to Riyadh, it is 736 NM from Dhahran to Tabuk, 590 NM from Riyadh to Tabuk, 394 NM from Riyadh to Jiddah, and 465 NM from Tabuk to Taif. In practical terms, this means that refueled F-5 fighters cannot safely reinforce any main Saudi combat operating base from any other base. Even F-15s and Tornados cannot provide the loiter time necessary to provide air defense coverage from any other base without the added fuel provided by conformal fuel tanks and additional in flight refueling.

By reducing its air coverage of one front to strengthen the defense of another, Saudi Arabia can develop a limited concentration of force. Even so, Riyadh is 250 NM from Dhahran and 394 NM from Jiddah. This means that the only additional major Saudi air base that can cover the oil fields at Dhahran is outside the range where an F-5 can provide effective air defense without refueling, and that an F-15 without conformal fuel tanks will still lack the loiter time to fly effective CAP missions. Even Khamis Mushayt and Taif are 230 NM apart--too far for effective fighter cross reinforcement much beyond the other base.

Saudi Arabia also faces the problem it may have to move combat aircraft forward from their normal bases to military air strips in the same general area. Saudi Arabia does not have the air strength to permanently base combat aircraft at its key dispersal strips at Hafr al-Batin, or Sharurah.

These size and coverage problems mean the Saudi Air Force will be strained to defend its vital areas even with the most advanced fighters, support system, and C³I/BM capabilities. Saudi Arabia cannot, however, rely simply on point defense. It must be able to maintain a perimeter defense against the Yemens, Iraq, Jordan, Syria, and Israel, and be able to concentrate its air forces to defend its "strategic axis". This strategic axis extends south from the Saudi oil facilities and cities on the Gulf (Jubail, Juaymah, Ras Tanura, and Dammam) to cover the capital at Riyadh, Makkah, Taif, and the key coastal ports of Jiddah and Yanbu. It adds still another requirement for high performance fighters.

It is particularly important that the Saudi Air Force should be able to defend key population centers. Saudi Arabia's modernization has made Saudi cities acutely dependent on a limited number of water, desalinization, gas, and electric power facilities and on the use of a limited number of airports for food supplies. As is the case with the Saudi oil fields, past economies of scale have led Saudi Arabia to buy extremely large one-of-a-kind facilities. An air attack on such facilities could deprive a given Saudi city in the core area of essential human services, and this vulnerability is growing steadily as more and more of the Saudi population become dependent on modern urban utilities.

The key interest that unites both the West and Saudi Arabia, however, is the need to protect Saudi Arabia's oil facilities. The total oil area covers about 850,000 square miles, but Saudi oil facilities are concentrated largely in a 300-by-100 mile "core area". Although Saudi Arabia has 47 oil fields scattered from west to east in the Gulf and near the Gulf coast, it's core area ranges along a 250-mile axis that extends from the offshore field at Safaniya (the world's largest offshore field) to Ras Tanura and Berri on the coast to the southern tip of the Ghawar oil field (the world's largest onshore field). If various peripheral territories are included, the core area covers 10,000 square miles, or twice the area of the state of Connecticut. Depending on world demand, the facilities in this area must produce, distribute, and ship up to 9.6 million barrels a day and 3,500 million barrels a year.

Aside from the offshore portion, almost all of this core area is located on dry exposed plains with no natural cover or protection. During most of the year, oil targets are easy to locate by air, and there are long periods during the day when such Saudi oil facilities produce enough image contrast for even first-generation air-to-surface missiles to be effective. Many such facilities are vulnerable to area bombing or to heliborne raids, and many key facilities are vulnerable to a single bomb and a few are even vulnerable to light, shoulder-fired anti tank rockets like the RPG-9 or to light anti tank guided missiles like Milan or Dragon.

The terrain favors terrorist raids and air and sea operations. The coastal area is covered by shallow sand flats and small hummocks that severely limit rapid movement by armored vehicles except along a limited number of roads. The shoreline is generally too shallow for amphibious landings, and the waterfront can shift back and forth by several miles in some places, depending upon the wind and the tide. Salt flats are common and can become impassable with even limited rain. Coastal marshes often merge with the sea and create major mobility problems. Away from the coast, the dunes near the shore give way to the Jafura sand desert.

This desert terrain, a lack of water and facilities, and temperatures well over 100 degrees limit the ability to rapidly seize the Saudi oil fields. In contrast, a successful air attack or amphibious assault on the oil facilities within 40 miles of the Saudi coast--or even a raid on Abqaiq, Ras Tanura, and their sea islands--could destroy or seize most of Saudi Arabia's oil-loading and/or processing capabilities.

Weather conditions complicate the problem of providing air defense for the core area. In the summer, prevailing northwest winds, called "shamal," create summer sandstorms. Line squalls are common, and visibility at the ocean surface can drop to zero. Thermal currents create a ducting phenomenon that can "blind" or obscure most radars. By taking advantage of these weather conditions, an airborne or seaborne attacker could hit Saudi oil facilities at a time when radars on the ground would be virtually "blind" and have difficulty operating surface-based sensors and missile defenses.

Critical targets for air or sea attack are scattered throughout the core area. Most of the roughly 650 onshore wells in Saudi Arabia require water injection to maintain pressurization. While the individual wells are scattered targets, a more limited series of air attacks on key high output wells would have a considerable effect on Saudi oil production, as would destruction of key components of the water-injection system.

Similarly, much of the Berri field is under water and feeds into 11 offshore platforms that regulate four to six wells each. Eight more offshore platforms maintain the water well and injection system. These are connected by 25 miles of undersea pipeline ranging from 10 to 24 inches. Much of this piping is vulnerable to sabotage by ordinary scuba divers. Each of these platforms is an attractive target, and carefully planned air strikes against a few of them could halt production from the entire Berri field. An attack on Saudi Arabia's 12 offshore drilling and workover rigs could also affect production, in the long run. So could an attack on the small island of Abu Ali, which is 20 miles off the Saudi coast, and where several main well and water-injection facilities are centralized, in addition to those for gas-oil separation.

The Saudi oil and gas collection system is vulnerable to air attack. Crude petroleum from all the Saudi fields, and a considerable amount of gas, converge on Ras Tanura through well over 1,200 miles of pipe. Pipe diameters fluctuate between 12 and 48 inches, and many increase dramatically in size as lines pass gathering points. The overall security problems in protecting such facilities are less difficult, however, than the total pipeline mileage indicates. The length of the major pipelines in the Kingdom exceeds 6,160 miles, and many redundant or back-up links exist.

Large pipes are difficult to destroy and small ones are easy to repair or replace. More than eight pipes share the same route from Abqaiq to the Qatif junction, five continue to the coast, and four pipes parallel the seaboard south of Khursaniyah. This redundancy makes them resistant to air attack and sabotage.

There are, however, many vulnerable choke points. Saudi production depends on up to 12.5 MMBD of processed, nonpotable saline water. A single plant, the Quarayyah Seawater Plant, processes more than 4.2 MMBD of filtered and conditioned sea water. This is a highly vulnerable "one-of-a-kind" facility that could take up to two years to replace.

The Saudi power plants that service the fields are extremely large, and the loss of key plants could shut down large parts of Saudi oil operations. Destruction of the 400+ megawatt facility at Ras Tanura might severely limit shipments from the port, as would hitting key power distribution points. The electric power available in the eastern Province increased from 1,200 megawatt in 1976 to 2,928 megawatt in 1981, and four new 400 megawatt plants have been built at Ghazlan, but there are still only a limited number of high-payoff targets.

The evolving Saudi power system is also highly dependent on a single central computer facility located in Dammam. A successful attack on this facility might paralyze key aspects of Saudi oil production for months. A wide range of other computer centers controlling key oil facilities are equally vulnerable, and their destruction or seizure could have serious effects. These include key computerized facilities such as the EXPEC Computer Center and the Supervisory Control and Data Acquisition (SCADA) installation which provides remote management of more than 90 wells and platforms for the Berri oil field.

The Saudi oil pipeline system is now over 19,000 kilometers long and depends on less than 50 major pumping stations, dotted anywhere from 5 to 50 miles apart. One new pumping station at Abqaiq alone processes 1.7 MMBD. One natural gas generator activates three pumping stations with three pumps each east of Abqaiq, and all nine pumps would be inoperative if the turbine failed. Other sensitive facilities are even more critical, and a loss of power to these facilities, or their sabotage, would virtually halt Saudi oil production.

These power plants that provide electrical current for a comparatively limited number of gas-oil separators (GOSPs), desalting facilities, pumps, and other purposes are controlled from a single dispatch center at Dhahran. If this center were destroyed, the ability to distribute power in the Eastern Province would be severely limited. Ain Dar is the gathering place for all petroleum produced in northern Ghawar, plus Khurais on the west flank. Lines from Ain Dar and Haradh (in southern Ghawar) funnel into Abqaiq. Even more critical junctions lie farther east at Dhahran, Qatif, and Ras Tanura, and each of these centers has special vulnerabilities.

A new major "target complex" has been created at Shedgum at the north end of the Ghawar field, the center of the new transpeninsular gas and oil pipelines. This center has a new gas plant which processes 1.5 billion cubic feet a day, and a twin plant which was completed at Uthmaniyah in 1983. Each of the four gas modules at Shedgum is a target that processes 375 million cubic feet a day, and 237 kilometers of vulnerable high-pressure gas piping feeds the facility. The combination of gas, oil, and pipeline facilities--many of which use one-of-a-kind equipment with long replacement lead times--will eventually make Shedgum a target almost as attractive as Ras Tanura or Juaymah.

The new petrocity at Jubail, at the southern end of the Berri field, is also an important target complex. Jubail combines a new coastal population center with plants using gas fuel and feedstock. It can process over 270,000 barrels per day (BPD) in gas products, as can Yanbu on the Red Sea. Jubail and Yaubu will not be as attractive as the previous targets, but they will still require Saudi Arabia to extend its air defense perimeter.

Saudi oil terminals are vulnerable, as Iraq's recent attacks on Iran's much better dispersed facilities at Kharg Island has demonstrated. About 2,700 to 4,000 ships a year call at the marine terminals at Ras Tanura, Juaymah, and Yanbu. The main terminal facilities that serve all Saudi oil fields occupy a 50-mile arc along Tarut Bay between Ras Tanura and Al Khobar. They shipped nearly 80% of Saudi production in 1984, with about 5% going to the Ras Tanura refinery and the rest going to the crude oil export terminals.

The Ras Tanura refinery and loading facility plays a critical role in ensuring the smooth flow of Saudi oil production. The refinery has a capacity of 450,000 BPD and processed 416,421 BPD of oil and 254,300 BPD of natural gas liquids (NGL) during the peak export period in 1981. Equally critical are the stabilization plants on adjoining land, particularly those at Abqaiq, which remove poisonous and corrosive hydrogen sulfide from crude petroleum before it is piped aboard tankers.

Crude oil and refined products awaiting shipment are stored in four great tank farms at Abqaiq, Dhahran, Ras Tanura, and the new port complex at Juaymah. The latter location includes 5 containers holding 1.5 million barrels each, and 14 that hold 1.25 million barrels each. Including pipelines and smaller storage facilities, the location stores up to 30 million barrels. The major storage facilities are extremely vulnerable to air or other attack.

Ras Tanura is the world's foremost oil port. It shipped over 175 million barrels of oil and gas product in 1984, and has shipped peak levels of 256 million barrels. It can berth 18 tankers. Its T-shaped northern loading pier can berth 6 tankers simultaneously, and its south pier can handle 4 more. An artificial "sea island," a mile farther out, can accommodate five supertankers up to 200,000 tons deadweight, as propane gas (LPG) facilities have "layered" tanks and pipelines over the existing crude oil facilities and placed LPG tanks near new 1.5 MMBD oil storage tanks, there is an acute risk that a major air attack could cause a massive "chain reaction" of explosions. Ras Tanura's loading facility may be the most attractive conventional bombing target in the world.

ARAMCO off-loads Arabian light crude oil at Juaymah, and Juaymah's capacity is steadily expanding. In addition to a new 10 kilometer offshore trestle and LPG twin-berth loading facility, Juaymah has single-point moorings (SPM) in deep water about 11 kilometers offshore. These can handle 500,000 deadweight ton (dwt) tankers with 95 foot drafts (currently the world's largest). The Ras Tanura terminal is limited to 65 foot drafts.

Juaymah can simultaneously provide several grades of oil to six vessels. A pair of 56 inch pipes now connects the oil storage tanks on shore with a giant metering platform in 45 feet of water, and this platform can shunt oil to waiting ships at rates of over 140,000 barrels per hour. Juaymah started loading LPG in 1980, and its 30,000-barrel-per-hour loading facilities can handle 200,000-cubic-meter tankers. The key facilities at Juaymah are concentrated, exposed, and might also "chain react" as the result of a large scale air attack. The throughput capacity at these two ports serviced 4,067 tankers in the peak year of 1981, and loaded 3.2 billion barrels of crude oil product and natural gas liquids.

These Saudi defense problems are compounded by several other factors. Many of the facilities in the Saudi core area are pressurized systems. Unless Saudi Arabia can protect its oil systems with confidence, it must respond to a major threat of air attack by shutting in--or depressurizing--a wide range of facilities. Saudi Arabia also cannot produce more oil or gas than any given choke point allows, and most of these choke points depend on a few items of tightly grouped and specially fabricated equipment that were designed for maximum economy of scale and were located without any regard to vulnerability to military weapons. There is little or no redundancy or in-country repair capability for such equipment, and most such key items are not readily available on the world market. They must be specially fabricated to order, which can take up to two years.

This Saudi vulnerability extends beyond Saudi territory. Saudi Arabia is dependent on the free movement of tankers to ship its oil. Virtually all of these tankers now move in and out of the Gulf through its narrow eastern opening at the Strait of Hormuz. Approximately 50 to 65 ships move through the Strait each day. About 25 to 40 of these ships are loaded outbound tankers. During peak production periods in 1981, an average of 11 tankers, carrying 8.9 MMBD of gas, oil, and petroleum products, came from Saudi Arabia. Another 0.2 MMBD, or 2.2% of total Saudi production, was shipped from the refinery at Bahrain.

Saudi Arabia now has only two possible alternatives to the Gulf route--both of which have vulnerabilities to air and sea attack of their own. The first such alternative has little practical value. It is the "Tapline" pipeline, with

470,000 BPD capacity, that runs from Dhahran and Qaisumah through Jordan, Syria, and Lebanon to a port and 17,500 BPD refinery south of Sidon.

The "Tapline" was built in 1950, and it requires exceptionally large amounts of manpower and service by modern standards. It is not economic in comparison with tanker shipment through the Gulf, and it has been made even less economic through the lack of modernization and service that has resulted from the long series of disputes over transit fees.

The Tapline's operation has also been highly erratic. It intermittently shipped about 50,000-60,000 BPD from 1979 to 1982, a total of 20-29 million barrels--only about 0.62-0.83% of Saudi crude production. The main impact of the pipeline is that roughly 36,000 BPD has been shipped to support a refinery in Jordan. Even when the rest of the line has operated, it has done little more than support a refinery in Sidon. There have been no significant exports to the West. In fact, the Tapline is virtually useless. The link to Lebanon was cut during the fighting in 1981, and by the Israeli invasion in 1982, and has never flowed since. While the line could be restored to 470,000 BPD, major investment would be needed to upgrade the line, repair port facilities, improve efficiency, and improve security against sabotage. ARAMCO officials privately regard such an effort as a waste of money.

The second--and far more meaningful--alternative is a pair of 1,170 kilometer "East-West" pipelines from Shedgum in eastern Saudi Arabia to the new petrocity at Yanbu on the Red Sea. One of these lines, the "Petroline", is a 48 inch pipeline with 1.85 MMBD normal capacity, and a peak capacity of 2.35 MMBD. The other is a 26-30 inch oil gas line with an initial capacity of 270,000 of gas liquids. A second oil line will be added, with a capacity of between 1.15 and 1.35 MMBD. This line runs parallel to the existing line, and will be completed in March, 1987. It was rushed ahead at a cost of $600 million because of the threat of an escalation of the Iran-Iraq War.

There is also a strong possibility that Iraq will build a full pipeline to the Red Sea, rather than simply connect to the Saudi line. This, however, would shift Saudi vulnerability to an increasingly unstable Red Sea area, and strain the limited Saudi air defense forces based at Tabuk.

Saudi Arabia would also still be heavily dependent on the free movement of tankers through the Gulf and on its ability to persuade tanker owners and captains that they can safely move through Gulf waters. The new pipelines will make the Kingdom dependent on convincing such owners and captains that they can safely move through the Red Sea.

The new pipelines and pumping stations along the route to Yanbu also open up new opportunities for sabotage and long-range air strikes that would bypass Saudi Arabia's $C^3I/BM$ and E-3As and other air defenses along the Gulf coast. The large 130,000 barrel an hour shipping pumps at each of

## The Pivotal Role of the Saudi Air Force

Yanbu's three berths would be good targets. So would the polyethylene plant. The new complex at Yanbu forces the small Saudi Air Force to defend two coastal areas more than 1,000 miles apart, and this defense burden will increase when Iraq connects to the Saudi Petroline in 1986. It will be further heightened if Iraq goes on to construct its own Red Sea pipeline to a new facility near Yanbu. Current plans indicate this line will have a capacity of over 1 MMBD, and it could link Saudi Arabia to any future attacks on Iraq.

Finally, Saudi Arabia also plans to provide air and maritime defense for the other GCC states. Iran's air attacks on Kuwait, and air raids on tankers east of Qatar, have shown that an attacker might well choose to put pressure on Saudi Arabia by attacks on urban facilities in each of the smaller conservative Gulf states, or on the wider range of oil facilities located in a broad arc along the southern Gulf from Kuwait to Oman. As a result, Saudi Arabia publicly declared in June, 1986, that it would help defend Kuwait against an Iraqi attack.

Like the Saudi facilities, the other major GCC oil facilities have generally been designed as one-of-a-kind installations on the basis of purely economic criteria. They tend to use extremely large individual equipment items, without redundancy, to achieve economies of scale. The destruction of a few targets in the form of pumping stations, gas-oil separators, or other key equipment could lead to major cuts in production and in the loss of equipment that can take up to two years to replace fully.

## THE IMPACT OF SAUDI VULNERABILITY ON SAUDI MILITARY MODERNIZATION

These vulnerabilities explain why the U.S. and Saudi Arabia paid so much attention to improving Saudi air defenses after the Shah's fall in 1979, why Saudi Arabia pressed the U.S. so hard for the sale of advanced air combat equipment, and why the Kingdom was so quick to turn to Britain when the sale fell through. Saudi Arabia's mix of vulnerabilities created the need for an exceptionally efficient and credible Saudi air defense system. To be effective as a deterrent or defense, this system had to be able to guard against sudden raids or saturation attacks on a 24 hour basis and to offer broad coverage over a wide area.

While the most critical part of the Saudi core area in the northern oil fields occupies only 10,000 square miles, the total critical air space to be defended in northern Saudi Arabia must include its cities in the area, and this creates a critical air space of over 30,000 square miles. If the offshore fields and Neutral Zone are included, the area to be defended becomes at least 70,000 square miles, and the relevant airspace of friendly Gulf states adds another 35,000 square miles. Moreover, the Saudi defense problem is not simply one of detecting and intercepting against offshore and shoreline facilities, which means that ships have to be tracked and characterized.

## The Pivotal Role of the Saudi Air Force

The Saudi Air Force faces major resource constraints in creating an effective air defense. It must rely on limited numbers of fighter aircraft, sensors, and surface-to-air missiles to cover this territory in a way that does not lock its forces into a "one-front" defense that can only cover the Gulf. It must deal with special terrain problems. No mountains or high points exist near the Gulf coast. The terrain rises an average of only 5 feet for every mile from the high-water line until it reaches the Summan Plateau, which is too far inland to be useful in covering the Gulf. As a result, ground based Saudi radars in the Gulf area can only provide about 30-50 nautical miles of low-altitude coverage or 2-4 minutes of warning.

Saudi Arabia's resource constraints mean its air defense system must rely on the Kingdom's five existing major air bases, and their related sectoral radar and ground-based air defense centers, to cover the entire country. The air base at Dhahran is especially critical in defending against Iran. It must cover all the major oil facilities in the Gulf, the Saudi cities in the area, and those of the other conservative Gulf states.

These five main Saudi air bases do have Improved Hawk surface-to-air missiles and 35 mm anti aircraft (AA) guns. They are also being sheltered with aircraft shelters and underground command facilities superior to those in NATO. The first such shelters were completed at Dhahran in late 1981. Similar facilities have now been completed at Khamis Mushayt, and will eventually be completed at Tabuk and the other major Saudi bases.

The Saudi shelters allow four aircraft to be worked on in each shelter, with a fifth on quick-reaction alert (QRA). They are twin-door shelters with shielded, camouflaged entrances and exits and four taxiways each, and they can house air and service crews for 30 days without resupply. Dispersion is excellent, and the taxiways from each shelter are long enough to serve as runways. The Saudi munitions and fuel facilities are equally well sheltered, as are certain classified service facilities as well as the battle management or sector coordinating center (SCC).

Saudi bases can fully shelter two squadrons in this manner, and this capability is being expanded and supplemented by dummy shelters. The base construction teams also have a rapid runway repair capability, and Saudi Arabia is constructing dummy shelters and expanding its taxiways and alternative air strips to help deter the use of penetrators or air field suppression munitions.

This base design reduces Saudi Arabia's problems in relying on a single base per sector, and the Air Force can deploy to civil air fields as a dispersal measure. Saudi Arabia has 55 additional airfields with paved runway and taxiway facilities, 5 with runways over 3,659 meters, 22 with runways over 2,440-3,659 meters, and 28 with runways less than 2,440 meters.[2]

Passive and active base defenses cannot, however, protect Saudi airfields against new air base suppression techniques, such as earth penetrators, cluster or modular glide bombs with minelets, or sensor weapons. They cannot protect such bases against updated versions of the hard-point munitions that Israel first used against Arab targets in 1973, and which are now becoming commercially available in Western Europe. They also cannot fully protect all the key facilities on these bases against conventional munitions delivered with the accuracy Israel demonstrated in its attack on the Iraqi Osirak reactor.

All these factors shaped Saudi perceptions in 1979 and 1980. Saudi planners had to consider the risk that Saudi Arabia might lose a forward air base like Dhahran, and most of its fixed ground radars in a given area, by the late 1980s or early 1990s. This situation imposed requirements almost as demanding as the sensor coverage problem discussed earlier. The Saudis also faced the problem of deploying and operating a reasonable number of individual radars. Even if their air bases could survive, their effectiveness depended on land-based radars. Virtually all of these had to be sited in fixed and exposed positions dictated by the need to maximize low-altitude coverage. Both U.S. and Saudi planners concluded that no expansion of Saudi Arabia's land-based radar system could eliminate the problems of vulnerability and the possible "blinding" of a large part of each base's defense zone by anti-radiation missile (ARM) attacks on its radars.

The main radar at Dhahran, for example, was permanently fixed on an artificial hill, and many other main radars were similarly fixed in a position to allow rapid data transmission to each of the five sector operating centers serving the local air base and army air defense control center (ADC). Even the base at Khamis Mushayt--whose main radar is located on a sawed off mountain top had limited low altitude surveillance capabilities.

Further, Saudi planners had to consider that if they lost the use of the base at Dhahran, they would have to use remote sensors and the air bases at Taif and Khamis Mushayt to cover the Gulf, which would mean flying fighter missions of 600-800 miles. This is a longer operational radius than Israeli fighters had to fly in attacking the Osirak reactor, and is roughly equivalent to attempting to defend Chicago from Wichita or Dallas or London from Athens. Any such Saudi sorties would also be meaningless without local radar coverage, since the reinforcements would be too blind to be effective.

## THE NEED FOR THE AIR DEFENSE ENHANCEMENT PACKAGE

These factors shaped the Air Defense Enhancement Package the USAF and Saudi Arabia developed in the late 1970s and early 1980s. The details of this package are shown in Table 6.1, and the package represented the only logical way of making Saudi Arabia's fighters effective enough to meet its complex and demanding air defense system requirements.

## The Pivotal Role of the Saudi Air Force

Table 6.1: The Saudi Air Defense Enhancement Package

- o <u>5 E-3A AWACS Aircraft:</u> The aircraft were to be delivered within four years. The procurement cost of $3.7 billion included three years of spares and support equipment, plus logistical, maintenance, training, and technical support.[a] The E-3A is highly sophisticated and requires 170 aircrew and 350 maintenance personnel for 7 days of 24 hour flight. The initial requirement for U.S. support manning was 480 contractors and 30 U.S. government personnel.

- o <u>Ground Defense Environment</u>: 22 major system elements of hardened command and control facilities, data processing, and display equipment, new radars, and ground entry stations were to be procured as the result of a 2 year USAF study over a period of six years at a cost of $2.1 billion. This was the first major modernization of the Saudi air control and warning system since the 1960s. The RSAF was to operate 10 sites, and the Civil Aviation was to operate 12.

- o <u>6-8 KC-707 or KE-3A Tankers:</u> The tankers were to be delivered over 40-44 months at a total cost of $2.4 billion or $120 million each.[b] The price included two years of spares plus training, maintenance and support. Saudi Arabia also obtained the option to buy two more tankers. The aircraft required 96 aircrew and 320 contractor support personnel during the initial phase of delivery. They had parts, engine, and air frame commonality with the E-3A.

- o <u>101 Sets of Conformal Fuel Tanks or "Fast Kits":</u> These were to be delivered over a 27 month period at a total cost of $110 million, or $900,000 per unit. The cost included related spares; support for the F-15; and equipment, training, and publications. Saudi Arabia informally agreed that the F-15s using the tanks were to be deployed at Dhahran, Taif, and Khamis Mushayt.

- o <u>1,177 AIM-9L Missiles:</u> These new air-to-air missiles supplemented Saudi Arabia's existing stocks of AIM-9F-3 and AIM-7F missiles, and were to be delivered over 30 months as the USAF replaced them with stocks of AIM-9M missiles. The total cost was $200 million, or $98,000 per missile. The price included 42 months of contractor training, maintenance, and logistic support. No new Saudi personnel were required. Nine U.S. contractor personnel were required during the first three years of conversion.

Source: Department of Defense

a. The total price of the AWACS portion of the program was $5.8 billion. The price for 5 aircraft was $1.2 billion (including software modifications, engineering change orders, and an avionics integration laboratory). The price of spares was $536 million, support equipment was $44 million, contractor support and training were $1.3 billion, and miscellaneous program expenses were $664 billion. The price for upgrading the ground radar network was $2.0 billion.
b. The total price for the tankers was $2.4 billion. This included $962 million for 8 aircraft ($120 million each, and included extensive engineering, design, and test work to make the aircraft into a tanker), $316 million for spares, $34 million for support, $700 million for contractor support and training, and $387 million for miscellaneous program expenses.

Ambitious as the Air Defense Enhancement Package was in many ways, it was a vital step in dealing with the problems posed by the threat from Iran. The collapse of the Shah's regime had added 432 fighters to the threat

## The Pivotal Role of the Saudi Air Force

against Saudi Arabia, including 188 F-4D/Es, 166 F-5E/Fs, and 77 F-14As. While many Iranian fighters ceased to be fully operational once U.S. support was withdrawn or were lost in the Iran-Iraq War, the U.S. and Saudi Arabia had to plan for Iranian re-equipment and for the possibility that Iraq might come under hostile rule.

The Carter administration had never considered this possibility when it pledged not to deploy additional advanced air defense weapons to Saudi Arabia in 1978, and far more was involved than force numbers. As a staff report which the Senate Foreign Relations Committee issued on the E-3A sale pointed out, the Iranian threat posed an incredibly demanding problem in defending the Saudi core area.[3]

Defending the marine terminals at Ras Tanura and Juaymah was particularly difficult. These terminals trans-shipped over 90% of Saudi crude oil exports, and were situated at points on Saudi Arabia's coast that faced the Iranian air bases at Bushihr and Shiraz. The key processing and distribution facilities at Abqaiq and Saudi Arabia's multibillion dollar natural gas development project, the Master Gas System, were only minutes further inland.

This combination of geography and threat created an extremely difficult time and distance problem for Saudi and U.S. military planners, and remains a driving factor behind Saudi Arabia's effort to upgrade its F-15C/Ds, its purchase of the Tornado and its request for additional F-15s.

An Iranian F-4, flying at 200 feet and 480 knots, can bomb the Sea Island at Ras Tanura or the offshore mooring stations at Juaymah with a payload of over 5,000 lbs of munitions only 16 minutes after taking off from Bushihr. If such an enemy fighter loiters peacefully within Iranian airspace over the Gulf and then suddenly veers directly for Ras Tanura, the Saudi reaction time is reduced to 8-9 minutes.

An F-4, however, is a relatively slow-flying and limited-range attack fighter. It was clear even in 1981 that the threat aircraft of the mid-1980s were likely to be faster, have much more lethal avionics and munitions, and have greater range and endurance. This has since been proven all too clearly by Soviet deployment of the new Su-24, Su-27, and MiG-29 fighters discussed in Chapter IV, which have the ability to carry conformal or internal attack munitions at supersonic speeds and can substantially cut the warning and reaction time available to Saudi forces.

In addressing this problem, both Saudi and U.S. Air Force planners had to take into account the fact that intercepting an enemy air attack involved more than the intercept itself. The Saudi Air Force had to be able to perform several other tasks to provide an effective air defense for its cities and oil fields. These tasks are summarized in Table 6.2, and they still describe the basic tasks the Saudi Air Defense system must perform.

<u>Table 6.2: The Military Tasks Necessary for Effective Saudi Air Defense</u>

## The Pivotal Role of the Saudi Air Force

- <u>Detection</u>: Recognize that a potentially hostile target is airborne. This task must be accomplished using radar. Radar detection, however, is a function of target altitude, size, and range. The higher the target, the greater the distance at which it can be "seen" by the radar; the larger the target, the better the chances become of receiving a usable radar return. Radar operates on a "line of sight" principle, and a low-flying fighter aircraft is screened by the curvature of the earth at ranges beyond 25-30 miles. Only by elevating the antenna or sensor system could Saudi Arabia extend the horizons of its radars significantly beyond this distance.

- <u>Identification</u>: Identify all aircraft. Once a radar operator "sees" a target on his scope, he must attempt to determine its identity or at least to categorize it as "potentially" or "probably" hostile. In wartime, one can assume that any target detected coming from a certain area is probably hostile. In peacetime, however, a specified sector of airspace is likely to be filled with numerous commercial, private, and military aircraft. By using identification of friend or foe and by cross-referencing filed flight plans and pilots' radioed position reports, a certain number of targets will remain unknown, however, and the determination of possible threats must rest on a more subjective reading of likely intent.

- <u>Decision</u>. Decide whether to intercept. A decision order an intercept of an unidentified target can be pegged to an arbitrary rule: Any "unknown" aircraft enters a certain zone will be intercepted. This is the approach used by the United States, which has established an Air Defense Intercept Zone, or ADIZ, which extends up to 300 miles beyond its east and west coasts. In the Saudi case, geography does not permit the luxury of such an extensive air defense zone. It had to be kept within its borders or the limits of territorial waters in the Gulf and the Red Sea. The Gulf is just over 100 miles wide opposite Dhahran, and major air routes--connecting Baghdad, Bahrain, Abu Dhabi, Tehran, and other major cities to the northwest and southeast--lie just miles off the Saudi Gulf coast. To be sure of intercepting any unidentified aircraft flying as close as 100 miles from the oil fields, the RSAF had to be ready to fly around the clock.

- <u>Combat Air Patrol and Scramble</u>: Have sufficient forces to maintain combat air patrol and to scramble. Saudi F-15 sorties take 3-5 minutes to launch. Fighter reaction time could be cut by several minutes by keeping the pilots in the fighter cockpit with the aircraft engines running, or by using new quick-reaction laser gyros, but Saudi F-15s normally must fly combat air patrol and loiter in the air to be sure of being able to react in time.

- <u>Intercept</u>: Make successful intercepts. Once fighters are airborne, they must be able to engage the enemy, which means both closing on the target (Dhahran air base is about 30 miles from Ras Tanura) and maneuvering into a position from which short-range missiles can be fired. As a general rule, it takes much longer to get maneuver behind an attacker means that the defending fighter must expose itself to hostile fighters. While an RSAF F-15 could also launch radar-guided AIM-7 Sparrow missiles from beyond visual range, it must then track the enemy until the missile hits. This method would mean tying up the Saudi fighter while other hostile fighters could fly through or attack the Saudi aircraft.

## The Pivotal Role of the Saudi Air Force

These requirements made it plain that the Saudi Air Defense Enhancement Package had (1) to improve the Saudi sensor and air control and warning systems, (2) to improve Saudi head-on intercept capability, and (3) to improve Saudi air endurance and deployment capability. Without an airborne sensor platform as capable as the E-3A, the Saudi Air Force would have to rely on fixed, ground-based radars in the Dhahran-Juaymah area.

Even once an Iranian F-4 was detected, it would still take the Saudi Air Force 12-15 minutes to intercept it east of Ras Tanura, and again, US and Saudi planners had to consider that the fighters of the mid-1980s would be much faster and to be able to penetrate at lower altitudes using low conformal munitions.

This meant Iranian fighters could be over the target within 3 minutes of the time Saudi ground radars could detect them. Even under optimal assumptions, a Saudi intercept based on warning from ground radars would then occur 10 minutes too late. This then would force the Saudis to defend the target with only surface-to-air missiles and anti aircraft guns.

While the Ras Tanura-Juaymah-Dhahran area was defended by army air defense battalions made up of Hawk and Crotale missile batteries and 35 mm Oerlikon guns, the Hawk batteries normally need about 10 minutes warning to fire effectively, and the Crotale and Oerlikon weapons systems would probably be able to fire only as the attacker left the target. Even with extensive warning available with the AWACS, and additional short range systems like the Shahine, the Saudis could not afford to rely on ground-based defenses.

The theoretical sensor range of Saudi Arabia's land based air defenses had no practical meaning in the face of low altitude threats. The Hawk could theoretically detect fighter sized targets at a range of 120 Km, the Shahines and Crotales could detect such targets at 70 Kms, and the 35 mm Oerlikon guns at ranges of up to 40 Kms. At low altitudes, however, detection ranges rarely exceed 30 Kms, and the ground-based radars associated with each air defense weapon must work perfectly in detecting small, low-altitude targets to provide even 3 minutes of warning.

In practice, however, ground-based radars operating in the Gulf experience serious performance degradations about 75% of the time due to the temperature gradient between the air mass above the hot desert in Saudi Arabia's Eastern Province and the cooler air over the Gulf. This phenomenon is known as "ducting" and often impedes target detection until the enemy fighter is virtually on top of a ground-based radar. While Ferranti has developed technology that can detect its existence, only an air borne platform can take advantage of the fact that radar coverage will continue at other altitudes even when ducting shortens radar range at sea level.

The potential threats to Saudi Arabia's other key border areas are only marginally less demanding. For example, the South Yemeni Air Force which attacked in the Sharurah area as recently as 1973, has since been equipped with Soviet MiG-21s and Su-20/22s, and has more advanced aircraft on order. Its fighters have the combat radius to strike at most targets in southwest Saudi Arabia, although Makkah, Riyadh, and the oil fields in the east are too distant for current Yemeni fighters.

The key Saudi base defending against the Yemens at Khamis Mushayt is supported by ground-based radars, as is the base at Dhahran. Ground-based radar coverage at Khamis Mushayt and Sharurah is limited, however, because of the mountainous terrain. This potentially allows low flying Yemeni fighters to penetrate deeply into Saudi Arabia without detection. Saudi officials were already highly impressed with the U.S. AWACS' performance during a deployment in 1979, and with its superior capability to look over the mountains into South Yemen and provide advance warning of aerial activity during a burst of fighting between North and South Yemen.

SELECTING THE E-3A

All of these factors contributed to the selection of the E-3A. Work done by USAF Studies and Analysis in the "Air Feasibility Study" of July 1980 concluded that it would take a minimum of 48 large, fixed, and vulnerable radars to cover all of Saudi Arabia's borders without an airborne warning and control system. These radars would still leave major penetration gaps, provide only 20-30 miles of low-altitude coverage, and give only token maritime surveillance capability.

The USAF also found it would take 11-15 E-2C Hawkeyes and 34 ground radars to provide minimal coverage of the Gulf. Even this force could not provide 24-hour surveillance of Saudi Arabia's oil facilities for a 7-day period. Moreover, the E-2C could not effectively control Saudi fighters in the face of a large-scale attack over Saudi airspace, which is over 100 times the airspace of Israel, and the E-2C had electronic intelligence (ELINT) capabilities that would be useful in Saudi land and air offensives against Israel.

In contrast, the USAF estimated that 5 E-3A and 18 ground radar installations could provide a single-front coverage of the oil facilities and cities in the Gulf--even under the assumption that one E-3A aircraft would be in a constant overhaul and refit status, another would be in regular maintenance, and three would be fully operational. Each E-3A could provide a minimum of 175 nautical miles of low-altitude and maritime coverage and extend warning of an air attack on the Gulf front to a minimum of 7 minutes.

This warning did not solve all of Saudi Arabia's $C^3I$ problems, but it was sufficient to allow the E-3A to vector in Saudi fighters in time to make at least one pass on an attacker before it hit a critical oil facility. It was sufficient to allow the Saudi Army to vector the acquisition radars of its Hawk batteries to enable them to engage effectively and would allow the F-

## The Pivotal Role of the Saudi Air Force

5E to play a back up role. Further, 5 AWACS could cover the entire front over the Gulf.

USAF planners estimated that even this small number of E-3As would also be survivable in defending the forward area over the Gulf front because there would be virtually none of the terrain masking at low altitudes that exists on Saudi Arabia's western border with Israel and Jordan, and the E-3As could operate far enough to the rear to withdraw if attacked. Moreover, the long flight times and limited air density of the Gulf would allow the E-3As to know they were under attack in time to react. Saudi fighters could then cover the AWACS; the E-3A could retreat or it could "pop down" below the coverage of most fighter radars.

An individual E-3A could also fly for 11 hours before refueling. This long flight time allowed a crew of 17 men per aircraft (13 in the actual electronics role) to carry out the air control and warning mission more efficiently. USAF studies showed that the E-3A had more than three times the endurance of a force using the E-2C plus added ground radars, and would require far fewer technicians.

Most important, the E-3A had the radar power and side lobe suppression to be highly jam-resistant, to track large, medium-altitude targets at 360 mile ranges, and to identify even small cross-section fighters flying at altitudes above 200 feet at ranges of up to 175 miles ("cross-section" refers to the minimal radar profile of the aircraft, usually expressed in square meters).

These features allowed the AWACS to fly about 50-100 miles inland from the Gulf coast and still provide a minimum of 5 minutes warning before the required moment of intercept. Each AWACS could independently track up to 300 targets and accept data on up to 200 more from another AWACS or ground radars. Under ideal circumstances an E-3A could engage and characterize up to 240 targets in terms of size, altitude, identity, speed, and direction. It could also direct 6-8 closely spaced intercepts and 3-6 simultaneous intercepts.

### THE ISSUE OF TECHNOLOGY TRANSFER

The USAF also concluded that the configuration of the AWACS sold to Saudi Arabia could omit the frequency-agile, secure voice and the jam-resistant joint tactical information distribution system (JTIDS) necessary to manage an air battle of the density that would be common in a NATO-Warsaw Pact or Arab-Israeli environment. The USAF was able to tailor the E-3A to meet Saudi needs, concluding that such a configuration would be able to avoid creating a potential threat of technology loss to the U.S.--or military threat to Israel--but still be able to handle most Gulf threats through the late 1980s.

This "tailoring" sets an important precedent for current and future U.S. and European efforts to meet Saudi Arabia's current arms needs from the West, and it is interesting to note the details:

## The Pivotal Role of the Saudi Air Force

o No advanced secure digital data links such as the JTIDS were to be provided.
o The computer software was tailored to limit capability against U.S. made fighters of the kind flown by the USAF and Israel.
o Training and software support were optimized for defensive missions in the Gulf and Red Sea areas only.
o Major overhauls, annual service, and all modifications were to be performed in the U.S.

At the same time, Saudi Arabia agreed not to fly the E-3A outside its own borders without U.S. consent, to protect all classified systems using U.S. procedures, to U.S. approval of its security plan, to the computer software remaining U.S. property, to a new information security agreement, and to limiting access to all sensitive documentation. It agreed to share all E-3A data and to refuse to allow third country personnel to fly on, modify, or maintain the E-3A--or to have access to E-3A data without U.S. consent.

Equally important, the U.S. estimated that the first E-3A configured to Saudi needs could be delivered in 1986, and the other four at two-month intervals thereafter. The Saudis would thus be able to operate without U.S. crew support as early as 1988-1989, and such Saudi operation of the E-3A was absolutely critical. Any other long-term arrangement for deployment of the AWACS or basing of U.S. combat forces in Saudi Arabia would have presented impossible political problems in terms of Saudi sovereignty, internal political stability, ability to lead the other conservative Gulf states, and provocation of hostile reactions from the more radical Arab states.

The U.S. also concluded that it could sell the AWACS to Saudi Arabia with little fear that it would be hijacked or operated in ways hostile to U.S. interests. The E-3A aircraft could not be flown for more than a month without the full cooperation of the U.S. support personnel in Saudi Arabia, and all depot-level maintenance would have to be done in the U.S. Because of sensitive radar design and operating requirements, the key equipment on the AWACS could not be operated without U.S. support for more than a few days.

The E-3A's mean time before service is required to deal with major system failures is 27.4 hours. The variant of AWACS sold to Saudi Arabia could meet all Saudi requirements and still be left vulnerable to sophisticated U.S. communications jamming and to jamming by Israel. The E-3A could also be sold without the sophisticated ECM gear or any of the ELINT capability of the four Grumman E-2C Hawkeyes now in Israel.

The sale of the E-3A presented little risk of technical compromise because of its age and the special character of its technology. The AWACS was first flown in 1971. Only 10 of the more than 1,000 AWACS technical manuals were classified, none was classified higher than "secret," and all had already had broad release in NATO. The basic radar design of the E-3A was not sensitive--only the equipment used to produce it. This design could not be compromised by reverse engineering through acquisition of the aircraft. The production equipment involved vast amounts of software that would not leave U.S. hands and that represented an investment in special manufacturing capabilities of well over $1 billion.

In fact, since the first E-3A would not be delivered to Saudi Arabia until 1986, it seemed likely that the Soviets would be in the process of deploying their new AWACS variant of the Il-76 Candid by the time U.S. aircraft deliveries ended. The rest of the electronics in the E-3A dated back to the late 1960s and would also be well within Soviet technical capabilities at the time the aircraft was transferred to Saudi Arabia. The E-3A's basic ECM defense and its key characteristics--operating frequencies, pulse repetition rates, pulse widths, side lobe characteristics, effective radiated power, antenna gain, transmitter power, scan rates, and receiver dynamic range--had already been acquired by Soviet ELINT systems.

THE IMPACT OF THE AIM-9L MISSILE

The sale of 1,177 AIM-9L missiles contributed to the Air Defense Enhancement Package by giving Saudi Arabia an all-aspect air-to-air missile with the shoot-down capability that it could use in "head-on" intercepts against low-flying attackers, without having to sacrifice the time and probability of intercept necessary to maneuver into a long, stern chase or "dogfight" position. Such a capability was essential given the limited warning time the AWACS could provide and the need for each Saudi F-15 to be able to engage more than one attacking fighter per encounter.

Although the Saudis already had 2,000 second-generation AIM-9J air-to-air missiles, 600 fourth-generation AIM-9-P3s, and large stocks of "product-improved" AIM-7F radar-guided Sparrows, these missiles lacked the multi-aspect capability to enable the F-15 to avoid time consuming and complex fighter maneuvers in meeting an attacking aircraft and lacked the energy of maneuver to be lethal at very low altitudes. While the sale of the AIM-9L did create some risk of technology transfer, no other missile in the U.S. inventory had the requisite capabilities, and the U.S. gained compensating advantages.

PROVIDING ENHANCED RANGE AND REFUELING CAPABILITY

The sale of 101 sets of conformal fuel tanks or "FAST" kits (two tanks per aircraft) for Saudi Arabia's F-15 fighters solved another problem. It gave individual Saudi fighters the endurance and range to maintain combat air patrol with a comparatively limited number of fighters and the ability to mass in the Gulf area for short periods even if Saudi Arabia should lose most of the facilities on its air base at Dhahran. The FAST kits gave the Saudi F-15 about 1,500 gallons more fuel per set. They extended the F-15s radius by 79% in the air-superiority mode and 93% in the interdiction mode and increased endurance by 65% in the CAP mode. They also allowed the F-15 to retain its capability to carry four AIM-7F radar-guided missiles.

This increase in range was essential if Saudi Arabia was to use the F-15 in anything other than a relatively short-range point defense mode. Without the FAST tanks, the F-15 remained a relatively short-legged and low-endurance fighter. It was for this reason that the U.S. Air Force studies in 1978, which had led the U.S. to encourage Saudi Arabia to buy the F-15 rather than the F-14 or F-18, had recommended that Saudi Arabia be given these tanks. The kits also had the advantage that they could be provided in a form that would not allow Saudi F-15s to carry offensive attack munitions without U.S. technical support, since Saudi Arabia could not modify them unilaterally in ways that would allow a loaded F-15 to sustain its speed and maneuverability.

## THE NEED FOR A FULL $C^3I/BM$ SYSTEM: THE GENESIS OF "PEACE SHIELD"

The precise interface among the Saudi version of the E-3A, its air defense guns, and its Shahine and Improved Hawk missiles was not decided upon when the USAF study was completed, and was still under study when the U.S. Congress debated the Air Defense Enhancement Package. In fact, the actual award of the first phase of the Peace Shield contract was not made until late February, 1985. Nevertheless, it was planned from the outset that Saudi Arabia would acquire data terminals at each major air defense site with digital processing capability and commercial encryption gear similar to the U.S. TADIL C.

The radar problems discussed earlier made it essential that Saudi Arabia's limited fighter strength be able to "net" its fighters and Hawk surface-to-air missiles through the six ground-based sector coordinating centers and army air defense control centers (ADCs), so that the data collected by AWACS could be interpreted and transformed to provide the Hawk units with the search data they needed to back up the fighter screen. This combination of air and ground defenses could protect its Hawk against much of the ECM gear likely to be common in the Gulf in the mid-1980s. Similar terminals planned for selected Saudi, short-range air defense systems were too limited in range, $C^3$ flexibility, and electronics sophistication to benefit greatly from AWACS data.

As the Saudi Air Defense Enhancement Package progressed through the Pentagon, the U.S. added further features to improve the Saudi $C^3$ system and make optimal use of the improvements planned in Saudi Arabia's sector operating centers and General Operating Center (GOC) near Riyadh. These efforts drew on the Peace Hawk VII study and other studies begun after the sale of the F-15 to Saudi Arabia in 1978.

Such an upgrading was vital. Many elements of the existing Saudi $C^3$ system dated back to the abortive Anglo-U.S. air defense system of the

1960s, and major improvements were required to make effective use of the AWACS. These improvements included new hardened command and control facilities, new data-processing and display equipment, links to the new al-Thaqib package of Shahine missiles and other land based defenses France sold the Saudi Army, and improvements to the ground radar surveillance network through replacement of existing radars and the addition of new radar sites to extend coverage. Special ground entry stations also had to be provided to allow optimal communications with the AWACS.

In any case, a contract award went to a consortium headed by Boeing Corporation in March, 1985, for the first phase of the Peace Shield command, control, communications, and intelligence ($C^3I$) system. This contract was worth about $1.18 billion, and the entire system was costed at roughly $3.7 billion. The deal also illustrated the commercial as well as the strategic importance of Western military ties to Saudi Arabia.

About 75% of the Peace Shield contract went to subcontractors, including Westinghouse (displays and software), ITT (communications engineering and long haul communications), Standard Electric of the FRG (communications switching and mobile telephones), BDM (engineering support), Frank E. Basil (personnel support services), General Electric (radar installation services), and the Saudi Amoudi Group (in country support).

The award involved three contracts to be managed by different elements of the USAF. One was for $848 million to be managed by the USAF Electronic Systems Division for equipment and system integration, a second was for $331 million to be managed by the Air Force Logistics Command for organizational and intermediate maintenance, personnel support services, and on the job training, and the third was for $3 million to be managed by Air Force Training Command for initial operations and maintenance training. Separate contracts had already gone to General Electric for radars ($330 million), and to other firms for design, training support, etc. The Boeing awards also did not include an estimated $900 million in additional construction contracts.

Interestingly enough, the award involved a new feature in U.S. and Saudi relations. The bidding companies had to offer a 35% offset for programs to create a high technology industrial infrastructure in Saudi Arabia. These will fund increased Saudization of the Kingdom's defense support as well as such activities as jet engine overhaul and long distance telecommunications. It seems likely that most future U.S.-Saudi military contracts will have similar features.[4]

The main features of the final Peace Shield system are shown in Figure VI-1, and they included:

o A fully integrated network of control centers.

## The Pivotal Role of the Saudi Air Force

- o 17 modified "minimally attended" AN/FPS-117 ground based surveillance radars based on the "Seek Igloo" radars the USAF used in Alaska as part of the NORAD defense system.
- o Upgrading of the centralized Command Operations Center that already exists in Riyadh.
- o Building of two Base Operations Centers to coordinate country-wide air activities such as aerial refueling and search and rescue.
- o Creation of five Sector Command and Operations Centers with fully automated computer capabilities. Each center will be located at a major Saudi Air Base and is capable of surveillance, control, and management of air operations for a given sector and is linked to the COC in Riyadh.
- o Eventual growth to provide improved data links and $C^3I$ links to the Air Defense Corps Improved Hawk missiles and to the Shahines in the al-Thaqib air defense package of 1984.

Peace Shield is specifically designed for defense against attacks from across the Gulf, attacks by Yemen, and attacks from across the Red Sea. Like the AWACS, it will be heavily dependent on continued U.S. technical support throughout the 1980s and uses U.S. communications systems and operating concepts. This will help ensure that Saudi air units will be directly interoperable with USCENTCOM forces in spite of the Saudi purchase of Tornado. It also reduces the risk that Saudi air units can be used unilaterally against Israel.

The Peace Shield air defense system has the further advantage that it can be modified to interface with the ships in the Saudi Navy. It can link their radars and surface-to-air missiles to Saudi Arabia's other air defenses and conduct joint sea-air operations against any seaborne attacking force. The E-3A has 35-108 nautical miles of range in the maritime surveillance mode against metal ships of 40 feet or more length, operating in a normal sea. Given the probable proficiency of the Saudi Navy in the 1980s, such a battle-management system may be essential if Saudi Arabia is to use its new vessels with any effectiveness.

Although it is not part of the present Peace Shield, Saudi Arabia will also have the option of using the AWACS to monitor transponders on Saudi Army vehicles and helicopters and potentially those of the National Guard. This capability would allow the Saudi Army and Air Force air support for the land forces defending the Saudi oil fields and other critical facilities. Finally, Peace Shield has a significant potential improvement in the ability to coordinate Saudi defenses against guerrilla or larger-scale terrorist attacks. Such combinations of ground, helicopter, and fighter operations are exceedingly difficult to coordinate even for Western armies, and the AWACS provides a potential battle-management and communications center for the kind of small-scale but delicate operation that would be involved in actions against guerrillas and terrorists.

## THE ADVANTAGES TO THE WEST

Each of these elements of the 1981 Saudi Air Defense Enhancement Package contributed to a system that would upgrade Saudi air defense capabilities and lay the cornerstone of the deterrent Saudi Arabia had sought since the early 1960s. The West had a great deal more to gain from the sale, however, than simply strengthening Saudi ability to protect the oil fields. In the course of the negotiations, the U.S. acquired potential over-the-horizon reinforcement capability far more important than the full time bases it had sought at the end of the Carter Administration, and which was far better suited to the region.

In fact, the advantages to the West of the U.S. sale of the Air Enhancement Package closely parallel those that will be provided by the British sale of the Tornado and advanced air munitions. They are listed in Table 6.3, and provide a detailed illustration of the ways in which Western and Saudi objectives can coincide.

### Table 6.3: The Advantages to the U.S. of the Saudi Air Defense Enhancement Package of 1982

- o The Air Defense Enhancement Package gave Saudi Arabia a credible local deterrent and defense capability against the most probable regional threats that could affect its security or the West's supplies of oil.
- o The package gave Saudi Arabia the military power and status it needed to act as a counter weight to Iran and Iraq. It meant that the other smaller Gulf states could turn to Saudi Arabia for a credible strengthening of their air defense. It was an ideal form of "linkage" between Saudi Arabia and the smaller conservative Gulf states, which had something like 50% of Saudi Arabia's oil production capacity. It gave them the defensive coverage they need without threatening them and was an ideal means of uniting them behind the Gulf Cooperation Council and its nascent National Security Council.
- o The package was a partial solution to the long-standing problem of convincing Saudi Arabia, particularly the Saudi military, that the country's military expenditures would be effective and would not jeopardize Saudi sovereignty, and that the Saudi government had not miscalculated in maintaining its ties to the U.S. No single factor had been more important in destabilizing Third World military forces than the perception that their governments have failed to provide a credible basis for national defense and for maintaining national strength and independence.
- o The package avoided formal military ties between the West and the conservative Gulf states, which half a century of Arab nationalism, the Arab-Israeli conflict, and the political history of Saudi Arabia had made untenable. It provided the U.S. with a means of strengthening Saudi Arabia while simultaneously preserving Saudi Arabian sovereignty and stability.
- o The resulting Saudi-U.S. agreement gave the U.S. continued direct access to the information gathered by the AWACS while retaining control over transfers to third nations. Direct digital look down links were to be available to the U.S.; these included data not only from the AWACS, but from the full range of sensors that make up the Saudi air defense system, many of which were not otherwise available.

## The Pivotal Role of the Saudi Air Force

- o The resulting improvement in Saudi capabilities greatly reduced the risk of having to send U.S. or other Western forces to deal with local or low-level threats. It also decreased the destabilizing effects of any such U.S. deployment without a threat great enough to unite the conservative Gulf states and moderate Arab opinion in support of such U.S. intervention.
- o At the same time, the Air Defense Enhancement Package gave the U.S. the ability to deploy up to two wings, or roughly 140 USAF fighters, to support Saudi Arabia and the conservative Gulf states in an emergency. In fact, each main Saudi air base had the basic support equipment for 70 U.S. F-15 fighters in addition to supplies for its own F-15s. The package meant that Saudi Arabia would have all the necessary basing, service facilities, refueling capability, parts, and key munitions in place to accept over-the-horizon reinforcement from USAF F-15 fighters. No conceivable improvement in U.S. airlift or USAF rapid deployment and "bare basing" capability could come close to giving the U.S. this rapid and effective reinforcement capability.
- o The package allowed the U.S. Navy to use its airpower effectively in the Gulf. For example, U.S. carriers were too vulnerable to deploy into the Gulf, during the start of the Iran-Iraq War in 1980. The TF-70 Task Force the U.S. sent to the region had to stay in the Gulf of Oman because of the threat posed by Iranian forces, and carrier-based fighters lacked the range and AC&W capability to overcome the problem of having to deploy from outside the Gulf.
- o None of the key elements of the system would be operable without U.S. support throughout their useful life.
- o The facilities that would become part of the Saudi system would also help to strengthen U.S. ability to deploy forces from the eastern Mediterranean and project them as far east as Pakistan in those contingencies that threatened both U.S. and Saudi interests. No conceivable buildup of U.S. strategic mobility, or of U.S. staging bases in Egypt, Turkey, Oman, Somalia, or Kenya, could act as a substitute for such facilities in Saudi Arabia. The closest other U.S. facility in the region was at Diego Garcia, which is as far from the western Gulf as is Dublin, Ireland.
- o The systems' maritime mode provided a potential method of solving many of the problems in Saudi Arabia's naval defense and the modernization of its naval forces and in improving the coordination of its diverse U.S. and French vessels and equipment.
- o The package solved the critical problem of financing the defense of the Gulf by having Saudi Arabia assume the full cost of the system. The Air Defense Enhancement Package was projected to cost $8.5 billion in current dollars, with only three years of spares and support. Even this cost estimate depended on exceptionally efficient U.S. assistance in managing the construction and training effort. Allowing for a 10-year life-cycle, systems growth, and normal cost growth, the true cost was projected to be at least $15 billion. The package also built on past and future U.S. military assistance expenditures, which then totaled $33-38 billion, some $20-25 billion of which was still to be delivered, and it meant the dollars were to be spent in the U.S. rather than in France or Britain. At least 50% of this expenditure was to be on construction, and some 80% of it will contribute directly to the defense of the Gulf's oil exports. The U.S. lacked the financial resources and the forces to create any credible alternative.
- o The package was inherently defensive in character and did not threaten other regional powers. At the same time, the Saudi ground stations, SAM defenses, E-3A, and other elements of the package could be upgraded in the future in direct proportion to any growth in the threat.

The Pivotal Role of the Saudi Air Force

SETTING THE STAGE FOR THE ARMS SALE CRISIS OF 1985-1986

These developments shaped the pattern of Saudi Air Force modernization up to the time of Saudi Arabia's request to the U.S. for additional F-15 aircraft, air munitions, and other force improvements. They represented major progress. In fact the merits of Air Defense Enhancement Package of 1981-1982 have already been demonstrated. U.S.-flown E-3As worked with Saudi fighters to shoot down Iranian F-4s that intruded into Saudi space on June 5th, 1984. The Saudi F-15s were vectored to their target by USAF E-3As, and were refueled by USAF tankers, and the incident unquestionably played a major role in deterring Iranian attacks on tankers moving through the Southern Gulf.[5]

At the same time, the Air Defense Enhancement Package and Peace Shield failed to deal with several key issues. First, it did not provide Saudi Arabia with a balanced mix of air defense and air attack capabilities. Second, they did not provide the combat aircraft numbers Saudi Arabia would need in the future. Finally, they made a number of serious compromises in the $C^3I$ equipment it made available to the Kingdom.

The limits in $C^3I$ capability were least important. The Saudi configuration of the E-3A lacked the JTIDS, secure digital data links, the Have Quick and Seek Talk frequency agile voice links, and the five extra data-display consoles in the USAF versions of the E-3A. This made the Saudi E-3As potentially vulnerable to the level of ECM-capability electronic warfare that neighboring powers could acquire in the late 1980s.

This risk, however, has largely been addressed in the years that have followed, and the U.S. has found ways of tailoring its technology transfer to meet Saudi needs without compromising key Western military technology or increasing the threat to Israel[6]:

o Secure radio teletype equipment and software for the E-3A were ordered in May, 1983, that were superior to commercially available software, and compatible with the NATO data links, but which did not present a risk of technology loss to the U.S.

o UHF relay equipment was ordered at the same time. This will greatly improve data transfer over the use of the E-3A's radios, but it is oriented to the ground links in the Peace Shield system and will not threaten Israel.

o Color display monitors were added in September, 1984, when the USAF ordered such equipment. These help compensate for the limited number of stations on the Saudi AWACS.

o Infrared countermeasure sets were added similar to those installed on other Saudi aircraft in August, 1984. These were provided in the "tailored technology" form releasable to other foreign countries.

## The Pivotal Role of the Saudi Air Force

These compromises present some military risks to Saudi Arabia in a high intensity conflict, although Britain may now be able to supply some of the missing capabilities as part of its follow-on sales to the Tornado package. The lack of JTIDS digital data link and Have Quick secure voice link reduces the capability of the Saudi E-3A to handle high-density attacks because of the need to rely on slower communications with less security. The Saudis have been sold sanitized, Modes 1, 2, and 3, identification of friend and foe (IFF) capability, rather than U.S. military secure Mode 4 IFF cryptographic equipment. The Saudi E-3As are not to be provided with the computer software needed for TADIL C data links with interceptors or U.S. Navy F-14 fighters; and the Saudi F-15s still lack the advanced air-intercept program support package to be provided on U.S. F-15C/Ds.

Even with these limitations, however, the revised Saudi air defense system offers Western and Saudi air forces a substantial degree of interoperability. For example, the Saudi E-3As will be able to transmit or receive digital data using TADIL A high frequency links with the U.S. AWACS, U.S. Navy ships, or air force ground-based tactical reporting and control posts (provided the formatted data is not passed through the incompatible Saudi and U.S. cryptography equipment).

The Saudi E-3As will also be able to communicate by voice with U.S. E-3As and fighters using UHF radio (again provided that neither side passes transmissions through incompatible secure voice equipment). The Saudi E-3A will also be able to interrogate U.S. E-3As, E-2Cs, and U.S. and British fighter IFF transponders using Mode 3 (but not the secure Mode 4). Further, the communications equipment on the Saudi E-3As is designed to have "form, fit, and function" interchangeability with the USAF E-3A, which means that Saudi interoperability with U.S. forces can be significantly upgraded with modifications that can be quickly and easily performed in the field.

In an emergency, the Saudi Air Force secure voice and IFF equipment can be removed and replaced with U.S. "black boxes" in about four hours, giving both air forces fully compatible secure voice data and IFF capabilities. Alternately, the U.S. AWACS could replace the gear with Saudi "black boxes". U.S. Air Force mission tapes and TADIL C software can quickly be programmed into the RSAF AWACS computers. Only the installation of JTIDS and Have Quick requires depot-level installation in the U.S.

It is also worth noting that one follow-on modification to the Saudi E-3A has been of direct benefit to the U.S. The Saudi purchase of the CFM International CFM56 engines for the E-3A, instead of the Pratt and Whitney TF33-PW-100A, in October, 1983, gave Saudi Arabia improved fuel efficiency and thrust. This results in longer unrefueled time on station, a slightly higher optimal cruising altitude, and faster or shorter takeoffs. The R&D and design costs for this substitution were paid for solely by the Saudi government, but have had the side effect of saving the U.S. Navy $50-60 million on its Boeing E-6 program.[7]

Saudi Arabia's new Tornados should be able to integrate smoothly into this system. British and U.S. air control and warning concepts differ slightly in detail, but they are broadly compatible. The air defense variant of the Tornado can interface effectively with the E-3A, and its basic IFF and secure communications systems should be compatible with Peace Shield. The uncertainties lie more in the efficiency of the interface between Peace Shield and the Tornado IDS attack fighters, which may require some software and training changes in both the Saudi use of the E-3A and ground based $C^3I$ system, and in determining the best way to provide the Tornado with full intercept data in beyond visual range or complex intercept modes.

---

[1] These data are taken from CIA, The World Factbook, 1983, CR 83-11300.

[2] CIA, The World Fact Book, 1984, Washington, April, 1984. p. 199.

[3] Senate Foreign Relations Committee, The Proposed AWACS/F-15 Sale to Saudi Arabia, GPO 84-557-0, September, 1981.

[4] For a good detailed description, see Defense and Foreign Affairs Daily, May 21, 1984, June 11, 1984, March 4, 1985, and the Wall Street Journal, Washington Post, and New York Times, February 26, 1985

[5] Washington Post, New York Times, and Christian Science Monitor, June 6 and 7, 1984.

[6] Aviation Week, July 22, 1985, p. 21.

[7] Aviation Week, July 22, 1985, p. 22.

## VII. THE SAUDI ARMS SALE CRISIS OF 1985-1986

All of this patient effort by Saudi Arabia and the U.S. was shattered by the Saudi-U.S. arms sale crisis of 1985-1986. In spite of considerable patience in trying to preserve its military relations with the U.S., the Kingdom was forced to turn to Europe. The resulting events which shaped the original Saudi request to the U.S., the refusal of the U.S. Congress to grant the request, and the eventual Saudi arms purchase from Britain make a classic case study in both the strengths and weaknesses in the strategic ties between Saudi Arabia and the West.

### THE ORIGINAL SAUDI ARMS REQUEST: THE "F-15 PACKAGE"

Saudi Arabia originally sought to continue the modernization and expansion of its Air Force by obtaining arms from the U.S. Even at the time of the E-3A debate, it was clear that Saudi Arabia would need to expand its F-15 force, acquire a more advanced attack missions capability, and begin to replace its aging F-5s at some point in the late 1980s to early 1990s. This led to a series of low level planning efforts by the Saudi Air Force and U.S. Air Force. After long consultation with the U.S. State Department and Department of Defense, the Kingdom developed an arms package which called for the further expansion and modernization of Saudi Air Defense capabilities, but which deferred the full modernization of Saudi attack mission capabilities, and involved a complex series of technical constraints to help protect Israel.

Both sides agreed that any new Saudi arms had to be deferred until after the Presidential election campaign of 1984. Shortly after President Reagan's sweeping re-election victory, therefore, both Saudi Arabia and the Administration began to move towards a formal Saudi request for additional arms and dealing with the Congressional debate that was certain to follow.[1] The Reagan Administration initially felt its new mandate was sufficiently strong to rush the sale through, and planned to announce the sale during King Fahd's planned visit to Washington on February 11, 1985.[2]

The details of this new Saudi arms request are shown in Table 7.1. The request involved $3,612 million in immediate U.S. FMS sales. It also involved a carefully crafted compromise in which Saudi Arabia gave up the acquisition of an advanced attack capability and access to some advanced air combat technology for an increase in the strength of the Saudi Air Force improved air defense capability, and a capability to deal with the naval threat from Iran and the growing naval threat in the Red Sea. The new "F-15 package" was a logical next step in eliminating the remaining gaps in the ability of the Saudi Air Force and providing a strong deterrent in the Gulf and Red Sea areas.

The key developments in the new arms package were the gradual conversion of Saudi Arabia's existing 60 F-15 C/Ds to more advanced versions of the aircraft, the purchase of additional F-15C/Ds and several major arms acquisitions. These new acquisitions included 40 more F-15 C/D with MSIP plus 8 additional aircraft to be held in the U.S. as an attrition reserve, 1,620 more AIM-9L/P missiles, and the remaining 800 Stingers out of a 1984 order for 1,200. Saudi Arabia also sought 100 Harpoon air-to-ship missiles for use on its F-15s, and 12 unarmed Blackhawk UH-60 helicopters, with an option to buy 12 more, to provide a limited amount of heliborne lift for its army.[3]

The upgrading of Saudi Arabia's F-15 force, however, was the key element of the new arms request and the Reagan Administration felt it could obtain sufficient support in the Congress to obtain the votes of one-third of the Senate, which is required to prevent a Senate resolution against an arms sale from going into force.

The key was the timing of the modernization and expansion of the Saudi F-15 force. While the U.S. could begin deliveries and conversions of the F-15C/D MSIP in 1988, it could only complete them by 1991-1992. This would not have allowed Saudi Arabia to fully absorb its new purchases and bring them on line in combat ready forces until 1993-1994. Many within the Reagan Administration felt this would defuse opposition by Israel's supporters, and Saudi Arabia agreed because both Saudi Arabia and the U.S. estimated that this would be in time to counter Iranian rearm and deal with the fact that radical Soviet supplied states would have large numbers of Soviet made aircraft roughly equivalent to Saudi Arabia's current version of the F-15 C/D.

The Saudi Arms Sale Crisis of 1985-1986

## Table 7.1 The Saudi Arms Request of 1985

o Conversion of Saudi Arabia's existing F-15C/D to the Multi-stage Improvement Program (MSIP).

-- Total cost: $250 million.
-- Conversion to be accomplished in batches of three in Saudi Arabia. Would require a team of 80 contract personnel.
-- Conversion would begin 46 months after signing letter of offer (1988), and be completed in three years (1991).

o Purchase of 40 additional F-15C/D MSIP with an additional eight fighters to be kept in the U.S. as an attrition reserve.

--Total cost: $2.8 billion.
-- Delivery would begin 40-46 months after signing letter of offer (1989), and be completed in 1990. Full operational training would begin in the summer of 1990 and be completed in 1992.

o Purchase of 980 AIM-9L air-to-air missiles for the F-15C/D, and 630 AIM-9P4 for the F-5E/F to round out previous purchases of 1,177 AIM-9L and 2,500 AIM-9P4.

--Total cost: $100 million for AIM-9L and $45 million for AIM-9P4.
--Delivery time is 30 months after LOA for AIM-9L and 34 months for AIM-9-P4.

o Purchase of 800 manportable Stinger surface-to-air missiles for the Saudi Air Defense Corps to complete a 1984 authorized program of 1,200, and provide defense for Saudi Arabia's ports, oil and other key facilities in its Eastern Province.

-- Total cost: $89 million.
-- Delivery time is 29 months after signing LOA.

o Purchase of additional 100 Harpoon missiles with air-to-ship capability for Saudi Arabia's F-15C/Ds to provide an improved maritime deterrent and defense capability once these complete MSIP conversion.

-- Total cost: $106 million.
--Delivery time is 30 months after LOA, but cannot be used until F-15 C/D MSIP is completed.
--Cannot be used against ground targets.

o Purchase of 12 unarmed Blackhawk UH-60 helicopters with an option to buy 12 more to provide the Saudi army with limited heliborne lift.
-- Total cost: $267 million.
--Maximum lift is 11-14 troops or 2,640 pounds of cargo. Maximum speed is 145 knots and range is 324 NM.

The Saudi Arms Sale Crisis of 1985-1986

THE STRATEGIC RATIONALE FOR THE NEW F-15 PACKAGE

It is important to understand the full strategic rationale for the Saudi arms request, however, because it not only illustrates why virtually every major foreign policy and defense official in the Reagan Administration at least privately agreed to the military need for the sale, but also the reasoning behind Saudi Arabia's decision to turn to Britain once it became clear that the U.S. could not go ahead with the sale. The previous chapters have made it clear why Saudi Arabia feels it must invest in the most advanced fighter it can obtain, and in one which is directly compatible with its existing force structure.

In broad terms, the new arms request offered Saudi Arabia the following advantages:

- o Superior air combat technology; The only way to impress its radical neighbors with its ability to use force quality to make up for its inferior force numbers;
- o The future option of upgrading its F-15s to provide superior air attack capability: The only way Saudi Arabia can compensate for its acute weaknesses in land force numbers relative to threats from the Northern Gulf and the Yemens;
- o A demonstration of U.S. support for Saudi Arabia: Which could give "over the horizon" reinforcement from USCENTCOM more credibility and military effectiveness;
- o Enhanced Saudi prestige and ability to lead the GCC states;
- o A demonstration of "balance" in the U.S. treatment of Israel and Saudi Arabia: This could help defuse the political and strategic backlash in the Arab world resulting from Saudi ties to the U.S.;
- o Adequate provision for the necessary lead time in force modernization: U.S. fighter deliveries lag at least 2-4 years behind U.S. approval of an order. This lead time--combined with 2-3 years it takes to fully convert to new aircraft and advanced technologies--means much of the advantage of advanced technology is lost by the time the equipment actually becomes fully operational.
- o Cost-effective force improvement: The marginal cost of buying the most advanced air combat technology is negligible in "life cycle" cost relative to the overall price of conversion and support, and buying the most advanced systems usually adds five years more life to a major weapons system relative to the improvement in potential threat systems. Coupled to investments in infrastructure and munitions, advanced technology purchases can save Saudi Arabia 30-50% in real life cycle costs over mid-level technologies.

## THE MAJOR TECHNICAL ISSUES

The rationale for the new request becomes even clearer when one examines the technical issues involved in each major part of the new arms package.

### THE UPGRADING OF SAUDI ARABIA'S EXISTING 60 F-15C/DS

Saudi Arabia was virtually forced to obtain some form of the multi-stage improvement program for its F-15C/Ds. The existing versions of the F-15C/Ds were going out of production, and Saudi Arabia faced major eventual increases in its training, munitions, and operating costs if it could not improve its F-15C/Ds to U.S. standards because the U.S. Air Force would cease to support some of the systems in the existing configuration of the F-15C/D as standard equipment.

The Saudi Air Force also had an obvious interest in upgrading the performance of its F-15C/Ds, and these upgrades were of considerable value in meeting its mission requirements. Table 7.2 shows what the MSIP program could add to Saudi Arabia's existing F-15C/Ds:

Table 7.2: Multi-Stage Improvement Program (MSIP) for the Saudi F-15C/Ds

- o A Programmable Armament Control Set (PACS) with:
  - --Improved signal data processing.
  - --Improved data processing.
  - --Multicolor displays.
  - --Conversion programs to allow more effective use of modern air armament.
- o An improved central computer with four times the memory and three times the processing capability of the existing computer.
- o A modified APG-63 radar with wider band width, frequency agility, and increased dynamic range.
- o Incorporation of MIL-STD 1760 wiring.
- o A modified Tactical Electronic Warfare System (TEWS) allowing for the use of advanced weapons such as the Aim-9M, Improved Aim-7, and AMRAAM--although none of these weapons are to be approved for release to Saudi Arabia.
- o Modifications to allow use of the Harpoon air-to-ship missile.
- o HF radio.
- o ALR-56 radar warning receiver (RWR).
- o ICS in Variant B with group A provisions.
- o Internal provision for JTIDS upgrading without JTIDS.

The Saudi F-15 MSIP was not, however, to include all the features in the USAF MSIP-2 program. The omissions from the Saudi MSIP package included the new dual mode threat warning system, secure voice system, full TEWS, new electronic warfare system (EWWS), Mode 4 identification of friend and foe (IFF), MER-200 multiple ejection racks, and Joint Tactical Information Distribution System (JTIDS). The omission of JTIDS was particularly important, and illustrates the extent to which the proposed arms package was tailored to protect Israel.

JTIDS is a key part of the USAF MSIP program. It provides the F-15 C/D MSIP with more than a secure communications system. On the improved F-15C/D, it replaces today's limited voice cueing, and sector scan radar, with far more advanced fighter control and communications. It provides digital communications and conversion of voice information; grid referenced TACAN and navigation information; automatically updated position, speed, and vector data on unknown and unfriendly aircraft; and coordination data for local flights and air-to-ground missions. It also allows the new tactical scope to display the equivalent of a 360 degree picture of the current combat situation including target and mission data. Expanded modes may also provide data on hostile surface-to-air missiles, allow automated coordination with other air defense fighters (an automated mini AWACS capability), and other features.

Even without JTIDS, however, the new 5X5 inch color cockpit display would still have provided Saudi Arabia with several important advantages. These would have included built-in test displays, graphic displays of armament stores to replace the existing armament control panel, and a video display of electro-optical sensor systems and weaponry.

Further, the Saudi MSIP did not include any of the features of the far more ambitious MSIP-3 program. The MSIP-3 is a full dual-role fighter conversion of the F-15C/D which includes many of the features of the F-15E. These include the APG-70 high resolution radar, a much more advanced HUD digital flight control, automatic terrain following modes, expanded weapons capabilities, and a 9 G flight envelope. It also did not include the full integrated flight/fire control system (IFCCS-1) which uses the Firefly III electro-optical sensor tracker to improve both air combat capability and allow far more survivable maneuvering attacks instead of standard pop-up attacks.[4]

The Saudi "MSIP" program could make the Saudi Air Force compatible with the USAF on a support and block improvement basis, but it scarcely represented a threatening transfer of technology either in terms of potential loss to the Soviet Union or in giving Saudi Arabia an edge over Israel.

This was particularly true because of the timing involved in the conversion of the Saudi F-15C/Ds. Even if the Congress had approved the sale as early as October 1985, and the letter of offer (LOA) had been signed the next day, the first conversions could not begin in Saudi Arabia until 46 months later because of contracting (6 months) and manufacturing (40 months) lead times. The 80 man contractor team to be sent to Saudi Arabia would then only be able to process three aircraft at a time, and will take three years to complete the conversions. The full conversion process would not have been completed until 1992.

## THE PURCHASE OF 40 MORE F-15C/D MSIP

The most expensive and controversial aspect of the Saudi arms request, and the one that did most to provoke Congressional resistance, was Saudi Arabia's desire to buy 40 more F-15C/D MSIP, plus eight more aircraft to be kept in the U.S. as attrition reserves. The issues affecting this controversy, however, were more apparent than real. It involved F-15s with the same performance, and technology transfer limitations, as the F-15 C/D MSIP conversions discussed above. It also involved similar lead times.

Even if the Congress had approved the sale in October, 1985, and Saudi Arabia had signed the LOA the next day, work on the new aircraft could not have started until April, 1986. The first aircraft could not have been delivered until February, 1989, and delivery could not have been completed until mid-1990. Even with preliminary training on the existing F-15C/Ds, or in the U.S., full squadron-level Saudi training could not have begun until the summer of 1990, and could not have been completed until 1991-1992. By this time, the new Saudi aircraft would face far larger regional hostile forces equipped with Soviet and European fighter types which would be far more comparable to the F-15C/D MSIP than today's hostile fighters are to the F-5EII and F-15C/D.

Further, Saudi Arabia did not have the option of buying more existing F-15C/Ds because the production line of these aircraft had already closed. Further, by 1992, many Saudi F-5s would be twenty years old. Nearly half will be at the end of their useful life, and restricted to a training role. As a result, the additional F-15s would not have represented a major increase in Saudi air strength, but would rather have served as replacement aircraft. In fact, Saudi Arabia could not have maintained its existing first line combat strength unless it had ordered 40-60 other fighters during this time frame.

## THE PURCHASE OF ADDITIONAL AIM-9L/P MISSILES

The 980 additional AIM-9L and 630 AIM-9P4 air-to-air missiles in the new Saudi request were designed to create a total stockpile of about 1,900 AIM-9Ls and 2,800 Aim-9P4s. While Saudi Arabia already had ordered 1,177 AIM-9Ls and 2,500 AIM-9P4s, deliveries of the new order would have been staggered over 30-34 months after the approval of the sale and signing of the letter of offer, and training would have used up a significant number of existing missiles in the interim. The timing involved is illustrated by the fact that only 250 AIM-9Ls have so far been delivered out of the 1981 order for 1,177.

These total future inventories were approximately half the original force goal that Saudi Arabia set based on USAF planning factors. These planning

The Saudi Arms Sale Crisis of 1985-1986

factors were based on target density, and the U.S. has since persuaded Saudi Arabia to accept goals based on (a) the need to disperse munitions throughout the Kingdom, (b) a 5-10 year life cycle and training attrition, and (c) probable maximum Saudi sortie rates and attrition against probable enemies. The resulting goals were conservative in that they make an informal allowance for U.S. ability to provide over-the-horizon reinforcement and compensate for Saudi losses in combat or lack of force numbers.

The new weapons were to be stored under U.S. security procedures, and could not increase the risk to Israel or the risk of technology loss. Saudi Arabia cannot hope to generate with Israel the additional sorties in air combat which it can achieve against a Gulf or Red Sea threat, and would not have enough surviving aircraft to use the additional missiles in a war with the Israeli Air Force.

THE REQUEST FOR 800 STINGER MISSILES

The Saudi request for 800 manportable Stinger surface-to-air missiles would have supplemented earlier deliveries of 400 missiles out of an order of 1,200, they would have been delivered 29 months after the signing of the letter of offer, or no earlier than 1989. The Reagan Administration first delivered the existing 400 Stingers under emergency conditions in May, 1984, at a time when Iran was constantly issuing threats to broaden the war into the Gulf. The delivery consisted of 200 shoulder-fired launchers and 200 missiles with a follow-on delivery of 200 improved Stinger missiles.

The Stingers would have filled a critical gap in Saudi Arabia's ability to provide close-in protection against air and helicopter attacks, and U.S. studies validated a total Saudi requirement for up to 5,000 missiles.

As has been explained in Chapter V, the Saudi Air Defense Corps' land-based air defense units do not match the Saudi Air Force in effectiveness, and have only a limited capability to make effective use of their Crotale and Shahine systems. This situation could not be corrected until the deployment of the Shahine II and the Saudi E-3As, and until Saudi Arabia's new Peace Shield system could integrate the Improved Hawks, French supplied short to medium range air defense missiles, and radar controlled AA guns into a true Saudi air defense system.

In addition, Saudi Arabia needed a quick reaction weapon for its ports, the oil facilities in the Eastern Province and Red Sea area, its ships, and its seven army brigades. Saudi Arabia cannot predict when Iran might launch air attacks, or use helicopters against Saudi Arabia. The Stingers could provide a highly mobile means of point defense, and one that can be used with only limited training. They have only moderate effectiveness against the kind of first line attack fighters the USSR is beginning to deploy, but they are effective at line of sight ranges against helicopters, the kind of aircraft now flown by Iran, and most of the hostile aircraft likely to be in inventory through the mid-1990s.

Once again, Saudi Arabia was already using U.S. security procedures to protect its existing Stinger missiles. The additional deliveries could have provided nation-wide coverage over a three to five year period without significantly increasing the risk of technology compromise or the number that would be usable against Israel.

While the Stingers would have commercial identification of friend and foe (IFF) capability, it is important to note that they did not have the passive optical seeker technique (POST) version of Stinger. This sensitive system had a dual infrared and ultraviolet (sometimes called "multicolor") counter countermeasure capability against flares and IR decoys, new mirror alignment technology, and improved electronic signal processing. This ensured that such systems cannot be used with high effectiveness against U.S. aircraft with advanced countermeasures, and gives the U.S. the option of transferring such countermeasure technology to Israel.

It was also clear that Saudi Arabia could buy roughly the same arms elsewhere. France, Britain, Italy, and the USSR were all developing or selling roughly equivalent systems to Middle Eastern countries. According to U.S. officials, the heavier SA-13 missiles the USSR had sold to Syria already had roughly equivalent counter-countermeasure and lethality characteristics to the Stinger, and a classified variant of a Soviet manportable weapon is available which also has similar capability.

At the same time, U.S. experts estimated that the USSR would not allow any other nation to have the countermeasure technology that Stinger POST is designed to be used against, and that the Stinger would fully meet Saudi needs over a 5 to 10 year period. The U.S. Army will only slowly convert to the POST variant--which is not yet in production--and it will only be deployed where first line Soviet threats seem likely.

### THE SALE OF 12 UH-60 BLACKHAWK HELICOPTERS

The sale of 12 UH-60 Blackhawk helicopters, with the option to buy 12 more, was the least controversial aspect of the Saudi arms request. The sale met an urgent Saudi army need for heliborne mobility discussed in Chapter IV. Each UH-60, however, can only carry 11-14 troops, or 2,640 lbs of payload, under typical Saudi mission conditions. Maximum speed is 145 knots and maximum range (not radius) is 345 nautical miles. The total purchase would have provided a total lift of only 132-168 men for all 12 helicopters, and the UH-60s were to be unarmed. This buy was adequate for urgent missions in support of other GCC states, to protect key facilities, and deal with terrorism or infiltrators, but scarcely presents a threat of a major Saudi airborne assaults.

### THE SALE OF 100 HARPOON AIR-TO-SHIP MISSILES

The sale of 100 AGM-84A Harpoon air-to-ship missiles was designed to supplement Saudi Arabia's existing stocks of ship-to-ship missiles with the ability to deliver air strikes on threats like the Iranian Navy, and the navies of the radical Red Sea states, and the other threats described in Chapter IV. It would also have helped give the GCC a rapid reaction capability against infiltrating ships, arms smugglers, sea borne terrorists, and small landing parties or raids.

The Harpoon missiles are highly effective against ships at ranges up to 90 Km, depending on the altitude and radar resolution/horizon of the launching aircraft but they cannot be used against land targets, and the U.S. would have retained all classified data on countermeasure technology. While the Harpoons could be delivered within 30 months of the letter of offer, the Saudi Air Force could not begin training to use the new missiles until the F-15C/D MSIP conversions were completed in significant numbers, and this would not have taken place until 1990 at the earliest. The Saudi Air Force could not have been fully effective in the anti-ship mission role until 1991-1992 at the earliest. By this time, it had to be prepared to face far stronger threat forces from both Northern Gulf and Red Sea states.[5]

## THE MISSING LINK: DUAL CAPABILITY FOR THE SAUDI F-15

The one key need the new arms request did not meet, and which was a powerful factor leading Saudi Arabia to buy 48 Tornado IDS attack aircraft, was strengthening the air-to-ground capabilities of the Saudi air force. In the long run, Saudi Arabia could not afford to try to defend solely by matching air force against air force. It had to have enhanced air-to-ground capabilities to make up for the weakness of Saudi ground and naval forces, and to use air power against the Northern Gulf states' overwhelming superiority in land force numbers.

Saudi Arabia's F-15C/Ds now use a relatively low quality attack munitions delivery device called the MER-10, which Saudi Arabia obtained from a third country with U.S. permission. The MER-10 does not allow accurate or high capacity attack munitions delivery, and forces the plane to fly at subsonic speeds which makes it extremely vulnerable to air attack in a high density air environment.

The upgrading of Saudi Arabia's F-15C/Ds to full attack mission capability would not have given the Saudi Air Force attack aircraft equal to the Tornado IDS, but it would have provided considerable air-to-ground capability. The improved F-15C/D MSIP could be equipped to carry up to 17,800 lbs of munitions to typical attack sorties. Conformal fuel tanks could be provided to carry ordnance tangentially to reduce drag, and the multipurpose color video screen and upgrades to the computer would support low altitude penetration and accurate weapons delivery against the probable threats in the Gulf and Red Sea areas.

The Saudi F-15s could carry up to three 30 mm gun pods, and electro-optical missiles such as the new imaging infrared version of the Maverick AGM-65D. The AGM-65D has already been cleared for technical release to

Saudi Arabia. While it is still experiencing some development troubles, it should be much more reliable and effective than Saudi Arabia's 1,600 existing AGM-65A/D. The new Tri-service IIR seeker would have allowed the missile to lock on in mist or poor contrast conditions, and the F-15s could be converted to use a FLIR pod or radar warning receiver to strike at standoff ranges against most of the systems that will be in Gulf and Red Sea forces.

The modifications to the F-15C/D MSIP would also have allowed them to deliver such advanced munitions as HARM, Harpoon, runway suppression systems, modular glide bombs, and "smart submunitions". Like the Tornado, the F-15 C/D had the heavy munitions "lift" and delivery technology to provide an advanced attack mission capability well into the 1990s.

Further, the F-15 C/D MSIP could have been equipped with an improved version of the existing light weight X-Band APG-63 Pulse Doppler Radar. The Improved APG-63 will be a significant upgrade of the original version. It has programmable signal processors with high density storage elements in the radar which make it possible for the APG-63 to reject ground clutter. While the precise success of these upgrades is uncertain, it seems likely that the Improved APG-63 should be able to provide a considerable increase in ground resolution under all weather conditions, and at slant ranges of up to 20 miles. The upgraded radar has been tested as accurate to 3 meters at ranges of 18 kilometers [10 feet at 11.5 miles] and had a radar mapping navigation accuracy of 127 feet at a possible range of 173 miles.

Such an upgrading would not, however, have made the F-15C/D MSIP competitive in the air-to-ground mode with the F-15s that will be in the USAF inventory during this period. Even fully equipped air-to-ground versions of the Saudi F-15 MSIP would not have approached the lethality of the USAF F-15C/D MSIP-3, full F-15E, or Tornado IDS. The key differences between the U.S. and Saudi versions would have been the lack of the F-15's additional weapons officer position, new radar, and tactical weapons system.

Combined with an expanded Tactical Electronic Warfare System (TEWS), the new APG-70 radar and computer system will have up to 1,000 times the memory of the present APG-63 and about three times the processing speed. The APG-70 can store up to four times as much data and will have far greater growth capability to handle improved munitions, more demanding mission profiles, and more sophisticated countermeasure requirements.

The second seat and dedicated weapons officer in the full F-15E will be able to use an integrated LANTIRN capability to provide a full all-weather/night attack capability, and the ability to simultaneously process both radar and FLIR data for attack missions. The imagery from the APG-63 can also be integrated with the FLIR system of Pave Tack, but the success of such integration is far more uncertain, and the "growth" capability to handle more complex munitions and mission profiles of the 1990s will be uncertain.

The weapons officer will be able to use the APG-70 and its associated computer and data links to allow the F-15E to (a) coordinate with other fighters, (b) use the F-15 radar to vector other fighters, (c) make optimal use of data from an AWACS or ground sensor system, (d) conduct anti-ship surveillance and attacks, (e) fight in beyond visual range (BVR) and non-dogfight intercepts, and (f) make optimal use of the AIM-9M, advanced AIM-7, AMRAAM, and successor air-to-air missiles.

### Table 7.3  Features of the F-15E Which Would *NOT* Have Been on the Saudi F-15C/D MSIP

- o Second seat and four multipurpose cathode ray tube displays, plus two hand controllers, for optimal weapons officer role in air-to-air and air-to-ground combat.

- o APG-70 radar and computer. High resolution Synthetic Aperture Radar (SAR) which is capable of all weather detection of tank sized targets at 30 NM, moving target detection, and of discriminating targets only 10 feet apart.

- o Tactical Situation Display with electronic moving map bearing orientation, threat status, navigation data, and sensor management information.

- o Advanced terrain following/terrain avoidance system.

- o LANTIRN target forward looking infrared (FLIR) for high resolution imaging and targeting.

- o Advanced ECM and other counter measure gear and Mode 4 IFF.

- o Combined gun/internal countermeasure set.

- o Increase to five air-to-ground store stations.

- o Optimal avionics and platform capability to use AMRAAM, the final form of the Advanced Joint Tactical Missile (JTACM), boosted/conventional glide bombs, and smart munitions dispensers and glide bombs.

- o Increase to 81,000 lbs maximum gross take off weight, and add internal fuel, permitting payloads to 24,500 lbs.

- o 9 G maneuver capability with payload.

## IMPACT ON WESTERN CONTINGENCY CAPABILITIES AND NEEDS

The West would have gained strategic advantages from meeting the Saudi arms request, as well as over $10 billion in total export earnings. The sale would have created larger interoperable stocks, facilities, and forces in an area 12,000 miles away from the U.S., and in the country best positioned to defend the West's oil assets. It would effectively have "prepositioned" more support facilities, maintenance and repair capabilities, and $C^3I$ assets of the kind that ease the deployment problems a U.S. force faces in moving to Saudi Arabia, and in covering the upper Gulf or lower Red Sea areas. The arms sale package would have allowed the U.S. to simultaneously build-up regional deterrent capabilities while improving its own contingency capabilities, and allowed the U.S. to do so at Saudi expense.

The fact that the Saudi Air Force would have operated a force of 100 F-15C/D/E MSIPs might have meant that the U.S. would have been able to fight with regional allies and not in isolation. Saudi Arabia will continue to equip the largest, most modern, and best sheltered air bases in the Middle East. It will also steadily improve the quality of its "Peace Shield" command, control, communications, and intelligence ($C^3I$), and air control and warning (AC&W) system in ways which will aid USCENTCOM deployment capabilities.

As has been touched on earlier, these Saudi air facilities can base up to two wings of U.S. Air Force fighters, and give them full munitions and service support. The bases could allow large amounts of U.S. air power to deploy to the most threatened areas in the Gulf in 48 to 72 hours. While Oman, Turkey, and Egypt provide useful contingency facilities on the periphery of the Gulf and lower Red Sea, they could not compensate nearly as well for the range and reinforcement problems USCENTCOM would face in defending the critical oil facilities in the Upper and central Gulf.

U.S. air power also has the greatest contingency impact of all the forces the U.S. can deploy. As Table 7.4 shows, the U.S. cannot hope to match the USSR or Iran in terms of land forces, and although it is steadily improving its ability to speed the deployment of USCENTCOM forces, it could still take more than a month to deploy its full strength. It can, however, deploy massive amounts of tactical air power within days. This air power may well be enough to offset the probable threat advantage in land forces provided that it can deploy to compatible bases, use the same munitions and support facilities, can use an advanced $C^3I$ system, and can operate with Saudi forces using the same tactics and doctrine.

## Table 7.4 Comparison of U.S. and Soviet Forces Available for A Gulf Contingency: 1986-1987

| U.S. Combat Forces | | | Soviet Combat Forces | | |
|---|---|---|---|---|---|
| Service | Units | Personnel | Service | Units | Personnel |

**1. Army**

| | | | | | |
|---|---|---|---|---|---|
| | 82nd Airborne | 16,200* | | 1 Tank Division | 11,000 |
| | 101st Air Assault | 17,000* | | 22 Motorized Rifle Divisions | 152,000 |
| | 24th (Lt. Mech) Division | 12,300* | | 1 Airborne Division | 9,000 |
| | Ranger Battalions (2) | 1,200 | | 3 Artillery Divisions | 15,000-18,000 |
| | Air Cavalry Brigade/ | | | | |
| | 5th Special Forces Group | 2,500 | | | |
| | 6th Air Combat Brigade | ? | | | |
| | 7th Light Division | ?* | | | |
| | 9th Light Division | ?* | | | |

**2. Amphibious Assault**

| | | | | | |
|---|---|---|---|---|---|
| | 1 Marine Amphibious Force (Division/Air Wing) | 47,500 | | 2 Naval Infantry Regiments | 5,000 |

**3. Air Force**

9th Air Force
   7 Wings Plus 3 Wings Reserve
   Including:
     F-15 (1 Wing)     72
     F-111A (1 Group)   144
     F-4E (1 Wing)     72
     A-10 (1 Wing)     <u>85</u>
                               373

   B-52H (2 Squadrons)     35

**Frontal Aviation**
o 2 TAAs with 6 fighter and 6 fighter-bomber regiments:
  - 6th TAA (Turkestan MD)
    with MiG-21, 23, 21R, Mi-8     175
  &
  - 34th TAA (Transcaucasus MD)
    with MiG-21, 23,27, Su-24,25,27     300

**Long Range Aviation**
Tu-95, Tu-16, Tu-22, Tu-26 Bombers 100+

Naval Aviation    Naval Bombers     100+

**4. Naval Forces**

| | | | | | |
|---|---|---|---|---|---|
| | 2-3 Carrier Air Task Forces | | | 1-2 ASW Carrier Task Groups | |
| |   Combat Aircraft | 258 | |   Combat Aircraft (VSTOL) | 28 |
| | 5 ASW Aircraft Squadrons | | | 2-3 Guided Missile Task Groups | |
| |   Prepositioned Ships | 17-21 | | | |
| | 1 MAB Amphibious Lift | | | 1 Naval Infantry Regiment | |
| | | | |   plus Amphibious Lift | |
| | ? Nuclear Missile Submarines | | | ? Nuclear Missile Submarines | |

The Saudi Arms Sale Crisis of 1985-1986

\* To be reorganized during 1986-1995 as part of Army's new light division concept. Decisions as to assignment of 7th and 9th Divisions are being re-evaluated.
Source: Adapted From Anthony H. Cordesman, The Gulf and the Search for Strategic Stability, Westview, Boulder, 1984, p. 818, and the IISS, Military Balance, 1985-1986.

In short, the Saudi F-15 package would have supported precisely the kind of broad strategic relationship with Saudi Arabia and the other moderate Gulf states that the West needs. It would have raised the threshold at which U.S. forces must be committed and allowed them to be far more effective when they were committed. It would have allowed U.S. forces both to stay "over the horizon" and to be effective. This would have minimized the political problems of maintaining a U.S. military presence in the Gulf area, yet still helped to ensure that such U.S. reinforcements had deterrent credibility.

WHY THE U.S. DENIED THE SALE

U.S. domestic politics, however, drove Saudi Arabia in a totally different direction. Even before King Fahd's visit to the U.S. in February, 1985, the Reagan Administration had rapidly learned it had seriously miscalculated the effort it would have to put into getting Congressional support for the sale. The problem was not so much one of winning the resulting debate in the House and Senate, it was one of being willing to pay the political price of a long and grueling political battle.

The domestic policy advisors in the White House, and senior Republicans in the Congress, were worried that any major arms sale to an Arab state would lead to a major fight with every supporter of Israel. They were concerned at the slow rate of progress in making new Arab-Israeli peace initiatives, at the impact on the President's ability to achieve tax and budget deficit reform, and at the potential cost in Jewish-American votes and support at a time when this part of the ethnic vote was turning towards the Republican Party and could be critical to maintaining Republican control of the Senate in the 1986 elections. A growing gap developed between the advocates of U.S. strategic interests and advocates of the President's effort to strengthen the conservative political movement within the U.S.[6]

The Reagan Administration never firmly came to grips with this division between the advocates of strategy and the advocates of domestic politics. By mid-January 1985, it had to warn King Fahd that it could not send the new arms request forward during his visit. This almost led the King to cancel his trip, until he was quietly promised that the President would make a personal commitment to him to send the sale forward at a future date.[7]

At the same time, however, the Administration was running into serious problems with a similar arms sale to Jordan. The Congress was increasingly demanding a clear picture of the Administration's arms policy towards the Middle East, and "linkage" between any sale to Saudi Arabia or Jordan and major progress on a Middle East peace settlement. For many supporters of Israel, this progress meant direct talks between Israel and Saudi Arabia and Jordan that excluded the PLO--a requirement that neither Saudi Arabia or Jordan could meet without isolating themselves in the Arab world and fundamentally undermining their security.

The result was that the Administration bought itself time by stating it would defer all new arms requests for the Middle East until it prepared a comprehensive report to the Congress on such sales. This announcement was made on January 31st, 1985, by Richard W. Murphy, the Assistant Secretary of State for Mideast Affairs, in testimony before the Congress. It was the result of considerable debate at the staff level, but Secretary of State George Shultz, Secretary of Defense Caspar Weinberger, and the President's National Security Advisor, William C. "Bud" McFarlane finally agreed they had no other choice. [8]

Senator Alan Cranston of California had already gathered some 51 signatures of U.S. Senators on a letter opposing the sale before the Administration had announced its terms or begun to defend it. Senator Richard Lugar, the Chairman of the Senate Foreign Relations Committee had warned the President he might lose a political battle over the sale, and McFarlane was particularly concerned about the impact on Republican control of the Senate after the 1986 elections. Further, it had become clear during Israeli Defense Minister Yitzhak Rabin's visit to Washington the week before that Israel would strongly oppose a sale to Saudi Arabia, in spite of the Administration's willingness to increase military aid to Israel to $1.8 billion in FY1986, a $400 million increase over the aid provided in FY1985.[9]

The timing of the Administration's announcement of a delay in arms sales to Arab states was acutely embarrassing because it came just before the King's visit, and was so clearly linked to Rabin's visit. Nevertheless, the Reagan Administration felt it had found a way to deal with Israeli and Congressional pressures. Several senior Administration sources agree that President Reagan felt confident enough to make a direct verbal promise to King Fahd that he would send the sale forward when the King visited Washington in February, 1985. Exactly what the President said is still unclear, but the Saudis certainly were confident enough in this promise so they slowed efforts to find a European alternative to the U.S. arms sale.

The Reagan Administration did not, however, use the time it had bought to push the sale forward. While the "Middle East arms sale study" continued to go on within the Administration at the staff level, regurgitating material and work that had actually been fully completed at least six months earlier, the Administration found itself in more and more trouble on domestic political issues. The various lobbying groups supporting Israel, and opposing not only the arms sale but U.S. strategic relations with Saudi Arabia, continued to work on the Congress without any serious opposition.

## The Saudi Arms Sale Crisis of 1985-1986

A well orchestrated press campaign was launched to oppose the sale, and the heavily Democratic House of Representatives became more and more vehement in opposing the sale.[10]

The Reagan Administration had originally planned to issue its arms sale report to the Congress in both classified and unclassified form in April or May, 1985, and then send it forward as the opening gun in a major political effort to support the sale. As time went on, however, domestic politics began to take more and more precedence over foreign policy and strategic interests, and the impact on Republican chances for control of the Senate after November, 1986, became the primary issue. While even a number of very senior Administration officials still pushed hard for the sale, including the Secretary of Defense, some of the White House and National Security Council staff began to push for killing it. Others simply stalled, hoping for some dramatic catalyst from the Iran-Iraq War or the Middle East peace process.

The Middle East Arms sale report was put on a distinct backburner. When it was finally issued, it was issued only in classified form and became one of the most unread documents in Washington. The U.S. Air Force was not allowed to conduct any meaningful briefing effort on the need for the sale, U.S. foreign policy and defense experts were not allowed to brief the hill, and U.S. defense industry was put on hold. The only lobbying effort for the sale consisted of small and badly organized pro-Arab groups which spent so much time defending the PLO and Libya that they did at least as much harm as good.

The Administration simply dithered, and the State Department and Defense Department had the same impression, and both prepared actively to present the new arms package to Congress until virtually the day President Reagan finally decided not to go ahead. Even officials at the Assistant Secretary level were so convinced of the President's continuing support for the Saudi sale that the State Department notified Saudi Arabia during Ramadan that the Administration was ready to give Congress informal notification of the sale.

When this notification was delayed by the White House, a whole series of false notification announcements followed. Indeed, senior State Department officials again gave Saudi Arabia a "green light" that the sale would go forward less than a week before the President's final decision not to proceed with the sale. The whole impression on the Saudis was one of an Administration in chaos, captive to its own fears and lobbying efforts, and unable to make a decision. Worse, even those Saudis who understood the U.S. best could never fully understand that getting the President's promise was not the same as getting a King's. The impression that the President was too weak or indecisive to act was reinforced by the Administration's inability to send clear and consistent signals to the Saudis even from the senior policy level.

## The Saudi Arms Sale Crisis of 1985-1986

The Administration did make one final attempt to help the sale go through in May, 1986, but this only made things worse. A senior Administration official called Prince Bandar bin Sultan, the Saudi Ambassador to the U.S., when he was already in London discussing options to buy the Tornado with the Thatcher government. The U.S. official stated that the U.S. would send the F-15 package forward to the Congress *if* the Saudi government agreed to support the Jordanian peace initiative, *if* the Saudis agreed to support a parallel U.S. arms sale to Jordan, and *if* the Saudis agreed to pay for the arms sold to Jordan.

After urgent consultation with King Fahd, the Saudis tentatively accepted the last two conditions. The first condition, however, threatened to drag them into the middle of a political battle between Jordan, the PLO, and Syria at a time when the Iran-Iraq war was escalating and Saudi Arabia was trying to promote Arab solidarity in dealing with Iran. Further, the whole offer rapidly proved to lack the President's support. When Bandar returned to Washington, he found that Schultz and McFarlane did not really support the plan, nor did President Reagan. The U.S. had sent another high level false signal to the Kingdom.[11]

By July 1985, the situation had gotten so bad and U.S. officials had sent so many conflicting messages and signals, that the Saudis finally asked President Reagan for a formal letter stating that the sale could not go through and that the U.S. would understand if Saudi Arabia turned elsewhere for arms. The President sent the letter, and this triggered a mad scramble between Britain and France to pick-up the Saudi market.[12]

When President Reagan's letter finally came, however, it arrived under conditions which were fully transparent to the Saudis and most other Arab embassies in Washington, and which were deeply embarrassing. It was clear that the President decided against the sale because of pressure from senior Republican members of the Senate, including Senator Richard Lugar, the Chairman of the Senate Foreign Relations Committee.

It was also clear to the Saudis and other Arab states that the Senators only gave this advice for one reason: the fear that the sale would lead to an additional punishing political battle in the midst of domestic political battles over the budget and national debt, and that the backlash from a public debate might produce enough hostile reaction from Israel's supporters to weaken Republican chances for control of the Senate in the 1986 elections.

Domestic political pressure had obviously taken clear precedence over Secretary of State George Shultz and Secretary of Defense Caspar Weinberger's support for the sale and their repeated reassurances to the Saudis. Senior officials in the National Security Council and several of the President's senior domestic political advisors opposed the sale only because of their concern for its impact on the 1986 elections. In fact, no major actor in the Administration's decision making process seriously challenged the merit of the sale from the viewpoint of U.S. national security. The only reason for blocking the sale was domestic politics and the desire to avoid a political fight with pro-Israel lobbyists.[13]

This political context added insult to injury. It virtually forced Saudi Arabia to turn to another arms supplier. It was a further step in a long U.S. history of rejecting or delaying Saudi arms requests that had already helped push Saudi Arabia to turn to Europe for equipment and advice for its Army and Navy. It capped the similar mismanagement of U.S. arms sales efforts to the other Southern Gulf states, and represented the virtual paralysis of efforts to improve U.S. military ties to the Gulf states, and contingency capabilities in the Southern Gulf.

It is hard to blame Israel or its supporters, however, for what happened. The problem lay in the Reagan Administration, in its initial failure to properly check Congressional opinion and then to even try to actively prepare the Congress for the sale. The White House failed when it decided it could wait until the last minute and then use the President's prestige to rush the sale through Congress. While the Administration did nothing, strong and well organized pro-Israel lobbying groups did what special interest groups are supposed to do in the U.S. and made every possible effort to block the sale. By the time the White House finally did decide to act, it was simply too late. The Congress had been thoroughly briefed and mobilized by supporters of Israel.

## THE SAUDI DECISION TO BUY FROM BRITAIN

This long series of uncertain U.S. signals, of "green lights" and rebuffs, helped keep Saudi Arabia's interest in buying from Europe alive, and helped shape the Saudi decision to turn to Britain. The Saudi Air Force had had other options to the U.S. sale since at least early 1983 and Saudi Arabia had begun to lay the ground work for buying substitute weapons and aircraft from Britain in early 1984.[14] Both the British and French realized they were unlikely to make any major fighter sale to Saudi Arabia as long as the U.S. was able to overcome its domestic political problems in providing such arms, but by late 1983, they had concluded that there was a good chance that the U.S. could not make further fighter sales. By early 1984, Britain and France had massive lobbying efforts under way both in Saudi Arabia and in their respective capitals.

In January, 1984, the British Minister of Defense, Michael Heseltine, went to Riyadh to meet with the Saudi Defense Minister, Prince Sultan ibn Abdul Aziz. Prince Sultan was normally considered strongly pro-French, but the British felt they had two good arguments for an aircraft sale. The first was that the Tornado was a much more sophisticated and survivable aircraft than the competing Mirage 2000, had two engines, and could fly much further and deliver a heavier payload. The second was that France had just won a major arms sale in the form of a $4 billion short range air defense system for the Saudi Air Defense Corps. The British had also done an excellent job of briefing some of the younger Saudi princes with experience in the Saudi Air Force, virtually all of which felt the Tornado was a more capable fighter. The result was that Prince Sultan signed a non-binding letter of intent to buy 40-50 Tornados.

This did not stop the French from competing, however, and France felt it had three major advantages: better contacts with the Royal family, a better sales team in France and in the Kingdom, and a cheaper aircraft that would allow the Saudis to buy the Mirage 2000 as a replacement for their U.S. made F-5s and then buy more F-15s when the U.S. political climate shifted.

The French made real headway when King Fahd visited the Cote d'Azur in April, 1984. The French Minister of Defense, Charles Hernu, flew down to see the King. He capitalized on Saudi dissatisfaction with the U.S. and British withdrawal from Lebanon, and persuaded the King to come to Paris to visit President Mitterand. The King's talks went so well that he left the French with the clear impression that he had agreed to the sale, although the Saudis feel he did no more than express his interest.

The French position seemed further strengthened between April, 1984, and March, 1985, as the U.S. sent new signals that it might sell Saudi Arabia the F-15 package. Saudi oil revenues had begun to decline and the Tornado was too expensive and too complex to be bought in addition to the F-15. The Mirage 2000, however, was a good replacement for the F-5 as second line fighter, and it seemed unlikely that the U.S. could both sell the F-15 package and make a timely later sale of an F-5 replacement. The French also were successful in entertaining a number of senior Saudi officers and officials, and in using Akram Ojjeh--a Saudi arms agent living in France--to reach Khalid bin Abdul Aziz al Ibrahim. Ibrahim was the brother of the King's favorite and most recent wife.

The British, however, launched their own entertainment and briefing battle during this period, and they used Wafiq Said, a Syrian born Saudi national, with good contacts within the Saudi Ministry of Defense. Said normally worked with the French, but had helped arrange Sultan's signature on the British letter of offer, and was in an excellent position to brief the Saudis on every problem in the French offer.

Prince Sultan's son, Prince Bandar, wanted the Tornado for both technical and strategic reasons. While some Saudi Air Force officers saw the sale only in terms of an F-5 replacement and strongly supported the Mirage 2000, the French fighter lacked military impact and political prestige. Both Sultan and Bandar did not like the French use of agents to pressure the King and try to win influence with the Saudi officer corps. Further, Prince Bandar who was not only the Saudi Ambassador to the U.S. but an ex-British trained fighter pilot, was increasingly worried that the U.S. F-15 sale might fall through.

Prince Bandar arranged for Prime Minister Thatcher to visit King Fahd in Riyadh in April, 1985, on her way back from a trip to the Far East. The

The Saudi Arms Sale Crisis of 1985-1986

Prime Minister brought the prestige of having won in the Falklands and strongly impressed the King. This gave Prince Sultan the influence to cancel a meeting on the Mirage sale with Hernu in May, 1985, and led Prince Bandar to begin to spend almost as much time trying to close the Tornado sale in May and June, 1985, as he did trying to salvage the F-15 package. His efforts were aided after June by both the U.S. inability to make the F-15 sale and by the fall in oil prices. Britain proved ready to deal in oil, and even to offer a limited "buy back" of Saudi Arabia's obsolete British Lightnings. The French did not prove to be good oil traders, and already had problems in disposing of Gulf oil because of their previous refinancing deals with Iraq.[15]

The groundwork for the sale was well prepared, therefore, when Saudi Arabia began the final negotiations with Britain in September, 1985. What was a surprise was the extent to which Saudi Arabia expanded the original offer to buy 48 Tornados into a 132 aircraft package that raised the cost from around $4 billion to $7 billion, and shifted the entire structure of the Saudi Air Force from dependence on the U.S. to dependence on Britain.

The Saudis seem to have concluded that they had no real hope of a future major U.S. sale until after the 1988 elections, and then only after a new President had had some time in office. They also concluded that the Reagan Administration would not see a major purchase from Britain as in any way hostile, and was actually encouraging the Saudis to distance themselves from the problems of U.S. domestic politics.[16]

The Saudi negotiating team had been in London for about eight weeks before the public announcement of the sale on September 26, 1985. It was only on September 24th, however, that the chief of the Saudi Air Force received instructions from Prince Sultan to expand the sale from 48 attack versions of the Tornado to include 24 air defense versions of the Tornado, and 60 trainer aircraft, including 30 British made Hawks and 30 Swiss-built Pilatus PC9s. The catalyst seems to have been a new package offer that offered more rapid delivery of the Tornados at the expense of the RAF and which was linked to a deal in which Shell Transport and Trading Company and British Petroleum were to work with ARAMCO over the next three years to market the necessary oil to pay for the all 132 aircraft.[17]

The final letters of offer and acceptance were signed on February 17, 1986. The British also agreed to invest 35% of the technical content of the contract in Saudi Arabia under the same kind of offset arrangements the U.S. provided as part of the Peace Shield sale. Further, the contract allowed renegotiation of the timing and volume of the oil to be sold to protect Saudi Arabia against a further drop in oil prices. This became important in April, 1986, when oil had fallen from $26 per barrel at the time of the sale to $12.25 a barrel and the Saudis threatened to reduce their aircraft purchases. In May, 1986, the British Secretary of State for Defense, George Younger, rushed to Riyadh, and in June, Chancellor Nigel Lawson renegotiated the deal to increase the volume of oil and stretch the repayment period out over six years to allow Saudi Arabia to remain within its OPEC quota. By that time, the Kingdom had already paid the U.K. some $300 million worth of oil and the British had already delivered six Tornado GR.1 attack fighters.[18]

## U.S. EFFORTS TO MAINTAIN STRATEGIC RELATIONS

The final act in the arms sale crisis of 1985-1986 was a U.S. effort to rebuild its strategic relations with Saudi Arabia after the failure of the F-15 Package and the Saudi decision to buy from Britain. By mid-1985, the Reagan Administration had begun to consider a smaller arms package that would at least modernize the Kingdom's F-15s, and provide most of the munitions the Kingdom had requested in the original F-15 Package. It became clear during the course of the rest of 1985, however, that the Reagan Administration could not obtain solid political support for any major new arms sale to Saudi Arabia, including the modernization of Saudi Arabia's existing 60 F-15C/Ds, without having to sacrifice some of its domestic political support. The Administration was also forced to let a major arms sale to Jordan die without full Congressional debate or action.[19]

The Congress kept putting added pressure on the Administration, limiting sales to the Arab world. In July, 1985, the Senate introduced legislation that forced the Administration to report every major technical upgrade in the equipment it sold to foreign nations. This was clearly targeted towards Saudi Arabia since there had been some minor changes to the E-3A AWACS being sold to the Kingdom. These included better secure teletype equipment and software, because commercial equipment had proved unable to communicate with NATO teletype data links, better UHF equipment, the same color data displays that had become standard on all U.S. E-3As, and infrared countermeasure equipment of a kind already released for use on all other Saudi aircraft.[20]

Several members of the Congress, led by Senator Cranston, then began a low level effort to try to block the actual transfer of the E-3As that Saudi Arabia had bought on October 28, 1981. A section was inserted to the International Security and Cooperation Act of 1985 that required the President to make fully public all the details of his certification and of the precise ways in which the Saudis would meet U.S. conditions for buying and using the E-3As.[21] Some of these provisions were embarrassing to the Saudis, including "continuously and completely" sharing all data, prohibitions on the transfer of data to third countries, and limitations on its use to flight over Saudi territory. The intent of the opposition, however, was not to embarrass the Saudis with more publicity, but to lay the ground work for challenging the President's certification, and try to get enough votes in the Senate to block the sale.[22]

The Reagan Administration then began to fight back. The certification problem threatened to totally shatter every aspect of U.S. policy and military relations in the Gulf. It was also clear that a token arms package had to be pushed through the Congress to ease the growing internal pressure on the Senior Saudi officials that supported strong ties to the U.S., including Prince Sultan.[23]

On March 11, 1986, the Administration decided to send forward a token arms package of missile systems. This new arms package included 995 AIM-9L air-to-air missiles ($98 million), 671 AIM-9P4 air-to-air missiles ($60 million), 100 Harpoon air-to-sea missiles ($107 million), and 200 Stinger man-portable surface-to-air missile launchers and 600 reload missiles ($89 million). The total value of the new arms package was $354 million. The Administration used the excuse that the Iranian victory in Faw in early 1986 had led Saudi Arabia to urgently request additional missiles to improve its defenses against Iran. In fact, however, this was simply a Reagan Administration political cover to justify announcing the sale.[24]

The new "mini" package was carefully designed to minimize the political cost of sending it forward. The Reagan Administration could defend the package on the technical and military grounds described earlier for these portions of the F-15 Package, and on the basis that Saudi Arabia already had most weapons systems in inventory and had demonstrated its ability to provide security from espionage and terrorists. It could quietly make it clear that the reason for the high number of munitions was as much to provide stockpiles to enhance U.S. contingency capability in the Gulf as to meet Saudi needs.[25] The only systems that were even slightly different were the AIM-9P4 and air-to-surface version of the Harpoon. The AIM-P4 was only a slight upgrade over the AIM-9P3 already in Saudi Arabia, and Saudi Arabia already possessed a surface launched version of the Harpoon.

The Reagan Administration also adopted a strategy based on a very low profile lobbying effort for the sale, and on trying to make a tacit bargain with pro-Israel lobbying groups to support a high level of aid for Israel and strengthen U.S. and Israeli strategic relations in return for limited opposition to the sale. This strategy, however, backfired. The lobbying effort was so low level, so badly organized, and so confused by the efforts of various pro-Arab lobbying groups whose real goal was to defend the PLO, that it almost collapsed. The various pro-Israel lobbying groups saw no reason in an election year to make any bargains and became even more active than ever.

As a result, the Reagan Administration met so much Congressional resistance to the sale that it was forced to drop the Stinger man-portable surface-to-air missile from the package in spite of the fact (a) the Saudis already had the Stinger and had proved they could preserve its security, (b) an independent study by the Congress General Accounting Office conducted in Saudi Arabia indicated the arms were safe in Saudi hands, and (c) Soviet SA-14 missiles of similar capability were being delivered to Syria and other Arab countries. It faced a situation where 64 Senators had already joined Senator Alan Cranston in signing a resolution against the sale, and about 290 members of the House were ready to vote against the existing package. This was enough votes in the Senate to block the sale without a President veto and enough votes in the House to override the veto if the President made it.[26]

The Reagan Administration was forced to recognize that it could never get the support of the House of Representatives, and that the President could never get enough of the Senate to support the sale on his first try. Under U.S. law, his only way of making the sale was to accept the fact the Senate would pass a resolution against the sale, but use his influence to prevent the Senate from overriding a Presidential veto of the Senate bill. This meant the President would only need the support of one-third of the Senate.

When the first real key vote came on May 6, 1986, four-fifths of the Senate voted for a bill opposing the sale. This forced the President to rely on his ability to sustain a veto of the Congressional legislation blocking the sale. Ironically, the vote against the sale also illustrated the clumsiness of the Administration's lobbying effort even at the highest levels. The President's new National Security Advisor, Admiral John A. Poindexter, wrote an editorial in the Washington Post designed to influence the Senate vote on the sale, but Administration lobbyists knew so little about the oppositon that the editorial only appeared a day *after* the Senate vote.[27] The signal to both the Congress and the Saudis was that the Administration simply did not know what it was doing.

This again raised the specter of the Congress voting against the transfer of the E-3As as well and catalyzed a more intensive effort by the President.[28] The problem became one of whether the President could now salvage the sale even if he did commit all his personal prestige. After weeks of political arm twisting, however, President Reagan finally did win enough support to sustain his veto. When the vote came on June 5, 1986, however, President Reagan only won by a single vote. This victory was so minor, so uncertain, and involved so many Congressional attacks on Saudi Arabia, that it did almost as much to undermine U.S. and Saudi relations as to strengthen them.[29]

The only positive event in two years of U.S. and Saudi strategic relations was that the battle over the "mini" arms package was sufficiently bitter and exhausting so that the pro-Israel lobbyists chose to give priority to increased U.S. aid to Israel over yet another battle over the AWACS. Saudi Arabia formally agreed to comply with all the conditions the U.S. had set for using the E-3As in a signed agreement with the U.S. in mid-June, 1986.[30] As a result, the President was able to transfer the first of the five E-3A AWACS that Saudi Arabia had bought three years earlier in with a simple letter of certification later that month. The President's certification, however, was scarcely a triumph. The U.S. had clearly reached the point where it was unable to maintain full scale strategic relations with Saudi Arabia, and with any other moderate Arab state in the region except Egypt.

## THE STRATEGIC IMPACT OF THE ARMS SALE CRISIS OF 1985-1986

The strategic impact of the arms sale crisis of 1985-1986, and of the growing shift in Saudi military relations to dependence on Europe, becomes clear when the results are examined for each of the major actors involved. These impacts and trends are scarcely disastrous for the West, and can still be transformed into an effective structure of military relations, but they have unquestionably weakened Western military contingency capabilities in the Gulf. Ironically, they have also weakened Israel.

### IMPACT ON BRITAIN

Britain will get major benefits from the sale, and faces only indirect and long term risks. Britain will get a minimum of some $4-6 billion in additional exports. The sale will probably provide at least another $2-4 billion in support costs and other benefits, and could lead to substantial additional exports. This is of special importance to Britain because its arms exports have dropped from 2.7% of all exports in 1981, to less than 1.5% in 1984, and the value of its arms exports have dropped from $2.8 billion in constant 1982 dollars to under $1.5 billion.[31] The sale to Saudi Arabia re-establishes Britain as a serious competitor in the world sales of military electronics and aviation.

The first of the risks to Britain is that it must now demonstrate that it can actually provide the support and training necessary for Saudi Arabia to operate one of the world's most advanced fighter aircraft. Britain has not performed this role recently, although it has long provided much of Saudi Arabia's air training and services and has supported Saudi operation of the Lightning and BAC-167 fighters.

More significantly, Britain faces the risk that any erosion of U.S. military influence in Saudi Arabia weakens U.S. ability to deter threats against the Gulf and Europe's key future source of oil imports. This risk, however, is a long term risk and uncertain. It must be balanced against the fact that Britain's aviation and defense electronics industries desperately needed the sale to Saudi Arabia to avoid massive layoffs in the late 1980s.

### IMPACT ON SAUDI ARABIA

The risks to Saudi Arabia are also limited. Saudi Arabia must trust in Britain's ability to provide the support it will need, although Britain lacks America's recent experience in managing large scale foreign military sales programs. More significantly, the Kingdom runs the risk that the new turn of events will diminish the military assistance the U.S. can provide in an emergency.

U.S. ability to provide immediate "over-the-horizon" reinforcements is heavily dependent on U.S. air power, and the effectiveness of U.S. air reinforcements is heavily dependent on the extent to which Saudi Arabia

## The Saudi Arms Sale Crisis of 1985-1986

already can provide interoperable bases and forces. Nevertheless, Saudi Arabia will not experience any such loss in U.S. reinforcement capabilities as the result of buying the Tornado until the late 1980s and early 1990s, when the 40 additional U.S. F-15s would have been delivered. By this time, oil prices are likely to have recovered and U.S. policy may change.

The Saudi Air Force will also get major offsetting benefits in return for any risks the Kingdom will run. It will get a total of 72 first line Tornado fighters, rather than 40 F-15C/Ds--and the option of buying more whenever the Kingdom needs them and without future political restraints. It will get 30 Hawk light attack trainers as part of the package, and a wide range of technologies that were not available from the U.S.

The U.S. had not planned to provide advanced attack mission capability, or dual-capability in the attack role on the variant of the F-15 C/D MSIP, all of which were to be heavily optimized for the air defense mission. The Saudi Air Force now will get 48 Tornado GR.1 or IDS (Interdictor-Strike) fighter-bombers. These Tornados can fly missions at ranges over 500 nautical miles in LO-LO-LO profiles, over 700 NM in close air support missions with one hour of loiter near the FEBA, and over 850 NM in HI-LO-HI interdiction missions.

The Tornados have one of the most advanced terrain following systems in the world, full fly-by-wire capability, an excellent combined radar and map display for precision bombing, an advanced radar warning receiver, and the avionics, data display, and laser to make effective use of virtually any air-to-ground munitions including virtually all of NATO's "emerging technology systems" like the MBB MW-1 munitions dispenser and GBU-15 laser guided bomb. They will be sold with full ECM gear, and have excellent ability to penetrate below ground based radar coverage and to use terrain masking to minimize the "look down" capability of advanced fighters.[32]

The Tornado IDS will give the Saudi Air Force the advanced attack mission capability it has sought from the U.S. for a decade. Britain will also sell Saudi Arabia the Sea Eagle antiship missile (the Tornado has a 700 nautical mile Hi-Lo-Lo-Hi range capability to deliver this missile including a terminal supersonic dash), the Dynamics Alarm anti-radiation missile, and far more advanced attack munitions than the U.S. was willing to provide. These will include many advanced or emerging technology weapons such as the new JP-233 air base suppression system and smart submunition weapons Britain has under development.[33]

Moreover, the Saudi Air Force also gets 24 Tornado ADV air defense fighters with more advanced air defense avionics and munitions than the U.S. was willing to release for the F-15. These will include full all-weather capability, more advanced tactical air displays, a multiple target track with scan radar and more advanced computer with up to a 100 mile look down-shoot down and BVR missile capability, excellent ECCM capability, and the

## The Saudi Arms Sale Crisis of 1985-1986

ability to carry and fire four state of the art air-to-air guided missiles like Skyflash and fire them in a near "ripple" mode.[34]

The comparative performance specifications of the Tornado, the F-15, and the F-5E are shown in Table 7.5, and it should be clear even to the layman that the Tornado has excellent performance specifications.

## Table 7.5 Comparative Performance Characteristics of Key Fighter Aircraft Affecting the Saudi Air Force Modernization Program

### Part One-Aircraft Performance

|  | F-5E | F-15C/D | F-15E | Mirage F-1C | Mirage F-2000 | Tornado |
|---|---|---|---|---|---|---|
| **Mission Distance (NM)** | | | | | | |
| Air-to-air Radius | 360 | 720 | 720 | 400+ | 454 | 500+ |
| Ferry Range | 1,340 | 3,450 | 3,450 | 2,050 | 1,754 | 2,400 |
| **Attack Radius (NM)** | | | | | | |
| Hi-Lo-Hi | 480 | 750 | 750 | 400 | 465 | 863 |
| Hi-Lo-Lo | - | 580 | 580 | 340 | 390 | 750 |
| Lo-Lo-Lo | 325 | 450 | 450 | 205 | 260 | 400 |
| **Payload (Lbs)** | | | | | | |
| Max. | 8,000 | - | - | 8,820 | 16,758 | - |
| W/ Full Internal Fuel | 8,000 | 16,000 | 16,000 | - | 13,225 | 16,000 |
| **Air-to-Air Armament** | | | | | | |
| Gun | 2XM39 | M61A1 | M61A1 | DEFA 30mm | DEFA 30mm | 2X 27mm |
| IR Missile | 2XAIM-9 | 4XAIM-9 | 4XAIM-9 | S-550 | S-550 | 6XAIM-9 |
| Radar Missile | No | Yes AMRAAM | Yes AMRAAM | S-530 | S-530 | Yes AMRAAM |
| Maximum Endurance/Loiter in CAP Missions (Hrs.) | - | - | - | 3.7 | - | 3+ |
| Absolute Ceiling (Ft) | 51,500 | 100,000 | 100,000 | 60,695 | 65,000 | 51,000+ |
| **Maximum Mach** | | | | | | |
| Optimum Altitude | 1.64 | 2.5+ | 2.5+ | 2.12 | 2.4 | 2.2 |
| Sea Level | 1.04 | - | - | 1.2 | 1.2 | 1.1 |
| **Maximum Turn Rate** | | | | | | |
| 8 M at 15,000' | 18.5 | - | - | - | 15.81 | 14 |
| Wing Loading (lbs/ft.) | 72 | - | - | 76.1 | 83.7 | - |
| Thrust to Weight Ratio | 0.75 | 1.4 | 1.4 | 0.73 | 0.77 | - |
| Maximum Load Factor | 7.33 | 9.0 | 9.0 | - | 8.0 | 7.5 |
| **Sea Level Rate of Climb** | | | | | | |
| (Ft/Min) | 34,300 | - | - | 41,930 | 59,050 | 46,500 |
| **Maximum Climb to** | | | | | | |
| 40,000' (Min) | 3.4 | 1.0 | 1.0 | - | 1.5 | 3.1 |
| **Subsonic Turn** | | | | | | |
| Radius (Ft) | 4,700 | - | - | - | - | - |
| **Loiter Time** | | | | | | |
| (Min at 100 NM) | - | - | - | - | - | 170 |
| Landing Distance (Ft) | 2,450 | 2,500 | 2,500 | 1,700 | - | 1,200 |

## Table 7.5 Comparative Performance Characteristics of Key Fighter Aircraft Affecting the Saudi Air Force Modernization Program

### Part Two-Avionics and Maintenance Performance

| | F-5E | F-15C/D | F-15E | Mirage F-1C | Mirage F-2000 | Tornado |
|---|---|---|---|---|---|---|
| Radar | APQ-159 | APG-64/5 | APG-70 | Cryano | CSF | British |
| Detection Range 5M$^2$ | | | | | | |
|   Up (NM) | 14 | 80-120 | 80-120 | 30 | 50 | 50 |
|   Down (NM) | No | 47 | 47 | 15 | 20 | 30 |
|   Shoot down | No | Yes | Yes | Lim | Yes | Yes |
|   Ground Mapping | Lim | Lim | Yes | Lim | Yes | Yes |
|   Doppler Beam Sharpening | No | Yes | Yes | No | Yes | Yes |
|   BVR Missile Capability | No | Yes | Yes | No | Yes | Yes |
|   Terrain Avoidance | No | No | Yes | No | Yes | Yes |
|   Moving Map Display | No | No | Yes | No | Growth | Yes |
|   Track While Scan | No | Yes | Yes | No | Yes | Yes |
|   Raid Assessment | No | Yes | Yes | No | No | Yes |
|   Radar Ground Track | No | No | Yes | No | Yes | Yes |
|   Radar Altitude | No | Yes | Yes | No | Yes | Yes |
| FLIR | No | No | External | No | External | Optional |
| Laser Desingator | No | No | External | No | External | Yes |
| Fire Control | | | | | | |
|   Memory/Speed | No | 64K/500K | - | - | 64K | - |
|   HUD | No | Yes | Yes/TV | Yes | Yes | Yes |
| Displays Conv. | 2 CRT | 3 CRT | Conv | 3CRT | Multi | Multi |
| INS | Litton | Litton | Laser | No? | Yes | Yes |
| Radar Warning | No | ALR-67 | ALR-67 | - | Yes | Yes |
| ECM | No | Conformal | ASPJ | Pod | Pod | Internal |
| Data Transfer | Voice | Automatic | Advanced | Voice | Manual | Advanced |
| Built-in Test | No | Yes | Yes | Yes | Yes | Yes |

While the British Aerospace Hawk P.1182 T.1 is not an advanced combat aircraft, it is a relatively long range light fighter with transonic speed capability. It carries a 30mm gun and two AIM-9L and has effective enough avionics to act as light day interceptor. It also can carry up to 6,800lbs/3,085 kgs worth of attack munitions, and can fly patrol missions for up to 3 hours or fly over 200 NM HI-LO-HI attack profiles. While it lacks an advanced radar, its avionics are adequate for locating nearby fighters at medium to high altitudes.[35]

Finally, the Saudi Air Force will get its new British aircraft two to four years earlier than if it had ordered 72 F-15s from the U.S. While it has stated that it will not initially base its Tornados in Tabuk, the Saudi Air Force will also have more long term flexibility in basing the Tornados anywhere in Saudi Arabia--which the U.S. would have prohibited in the case of the F-15 because of opposition by Israel. It will be free of U.S. restraints on the employment of its aircraft and on the release of emerging technology that will allow the Saudi Air Force to equip itself with force multipliers.

IMPACT ON THE U.S.

It is the U.S. and its military capabilities which will suffer most. In the case of the U.S., the risks and costs will be strategic and financial. The main strategic risks are the erosion of U.S. military relations with Saudi Arabia, and the loss of interoperable bases, forces, and equipment. The main financial risks are the loss of a major arms sale worth an immediate $2.8 billion in new F-15 sales with the probable loss of $3-6 billion more in follow-on support sales, plus some $7-14 billion for replacing Saudi Arabia's F-5E-IIs. In addition, the U.S. will inevitably lose more civil sales in what has recently been a $4-5 billion dollar annual market for U.S. commercial exports.[36]

It is hard to say whether the damage to U.S. and Saudi military relations or that to U.S. contingency capabilities in the Gulf will be more significant. There is no question that the manner in which the U.S. failed to support the F-15 sale has eroded a great deal of Saudi and moderate Arab confidence in the Reagan Administration, and in its ability to maintain military relations with the Gulf states. The U.S. decision also came at a uniquely bad time. The Saudis not only had at least some reason to believe that the U.S. had broken a Presidential promise to the King, the U.S. rejection of the F-15 sale occurred within days of New York Times and Washington Post leaks of a classified U.S. study that mentioned that Saudi Arabia had made secret agreements for U.S. contingency use of Saudi bases.

The Saudi Defense Minister, Prince Sultan, did announce immediately after the signing of the agreement with Britain that the Tornado sale did not mean the Kingdom was turning away from the U.S., and stated he still had an interest in buying up to 50 more F-15s. He also visited Washington in early October, 1985, to negotiate the modernization of Saudi Arabia's existing F-15s and some additional arms purchases. Nevertheless, the Kingdom cancelled several other arms requests, and it was clear that the U.S. denial had left a distinctly bitter political aftertaste.[37]

Even if Saudi Arabia does not quietly distance itself from the U.S. even further, the sale alone will affect U.S. contingency capabilities in the region. There has never been any question that Saudi bases could be vital in a U.S. effort to defend the West's oil supplies. The issue has always been their availability and their interoperability with U.S. forces. Until now, the U.S. has made steady progress in both areas. A Saudi shift to British aircraft will reduce U.S. ability to use Saudi facilities in both political and military terms. It makes it steadily more politically difficult for Saudi Arabia to plan with the U.S. or to accept U.S. reinforcements, and it will undercut the interoperability between U.S. and Saudi forces.

IMPACT ON ISRAEL

While it is tempting to blame many of these problems on Israel or its supporters, the blame must rest with the U.S. No political group in the American political system can be blamed for having an effective lobby or for advancing its own self interest. The blame lies with those in the Reagan Administration and the Congress who are charged with serving the U.S. national interest--and that of the free world--even at the cost of domestic political advantage.

At the same time, it is clear that the efforts to serve Israel's interests have ended in damaging Israel's strategic interests as well as those of the U.S As has been mentioned earlier, this damage has taken three forms: It has increased the barriers to Saudi participation in the peace process, it has reduced U.S. ability to influence Saudi policy and military actions, and it has increased the theoretical military threat that Saudi forces could present to Israel in some future war.

The first form of damage is unquestionably the most important. Saudi Arabia is not, and has never been, a serious military threat to Israel. It faces immediate threats in the Gulf, in the Red Sea, and in the Yemens, and its role in the Arab-Israeli conflict is limited to political and economic support of Arab causes. The problem the U.S. faces in persuading Saudi Arabia to make peace with Israel is essentially one of making the political risks of such a peace acceptable. King Fahd long ago advanced a peace plan of his own, and no key Saudi official privately objects to King Hussein's peace initiatives.

Saudi Arabia is not, however, going to readily take the risk of joining a peace process which will alienate Syria, a radical state and a powerful military presence near its northwestern border. It is not easily going to take the risk of having its political and religious legitimacy thrown into question by Iran or the other radical states that would capitalize on its support of what remains a highly uncertain peace process. Above all, it is not going to take the risk of seeming to support the U.S. at a time when the U.S. conspicuously refuses to provide it with the arms it needs and does so under the political influence of Israel.

This lack of Saudi support for the peace process, and improved Arab relations with Israel, is a far more real problem than the theoretical capability of Saudi forces to join in an Arab attack on Israel. At the same time, the previous analysis has shown in detail that U.S. refusal to sell Saudi Arabia the F-15, and the Saudi purchase of the Tornado, have unquestionably increased Saudi Arabia's theoretical capability to engage Israel.[38]

## BROADER IMPACT ON WESTERN STRATEGIC RELATIONS WITH THE GULF

The U.S. refusal to sell Saudi Arabia the arms package it requested has an impact which goes far beyond U.S. interests or even the damage done to Western military relations with Saudi Arabia. In combination with the U.S. refusal to sell arms to Jordan, it represents the culmination of similar problems in dealing with the other Southern Gulf states. Although none of these states are a threat to Israel, the Reagan Administration's fear of domestic political problems has led it to delay, block, or mishandle every major opportunity to sell U.S. equipment or air defense fighters. The U.S. has lost every major market in the Gulf to France and Britain except Bahrain's small air force.

This has not only cost the U.S. billions of dollars in exports, it has prevented the creation of effective U.S. military relations with most of the smaller Southern Gulf states. The resulting diversification has helped ensure that many of their forces are not interoperable with each other, and the general Western failure to ensure they are interoperable with U.S. forces has severely reduced the potential effectiveness of any over-the-horizon reinforcements from the U.S. Navy and USCENTCOM. This is illustrated all too clearly in Table 7.6, which shows just how chaotic the efforts of the Gulf Cooperation Council states to create an effective air deterrent have become.

The Saudi Arms Sale Crisis of 1985-1986

## Table 7.6: The Lack of Standarization in the Air Forces of the GCC States

| Air Defense Systems | | Aircraft | | SAM Missiles | |
|---|---|---|---|---|---|
| Type | Supplier | Type | Supplier | Type | Supplier |
| **Kuwait** | | | | | |
| Radars*($12M) | Thomson CSF | 19 Mirage F-1 (24 F-1C in delivery)** | Dassault (France) | 1 IHawk Bn | Raytheon (US) |
| AN/TSQ-73* | Litton, ITT (US) | | | SA-7 Missiles | USSR |
| $C^3$ System** | ($8.2 M) U.S. | 30 A-4KU | U.S. | SA-8 Missiles | USSR |
| **Saudi Arabia** | | | | | |
| 5 E-3A AWACS and air, ground $C^3I$ links | Boeing (US) | 48 IDS & 24 ADV Tornado* | U.K. | 2 Shahine Btes. | Thomson CSF (France) |
| | | 30 Hawk Lt. Attack* | U.K. | | |
| | | 30 Short PC-9 Trainer* | U.K. | | |
| $C^3$ System | Litton Data (US) ($1.6B) | 62 F-15A/B w/AIM-9L | U.S. | 16 IHawk Btes. | Raytheon (US) ($270M) |
| Peace Shield | Boeing consortia $C^3$ (U.S) ($3.9B) | 65 F-5E | U.S. | 400 Stinger | GD (US) ($30M) |
| 17 Seek Igloo Radars ($330M) | General Electric (US) | 40 F-5B/F | U.S. | 30mm SP AA guns AMX-30SA | France |
| 5 Underground Centers ($184M) | CRS-Sirrien, Metcalf & Eddy (US) | 15 Lightning | U.K. | | |
| Al Thaqib System with 100 radars and 100 missiles | Thomson CSF (France) ($4B) | | | 12 Shahine Btes. and Crotale point and naval defense | |
| **Bahrain** | | | | | |
| Teleprinter data Link to Saudi Arabia | | 12 F-5F w/AIM-9P2* | Northrop (US) | 6 RSB-70 Btes. | Sweden |
| | | | | IHawk*** | Raytheon (US) |
| **Qatar** | | | | | |
| Negotiations on $C^3I$ System | France, U.S. | 13 Mirage F-1 | Dassault (France) | Rapiers 5 Tigercat | British Aerospace (UK) |
| | | 14 Mirage F-1*** | | | |
| | | 8 Alphajet | FRG | | |
| | | 2 Hunter | BA (UK) | | |
| **UAE** | | | | | |
| Project Lambda*** air defense $C^3I$ and Electronic Warfare with C-130s ($422M) | U.S. | 18 Mirage 2000 | Dassault (France) | Rapiers Crotale | BA (UK) Thompson CSF (France) |
| | | 18 Mirage 2000* | | 24-42 I Hawk | Raytheon (US) |
| | | 30 Mirage 5 | Dassault | RSB-70 | Saab (Sweden) |
| | | 6 Alphajet | FRG | Skyguard 35mm | Contraves (Italy-Swiss) |
| **Oman** | | | | | |
| 28 Blindfire Radars | Racal (UK) | 8 Tornado | UK ($280M)* | 28 Rapiers | BA (UK) |
| | | 24 Jaguar | BA (UK) | | |
| | | 16 Hunter | BA (UK) | | |
| | | 12 BAC-167 | BA (UK) | | |

\* Ordered  \*\* Planned  \*\*\* Discussion only.
Sources: IISS, The Middle East, SIPRI, Defense and Foreign Affairs

# The Saudi Arms Sale Crisis of 1985-1986

This is not the kind of military chaos either the U.S. or Western Europe can afford to encourage. The West faces very real threats in Southwest Asia. It cannot predict the nature of the threat Iran poses to the other Gulf states and the flow of Gulf oil, or what will happen to Iraq as a result of the Iran-Iraq War, or the threat posed by the growing radicalism in several Red Sea states.

The USSR may not be a pressing threat in the Gulf today, but it will face major oil problems in the 1990s. It has already established a permanent naval base in Dahlak off the coast of Ethiopia and major naval and air facilities in South Yemen. It will certainly capitalize on any opportunity that may come out of the political turmoil in Iran or the Iran-Iraq War, and its freedom of action will greatly increase if it can win in Afghanistan or if Ethiopia can finally suppress its various rebel movements.

This makes it vitally important to Western strategic interests that the conservative and moderate Gulf oil exporting states--Kuwait, Bahrain, Qatar, Saudi Arabia, the UAE, and Oman--should create an effective deterrent. They are now linked together in the Gulf Cooperation Council, but they cannot develop strong enough naval and air forces to build a meaningful regional deterrent without U.S. aid. It is equally important that U.S. Navy and USCENTCOM forces should have a contingency access to friendly bases in as many Gulf states as possible, and have interoperable facilities, stocks, and major combat equipment.

## LESSONS OF THE ARMS SALE CRISIS

The lessons to the West of the Saudi arms sale are all too obvious, and virtually all are lessons that come from American mistakes. Britain's willingness to sell Saudi Arabia the Tornado has minimized the overall impact on the West and friendly Gulf states of U.S. political decisions which failed to benefit either Israel or the U.S. Western Europe, however, cannot make up for the collapse of U.S. military relations with key Arab states like Saudi Arabia.

It is one thing for the U.S. to make hard choices between aiding one friend at the cost of threatening another. It is another for the U.S. to make choices that damage a friend like Saudi Arabia without aiding a friend like Israel. Worse, it is absurd to damage the strategic interests of the U.S. at the cost of damaging the security of Israel when Israel is the very friend that the U.S. actions were intended to protect.

Both U.S. politicians, and Israel's friends and supporters, need to look beyond narrow and short sighted definitions of Israel's security, and avoid the kind of thoughtless "taking sides" that blocked the U.S. F-15 sale to Saudi Arabia. There also is a clear need for more leadership from the Reagan Administration. It is far from clear that the Administration ever chose to make the true nature of the U.S. sale clear to Israel's supporters or the Congress, and it is equally far from clear that the Administration ever honestly faced the consequences of what its area experts were telling it about the prospects for a British or French sale if the U.S. did not sell the F-15.

Debates over major arms sales are inevitable in any Western country. The problem with U.S. treatment of the Saudi sale did not lie in the fact the Reagan Administration faced a political battle, it lay in the fact that it failed to fight it. If the U.S. is to salvage anything from the resulting debacle, the Reagan Administration is now going to have to take the lead in working with Britain and France, in trying to rebuild U.S. credibility in Saudi Arabia and the Gulf, and in trying to create a better understanding of the need for U.S. military relations with the moderate Arab states on the part of the Congress and Israel's supporters in the U.S.

It is also unclear how much time the U.S. really has to try to restore its relations with Saudi Arabia. Saudi Arabia still has the equivalent of a letter of offer from France offering 46 Mirage 2000 fighters for 73 million barrels of oil plus a cash payment. While the Mirage 2000 variant offered would not be equivalent to the F-15E in payload, range, flight performance, or some of its more sophisticated avionics, the total cost would be around $3 billion or half the cost of the Tornado deal, and the Saudis would get another sophisticated attack fighter with most of the features in the Mirage 2000N nuclear strike fighter now being delivered to French forces and F-16s now in Israeli hands, and virtually all of the air-to-ground features of the upgraded F-15 MSIP.[39] This sale may well go forward when Saudi Arabia's oil revenues recover in the late 1980s, and would virtually destroy any future hopes of rebuilding standardization and interoperability between Saudi, Gulf, and U.S. power projection forces.

European arms sales to Saudi Arabia or other friendly states in the Middle East generally serve the West's strategic interests and reduce the impact of the Arab-Israeli conflict. If Saudi Arabia should turn to Europe for *all* its fighters because of its political problems with the U.S., however, this would have strategic implications which go far beyond that of an aircraft sale. The net impact of full Saudi reliance on European aircraft would be to weaken or break the one major remaining military relationship between the U.S. and Saudi Arabia, and the one most critical to USCENTCOM's deployment capability in terms of interoperable stocks, bases, and combat service facilities. Since no other Western state can assume the U.S. role in power projection in the Gulf, the result would be far more serious than the present Saudi shift to Britain.

[1] New York Times, November 18, 1984, p. A-12.

[2] Washington Post, January 24, 1985, p. A-18; Chicago Tribune, January 28, 1985, p. I-1; Washington Times, January 29, 1985, p. 1A, and January 30, 1985, p. 6A.

[3] The original sale of the F-15 had been approved on May 15, 1978, by a Senate vote of 54 to 44, and after a long political battle.

[4] See "Integrated Systems Evaluated on F-15", Aviation Week, April 11, 1985, pp. 47-57, and "F-15C/D Display Nears Test Stage", Aviation Week, February 20, 1985, pp. 77-81

[5] For a good description of the role of the current version of Harpoon see John F. Judge, "Harpoon Missile Targets Ships and Cost", Defense Electronics, April, 1985, pp. 92-98. Also see Bill Gunston, Modern Airborne Missiles, ARCO, N.Y., 1983, pp. 104-107.

[6] Washington Post, January 24, 1985, p. A-18; Chicago Tribune, January 28, 1985, p. I-1; Washington Times, January 29, 1985, p. 1A, and January 30, 1985, p. 6A.

[7] Washington Times, January 29, 1985, p. 1A, and January 30, 1985, p. 6A; Chicago Tribune, January 28, 1985, P. I-1, January 31, 1985, p. I-5, February 1, 1985, p. I-2; Baltimore Sun, January 31, 1986, p. 2A; New York Times, January 31, 1985, p. A-1; Washington Post, February 1, 1985, p. A-25.

[8] Chicago Tribune, January 31, 1985, p. I-5, Washington Post, February 1, 1985, p. A-25.

[9] New York Times, January 31, 1985, p. A-1; Boston Globe, February 3, 1985, p. 1.

[10] For typical reporting see Washington Times, February 5, 1985, p. 7B, February 11, 1985, p. 1D; Los Angeles Times, February 10, 1985, p. IV-5, February 12, 1985, p. II-5; February 13, 1985, p. I-1; New York Daily News, February 13, 1985, p. 24; Economist, February 9, 1985, pp. 25-26; Aviation Week, July 22, 1985, p. 21.

[11] John Newhouse, "Diplomatic Round", New Yorker, June 9, 1986, pp 52-54.

[12] Ibid.

[13] Ibid.

[14] See Anthony H. Cordesman, "The Saudi Arms Sale: The True Risks, Benefits, and Costs", Middle East Insight, Volume 4, Numbers 4 and 5, pp. 40-54 and "U.S. Middle East Aid: Some Questions", Defense and Foreign Affairs, June, 1986, pp. 15-18; and John Newhouse, " The Diplomatic Round, Politics and Weapons Sales", New Yorker, June 9, 1986, pp. 46-69.

15 International /Defense Intelligence, Volume 6, No. 53, December 31, 1984, pp. 1-2; Sunday Times, September 15, 1985; New York Times, September 16, 1985; Financial Times, December 21, 1984 and September 16, 1985; Aviation Week, September 30, 1985, p. 29, October 21, 1985, p. 73-74, March 24, 1986, p. 59; Defense and Foreign Affairs Daily, October 22, 1985, p. 1.

16 See Newhouse, "Diplomatic Round", pp. 60-61.

17 Sunday Times, September 15, 1985; New York Times, September 16, 1985; Financial Times, December 21, 1984 and September 16, 1985; Aviation Week, September 30, 1985, p. 29, October 21, 1985, p. 73-74, March 24, 1986, p. 59; Defense and Foreign Affairs Daily, October 22, 1985, p. 1.

18 Jane's Defense Weekly, June 14, 1986, p. 1075.

19 Washington Post, February 13, 1986, p. A-1, February 27, 1986, p. A-14, May 6, 1986; Wall Street Journal, February 23, 1986, p. 34, February 28, 1986; New York Times, March 1, 1986, p. 3, March 5, 1986, p. B-6; Aerospace Daily, April 22, 1986, p. 123.

20 Aviation Week, July 22, 1985, p. 21.

21 Section 131 of U.S. Public Law 99-83, August 8, 1985.

22 Wall Street Journal, 13 February, 1986, p. 34; Washington Post, February 13, 1986, p. A1.

23 The decision was not totally divorced from trying to preserve a market of immense value to the U.S. As of September 30, 1984, the Saudis had signed foreign military sales agreements worth a total of $47.7 billion, including $19.9 billion in construction and design services. U.S. FMS sales were averaging $4 billion annually with some $20.2 billion in sales still to be delivered.

24 Washington Post, February 27, 1986, p. A-14.

25 The sale raised the total Saudi inventory of U.S. AIM-9P and AIM-9L air-to-air missiles to 5,407. It raised the ratio of AIM-9Ls to Saudi F-15s (the only Saudi plane aside from the Tornado that could fire the AIM-9L) to 37:1 versus 6:1 for Israel and less than 10:1. The Saudis realized as well as the U.S. that Saudi fighters would never survive long enough in combat intensive enough to require such stock levels. The rationale was enhancing U.S. over-the-horizon capabilities.

26 New York Times, March 1, 1986, p. 3; Wall Street Journal, March 21, 1986, p. 28; Philadelphia Inquirer, May 5, 1986, p. 11A; Washington Times, May 5, 1986, p. 3A; Washington Post, May 5, 1986, p. A.5.

27 Washington Post, May 7, 1986, pp. A-1 and A-23.

28 Aviation Week, May 12, 1986, pp. 30-31.

[29] Wall Street Journal, June 6, 1986, p. 29; New York Times, June 6, 1986, p.1; Washington Post, June 5, 1986, p. A-35, June 6, 1986, p. A-1; Chicago Tribune, June 5, 1986, p. I-4; Baltimore Sun, June 5, 1986, p. 17A.

[30] Wall Street Journal, June 16, 1986, p. 37; New York Times, June 15, 1986, p.1.

[31] Estimate based on ACDA, World Military Expenditures and Arms Transfers, 1973-1983, Washington, GPO, 1985, p. 127.

[32] See D. Fiecke, B Kroqully, and D. Reich, "The Tornado Weapons System and Its Contemporaries", International Defense Review, No. 2/1977, and current Panavia brochures.

[33] Aviation Week, 30 September, 1985, p. 29.

[34] D. Fiecke, B Kroqully, and D. Reich, "The Tornado Weapons System and Its Contemporaries", International Defense Review, No. 2/1977, and current Panavia brochures.

[35] Bill Gunston, NATO Fighters and Attack Aircraft, ARCO, New York, 1983, p. 40

[36] For fuller details see U.S. Department of Commerce, Saudi Arabia, Foreign Economic Trends and Their Implications for the U.S., FET 84-80, July, 1984. Recent British reports have raised the total value of the sale to Britain to $7 billion, although the offset provisions involving oil make any analysis of its value uncertain.

[37] Washington Post, September 30, 1985.

[38] For further technical details, see "Integrated Systems Evaluated on F-15", Aviation Week, April 11, 1985, pp. 47-57, and "F-15C/D Display Nears Test Stage", Aviation Week, February 20, 1985, pp. 77-81; and "Saudis, British Define Terms of Tornado Sale", Aviation Week, September 30, 1985, p. 29

[39] For a "hands on" description of the Mirage 2000, see "Mirage 2000 Fighter", Aviation Week, June 24, 1985, pp. 38-39.

# VIII. KEY ISSUES AFFECTING WESTERN AND SAUDI RELATIONS

The arms sale crisis of 1985-1986 now divides the U.S. and Saudi Arabia to the point where it threatens to make any cohesive Western policy towards Saudi Arabia and the Gulf impossible. This is not simply a matter of access to weapons, it is a matter of U.S. and Western ability to preserve a proper balance in its treatment of both Israel and the Arab world. The Saudi search to buy advanced arms is surrounded by broader issues that affect virtually every aspect of Western and Saudi military relations. These issues include Western fears regarding Saudi internal stability and political alignments, Western concerns regarding the informal nature of the West's strategic ties to Saudi Arabia, and the potential military threat the Kingdom's military forces could pose to Israel.

## THE PROBLEM OF SAUDI STABILITY

No one can deny that Saudi Arabia faces major challenges as its society adapts to the sudden shifts in the nation's oil wealth, and to the forces of modernization. Regardless of any external threats, Saudi Arabia's future will be determined by such internal issues as whether it can continue to modernize in a way that maintains internal stability, and whether the ruling elite will share its power and the nation's wealth.

Fortunately, there are good prospects that Saudi Arabia will be able to continue to modernize in spite of the drop in its oil revenues, and with only limited internal strain and unrest. If anything, Saudi prospects for stability may be considerably better than those of most of the nations the U.S. depends upon for its strategic position in the developing world. There seems little near term prospect that the U.S. will run significant risks in furnishing high technology weapons to Saudi Arabia.

## THE "STABILITY" OF "INSTABILITY"

Saudi Arabia has long been one of the world's most stable "unstable" countries. The literature on the Near East in general, and on Saudi Arabia in particular, is littered with the bones of predictions regarding the instability of the Saudi Royal Family, Saudi society, Saudi international alignments, and Saudi Arabia's strategic position.

These predictions had a good grounding in fact when Nasser was at the height of his power and influence, but they now owe more to historical momentum than any indications that Saudi Arabia is confronted with internal problems it cannot master. In fact, there are a number of very real forces that seem likely to maintain Saudi stability during the next decade:

o In spite of occasional tension between the Sudairi and the other branches of the Royal Family, and between the Royal Family and senior ministers (such as the departure of Minister of Health Dr. Ghazi Algosaibi in April, 1984), the succession seems stable, and should shift smoothly from King Fahd to Prince Abdullah and then Prince Sultan. At the same time, the senior members of the Royal Family seem willing to place increasing reliance on technocrats and Ministers outside the Royal Family in every area except the armed forces, foreign relations, and internal security-- areas traditionally the province of the Royal Family.

o Saudi Arabia may not have any form of popular representation in the Western sense, but the Royal Family and their various Majlis offer a considerable amount of practical pluralism. While experts may debate whether the Saudi Royal Family should be counted as having 300 senior princes, 3,000 princes, or 5,000 members, the fact remains that it is so big and so politically and regionally diverse that its various factions tend to stabilize Saudi Arabia's strategic position, rather than weaken it. Various factions in the Royal Family and their supporters in the government limit major policy and strategic shifts. Opposition factions tend to become coopted. Internal tensions are resolved in the Royal Family's dialectic.

o The Royal Family always has the option of opening up its decision making beyond the traditional majlis, and to appoint a representative consultative council. While the promises to create such a body now date back at least ten years and remain uncertain, it is interesting to note that the government awarded a construction contract in September, 1984, for a building to hold a National Consultative Council (Majlis as Shura) as well as the King's Office and Council of Ministers.

o Saudi Arabia's wealth (a $10,000 per capita income even in a period of low oil revenues) and small population (8-10 million) act to unite and stabilize Saudi behavior. Regional, class, tribal and other tensions are offset by both the Kingdom's wealth and by a consciousness of its vulnerability to outside pressure.

o Saudi Arabia's economy is not impervious to changes in oil prices, nor is its society and strategic position. Virtually all Saudi economic data indicate, however, that the Kingdom can maintain its social programs and living standards in spite of the cuts in oil revenue. The Kingdom would have to cut back massively on show piece development projects and military expenditures (although most potentially hostile powers would have to cut back far more), but its combination of continued oil revenue and investment income should be adequate to deal with any near term social needs.

o The contraction of the Saudi economy will cause economic problems for a number of Saudi entrepreneurs--as well as a number of foreign companies. Some Saudi firms (National Chemical Industries, Ali and Fahd Shobokshi, and Carlson Al Saudia) ran into such problems in 1984, and more are certain to follow. The Kingdom will probably also have to cut back in areas like petrochemical development and agriculture. Nevertheless, a mild contraction is, if anything, desirable and it seems doubtful that many ordinary Saudis (or wealthy ones for that matter) will be hurt in ways which lead to unrest. It is also unlikely that there will be any broad loss of confidence in Saudi Arabia's economic future, given the number of experts predicting that oil revenues will begin to recover in the late 1980s or early 1990s.

o Saudi Arabia has already survived the most explosive period of political change in the Arab world. Saudi Arabia's modernization, and the rising political consciousness of its population, comes after the failure of Nasser, the Baath, Marxism, military elites, and most of the competing secular ideologies and regimes that might have threatened a rapidly changing Saudi society a decade earlier.

o Although many Westerners tend to discount the Saudi government's claim to acting as the protector of Islam, the fact remains that Saudi Arabia has gone to considerable lengths to reinforce its Islamic character since the uprising at the Grand Mosque in 1980. The Saudi government seems to have done a good job in balancing the desire for modernization against the desire for a return to a more traditional Islamic society. While other Islamic states or movements may be more extreme, it is unclear that their example is broadly attractive to any element of Saudi society.

o The radical political opposition to the Saudi Royal Family and government from groups like the Saudi Communist Party, the various Ba'athist radical groups, and elements of the Arab Nationalist Movement is extraordinarily weak. The Socialist Labor Party is probably the strongest radical party but has no popular following and no real political impact. The Saudi military is now virtually free from the kind of pro-Nasser or pro-Ba'athist elements that were a limited threat in the 1950s and 1960s. While some incidents and bombings seem inevitable, particularly in view of Iran and Libya's active support of various terrorist groups, they do not seem to reflect any broad movements within Saudi Arabia.[1]

o Saudi Arabia has undergone, and is undergoing, rapid social change, but this has stabilizing effects as well as destabilizing ones. While Saudi Arabia is an extremely young society (the population growth rate is over 3.3%, and more than 50% of the population is under 18), and has experienced rapid modernization and "urbanization", the government has created an exceptional set of social and financial incentives for the younger Saudis, and has done a reasonably good job of depolitising education and most career paths. This, coupled to the demand for skilled Saudi labor and the government's interest in coopting the more politically active university graduates, has helped defuse the effects of change.

o Saudi Arabia seems to have done a good job of adjusting to the complaints of its Shi'ite minority (about 300,000 or 3% of the population) since the riots in the Qatif oasis in late 1979 and early 1980. Khomeini seems to have lost much of his allure, and the Saudi government has made important concessions in terms of job, development, and religious ceremonies. Both the Governor of Qatif and the commander of the National Guard at the time of the riots have been replaced with new and far more progressive figures (Mohammed as Sharif and Prince Mishari lbin Saud bin Abdul Aziz). The Eastern province also has a new young dynamic governor.

o The impact of Saudi Arabia's dependence on foreign labor does not seem to have produced the internal security problems many experts predicted. If anything, the political impact of foreign labor was far more threatening 10-20 years ago--when such labor was more subject to influence from Nasser, radical Palestinian elements, and various Gulf liberation movements--than it is today. The number of foreign Arabs has been steadily reduced, while many of those who remain--particularly the Yemens--are being absorbed into Saudi society. Recent CIA estimates indicate that foreign workers are still about 50% of the work force and 17% of the population, but a steadily rising proportion are Asians on carefully controlled contracts who cannot bring their wives into the country and do not present a cohesive political threat. The number of Yemeni and other Arab workers in Saudi Arabia has fallen steadily since 1980.

Key Issues Affecting Western and Saudi Relations

EXTERNAL FORCES FOR INTERNAL STABILITY

These forces for internal stability are reinforced by other forces which affect Saudi Arabia's strategic position. While it is always easy to list the external threats to the Kingdom, it is important to note that:
- o The Kingdom's leadership is conservative. It rarely exposes itself or Saudi Arabia beyond carefully calculated limits, and it has decades of experience in balancing off the various radical Arab states, moderate Arab states, the U.S., and Europe.
- o Saudi Arabia's cautious foreign policy, and careful effort to maintain relations even with hostile radical states while using economic and political aid to develop good relations with nations like Syria and Iraq, is another major source of stability. The resulting ambiguities in Saudi policy often irritates Americans who would like to see more decisive Saudi action in the Gulf or on issues like an Arab-Israeli peace. They are, however, a remarkably successful way of allowing the Kingdom to maintain ties to the U.S. without becoming acutely vulnerable to radical pressure, and of reducing the threats the Kingdom faces. From a practical viewpoint, the U.S. almost certainly benefits far more from a cautious and secure Saudi Arabia than from a "brave" and vulnerable one.
- o Saudi Arabia has developed a high level of sophistication in using economic aid and political influence in countering the military and strategic pressures from its neighbors. It has also shown great resilience in recovering from political setbacks in dealing with its neighbors, and in gradually neutralizing or coopting radical leaders. Saudi dealings with Syria and South Yemen are good cases in point.
- o Saudi Arabia has been, and will remain, too valuable a prize for most threats to risk U.S. or Western reaction. Neither the USSR nor any major bordering state can pose a direct threat without reasonable assurance that the West will react.

This combination of internal and external forces is scarcely enough to inspire a panglossian confidence that Saudi Arabia can remain unscathed by the strategic effects of internal and external forces. Saudi Arabia faces very real threats, and the failure to provide the arms it needs to build a regional deterrent and to strengthen U.S. and Saudi military relations could gravely weaken the Kingdom's security and freedom of action. A weak Saudi Arabia would serve no one's interest--even that of Israel--since it would be forced to accommodate radical and extremist pressure. At the same time, a Saudi Arabia with close strategic relations with the U.S. is almost certain to continue to pursue a policy of moderation and stability.

## THE KEY VARIABLES

Several factors, however, could reverse the present trend towards internal stability. The Royal Family could expand its occasional tensions or feuds into a major struggle for power. More probably, it might make the mistake of attempting to keep too much of Saudi Arabia's wealth during a period of economic contraction, of keeping too many senior positions for the Royal Family that should go to career civilians and military, and/or of failing to shift from ruling to governing at the pace required. These mistakes do not seem likely, given the Royal family's flexibility and pragmatism over the last decade, but they seem to be more serious risks than Saudi Arabia's problems with its Shi'ites, Islamic fundamentalism, or youth *per se*.

The West must put these risks in careful perspective. Saudi Arabia is far more likely to evolve in the way the West desires if key Western nations maintain close military relations with the Kingdom. The transfer of Western arms is a key factor in ensuring that the Saudi regime will retain the confidence of the Saudi military, and that the dominant pro-Western factions in the ruling elite will continue in power.

Sustaining the informal alliance between the West and Saudi Arabia will also discourage external pressure on the Saudi regime, and strengthen the economic and educational contacts that have created a bridge between two very different societies and cultures. The West almost certainly runs more risk of creating Saudi instability from abandoning close military relations than it does from maintaining them.

## INFORMAL RELATIONS VERSUS IN-COUNTRY BASES

The West is faced with the practical reality that it cannot expect to transform its *de facto* alliance with Saudi Arabia into a formal treaty relationship, with U.S. or European bases in the Kingdom, or a major military presence. The political forces in the region simply do not permit such Saudi action, except in the face of a clear and present threat. Western military bases or a major Western military presence would probably do more to hurt the Western interests than to aid them. Such bases would be key targets for terrorism, and political attacks from Iran and other radical states, and an ideal point of leverage for external efforts to try to divide Saudi Arabia from Iraq and the other GCC countries.

The careful distinction that nations like Saudi Arabia and Egypt make between reliance on Western military advice and equipment, on Western technicians and support, and U.S. "over the horizon" reinforcements,--and any formal acceptance of a military treaty or western military base--may be difficult for many people in the West to understand. It is, however, a vital distinction in a part of the world where most Arab states have had to fight for their independence, where nationalism and anti-colonialism are the preconditions for political legitimacy, and where ties to the U.S. must be kept especially vague and low profile because of U.S. ties to Israel.

Saudi Arabia cannot hope to disguise its informal military ties with the West, but it can hope to clearly assert its sovereignty and independence. It can avoid the stigma of allowing formal bases on its soil or an active military presence. It can demonstrate to other Arab states that it is not a proxy for the U.S. or Europe, and maintain its religious and political legitimacy in the face of charges from hostile or radical political movements and nations.

At the same time, the West fully accept the fact that the kind of basing arrangements and formal treaties that Britain and the U.S. used to contain the USSR in the 1950s and 1960s are probably no longer in the West's interest. Such arrangements have obvious legitimacy and value in the case of NATO, Japan, and Korea, but they present problems for virtually every developing or "Third World" country that aligns its interests too closely with the West.

The West also has every interest in having the GCC states assume responsibility for their own deterrence and defense to the maximum extent they can, and in avoiding the need to commit Western forces to military confrontations or low level conflicts. The West also has a strong interest in helping the rulers of the GCC states retain their political legitimacy within the Arab world, and in preserving Saudi Arabia's religious legitimacy in an area where Islamic fundamentalism remains a serious threat. An "over-the-horizon" reinforcement policy and a suitable arms sale policy, offer the West political and strategic advantages that more than offset any military disadvantages it incurs from not having forces or formal military bases.

## THE IMPACT OF SAUDI ARABIA'S ARMS NEEDS ON ISRAEL'S SECURITY

The fundamental reason that Western arms sales to Saudi Arabia are not a threat to Israel does not lie in the details of the arms Saudi Arabia is requesting, or their technology, but rather in the fact that Saudi Arabia will remain a relatively weak military power that must concentrate on deterrence and defense. Saudi Arabia faces more direct and much higher priority threats, and would never take the risk of a major conflict with Israel.

No senior Saudi official or military officer has any illusions about the consequences of such a conflict or the outcome of any Arab-Israeli conflict well into the 1990s. If anything, Israel may present a threat to Saudi Arabia because U.S. ties to Israel and U.S. domestic pressures have made it unnecessarily difficult to maintain a strategic relationship between the U.S. and Saudi Arabia, and have delayed and complicated Saudi Arabia's military modernization.

### LIMITATIONS ON THE SAUDI THREAT TO ISRAEL

Saudi Arabia lacks any common border with Israel, and the previous chapters have shown that it lacks the military strength and manpower to engage Israel unilaterally at any time in the foreseeable future. It can at most provide the same symbolic forces in support of the Arab cause that it has provided in the past.

Saudi Arabia did not contribute any significant forces to the 1948 or 1956 Arab-Israeli conflicts. It supplied about 4,500 men, 10 tanks, and 40 aircraft to assist in the defense of Jordan in 1967, out of a total Arab strength of over 250,000 men 2,000 tanks, and 950 aircraft. Saudi forces, however, arrived only after the lightning pace of the Six-Day War had already ensured a decisive Israeli victory. Saudi Arabia contributed 1,500 men, about one tank squad, and some replacement aircraft in the 1973 war, but in a defensive role in support of Jordan and Syria that resulted in only minor combat. Its contribution to the Arab forces arrayed against Israel has otherwise been limited to stationing troops in Jordan and the Golan during periods of peace.

Saudi Arabia's forces are far better developed today than they were in 1973, but Israel's forces have improved at least as quickly as those of Saudi Arabia, and Saudi forces still lag far behind the current capabilities of Israeli forces.

The Saudi Army is undermanned, dispersed throughout the Kingdom, and incapable of making its present seven brigade strength fully operational until the mid-1990s. Its diverse mix of armor leads to major problems in operational readiness and serviceability, and Saudi Arabia lacks the ability to provide logistical, service, and combat support to project a significant part of its forces. The rest of the Saudi Army is in the process of transition to new equipment and is unprepared to move against Israel in any strength. Further, the terrain in the Saudi-Jordanian border area, and the distances involved, would force any Saudi Army units to move towards Jordan along a very limited number of paved roads. They would be easily detectable and highly vulnerable during any such movements.

The Saudi Air Force is excellent by Gulf standards, but it can pose only a limited future threat to Israeli forces. Saudi Arabia's offensive air capabilities now consist of 65 F-5E and 24 F-5F fighters. The 24 F-5F have the avionics to use Maverick air-to-surface missiles. As has been discussed in Chapters V and VI, these F-5E/Fs are limited in range and avionics capability. While they are well configured to match most of the Soviet made aircraft in current Gulf and Red Sea air forces, they cannot compete effectively with the air defense fighters in the Israeli Air Force. They would also be hard pressed to compete in air combat with Iraq's Mirage F-1s, or the new Soviet fighters that will enter the forces of potentially hostile states in the late 1980s and early 1990s.

Saudi Arabia also has 16 F-5Bs in operational conversion units, and 8 RF-5E reconnaissance aircraft. The F-5Bs do not contribute materially to its strength, and the RF-5Es cannot conduct recce missions against the Israeli Air Force (IAF) and survive. Saudi Arabia's 38 BAC-167 trainer-COIN aircraft are no longer armed or usable in combat, and its 23 active Lightning fighters are obsolete and lack the avionics and performance to engage Israeli fighters.

Equally important, Saudi Arabia's ability to operate against Israel is severely limited by its basing structure. It currently has only three airstrips in the vicinity of Israel, and only Tabuk is equipped to operate military aircraft. The Saudi Army only has forces equivalent to one and one-half mechanized brigades at Tabuk, and the only operational brigade is manned largely by Pakistanis and is extraordinarily unlikely to be used against Israel. In fact, the vulnerability of these forces is demonstrated by constant Israeli overflights in the area.

These Israeli overflights go so far as to include simulated attacks on Saudi targets. For example, Saudi sources indicate that Israel flew a recce sortie into the "notch" area in the Saudi-Jordanian border on March 30, 1984. On May 13th, three Israeli aircraft flew through Jordan and Saudi Arabia and over the Red Sea. Thirteen aircraft were involved, and one recce fighter flew 30 miles into Saudi territory. IAF aircraft overflew Jordan and into Saudi Arabia on August 20, 1984. Israeli formations penetrated deep into Saudi airspace on November 19, December 4th, and December 12th. Two Israeli formations overflew Saudi Arabia on January 25, 1985. One flight of three stayed high in the air combat "ambush" position while another flight of four flew within 25-30 NM of Tabuk and then conducted a simulated air raid on a Saudi radio transmitter at the seaport at Dibah. While such Saudi sources may be controversial, they have physical evidence to back up their claims. There are 18 F-16 drop tanks collected at Tabuk, all of which have serial numbers showing they came from Israel.

The Saudi Army facilities at Sadada, Kar, Turki, Badana, and Rafha cannot support offensive armored operations. The new Saudi military city at Hafr al-Batin is more than 350 nautical miles from the Israeli border, and is designed to support defensive operations along the border with Iraq and Kuwait. Its structure is best suited for short operations with a limited logistic "tail", and the airstrip is totally unsheltered, and unequipped to support offensive ground or air operations against Israel.

Saudi Arabia's force posture and basing effectively limit it to providing support of Jordan, although it might be able to provide symbolic (reinforced battalion strength) deployments to Syria. The Saudi Army is not equipped or manned with the mix of tank transporters, mobile support equipment, and support forces it needs to operate at long distances from its main western support bases at Tabuk and Hafr al-Batin. While it can always make token deployments, and could operate in a reserve or static defense role in an area like the Golan, it could not support and sustain intensive armored combat.

The Saudi Army's breakdown rate, lack of recovery and repair capability, and lack of supply and support capability would quickly cause anything more than brigade sized forces to collapse. Even if Saudi forces operated out of Jordan and were supplied by the closest Saudi base at

Tabuk, it is 200 kilometers from Tabuk to Eilat and 450 kilometers to Jerusalem by air and roughly 350 kilometers and 600 kilometers by road. This is too long a "tail" for a force so dependent on central support bases and foreign personnel. The support facilities at Tabuk also can only support a maximum of two Saudi brigades in active armored combat--and even this assumes additional service and combat support by Jordan. The facilities at Tabuk could only support one brigade in the kind of sustained combat Saudi Arabia would have to fight with Israel without Jordanian support. Syria lacks the equipment and interoperable spares and ammunition to provide such support.

In terms of air operations, Tabuk can currently support a maximum of three Saudi squadrons, and its capacity will only expand to four squadrons when present base improvement plans are completed in the late 1980s or early 1990s. Tabuk is currently defended by three Hawk missile batteries, but it lacks shelter facilities. It will have four Improved Hawk batteries and the same shelters as the Saudi base at Dhahran by the late-1980s, but it will only have shelters for 36-48 fighters, and will be limited to a maximum operational strength of 60-75 combat aircraft. The only other main base that might be created near Israel is the option of converting the airfield at Hail to a main base at some point in the late 1980s or early 1990s. This now seems unlikely for budget reasons, and Hail is further from Israel. It is better positioned to defend against any attack through southern Iraq.[2]

The Saudi air strips near Jordan at Turayf and Gurayat are barely suitable for fighter dispersal and recovery, but lack all the facilities to act as main operating bases and will not acquire such capabilities in the foreseeable future. Aside from the runways at Hafr al-Batin--which will not be equipped or sheltered as a main air base--the nearest alternative main air base will be at Taif, nearly 1,000 kilometers away.

Saudi ability to conduct air combat would be severely limited by other factors. Saudi Arabia stated in 1978 that it did not plan to deploy its F-15s at either Tabuk or Hafr al-Batin. In practice, this means that as long as the Saudi Air Force is dependent on the U.S. for its first line fighters, support, upgrades, and munitions, it cannot move its dedicated support equipment for the F-15 C/D or F-15E, or use U.S. contract personnel at either base, without U.S. permission.

Even assuming that Saudi Arabia was willing to risk a cut off of U.S. technical support, it would take a month to move critical equipment to Tabuk, and this could not be done without providing warning and risking a pre-emptive Israeli strike. These factors would limit any Saudi "surprise attack" using the F-15 refueling at Tabuk and the limited numbers of forward sorties that could be backed by service at a rear base like Taif. This situation will not be materially affected by supplying KE-3A tankers or F-15 conformal fuel tanks to Saudi Arabia, although they might enable Saudi

Arabia to provide a limited fighter screen over eastern Syria or northeastern Jordan.

As for the aircraft Saudi Arabia will deploy at Tabuk in the future, it has already indicated it will not base its new Tornados at Tabuk, during at least the initial conversion phase of absorbing the new aircraft. While Saudi Arabia must replace its Lightnings, it will evidently do so with F-5s because it would otherwise risk increasing the political gap between itself and the U.S., and block any near term hope of future U.S. arms sales. The Saudis could not deploy the support and service equipment for the F-15s or Tornados without U.S. and British technical aid. Saudi Arabia could not sustain its aircraft in combat if the U.S. and Britain cut off support in response to any Saudi effort to unilaterally redeploy F-15 or Tornado support and repair equipment from other bases.

This means Saudi Arabia will probably be limited to deploying its aging F-5E fighters through 1990. It will be unlikely to buy any other new fighters for Tabuk from any third country before the late 1980s or make them fully operational before the early 1990s. British Aerospace already supports the Lightnings at Tabuk and has some 2,300 personnel in the country, but will evidently be shifting most of these personnel to other new bases to help with absorption of the Tornado.

Even if Saudi Arabia eventually purchases the Mirage 2000 as a replacement for its F-5s and deploys some of these aircraft at Tabuk, this is unlikely to have much effect on its actual warfighting capabilities. The Mirage 2000 would increase the theoretical threat to Israel because the Mirage would have a high capability relative to the Israeli fighters and forces then in service. It is important to note, however, that no probable mix of Saudi deployments of the Mirage 2000 or any other mix of Western fighters could reach sufficient strength to keep Tabuk from being vulnerable to Israeli raids using the advanced runway and air base suppression munitions now coming into service--some of which have stand off range relative to Saudi ground based air defenses. Such raids would deprive Saudi Arabia of its one major operating base within range of Israel.

There is also a massive practical difference between Saudi ability to engage other Gulf and Red Sea Air Forces, and to engage the forces of Israel. Although some Saudi pilots have logged over 1,000 hours, and have demonstrated excellent flight proficiency in flying against top-grade U.S. "aggressor" squadrons, the Saudi Air Force is simply not ready to fly air combat or offensive missions against Israel. It would lack the endurance, basing, air control and warning capability, and command structure to avoid extremely high loss-to-kill ratios.

Saudi Arabia also cannot approach Israel's skill in managing air combat or sophisticated electronic warfare capability. No foreseeable pattern of U.S. technology transfer will prevent Saudi Arabia from falling steadily further behind Israel's sophisticated electronic order of battle. Once again, the only factor that could shift this balance would be to drive Saudi Arabia away from the U.S. and lead it to buy its air systems from France or Britain. Both nations have much more permissive sales policies than the U.S.

Table 8.1 helps put this aspect of the Saudi "threat" to Israel in perspective. Although it covers only the small portion of Israeli electronic warfare capabilities that are public, it shows that these capabilities are far more sophisticated than those of any competing Middle Eastern state, and the advanced state of Israel's defense industry ensures that it not only will lead in hardware, but develop a steadily greater lead in software. Israel not only has proven its technical mastery in the 1982 fighting, it is the only state in the world committed to, and capable of, developing such software in a form tailored to regional combat needs and in a form proven by actual combat.

## Key Issues Affecting Western and Saudi Relations

Table 8.1: Comparative Middle Eastern Electronic Orders of Battle

| Electronic Mission Aircraft and AWACS | Other EW and Countermeasure Systems |
|---|---|
| **Israel** | |
| 4 Grumman E-2C Hawkeye AEW aircraft<br>1 ABCCC & 4 ELINT configured B-707s<br>6 Jamming configured TA-4H Skyhawk with AGM-45 ARM missiles<br>Tadiran multirole and EW RPVs<br>TC-2 Kfir jamming variants<br>Possibly Beechcraft RU-21 electronic surveillance aircraft with Guardrail SIGINT D/F system | EL/K-1250 20-510Mhz COMINT receiver<br>AN/ALR-73 ESM and upgraded ELINT<br><br>EL/L-8303 2-18GHz ESM system<br>EL/L-8310 0.5-18GHz COMINT receiver<br>EL/L-8312 60MHz-40GHz ELINT/ESM system<br>EL/L-8230 G-J band noise repeater jammer (on Kfir/F-16)<br>EL/L-8202 F-J band advanced jamming pod<br>AN/ALE & Israeli multiband chaff/flare dispensers<br>Elta EL/K-1250 and L-8310 COMINT receivers<br>Raport III(?) E-J band self-defense system and spot and barrage jammers<br>AN/ALR-45,56, & 62 radar warning receivers<br>Beechcraft RU-21 electronic surveillance<br>AN/ALQ-99, 126, 130, 135, and 151 jammer technology released<br>AN/ALQ-101 family of jamming pods<br>AN/ALQ-119 and 131 noise deception jamming pods covering E/F, G/H, and I bands and 2-20GHz |
| **Egypt** | |
| 2 ELINT configured C-130H<br>4 Grumman E-2C Hawkeye AEW with ESM pods and ELINT deception pods (2 on delivery)<br>Westland Commando ELINT/Jamming helicopters with Selenia IHS-6 ELINT/Jamming systems | AN/ALQ-119 noise/deception jamming<br><br>AN/ALQ-131 2-20GHz modular noise |
| **Iran** | |
| 3 ELINT configured C-130H | Types and details unknown |
| **Iraq** | |
| None | Extensive, but types and details unknown |
| **Jordan** | |
| None | Very limited. Largely last generation. |

## Key Issues Affecting Western and Saudi Relations

**Kuwait**

Data link to Saudi E-3A on order

**Libya**

MiG-25D ELINT fighters based at Okba Ben Naif and probably flown by Soviet pilots

Extensive Soviet-supplied system

**Saudi Arabia**

5 E-3A Sentry AWACs on order
Study of purchase of 2 maritime patrol aircraft with ESSM capability

Limited British and French ESSM gear tied to ground based radar net.

**Syria**

Uncertain. Some Hip-8 ELINT/Jammer helicopters

Extensive Soviet supplied system, but types and details unknown

**UAE**

4 ELINT Configured CASA C-212
Study of purchase of E-2C or similar AEW aircraft

Adapted from Jane's Defense Weekly, June 22, June 29, and July 6, 1985, and the DMS data base as of June, 1986.

Perhaps most important of all, Saudi Arabia will lack the aircraft strength and pilot numbers to accept the losses it would suffer in any air combat with Israel without crippling its air capabilities and its ability to defend its oil fields for years to come. The fact that the Kingdom is moving toward a considerable self-defense capability against air threats in the Gulf area does not indicate that it will acquire a significant capability against Israel or that it could afford to send more than token forces against Israel without the risk of catastrophic losses.

## THE COMBINED IMPACT OF CURRENT AND NEAR TERM U.S. ARMS SALES

The delivery of Peace Shield, the E-3A, conformal tanks, AIM-9Ls, and the sale of upgraded and additional F-15C/Ds to the Kingdom, will do relatively little to enhance Saudi offensive operations against Israel, although it might have a significant effect in deterring Israeli strategic strikes on or through Saudi Arabia.

### THE IMPACT OF THE E-3A AND PEACE SHIELD

The E-3A and now Peace Shield $C^3I$ system will not be operational until the late 1980s, and it will then require U.S. support for the life of the aircraft. The Saudi E-3As have a systems mean time between failure of 27.4 hours and will need U.S. support at maximum intervals of three days to stay operational. There are also sound technical and operational reasons why the E-3A will not be a threat to Israel.

The capabilities and "noncapabilities" of the E-3A are summarized in Table 8.2. This table shows that, although the E-3A is of major value to Gulf air defense, it has far less value in air operations against Israel. It has none of the signals intelligence capability provided on the Nimrod or Israeli-operated E2-C Hawkeye. Saudi Arabia could not acquire such a capability covertly, and the U.S. personnel operating the E-3A would be provided with at least a year of warning during the period in which Saudi Arabia learned how to operate it.

# Key Issues Affecting Western and Saudi Relations

## Table 8.2: The Mission Capabilities of the Saudi E-3A and Peace Shield

### The System Has Capability To:

Detect and track all aircraft, even at low altitudes, provided they are moving faster than 120 NMH and are above the radar horizon line
- o 175 NM for MiG-21 sized targets
- o 240 NM for SU-24 sized targets
- o 360 NM for Backfire

Detect fighter aircraft above the horizon line beyond 208 NM for range only

Detect ships and low speed aircraft over water
- o Virtually all of Israel is immune unless E-3A moves too close to survive
- o 35-208 NM range
- o Ship must be metal and larger than 40 meters
- o Depends on sea conditions

Analyze and manage Gulf, Red Sea, and Yemen sized war using Peace Shield ground based system

Provide secure data links against Gulf and Red Sea threats

Link Saudi fighters, ships, and ground based air defenses
- o Make optimal use of F-15 as air defense fighter

Collect SIGINT or ELINT

Downlink to USN and USAF fighters and ships

Identify "friendly forces" with proper IFF transponders

### The System Has No Capability To:

See any moving target on the ground
- o Cannot see ground force equipment such as tanks, artillery, and troops

Cover most helicopter movements
- o Can pick up occasional rotor movement

Cover any moving object not within a prolonged radar line of sight
- o Virtually all of Israel is immune unless the E-3A moves too close to survive

Operate with maximum effectiveness in air combat mode against Israel without U.S software programs which are not released to any foreign country.

Predict fighter movements or actions beyond their current vector

Provide secure data and IFF links in combat against Israel

Aid in munitions delivery against tactical ground targets

Provide radar mapping of ground

Collect intelligence such as SIGINT, ELINT, or ESSM

Fully analyze air war over Israel without new software

Operate with maximum effectiveness except with fighters in Saudi Air Force. No software provided for most efficient air-to-air combat modes against U.S. fighters other than F-4 and F-5E, or to support fighters types other than those in Saudi Air Force.

Saudi Arabia also cannot acquire the kind of advanced Electronic Support Measures (ESM) and infrared (IR) sensors necessary to upgrade its E-3As against improved jammers and other countermeasures without U.S. support and at the rate the U.S. permits. USAF studies of the improvements necessary to make the AWACS viable in the late 1980s and 1990s show that a continuing process of technology transfer will be required to meet the Warsaw Pact threat. As Britain has learned in trying to develop the Nimrod, no other Western state has the combination of technology base and resources necessary to produce the fully integrated and sophisticated systems needed for the E-3A. Saudi Arabia will remain dependent on the U.S. for a phased technology transfer program well into the mid-1990s.

As has been discussed in Chapter VI, the Saudi version of AWACS will lack the advanced Have Quick and Seek Talk jam-resistant, frequency-agile voice links and the JTIDS digital data links necessary to prevent the Israeli use of electronic countermeasures. The APY-2 radar of the AWACS will have no value in detecting movements by land force equipment. As a result, the AWACS cannot be used to assist in attack missions or in analyzing army operations.

The confusion that emerged during the 1981 debate over the AWACS sale about the inability of AWACS to cover ground targets stemmed from the difference between the collection capability of the radar on the E-3A and its ability to process and analyze the resulting signal. The APY-2 radar will collect all movements by any object capable of radar reflection within its line of sight when it is operated in the high-PRF pulse-Doppler mode. In doing so, however, it collects a large volume of "clutter" signals from land objects that cannot be processed and interpreted by the IBM CC-2 computer and radar correlator on the aircraft.

This limitation forces the electronics and computer on the E-3A to reject all radar data reflected by land objects moving at less than 80 nautical miles an hour and to treat as "ground clutter" most objects moving at less than 100 NM per hour at altitudes of less than 200 feet. For obvious reasons, no army operates, or has in design, land weapons that operate at these speeds and altitudes. In fact, the E-3A is extremely erratic in tracking low-altitude helicopter movements, although it can occasionally track the motion of large rotor blades.

The Saudi version of the AWACS also has the capability to use its radar to receive signals from medium-sized or large metal ships at sea moving at speeds above 10-15 knots by using the radar's low-PRF, compressed-pulse mode. This coverage is dependent on the sea state, and it has no value over land since it produces a chaotic mixture of information and false signals, or "noise." The "interleave" mode of the AWACS allows near-simultaneous air and maritime coverage, but no land coverage. No upgrade or refit of the E-3A can give it land coverage.

The Saudi E-3As can do little, if anything, to enhance the Arab threat to Israel until they are actually deployed to the northern area. They cannot collect data on Israeli air movements or other intelligence from their patrol areas in the Eastern Province. They could not, for example, cover the Israeli raid on Iraq's Osirak reactor without being deployed further west, much less Israeli air operations over Jordan and Syria If they are deployed to the west, the Saudi Air Force will face massive survivability problems if Saudi Arabia attempts to use them to support air combat over Israel and most of Jordan and Syria.

Unlike the relatively flat terrain of the Gulf, the terrain of Israel, the Sinai, Jordan, Syria, and Lebanon is filled with ridges and mountains. These terrain barriers severely "shadow block", or limit, the line-of-sight coverage of the E-3A at low altitudes. Thus a Saudi E-3A would have to fly over Jordan or Syria to provide reasonable low-altitude coverage of Israel. Since Israel's E-2Cs can passively detect the operation of the E-3A at ranges of up to 400 NM, the Saudi AWACS would be a "sitting duck" and would have to fly well within the kill range of Israeli F-15s.

USAF studies have shown that even if the E-3As operate north of Tabuk in the "notch" in the Saudi-Jordanian border area close to Israel, their low-altitude coverage of Israel would be severely reduced by terrain-shielding. It would offer only limited additional coverage beyond that provided by land-based radars in Jordan and Syria.

Since Israel will operate an air force of roughly 600 first line combat aircraft from a territory with less than 1% of the airspace of Saudi Arabia, most Israeli sorties could not be determined as attacks on the AWACS until they were within minutes of reaching it and were virtually assured of a kill. Further, Israel would have the electronic warfare capabilities to jam any AWACS flying in such fixed predictable orbits, to jam or read its communications, and to enter its IFF system as "Saudi aircraft". These capabilities could expose the Saudi E-3As to instant attack.

UPGRADING SAUDI ARABIA'S EXISTING 60 F-15C/DS

If the U.S. does finally sell Saudi Arabia the MSIP upgrade for its F-15 C/Ds, this will not significantly affect Saudi Arabia's ability to engage Israel in air combat by the time the conversions become fully operational. Saudi Arabia will lack the basing and support capability to use the F-15s at Tabuk, and the improvements in the F-15C/D will not keep pace with similar qualitative improvements in the Israeli F-16s and F-15s, and its acquisition of a new Lavi or similar force structure fighter. By the time the Saudi Air Force fully absorbs its new Tornado air defense fighters in the early 1990s, and Saudi Arabia is ready to exploit more and/or better F-15s, the Israeli Air Force will have improved to the point where it has expanded, rather than simply maintained, its overall edge over the Saudi Air Force.

The E-3A and additional F-15C/D MSIPs could only offer Saudi Arabia more significant benefits in an air war with Israel if the U.S. agreed to support F-15 operations at Tabuk and if the E-3As operated in defense of Saudi airspace.

If the E-3As flew in a patrol area centered on an axis north from Tabuk and about 150 nautical miles within the Saudi border, it could provide both low-altitude coverage and survivability. The AIM-9Ls would add an increase in dogfight capability, and the KE-3A tankers and conformal fuel tanks would give the F-15C/D MSIP the endurance and range to maintain a significant air screen. The package would thus allow Saudi Arabia to deploy its fighters effectively in defending its border area, reduce the need for combat air patrol, and provide warning and vectoring for air-to-air combat in defense of Saudi airspace from about 6-9:1 in Israel's favor to 3-6:1--a significant increase in the effectiveness of Saudi air defenses.

Even in such a defensive role, however, the E-3A and Saudi F-15s would be vulnerable to Israeli saturation and pre-emptive Israeli attack. Further, any substantial F-15 and F-5E losses will mean a critical loss of first-line Saudi Air Force pilots. Saudi Arabia would also risk the loss of U.S. technical support and of its future ability to operate the bulk of its Air Force equipment unless it was fighting purely in self-defense.

The combination of the Saudi E-3A, improved F-15 forces, F-5E, AIM-9L, Peace Shield and Improved Hawk would, however, almost certainly be formidable enough to discourage any Israeli attack on Saudi Arabia, and the Israeli Air Force would experience far more severe problems in conducting selective strategic air strikes against Saudi ports, cities, or oil facilities of the kind that IDF planners have discussed since 1973 and executed against Iraq in the Osirak raid of 1981. This would only be true, however, of comparatively deep Israeli penetrations into Saudi Arabia, where they might lose much of their advantage in numbers, $C^3I$, and electronic warfare.

The F-15 improvements would also do little to help the Saudi Air Force support a land attack on Israel. Saudi acquisition of the E-3A, the AIM-9L, the KE-3A, conformal tanks, and MSIP improvements will allow the Saudi F-15s to fly far better air cover over Saudi Army forces in the Gulf and to "net" or link the Saudi fighters with the Saudi Hawk and Shahine missiles operated by the army. They would not, however, give the Saudi Army much aid in large-scale offensive operations against Israel. The E-3A AWACS cannot survive if it operates near Israel, and Saudi Hawk missiles will not have suitable mobility to provide forward air defense.

## THE TORNADO PURCHASE AND FUTURE SAUDI AIR MODERNIZATION

The impact of Saudi Air Force purchases of 24 Tornado air defense fighters, of 48 Tornado attack aircraft, full dual capability for the F-15C/D MSIP and of a more advanced light fighter like the Mirage 2000 on Saudi capabilities is more difficult to analyze. It is interesting to consider the effect of an incremental purchase of 80 new advanced fighters as an example of the largest purchase Saudi Arabia could fully absorb by the mid-1990s.

By this time, Saudi Arabia would not be able to make much use of its F-5E IIs and F-5Fs in any war with Israel These planes are good short-range fighters with good dogfight and moderate attack capabilities, but they lack the avionics and data display to allow effective netting with the digital system on the AWACS. They require the pilot to fly relatively vulnerable attack profiles in order to use Maverick or other advanced air-to-ground munitions of a kind unsuited for combat with Israel. While modifications like ring-laser gyros will help keep the F-5E/Fs combat effective in a Gulf environment, they will lack the radar, data display sophistication, combination of thrust-to-weight ratio and wing-loading and air-to-air missile range to engage Israeli pilots

Timing will also be a critical factor reducing the impact of Saudi Arabia's buy of the Tornado and any follow-on purchases. Britain cannot complete delivery of the 48 Tornado IDS fighters before 1988, and cannot complete delivery of the 24 ADV fighters until several years later. It would normally take a NATO air force between three and five years to fully accomplish a conversion to such a new aircraft, assuming a suitable pool of pilots and ground crews, and suitable support and training facilities. It will take the Saudi Air Force a total of four to six years to acquire and fully absorb all 72 advanced fighters.

Any new buy of the Mirage 2000 could now only become fully operational in squadron sized or larger strength in the early to mid-1990s. Even if Saudi Arabia was given U.S. approval to buy dual capability for its F-15s in FY 1988, however, it would still be able to complete conversion to large numbers of new fighters only in the early or mid 1990s. Even then, giving Saudi Arabia the tangential tanks and multiple ejection racks (MER) necessary to make efficient use of its F-15C/Ds in the attack mission seems unlikely to pose much of a "real-world" threat to Israel.

While the F-15C/D and Mirage 2000 have a considerable range-payload in attack missions, the Mirages and the Saudi version of the F-15 C/Ds would lack the high payload-low altitude penetration capability and advanced avionics of the F-15E and Tornado IDS which are necessary to use sophisticated offensive munitions effectively. They would still be forced into vulnerable attack profiles in the target area. This factor would further enhance Israel's advantage in dog-fighting capability and its ability to use its longer-range AIM-7E and AIM-7F air-to-air missiles.

The Saudi F-15 C/Ds will be well suited for attack missions in the less sophisticated environment Saudi Arabia faces on its other borders, but they will lack the mix of computer capability, sensors, and avionics to penetrate Israel's far more capable air defenses. As has been shown in Chapter VI, the upgraded Saudi F-15 C/Ds will not approach the attack mission capabilities of the Tornado, F-16C, F-16E, or F-15E, which will have superior tactical situation displays, advanced terrain-following capability and synthetic aperture radars (SAR) to provide long-range target imaging and all-weather strike capability, forward-looking infrared, and LANTIRN capability to provide long-range infrared target identification.

Once the Tornado IDS is in full service it will have an impact because of its high payload, advanced terrain following capability, and long range in very low altitude attack profiles. Once again, however, Saudi numbers would be limited to 48 attack variants of the Tornado delivered sometime in the late 1980s and not fully operational until the early 1990s. Even if no progress is made towards a peace settlement, Israel will have at least half a decade in which to prepare for such a threat and to obtain the kind of avionics and advanced missiles necessary to deal with it. As will be discussed shortly, the U.S. can provide such technology to maintain Israel's edge.

As for replacing the F-5E/Fs, Saudi Arabia cannot accomplish this before the early 1990s, and any such conversion would directly compete for manpower and technical resources with Saudi efforts to absorb the additional F-15C/Ds or Tornados. In fact, Saudi Arabia will probably be unable to expand its current force much above 260 aircraft before 1995. This means the Saudi Air Force of the early to mid 1990s is likely to consist of about 100 F-15C/D MSIP; 48 Tornado IDS, 24 Tornados, 40-70 Mirage 2000s or some other F-5E follow-on; and 40-70 of its existing F-5EII/F/RFs.

Regardless of the details of this force mix, Saudi Arabia will be constrained by all the limitations discussed earlier. It is important to reiterate, however, that any force mix dependent on European fighters, rather than U.S. types, will increase the net threat to Israel. This is illustrated in Table 7.3, which supplements the data provided in Chapter VI, and shows how U.S. and alternative European aircraft compare in attack mission capability:

Key Issues Affecting Western and Saudi Relations

Table 8.3: Comparative Air to Ground Performance of Key Western Fighter Types

Ranking in Terms of Key Performance Capability

| Maximum Disposable Payload | Radius of Action | Lo-Lo-Lo Attack Radius | Terrain Following Capability | Attack Avioincs | Air to Ground Missile | Smart Sub-Munitions IDelivery Capability | Turbulence Vulnerability | Maneuver Capability |
|---|---|---|---|---|---|---|---|---|
| F-15E | F-15E | F-15E | F-15E | F-15E | F-15E | F-15E | F-20A(80) | F-15E |
| Tornado | Tornado | Tornado | Tornado | Tornado | F-16C/E | Tornado | Tornado | Tornado |
| F-15C/D | F-16C/E | F-15C/D | F-16C/E | F-16C/E | F-15C/D | F-16C/E | F-4(74) | F-15C/D |
| F-16C/E | F-15C/D | F-16C/E | M-2000 | F-15C/D | Tornado | F-15C/D | F-5(74) | F-16C/E |
| F-4 | F-16A | F-16A | F-15C/D | F-20A | F-20A | F-16A | F-16C/E(71) | F-16A |
| M-2000 | M-2000 | F-20A | F-20A | M-2000 | M-2000 | F-4 | F-16A(69) | M-2000 |
| F-16A | F-4 | M-2000 | F-16A | F-16 | F-16A | M-2000 | F-15E | F-20A |
| F-20A | F-20A | F-4 | F-4 | M-F1 | F-4 | F-20A | F-15C/D | F-4 |
| M-F1 | M-F1 | M-F1 | M-F1 | F-4 | M F1 | M-F1 | M-F1 | M-F1 |
| F-5E/F | F-5E/F | F-5E/F | F-5E/F | F-5E/F | F-5E/F | F-5E/F | F-5E/F | F-5E/F |

Notes: Attack avionics and air-to-ground missile ranking is determined by level of technical and operational sophistication. F-15C/D ranking aapplies to the full U.S. F-15C/D MSIP-3, and not to the variant to be sold to Saudi Arabia.

The key point in the technical data shown in Table 8.3 is that the F-15E and Tornado attack fighter are very close in terms of long range, high payload, high lethality, and survivability. The F-16 C/E ranks next. The F-15C/D ranks fourth. The F-16A, F-20A and Mirage 2000 rank together in a significantly less capable category, although the F-20A has excellent performance at shorter ranges. The Phantom F-4 and Mirage F-1 rank well below the previous aircraft, and the F-5E/F ranks well below the rest. It seems unlikely, therefore, that any Saudi F-5E/F replacement is going to threaten the Israeli Air Force of the mid-1990s.

MINIMIZING THE RISK TO ISRAEL OF AN ADVANCED SAUDI AIR FORCE

If an Arab-Israeli peace settlement does not materialize in the 1990s, and if Israel's military edge should erode, the West still has a number of options to protect Israel. The U.S. can sell Israel the F-15E with the APG-70 radar and give it a fighter with significant air-to-air and air-to-ground superiority over the F-15C/D MSIP. It will also be able to deliver F-16Cs and F-16Es. Further, the U.S. could release a wide range of other technologies it now restricts for foreign sale.

## Key Issues Affecting Western and Saudi Relations

These technologies are summarized in Table 8.4, and they provide an important cumulative technical capability to ensure Saudi Arabia can meet local threats without reducing Israel's defense capability.

## Table 8.4 Key Restricted U.S. Technologies Affecting the Saudi-Israeli Balance

Technology          Impact

- **LANTIRN:** Next generation forward looking IR technology and pod mounted navigation and targeting system which allows very low altitude penetration of enemy air defenses and night and under the weather operations.
- **AIM-9M:** Next generation IR air-to-air missiles with limited beyond visual range and greatly improved dogfight capability, particularly at low altitudes. Has greatly improved countermeasure resistance and no smoke to warn enemy pilots of attack.
- **AIM-7M:** All weather radar guided air-to-air missiles (AAM) with greatly improved countermeasure resistance over the AIM-7F, and much better look down/shoot down capabilities.
- **AMRAAM:** An advanced beyond visual range (BVR) missile which will be the first radar guided missile with a "launch and leave" capability. An aircraft carrying such missiles can simultaneously engage multiple targets under BVR conditions at night and in all weathers.
- **JITDS:** An advanced secure digital battle management and communications system capable of giving a major edge in managing a large number of fighters and air defenses. Particularly important in providing maximum air-to-air effectiveness with the F-15 MSIP and F-15E.
- **E-3X:** Advanced "fusion" variants of the E-3 with computers capable of integrating ELINT (ESSM), radar, and new IR detection systems.
- **APG-70:** An advanced radar computer system with decisive range, mission flexibility, and munitions control lead over the radar on the F-16C and F-15C/D MSIP.
- **HARM:** A High speed anti-radiation missile with range and kill capabilities much superior to previous versions.
- **PLSS:** An all-weather stand off location and strike system designed to target and characterize enemy emitters.
- **ASPJ:** A new airborne self protection jammer which will be internal to U.S. fighters and which has advanced programable features to prevent countermeasures.
- **MER-200 and Tangential Conformal Tanks:** The key attack munitions dispenser systems necessary to make the F-15 fully effective in the attack mission. Each MER-200 can carry up to six 500 lb. bombs. One fits under each wing, and one under the body of the aircraft. Two tangential conformal fuel tanks can be fitted to each aircraft, each of which is also able to carry up to 4,400 lbs of attack munitions without degrading the AAM and ECM load or flight speed and performance.

- o **New Submunitions**: Combinations of greatly improved runway killers, and smart submunitions for suppressing armor, area targets, and infantry which will be launched from on-board dispensers, Multiple Rocket Launchers, and stand-off missiles and glide bombs.
- o **MLRS**: Multiple rocket launchers with ranges in excess of 20 Km and capable of firing 12 rockets with 7,700 grenade-like munitions capable of covering an area equal to six football fields and destroying a tank company or battalion. Smart submunitions are in development.
- o **Stinger POST**: An improved version of the manportable Stinger air defense missile with passive optical technique countermeasures and "multi-color" targeting capability to defeat flares and IR countermeasures.
- o **Patriot**: A greatly advanced all-altitude surface-to-air missile with a multifunction phased array radar and simultaneous multiple target engagement capability under jamming conditions.

Proper Western control over the timing and nature of the release of these U.S. and equivalent European technologies could also be used to limit any security risks from the loss of an F-15C/D MSIP or Tornado aircraft to some radical Arab state, as well as defusing the issue of its potential use against Israel. Further, Iran's experience in trying to keep its U.S. supplied aircraft flying has demonstrated that suitable U.S., British, and French restraint in providing critical spare parts and cyclical maintenance capability can ensure that no coup in Saudi Arabia could allow a radical successor regime to continue to operate the aircraft.

The U.S. can also take advantage of its lead in electronic warfare to ensure that Israel has a lead in IFF and ECM protection. Developmental systems of this kind are too complex and highly classified to discuss in any detail, but the U.S. has tremendous technical capability to ensure Israel's security through electronic warfare and intelligence technology without depriving Saudi Arabia of superiority over all radical regional threats.

Finally, the U.S. can ensure a lead in Israeli air strength and fighter performance through its support of the Lavi program. It can also aid Israel in obtaining a suitably sophisticated mix of a next generation AWACS, electronic warfare, and ELINT/ESSM capability to ensure its current edge in battle management well into the year 2000. This Israeli lead in battle management is currently far more important in any war fighting than aircraft numbers or fighter performance.

IMPROVEMENTS TO THE SAUDI ARMY AND NATIONAL GUARD

The West will have to furnish additional arms and equipment to Saudi Arabia to meet the threat in the Gulf and help it integrate the equipment it buys into its force structure. Saudi Arabia will have to replace or supplement its F-5E aircraft by the middle to late 1980s, and the Mirage

2000, Eurofighter, F-20A or F-16C would be a logical replacement. The Saudi Air Force will also eventually need to give its F-15 dual capability in the attack role and/or buy more Tornados.

The National Guard will need to obtain more advanced equipment to strengthen its internal security and local defense capabilities, and the Saudi Army will need more modern armor and additional equipment to overcome the imbalances and obsolescence in its force structure. Western ability to provide such equipment will be a key to strengthening the West's ties to the Gulf.

The issue of future sales to the Saudi Army is easiest to deal with. The Saudi Army of the early 1990s will still be below strength and its units will still be broadly distributed among key bases and military cities at Sharurah, Khamis Mushayt, Hafr al-Batin, and Tabuk. Tabuk's U.S. supplied armor is moving to Hafr al-Batin, and Tabuk will be largely French equipped by 1987.

It is highly doubtful that Saudi Arabia can reach its present force goal of 11 brigades by the mid 1990s, and will be lucky to have seven full brigades. It will definitely continue to suffer from the equipment problems discussed in Chapter IV and be short of trained officers, NCOs, enlisted men, and technicians. It will have to use most new sales of armor to replace its existing equipment, and this will leave the Saudi Army far under the strength it needs to cope with the threats it faces from Iran and the Yemens, and thus with no hope of conducting any serious combat with Israel and avoiding the destruction of irreplaceable cadres of trained manpower.

Follow-on Saudi army equipment modernization is unlikely to pose any technical threat to Israel. Saudi Arabia will benefit from rationalizing its wide mix of equipment types and replacing its current AMX-30 tanks with types better able to deal with the T-72, T-80, and successor tanks that potentially hostile nations are likely to deploy in the late 1980s and early 1990s. However, Saudi conversion to a new tank like the AMX-40, Leopard II, Challenger, or Abrams M-1 is unlikely to be completed before the mid 1990s and would not produce major changes in Saudi armored capability relative to Israel until well after the mid-1990s.

## PLANNING FOR THE ABSENCE OF PEACE

All of these considerations interact with the broader social and political impact the Arab-Israeli conflict is having on Saudi strategic relations with the West. Time is not defusing the impact of the conflict on Saudi Arabia or its neighbors. The past antagonisms caused by the conflict are increasingly interacting with the emergence of a new young highly educated class in the Gulf states, and the internal and external threat of religious extremism.

The failure to reach a peace settlement is making Saudi Arabia's ties to the U.S. an increasing source of domestic problems, makes the Saudi government vulnerable to radical political attacks, and weakens the Saudi government's political and religious legitimacy as well as that of the other moderate Arab regimes that are its natural allies. At the same time, it is forcing Saudi Arabia to placate its more "hard line neighbors". This is a key reason the Kingdom has been forced to extend so much aid to Syria.

Further, Israel is as likely to suffer from the defeat of the Saudi request as the West. The U.S. has just proven it lacks the ability to deny Saudi Arabia the aircraft and weapons it needs for its defense. The West can obtain major strategic advantages, and preserve more leverage over Saudi Arabia's use of its forces, by providing the weapons Saudi Arabia needs than by trying to deny them. Even the supporters of Israel in the U.S. cannot gain any security from wasting political leverage in blocking an arms sale to Saudi Arabia. They certainly cannot obtain anything approaching the security for Israel which they can gain from using their political leverage to increase U.S. military and economic aid.

---

[1] For a good indication of the kind of opposition movements involved, see "The Arabian Peninsula Opposition Movements", MERIP Reports, February, 1985, pp. 13-19.

[2] Ironically, successful Israeli pressure against U.S. arms sales may tilt the balance in the other direction. Some Saudi planners would like to build a second base near Tayma to help defend the Red Sea area but will not do so as long as Saudi Arabia is dependent on U.S. air weapons and technology. Tayma is halfway between Tabuk and Makkah, but is closer to Jordan and Israel than Hail.

## IX. THE FUTURE OF WESTERN AND SAUDI STRATEGIC RELATIONS

In many areas of the world, the West can only improve its security through dramatic changes in policy. In the case of Saudi Arabia, the Gulf, and Southwest Asia, the challenge to the West is to enforce its existing policy consistently. The irony surrounding all the issues and problems discussed in this book is that so little really divides such a wide sweep of nations and cultures.

The problem is far more one of communication than policy. All of the actors involved, including Israel, needs to understand the strength and weaknesses of the position of the others. The issues involved are technically complex, and this understanding does not come easily, particularly at the political level. Nevertheless, a detailed analysis of the issues involved shows that Saudi, GCC, U.S. and European military capabilities are largely complementary, and can offset serious individual weaknesses. All share pivotal strategic interests, and the U.S. can cooperate in building sound military relations with Saudi Arabia and the other GCC states without threatening Israel.

### CREATING A REGIONAL STRATEGIC PARTNERSHIP

The balance of strengths and weaknesses involved in creating an effective strategic partnership are clear. Saudi Arabia has no real hope of developing a stable structure of deterrent and defense capabilities without support from the West. Saudi Arabia, the smaller GCC states, and Europe must also rely on the U.S. to deter any overt Soviet military action, and as the last resort in dealing with an all-out attack by Iran, any new regime in Iraq, or a Soviet backed radical Red Sea threat. Finally, the Kingdom must rely on the West to provide the forces that its smaller GCC neighbors lack, and must rely on the U.S. to secure it against any major multi-front threat.

In contrast, Saudi Arabia can build the military strength to provide internal security, deter low level threats, and help the other moderate Gulf states build a collective defense. With Oman, it is leading the effort to link Bahrain, Kuwait, Oman, Qatar, Saudi Arabia, and the UAE together in a Gulf Cooperation Council (GCC). Only Saudi Arabia has the manpower, financial resources, and geography to underpin such cooperative internal security and defense efforts.

The U.S. must keep its forces "over the horizon" to avoid involvement in local internal political matters, and in unpopular low intensity conflicts. It must also minimize the growing strain on its power projection forces stemming from a growing series of threats in Third World capabilities and a growing Soviet global presence. Even European powers must keep an increasingly low profile in the face of the resurgence of Islam.

The U.S. has, however, developed rapid intervention forces that can deploy to Saudi Arabia, and other friendly states like Oman. Britain and France can provide considerable support against terrorism and low level violence. *If* USCENTCOM and western naval forces can operate in cooperation with Saudi and other GCC forces, and *if* they can use bases in Saudi Arabia and Oman, the resulting combination of Western and regional strength should be able to secure the Southern Gulf against both larger scale threats from the Northern Gulf states and Soviet backed threats.

In practice, this requires three types of improvement in the way the West and Saudi Arabia conduct their military relations. Europe needs to take a more realistic attitude towards making its arms sales militarily effective, and structuring its sales and military assistance to include U.S. over-the-horizon capabilities. Saudi Arabia and the Gulf states need to face their need for mutual interdependence, and their ultimate dependence on the U.S. The U.S. needs to show the courage to put Western strategic interests before domestic political advantage.

BETTER COOPERATION IN ARMS SALES

The Gulf states and the West need to pay far more attention to the interaction between Western reliance on USCENTCOM, and the need to coordinate an overall arms transfer policy between the major Western suppliers to Saudi Arabia and the other GCC states.

This is not a U.S., British, or French problem. It is a problem for the entire West. European states sell roughly the same amount of arms to the region as the U.S. France, in particular, has become a major supplier to Iraq and the Southern Gulf states, and is now the principal arms supplier to all the smaller Gulf states except Oman. Britain's new sales to Saudi Arabia will reassert its role in the region, and the FRG may yet become a major supplier of armor.

There is, therefore, a high priority for finding ways in which Western arms sales can be coordinated to enhance U.S. power projections capabilities. While competition between arms sellers will always be inevitable, it should still be possible to work together to develop local forces that can fully cooperate on a regional basis, and which will be interoperable with USCENTCOM in an emergency.

The U.S. needs to work with Europe to ensure that European arms sales involve some degree of standardization or interoperability for U.S. over-the-horizon operations, and to consider whether they could back their arms sales with special reinforcements or high technology forces for contingency operations. Arms sales cooperation may be difficult in a West which is far more oriented towards sales than strategy, but it offers great long term potential.

## DEPENDENCE ON U.S. POWER PROJECTION CAPABILITIES

The Gulf states and Europe need to fully accept the fact that they are ultimately dependent on the U.S. for protection against mid and high level threats. They have to understand that the GCC cannot hope to develop more than a limited collective deterrent and defense capability before the year 2000, and the present limits on the threat from the USSR, the Northern Gulf, and radical Red Sea states, can vanish far more quickly than the facilities can be created that will allow USCENTCOM and U.S. Navy forces to deploy before a conflict begins or escalates.

Saudi Arabia and the other GCC states already seem to recognize these realities in a crisis. They have privately turned to the U.S. every time Iran has escalated its attacks on Iraq or Gulf shipping. Nevertheless they have made little real progress in standardization, in ensuring interoperability with USCENTCOM forces, or in creating the kind of $C^3I/BM$ systems that U.S. forces would need. Only Oman and Saudi Arabia have generally accepted the reality of their strategic situation, and they have often been erratic in looking beyond a given procurement or force planning issue. All the GCC states need to work harder to link the GCC states into a common defense posture, and to create tacit links to USCENTCOM.

At the same time, most of the blame for the failure to build sound Western strategic relations with Saudi Arabia and the other GCC states clearly lies with the U.S. The key problem is that the U.S. policy has been paralyzed by Congressional fears of a largely imaginary increase in the threat to Israel. This has virtually blocked Gulf standardization on key U.S. arms and $C^3I/BM$ technology, and made it difficult, if not impossible, for Britain, France, and the Gulf states to develop a cohesive regional force improvement strategy that can be linked to reliance on the U.S. and USCENTCOM.

## A BETTER BASIS FOR WESTERN ARMS TRANSFERS

A better U.S. arms transfer policy will scarcely solve all these problems, but it is an essential catalyst in creating a stable Saudi strategic relationship with the West and informal links between USCENTCOM and the GCC. As the previous analysis has shown, the U.S. refusal to sell Saudi Arabia the

F-15 package involves more than a debate over a single arms sale. It is also symbolic of much broader problems in the entire U.S. arms transfer effort to the Near East and Southwest Asia.

While the Department of Defense and the State Department have made repeated and well structured attempts to use U.S. arms transfers to support U.S. strategic interests in the Gulf and Near East, the Congress has virtually paralyzed U.S. national security policy. However well intentioned, the Congress has created an unhealthy mix of instinctive moral objections to any arms sales--regardless of their impact and necessity--and willingness to put domestic political pressure from various pro-Israeli lobbying groups before U.S. strategic interests.

Such Congressional attitudes have been responsible for forcing Saudi Arabia to turn to France for much of its army and naval equipment. They may well force it to turn to France or Britain for all its future Air Force equipment if they deny the present Saudi request. At the same time, they have weakened a moderate Jordan while doing nothing to weaken a radical Syria, and virtually halted the kind of fighter and $C^3I$ sales to the smaller GCC states that could be of critical value in achieving internal standardization within the GCC and interoperability with USCENTCOM.

Such policies are neither realistic in terms of the military trends and threats in the region, nor effective in denying Saudi Arabia and the other Arab states access to arms. In fact, the only effect of more Congressional vetos of the request for more F-15s would be to deny U.S. industry the sale, further weaken cooperation between the GCC and USCENTCOM, and undercut a still critical U.S. role in cooperating with Saudi Arabia's most critical armed service.

Congressional actions also undermine the entire U.S. FMS program. Saudi Arabia is unquestionably the key purchaser of U.S. arms in terms of actual cash transfers to the U.S. It signed well over $48 billion worth of FMS agreements and construction agreements during the period 1950-1983, of which about $27 billion worth have been delivered. Given Iran's default on roughly $2 billion agreements, and the fact that Egypt and Israel will almost certainly have to seek forgiveness of past FMS loans, this means Saudi Arabia will contribute more in cash payments for U.S. arms sales than all other Middle Eastern nations combined.

To put the importance of Saudi Arabia in further perspective, its FMS Agreements with the U.S. during 1950-1983 totaled roughly one third of the $64 billion worth of all US military sales agreements with the Middle East, all of Africa, and all the Indian Ocean states. Saudi Arabia also agreed to $19,873 million in FMS construction agreements during the period. As compared with FMS construction agreements with all other nations totalling only $22 million during this period.

In fact the whole trend of U.S. arms sales to the Near East has been one in which the U.S. has lost influence to the Soviet bloc. The U.S. has not affected the rate of arms transfers in the region, it has merely diverted them to other exporters. Most of these exorters are far less concerned with Israel's security and with creating effective regional deterrent and defense capabilities. This increases the probability that U.S. forces may have to intervene and decreases the probability that they can be effective.

## BALANCE INSTEAD OF TAKING SIDES

An effective Western arms transfer policy does not mean tilting away from Israel, or favoring the Arabs. The West will gain nothing from "taking sides" in the Arab-Israeli conflict. Its strategic interests depend on ties to both moderate Arab states and Israel. The West can only hope to achieve even a moderate degree of stability in the Near East and Southwest Asia if it preserves a proper balance in its commitments to all its friends and allies.

Again however, the problem is far more a U.S. problem than a European one, although largely by default. Europe has left the problem of military supply to Israel to the U.S., and concentrated on sales to moderate Arab states. This makes it even more difficult for the U.S. to strike a proper balance between the pressures of regional and domestic politics. Both the moderate Arab states and Israel demand too much of the U.S., and constantly ask it to take sides in regional quarrels and issues.

Their American supporters may make things worse. Far too many American Arabs and Jews are more extreme than the Arabs and Jews in the nations in the region. They push the U.S.--and particularly the Congress--to "take sides" in a manner that does nothing to contribute to peace and development, and a great deal to contribute to regional vulnerability and the prospect of future wars.

The resulting lack of balance and the failure to meet Saudi Arabia's arms needs has been a costly case in point. There are legitimate security issues involved in arms sales to the Gulf, and the technical and military trade-offs in providing Saudi Arabia with the air power it needs are complex and require careful judgment. At the same time, the myth that Saudi Arabia is likely to become a major military threat to Israel serves no one's interest. It ignores the consequences of the U.S. not providing the arms Saudi Arabia needs, it ignores the true impact of the moderate and conservative Arab states on the Arab-Israelii balance, and it ignores the importance of Western ties to both the Arab states and Israel in reducing the risks of another Arab-Israeli conflict. The issue for both the U.S. and Western Europe is not how to choose sides between the Arabs and Israel, it is how to build bridges between them.

## MAINTAINING THE SEARCH FOR PEACE

Finally, better efforts to create stable military relations between the West and the Southern Gulf states cannot be separated from the search for an Arab-Israeli peace settlement. It is not the purpose of this analysis to suggest some dramatic new peace initiative, or even to suggest that any solution is imminent. The fact remains, however, that the search for peace is another area where Western Europe cannot act as a proxy for the U.S. If the U.S. is to defuse the growing hostility of the Arab world, and give moderate Arab regimes a political basis for strengthening their military ties to the West, the U.S. must show the same balance in seeking peace that it must show in maintaining military relations with both the Arab states and Israel.

Above all, it is necessary that the U.S. should not visibly abandon the peace issue, or try to treat it with benign neglect. Most Arab leaders--and certainly all Arab leaders friendly to the U.S.--understand the special nature of the U.S. relationship with Israel. They know that these ties are more than a matter of domestic politics and will be an enduring aspect of American policy. At the same time, they know--as do most Israelis--that only a constant and politically visible U.S.-led effort can hope to bring peace to the region.

The U.S. can only keep the long term support and friendship of states like Egypt, Jordan, and Saudi Arabia, if the U.S. presses for a just and balanced peace settlement. Whatever the ironies involved may be, the West can only establish a sound strategic position in the Near East by forging both swords and plowshares.

At the same time, Saudi Arabia and the other GCC states cannot afford to show too much caution in joining in peace initiatives with the U.S., Egypt, and Jordan. Time is not on the side of territorial settlements on the West Bank, in Gaza or on the Golan. Saudi Arabia can play a unique role in creating a long term bridge between Syria and the peace process. While the U.S. may have been too demanding in seeking a linkage between Saudi Arabia and Camp David, and then Saudi Arabia and King Hussein's peace initiatives, there is a time for courage. There will never be an ideal conjunction of U.S., Israeli, and Arab willingness to move towards peace, but neither Western nor moderate Arab interests in the Gulf or Middle East can ever be secure until a just and balanced peace settlement is achieved.

# BIBLIOGRAPHY

Abdel, Majid Farid, ed., <u>The Red Sea: Prospects for Stability</u>, London, Croom Helm, 1984, pp. 84-94

Abir, Mordechai, <u>Oil, Power, and Politics: Conflict in Arabia, the Red Sea and The Gulf</u>, London, Frank Cass, 1974

--------, "Saudi Security and Military Endeavor", <u>The Jerusalem Quarterly</u>, 33 (Fall 1984), pp. 79-94

al-Farsy, Foud, <u>Saudi Arabia: A Case Study in Development</u>, London, Stacey International, 1978

Albrecht, Gerhard, <u>Weyer's Warships of the World 1984/85</u>, 57th ed., Anapolis, Md., Nautical & Aviation Publishing Co.,

Akins, James E., et al., <u>Oil and Security in the Arabian Gulf</u>, New York, St. Martins, 1981

Allen, Robert C. "Regional Security in the Persian Gulf," <u>Military Review</u>, LXIII, 12 (December 1983), pp. 17-29

Ali Sheikh Rustum, <u>Saudi Arabia and Oil Diplomacy</u>, New York, Praeger, 1976

Aliboni, Roberto, <u>The Red Sea Region</u>, Syracuse, Syracuse University Press, 1985

Amirsadeghi, Hossein, ed., <u>The Security of the Persian Gulf</u>, New York, St. Martin's Press, 1981

Amuzegar, Jahangir, "Oil Wealth: A Very Mixed Blessing," <u>Foreign Affairs</u>, 60 (Spring 1982)

Anthony, John Duke, "The Gulf Cooperation Council," <u>Journal of South Asian and Middle Eastern Studies</u>, 5 (Summer 1982)

ARAMCO <u>Yearbook</u> and <u>Facts and Figures</u>

ARCO Series of Illustrated Guides, New York: Salamander Books, ARCO

--------, <u>Weapons of the Modern Soviet Ground Forces</u>

--------, <u>The Modern U.S. Air Force</u>

--------, <u>The Modern Soviet Air Force</u>

--------, <u>Military Helicopters</u>

--------, <u>The Israeli Air Force</u>

Bibliography

---------, The Modern Soviet Navy
---------, The Modern U.S. Navy
Arlinghaus, Bruce, Arms for Africa, Lexington, Mass., Lexington Books, 1983
Armed Forces Journal International, various editions
Army, Department of, 1985 Weapon Systems, Washington D.C., Government Printing Office
---------, Saudi Arabia, A Country Study, DA Pam 550-51, Washington, D.C., 1985, pp. 32-322
---------, Soviet Army Operations, IAG-13-U-78, April 1978
Army Armor Center, Threat Branch, Organization and Equipment of the Soviet Army, Fort Knox, Kentucky, January 1981
Arnold, Anthony, Afghanistan: The Soviet Invasion in Perspective, Stanford, Calif., Hoover Institution, 1981
Auer, Peter, ed., Energy and the Developing Nations, New York, Pergamon, 1981
Aviation Week and Space Technology, "F-15C/D Display Nears Test Stage", February 20, 1985, pp. 77-81
---------, "Integrated Systems Evaluated on F-15", April 11, 1985, pp. 47-57
---------, "Mirage 2000 Fighter", June 24, 1985, pp. 38-39
---------, "Saudis, British Define Terms of Tornado Sale", September 30, 1985, p. 29
Axelgard, Frederick W., "The Tanker War in the Gulf: Background and Repercussions," Middle East Insight, III, 6 (November-December 1984), pp. 26-33
Ayoob, Mohammad, ed., The Middle East in World Politics, London, Croom Helm, 1981
Aziz, Tareq, Iraq-Iran Conflict, London, Third World Center, 1981
Bakhash, Shaul, "The Politics of Oil and Revolution in Iran," Staff paper Washington, D.C., Brookings Institution, 1982
Banks, Ferdinand, The Political Economy of Oil, Lexington, Mass., Lexington Books, 1980
Barker, A.J., Arab-Israeli Wars, New York, Hippocrene, 1980
Barker, Paul, Saudi Arabia: The Development Dilemma, Special Report 116, London, Economist Intelligence Unit, 1982
Bass, Gail, and Bonnie Jean Cordes, Actions Against Non-Nuclear Energy Facilities: September 1981-September 1982, Santa Monica, Calif., Rand Corporation, April 1983
Batatu, Hanna, "Iraq's Underground Shi'a Movements: Characteristics, Causes and Prospects," Middle East Journal, XXXV, 4 (Autumn 1981), pp. 578-594

## Bibliography

Baylis, John, and Segal, Gerald, eds, <u>Soviet Strategy.</u> Totowa, N.J., Allanheld, Osmun & Co., 1981

Be'eri, Eliezer, <u>Army Officers in Arab Politics and Society.</u> New York, Praeger Publishers, 1970

Beling, Willard A., ed., <u>King Faisal and the Modernization of Saudi Arabia.</u> Boulder, Colo., Westview Press, 1980

Ben Horin, Yoav, and Barry Posen, <u>Israel's Strategic Doctrine.</u> Santa Monica, Calif., Rand Corporation, September 1981

Benton, Graham M., and George H. Wittman, <u>Saudi Arabia and OPEC: An Operational Analysis.</u> Information Series no. 138, Fairfax, Va., National Institute for Public Policy, March 1983

Bernstam, Mikhail S., "Soviet Oil Woes", <u>Wall Street Journal</u>, January 10, 1986

Bertram, Cristoph, ed., <u>Third World Conflict and International Security.</u> London, Macmillan, 1982

Betts, Richard K., <u>Surprise Attack.</u> Washington, D.C., Brookings Institution, 1982

Bishara, Ghassan, "The Political Repercussions of the Israeli Raid on the Iraqi Nuclear Reactor," <u>Journal of Palestine Studies.</u> Spring 1982, pp. 58-76

Blake, G. H., and Lawless, R. E., <u>The Changing Middle Eastern City</u> New York, Barnes and Noble, 1980

Blechman, Barry M., Stephan S. Kaplan, <u>Force Without War</u>, Washington D.C. Brookings Institution, 1978

Bligh, A., and S. Plant, "Saudi Modernization in Oil and Foreign Policies in the Post-AWACS Sale Period," <u>Middle East Review</u>, 14 (Spring-Summer 1982)

Bloomfield, Lincoln, "Saudi Arabia Faces the 1980s: Saudi Security Problems and American Interests," <u>Fletcher Forum</u>, 5, no. 2 (1981)

Borowiec, Andrew, "Turks Seek Aid To Upgrade Army", <u>Washington Times.</u> May 16, 1986, p. 7

Bradley, C. Paul, <u>Recent United States Policy in the Persian Gulf.</u> Hamden, Conn., Shoe String Press, 1982

Braibarti, Raoph, and Abdul-Salam, Al-Farsy., "Saudi Arabia: A Developmental Perspective," <u>Journal of South Asian and Middle Eastern Studies.</u> Fall 1977, p. 1

<u>Brassey's Defense Yearbook.</u> (later RUSI and Brassey's Defense Yearbook), London, various years

Brodman, John R., and Hamilton, Richard E., <u>A Comparison of Energy Projections to 1985.</u> International Energy Agency Monograph Series, Paris, OECD, January 1979

Brossard, E.B., <u>Petroleum, Politics, and Power</u>, Boston, Allyn and Bacon, 1974

Brown, Professor Neville, "An Out of Area Strategy?", <u>Navy International</u>, October, 1982, pp. 1371-1373

Bibliography

Brown, William, Can OPEC Survive the Glut?, Croton-on-Hudson, N.Y., Hudson Institute, 1981
Bussert, Jim, "Can The USSR Build and Support High Technology Fighters?", Defense Electronics, April, 1985, pp. 121-130
Campbell, John C., "The Middle East: House of Containment Built on Shifting Sands", Foreign Affairs, 1981, pp. 593-628
Carlsen, Robin Woodsworth, The Imam and His Islamic Revolution, New York, Snow Man Press, 1982
Carroll, Jane, Kuwait, 1980, London, MEED, 1980
Carver, Michael, War Since 1945, London, Weidenfeld and Nicholson, 1980
Center for Strategic and International Studies, "The Economic and Fiscal Strategy of Saudi Arabia", Georgetown University, Middle East Conference, March 20-21, 1985
Chalian, Gerald, Guerrilla Strategies, Berkely, University of California Press, 1982
Chicago Tribune, various editions
Choucri, Nazli, International Politics of Energy Interdependence, Lexington, Mass., Lexington Books, 1976
Christian Science Monitor, various editions
Chubin, Shahram, "Gains for Soviet Policy in the Middle East", International Security, Spring 1982, pp. 122-173
---------, Security in the Persian Gulf: The Role of Outside Powers, London, International Institute for Strategic Studies, 1981
Chubin, Shahram, ed., Security in the Persian Gulf: Domestic Political Factors, London, International Institute for Strategic Studies, 1980
Cittadino, John, and McLeskey, Frank, "C$^3$I for the RDJTF." Signal, September 1981
Clark, Wilson, and Page, Jake, Energy, Vulnerability, and War, New York, W. W. Norton, 1981
Clarke, John I., and Bowen-Jones, Howard, Change and Development in the Middle East, New York, Methuen, 1981
Clemens, Walter C., Jr., The U.S.S.R. and Global Interdependence, U.S.A., American Enterprise Institute studies in Foreign Policy, 1978
Cleron, Jean Paul, Saudi Arabia 2000, London, Croom Helm, 1978
Collins, John M. and Mark, Clyde R., Petroleum Imports from the Persian Gulf: Use of U.S. Armed Force to Ensure Supplies, Issue Brief IB 79046, Washington, D.C., Library of Congress, Congressional Research Service, 1979
Collins, Michael, "Riyadh: The Saud Balance", Washington Quarterly, Winter 1981
Combat Fleets of The World 1986/87, Their Ships, Aircraft, and Armament, A.D.Baker III ed., Anapolis Md., Naval Institute Press, 1986

Bibliography

Commerce, Department of, "Saudi Arabia", Foreign Economic Trends and Their Implications for the U.S., FET 84-80, July, 1984
---------, "Saudi Arabia", Foreign Economic Trends and Their Implications for the United States, FET-85-79, September, 1985
Conant, Melvin A., and Fern Racine Gold, Access to Oil: The U.S. Relationship with Saudi Arabia and Iran, Washington, D.C., Government Printing Office, 1977
---------, The Oil Factor in U.S. Foreign Policy, 1980-1990, Lexington, Mass., Lexington Books, 1982
Congressional Budget Office, Cost of Modernizing and Expanding the Navy's Carrier-Based Air Forces, Washington, D.C., Congressional Budget Office, May 1982
---------. Rapid Deployment Forces: Policy and Budgetary Implications, Washington, D.C., Government Printing Office, 1981
Congressional Presentation for Security Assistance Programs, Vol 1 and 2, Fiscal Year 1987
Congressional Research Service, Library of Congress, Soviet Policy and the United States Response in the Third World, Washington, D.C., Government Printing Office, 1981
Conine, Ernest, "Soviets Sit on Oil's Power Keg", Los Angeles Times, February 17, 1986
CONOCO, World Energy Outlook Through 2000, April, 1985
Conway's All The World's Fighting Ships 1947-1982, London, Conway Maritime Press, 1983
Cordesman, Anthony H., "After AWACS: Establishing Western Security Throughout Southwest Asia", Armed Forces Journal, December 1981, pp. 64-68
---------.American Strategic Forces and Extended Deterrence, Adelphi Paper no. 175, London, International Institute for Strategic Studies, 1982
---------, "The Crisis in the Gulf: A Military Analysis", American-Arab Affairs, 9 (Summer 1984), pp. 8-15
---------, "Defense Planning in Saudi Arabia", Defense Planning in Less-Industrialized States, edited by Stephanie Neuman, Lexington, Mass., Lexington Books, 1984
---------, "The Falklands Crisis: Emerging Lessons for Power Projection and Force Planning", Armed Forces Journal , September 1982, pp. 29-46
---------. Jordan and the Middle East Balance, Washington, D.C., Middle East Institute, 1978
---------. "Lessons of the Iran-Iraq War." Armed Forces Journal, April-June 1982, pp. 32-47, 68-85
---------, "Oman: The Guardian of the Eastern Gulf," Armed Forces Journal International, June 1983
---------, "The 'Oil Glut' and the Strategic Importance of the Gulf States", Armed Forces Journal International, October 1983

## Bibliography

---------, "Saudi Arabia, AWACS and America's Search for Strategic Stability", International Security Studies Program, Working Paper no. 26A, Washington, D.C., Wilson Center, 1981

---------, "The Saudi Arms Sale: The True Risks, Benefits, and Costs", Middle East Insight, Volume 4, Numbers 4 and 5, pp. 40-54

---------, "U.S. Middle East Aid: Some Questions", Defense and Foreign Affairs, June 1986, pp. 15-18

Cottrell, Alvin J., and Robert J. Hanks, "The Strait of Hormuz: Strategic Chokepoint", In Sea Power and Strategy in the Indian Ocean, Beverly Hills, Calif., Sage Publications, 1981

Cottrell, Alvin J. and Michael L. Moodie, The United States and the Persian Gulf: Past Mistakes, Present Needs, New York, National Strategy Information Center for Scholars, 1981

Croan, Melvin, "A New Afrika Korps," Washington Quarterly, no. 3 (Winter 1980), 21-37

Cummings, J. H., Askari, H., and Skinner, M., "Military Expenditures and Manpower Requirements in the Arabian Peninsula", Arab Studies Quarterly 2 (1980)

Danziger, Dr. Raphael, "The Persian Gulf Tanker War", Proceedings of the Naval Institute, May, 1985, 160-176

Darius, Robert G., John W. Amos II, and Ralph H. Magnus, Gulf Security into the 1980s: Perceptual and Strategic Dimensions, Stanford, Hoover Institution Press, 1984

Davis, Jacquelyn K., and Pfaltzgraff, Robert L., Power Projection and the Long Range Combat Aircraft, Cambridge, Mass., Institute for Foreign Policy Analysis, June 1981

Dawisha, Adeed I., Saudi Arabia's Search for Security, Adelphi Paper no. 158 London, International Institute for Strategic Studies, Winter 1979-1980

---------."Iraq: The West's Opportunity", Foreign Policy, no. 41 (Winter 1980-81) 134-154

---------, "Iraq and the Arab World: The Gulf War and After", The World Today, March 1981

de Briganti, Giovanni, "Forces d'Action Rapide", Armed Forces Journal, October, 1984, pp. 46-47

Deese, David A., and Joseph Nye, eds., Energy and Security, Cambridge, Mass., Ballinger, 1981

Defense and Foreign Affairs, various editions,

---------, "France's Special Operations Forces", June 1985, pp. 32-33

Defense News, various editions

Defense Update, "Helicopter Special", Number 60, March 1985

de Galard, Jean, "French Overseas Action: Supplementary Budget", Jane's Defense Weekly, 14 December, 1985, p. 1281

De Gaury, Gerald, Faisal: King of Saudi Arabia, New York, Frederick A. Praeger, 1966

Bibliography

Dougherty, James E. The Horn of Africa: A Map of Political-Strategic Conflict, Cambridge, Mass., Institute for Foreign Policy Analysis, 1982

Dunn, Keith A., "Constraints on the U.S.S.R. in Southwest Asia: A Military Analysis", Orbis, 25, no. 3 (Fall 1981) 607-629

Dunn Michael C., "Gulf Security: The States Look After Themselves", Defense & Foreign Affairs, June 1982

Dupuy, Trevor N., Elusive Victory: The Arab-Israeli Wars, 1947-1974, New York, Harper & Row, 1978

Economist, various editions

Economist Publications, London and New York

---------, "Growing Pains, The Gulf Cooperation Countries, A Survey", February 8, 1986

---------, "Oil Turns Manic Depressive", February 15, 1986, pp. 61-62

Economist Intelligence Unit, The Gulf War: A Survey of Political Issues and Economic Consequences, London, Economist Publications, 1984

---------, EIU Regional Review: The Middle East and North Africa, 1985, Economist Publications, London, 1985

---------, EIU Regional Review: The Middle East and North Africa, 1986, London, Economic Publications, 1986

Epstein, Joshua M., "Soviet Vulnerabilities in Iran and the RDF Deterrent", International Security, Vol. 6, no. 2 (Fall 1981), 126-180

Eshel, David, Born in Battle, Series nos. 1, 3, 12, and 16, Tel Aviv, Eshel-Dramit, 1978

---------, The Israeli Air Force, Tel Aviv, Eshel Dramit, 1980

---------, Peace for Galilee, Special edition of the Born in Battle Series, Tel Aviv, Eshel-Dramit, 1982

---------, The U.S. Rapid Deployment Forces, New York, Arco Publishing, Inc., 1985

Evron, Yair, An American-Israel Defense Treaty, no. 14, Tel Aviv, Center for Strategic Studies, Tel Aviv University, December 1981

Farad, Abd al-Majid, ed., Oil and Security in the Arabian Gulf, London, Croom Helm, 1981

Fairlamb, David, "Why the Saudis Are Switching Investments", Dunn's Business Month, May, 1985

Faquih, Osama, "Similarities in Economic Outlook Between the U.S. and Saudi Arabia", February 22, 1985

Feldman, Shai, "A Nuclear Middle East", Survival, 23, no. 3 (May-June 1981), pp. 107-116

--------- Israeli Nuclear Deterrence, A Strategy for the 1980s, New York, Columbia University Press, 1982

Fesharaki, Feridun, and David T. Isaak, OPEC, the Gulf, and the World Petroleum Market, Boulder, Colo., Westview, 1983

Feuchtwanger, E. J., and Nailor, Peter, The Soviet Union and The Third World, London, Macmillan, 1981

Bibliography

Fiecke, D., B. Kroqully, and D. Reich, "The Tornado Weapons System and Its Contemporaries", International Defense Review, No. 2/1977
Financial Times, London and Frankfurt
Fischer, Michael M. J., Iran: From Religious Dispute to Revolution, Cambridge, Mass., Harvard University Press, 1980
Flavin, Christopher, World Oil: Coping With the Dangers of Success, Worldwatch Paper 66, Washington D.C., Worldwatch Institute, 1985
Forbis, William H., The Fall of the Peacock Throne, New York, McGraw-Hill, 1981
Fricaud-Chagnaud, General, "La Force d'Action Rapide", July 2, 1986
Fukuyama, Frances, The Soviet Union and Iraq Since 1968, Santa Monica, Calif., RAND, N-1524, AF., 1980
Furling, R.D.M., "Israel Lashes Out", International Defense Review (Geneva) 15, no. 8, 1982, pp. 1001-1003
---------, "Operational Aspects of the F-15 Eagle", International Defense Review, 3/1975, pp. 129-139
Gail, Bridget, "The West's Jugular Vein: Arab Oil", Armed Forces Journal International, 1978, p. 18
Ghassan, Salameh, "Saudi Arabia: Development and Dependence", Jerusalem Quarterly, no. 16, Summer 1980, pp. 137-144
Golan, Galia, The Soviet Union and the Israeli War in Lebanon, Research Paper 46, Jerusalem, Soviet and East European Research Center, 1982
Goldberg, Jacob, "How Stable Is Saudi Arabia?", Washington Quarterly, Spring 1982
Grayson, Benson Lee, Saudi-American Relations, Washington, D.C., University Press of America, 1982
Grayson, Leslie E., National Oil Companies, New York, John Wiley, 1981
Green, Richard, Editor, Middle East Review, 1986, London, Middle East Review Company, 1986
Griffith, William E., The Middle East 1982: Politics, Revolutionary Islam, and American Policy, Cambridge, Mass., M.I.T. Press, 1982
---------. "The Revival of Islamic Fundamentalism: The Case of Iran", International Security, 5, no. 4, Spring 1981, pp. 49-73
Grimmett, Richard F., Trends in Conventional Arms Transfers to the Third World By Major Supplier, 1978-1985, Washington, CRS Report 86-99F, May 9, 1986
Grummon, Stephen R., The Iran-Iraq War, Washington Paper 92, Center for Strategic and International Studies. New York: Praeger Publishers, 1982.
Gulf Cooperation Council. Cooperation Council for the Arab States of the Gulf, Information Handbook, Riyadh, Bahr Al-Olum Press, 1982
Gunston, Bill, Modern Airborne Missiles, ARCO, N.Y., 1983

# Bibliography

---------, Modern Soviet Air Force, ARCO, New York, 1982

---------, Martin Streetly, "Su-24 Fencer C; Major Equipment Change", Jane's Defense Weekly, June 22, 1985, pp. 1226-1227

Haffa, Robert P., Jr., The Half War, Planning U.S. Deployment Forces to Meet a Limited Contingency, 1960-1983, Boulder, Colo., Westview Press, 1984

Halliday, Fred, Arabia Without Sultans, London, Pelican, 1975

---------. "Yemen's Unfinished Revolution: Socialism in the South" MERIP Reports, various editions

Halloran, Richard, "Poised for the Persian Gulf," The New York Times Magazine, April 1, 1984, pp. 38-40, 61

Hameed, Mazher, An American Imperative: The Defense of Saudi Arabia, Washington, D.C., Middle East Assessments Group, 1981

Hanks, Robert, The U.S. Military Presence in the Middle East: Problems and Prospects, Cambridge, Mass., Institute for Foreign Policy Analysis, 1982

Hardt, John P., "Soviet Energy: Production and Exports", Issue Brief no. 12B75059, Library of Congress, Congressional Research Service, Washington, D.C., 1979

Hargraves, D., and Fromson, S., World Index of Strategic Minerals, New York, Facts on File, 1983.

Harkabi, Yehoshafat, "Reflections on National Defence Policy", Jerusalem Quarterly, no. 18, Winter 1981, pp. 121-140

Hartley, Keith "Can Britain Afford a Rapid Deployment Force?", RUSI Journal, Volume 127, No. 1, March, 1982, pp. 18-22

Hawley, Donald, Oman and Its Renaissance, London, Atacey International, 1980

Hedley, Don, World Energy: The Facts and the Future, London: Euromonitor, 1981.

Heikal, Mohammed, Iran: The Untold Story, New York, Pantheon, 1982 (also published as The Return of the Ayatollah), London, Andre Deutsch, 1981)

Heller, Mark, Dov Tamari, and Zeev Eytan, The Middle East Military Balance, Jaffe Center for Strategic Studies, Tel Aviv University, 1985

Helms, Christian Moss, The Cohesion of Saudi Arabia, Baltimore, John Hopkins University Press, 1981

Henze, Paul B., "Arming the Horn", Working Paper no. 43, Washington D.C., International Studies Program, Wilson Center, 28 July 1983

Herzog, Chaim, The Arab-Israeli Wars, New York, Random House, 1982

Hetherton, Norris, S., "Industrialization and Revolution in Iran: Force Progress or Unmet Expectation", Middle East Journal, 36, no. 3 Summer 1982, pp. 362-373

Hickman, William F, Ravaged and Reborn: The Iranian Army, 1982 Staff paper, Washington, D.C., Brookings Institution, 1982

Bibliography

Holden, David, and Johns, Richard, The House of Saud, London, Sidgwick and Jackson, 1981

Horwich, George and Edward Mitchell, eds., Policies for Coping with Oil Supply Disruptions, Washington, D.C., American Enterprise Institute, 1982

Hottinger, Arnold, "Arab Communism at Low Ebb", Problems of Communism, July-August 1981, pp. 17-32

---------, "Does Saudi Arabia Face Revolution?", New York Review of Books, June 28, 1979

Howarth, H. M. F., "The Impact of the Iran-Iraq War on Military Requirements in the Gulf States", International Defense Review, 16, no. 10, 1983

Howlett, Lt. General Sir Geoffrey, "NATO European Interests Worldwide- Britain's Military Contribution", RUSI Journal, Vol. 130, No. 3, September, 1985, pp. 3-10

Hunter, Shireen, ed., Political and Economic Trends in the Middle East, The Center for Strategic and International Studies, Boulder, Colo., Westview Press, 1985

Hurewitz, J. C., Middle East Politics: The Military Dimension, New York, Praeger Publishers, 1969

Hyman, Anthony, Afghanistan Under Soviet Domination, 1964-81, London, Macmillan, 1982

Ibrahim, Saad Eddin, The New Arab Social Order: A Study of the Social Impact of Oil Wealth, Boulder, Colo., Westview Press, 1982

International Defense Review, Switzerland, Geneva, various editions

International Defense Review, Special Series, various editions

International Energy Statistical Review, Washington, D.C., National Foreign Energy Assessment Center, CIA, various editions

International Institute for Strategic Studies, The Middle East and the International System, Parts I and II, Adelphi Papers no. 114 and 115, London, 1975

---------, The Military Balance, London, various years

International Journal of Middle East Studies, New York

International Monetary Fund, Direction of Trade Statistics, various editions

---------, Direction of Trade Yearbook, Washington D.C., various years

Isby, David C., "Afghanistan: The Unending Struggle", Military Annual London, Jane's, 1982, pp. 28-45

---------, "Afghanistan: 1982: The War Continues." International Defense Review, 11 (1982), pp. 1523-1528.

---------, Weapons and Tactics of the Soviet Army, New York, Jane's, 1981

Ismael, Tareq Y., The Iran-Iraq Conflict, Toronto, Canadian Institute of International Affairs, 1981

Bibliography

---------, Iraq and Iran: Roots of Conflict, Syracuse, N.Y., Syracuse University Press, 1982
Ispahana, Mahnaz Zehra, "Alone Together: Regional Security Arrangements in Southern Africa and the Arabian Gulf", International security, VIII, 4, Spring 1984, pp. 152-175
Iungerich, Ralph, "U.S. Rapid Deployment Force--USCENTCOM--What Is It? Can It Do the Job?", Armed Forces Journal International, CXXII, 3, October 1984
Jacobs, G., "Afghanistan Forces: How Many Soviets Are There?", Jane's Defense Weekly, 22 June, 1985, pp. 1228-1233
The Jaffe Center for Strategic Studies, The Middle East Military Balance, Tel Aviv, Tel Aviv University, various years
Jane's, All the World's Aircraft, London, various years
---------, Armour and Artillery, London, various years
---------, Aviation Annual, London, various years
---------, Combat Support Equipment, London, various years
---------, Defense Review, London, various years
---------, Fighting Ships, London, various years
---------, Infantry Weapons, London, various years
---------, Military Annual, London, various years
---------, Military Communications, London, various years
---------, Naval Annual, London, various years
---------, Naval Review, London, various years
---------, Weapons Systems, London, various years
Jenkins, Brian Michael, et al., "Nuclear Terrorism and Its Consequences", Society 17, no. 5, July-August 1980, pp. 5-25
Johany, Ali D., The Myth of the OPEC Cartel: The Role of Saudi Arabia, New York, John Wiley, 1982
Johnson, Major Maxwell Orme, U.S.M.C., The Military as an Instrument of U.S. Policy in Southwest Asia: The Rapid Deployment Joint Task Force, 1979-1982, Boulder, Westview, 1983
---------, "U.S. Strategic Operations in the Persian Gulf," Proceedings of the Naval Institute, February 1981
Jones, Rodney W., Nuclear Proliferation: Islam, the Bomb and South Asia, Washington Paper no. 82, Center for Strategic and International Studies. Beverly Hills, Calif., Sage Publications, 1981
---------, ed., Small Nuclear Forces and U.S. Security Policy, Lexington Mass., Lexington Books, 1984
Jordan, Amos, "Saudi Arabia: The Next Iran," Parameters: The Journal of the Army War College, 9 (March)
Jordan, John, Modern Naval Aviation and Aircraft Carriers, New York, Arco, 1983

## Bibliography

Joyner, Christopher C., and Shah, Shahqat Ali, "The Reagan Policy of 'Strategic Consensus' in the Middle East", Strategic Review, Fall 1981, pp. 15-24

Judge, John F., "Harpoon Missile Targets Ships and Cost", Defense Electronics, April, 1985, pp. 92-98

Jureidini, Paul, and McLaurin, R.D., Beyond Camp David, Syracuse, N.Y., Syracuse University Press, 1981

Kanovsky, Eliyahu, "Saudi Arabia in the Red", Jerusalem Quarterly, no. 16, Summer 1980, pp. 137-144

Kaplan, Stephen S., Diplomacy of Power, Washington D.C. Brookings Institution, 1981

Karsh, Efraim, The Cautious Bear, Boulder, Colo., Westview Press, 1985

---------, Soviet Arms Transfers To The Middle East In The 1970s, Tel Aviv, Tel Aviv University, 1983

Kazemi, Farhad, Poverty and Revolution in Iran, New York University Press, 1980

Keegan, John, World Armies, New York, facts on File, 1979

---------, World Armies, 2nd ed., London, Macmillan Pub., 1983

Kelly, J. B., Arabia, the Gulf and the West: A Critical View of the Arabs and Their Oil Policy, New York, Basic Books, 1980

Kerr, Malcolm, and El Sayed Yassin, eds., Rich and Poor States in the Middle East, Boulder, Colo., Westview, 1982

Klare, Michael T., American Arms Supermarket, Austin, Texas, University of Texas Press, 1984

Korb, Edward L., ed., The World's Missile Systems, 7th ed., Pamona, Calif., General Dynamics, Pamona Division, 1982

Kraft, Joseph, "Letter from Saudi Arabia," New Yorker, July 4, 1983

Krapels, Edward, N., ed., "International Oil Supplies and Stockpiling", Proceedings of a conference held in Hamburg, 17 and 18 September 1981, London, Economist Intelligence Unit, 1982

Kuniholm, Bruce, "What the Saudis Really Want: A Primer for the Reagan Administration", Orbis, 25, Spring 1981

Kurian, George, Atlas Of The Third World, New York, Facts on File, 1983

Kuwait, Annual Statistical Abstract, Kuwait City, Ministry of Planning, Central Statistical office, various editions

Kuwaiti News Service, The Gulf Cooperation Council, Digest no. 9 KUNA, Kuwait, Ninth issue, 3rd ed, Kuwait, Kuwaiti Universal News Agency, December 1982.

Lacey, Robert, The Kingdom, London, Hutchinson & Co., 1981

Lachamade, Pierre, "The French Navy in the Year 2000", Jane's Naval Review, London, 1985, Jane's, pp. 79-90

Lackner, Helen, A House Built on Sand: The Political Economy of Saudi Arabia, London, Ithaca, 1979

Laffin, John L., The Dagger of Islam, London, Sphere, 1979

Bibliography

Leites, Nathan, Soviet Style in War, New York, Crane, Russak & Co., 1982

Leltenberg, Milton, and Sheffer, Gabriel, eds,. Great Power Intervention in the Middle East, New York, Pergamon Press, 1979

Lenczowski, George, "The Soviet Union and the Persian Gulf: An Encircling Strategy", International Journal, 37, no. 2, 1982

Library of Congress "The Persian Gulf: Are We Committed?" Washington, D.C., 1981

Liebov, Robert J, "Energy, Economics and Security in Alliance Perspective," International Security, Spring 1980, pp. 139-163

Litwak, Robert, ed., Security in the Persian Gulf: Sources of Inter-State Conflict, London, International Institute for Strategic Studies, 1981

Long, David E. "Saudi Oil Policy", Wilson Quarterly, 1979

---------, "U.S.-Saudi Relations: A Foundation of Mutual Need", American-Arab Affairs, no. 4, Spring 1983, pp. 12-22

Looney, Robert E., Saudi Arabia's Development Potential, Lexington, Mass., Lexington Books, 1982

Los Angeles Times, various editions

Lottam, Emanuel, "Arab Aid to Less Developed Countries." Middle East Review, 1979-1980, pp. 30-39

Luckner, Helen A., A House Built on Sand: A Political Economy of Saudi Arabia, London, Ithaca Press, 1978

MacDonald, Charles G., "The U.S. and Gulf Conflict Scenarios", Middle East Insight, 3, no.1, May -July 1983, pp. 23-27

Maddy-Weitzman, Bruce, "Islam and Arabism: The Iraq-Iran War", Washington Quarterly, Autumn 1982

Mansur, Abdul Karim (pseud.), "The Military Balance in the Persian Gulf: Who Will Guard the Gulf States from Their Guardians?", Armed Forces Journal International, November 1980

Martin, Lenore G., The Unstable Gulf: Threats from Within, Lexington, Mass., D.C. Heath, 1984

McDonald, John, and Clyde Burleson, Flight from Dhahran, Englewood Cliffs, N.J., Prentice-Hall, 1981

McLaurin, R.D., "U.S. Strategy in the Middle East and the Arab Reaction," Journal of East and West Studies, XI, 2, Fall-Winter 1982

---------, Lewis W. Snider, Saudi Arabia's Air defense Requirements in the 1980s: A Threat Analysis, Alexandria, Va., Abbott Associates, 1979

McNaugher, Thomas L., "Arms and Allies on the Arabian Peninsula, Orbis, Volume 28, No. 3, Fall 1984, pp. 486-526

---------, Arms and Oil: U.S. Military Security Policy Toward the Persian Gulf, Washington, D.C. Brookings, 1985

---------, Shireen Hunter, ed., Gulf Cooperation council: Problems and Prospects, CSIS Significant Issues Series, VI, 15 (1984), pp. 6-9

Bibliography

--------, "Rapid Deployment and Basing in southwest Asia," In Strategic Survey (London, International Institute for Strategic Studies, April 1983), pp. 133-137

---------,"The Soviet Military Threat to the Gulf: The Operational Dimension", Working paper, Washington, D.C., Brookings Institution, 1982

Macksey, Kenneth, Tank Facts and Feats, New York, Two Continents Publishing Group, 1974

Makinda, Samuel, "Shifting Alliances in the Horn of Africa", Survival, January/February, 1985, pp. 11-19

Male, Beverly, Revolutionary Afghanistan, London, Croom Helm, 1982

Mallakh, Ragaei El, OPEC: Twenty years and Beyond, Boulder, Colo., Westview Press, 1982

---------, Saudi Arabia: Rush to Development, London, Croom Helm, 1982

Mallakh, Ragaei El, and Mallakh, Dorothea H. El., Saudi Arabia: Energy, Development Planning, and Industrialization, Lexington, Mass., Lexington Books, 1982

Mansur, Abdul Kasim (pseud.), "The American Threat to Saudi Arabia", Armed Forces Journal International, September 1980, pp. 47-60

Marcus, Jonathan, and Bruce George, "French Rapid Deployment Force", Jane's Defense Weekly, 28 April 1984, pp. 649-650

Masters, Charles D., "World Petroleum Resources--A Perspective", USGS Open File Report, pp. 85-248

Masters, Charles D., David H. Root, and William D. Dietzman, "Distribution and Quantitative Assessment of World Crude-Oil Reserves and Resources", Washington, USGS, unpublished, 1983

Meir, Shemuel, Strategic Implications of the New Oil Reality, Westview Press, Boulder, 1986, p.55

MERIP Reports, "The Arabian Peninsula Opposition Movements", February, 1985, pp. 13-19.

Mets, Lt. Colonel David R., "The Dilemmas of the Horn", Proceedings of the Naval Institute, April, 1985, pp. 49-57

Middle East, "Guarding Turkey's Eastern Flank", April, 1986, pp. 9-10

Middle East Economic Digest, London

---------, Oman: A Practical Guide, London, 1981

---------, Saudi Arabia: A Practical Guide, London, 1981

---------, UAE: A Practical Guide, London, 1981

Middle East Economic Digest Special Report Series, Bahrain, London, September 1981 and September 1982

---------, France and the Middle East, May 1982

---------, Oman, November 1982

---------, Qatar, August 1981 and August 1982

---------, UAE: Tenth Anniversary, November 1981

---------, UK and the Gulf, December 1981

Middle East Insight, various editions

## Bibliography

Middle East Journal, Washington, D.C., Middle East Institute, various editions

Middle East Review, 1985, World of Information, Saffron Walden, England, 1985

---------, 1986, World of Information, Saffron Walden, England, 1986

Miller, Aaron David, Search for Security: Saudi Arabian Oil and American Foreign Policy, 1939-1949, Chapel Hill, University of North Carolina Press, 1980

Moyston, Trevor, Saudi Arabia, London, MEED, 1981

---------, UAE, London, MEED, 1982

Mottahedeh, Roy Parviz, "Iran's Foreign Devils", Foreign Policy, no. 38 Spring 1980, pp. 19-34

Naff, Thomas, ed., Gulf Security and the Iran Iraq War, National Defense University Press, 1985

National Foreign Assessment Center, International Energy Statistical Review, Washington, D.C., Photoduplication Service, Library of Congress, 1978-1986

Natkiel, Richard, Atlas of The 20th Century, New York, Facts on File, 1982

Navy, Department of, Office of the Chief of Naval Operations, Understanding Soviet Naval Developments, Washington D.C., Government Printing Office, April 1985

"Nearby Observer", "The Afghan-Soviet War: Stalemate or Solution?", Middle East Journal, Spring 1982, pp. 151-164

Neuman, Stephanie, Defense Planning in Less-Industrialized States, Lexington, Mass., Lexington Books, 1984

Neumann, Robert G. and Shireen T. Hunter, "The Crisis in the Gulf: Reasons for Concern but not Panic," American-Arab Affairs, 9 Summer 1984, pp. 16-21

Nevo, Joseph, "The Saudi Royal Family: The Third Generation", Jerusalem Quarterly, no. 31, Spring 1984

Newhouse, John, " The Diplomatic Round, Politics and Weapons Sales", New Yorker, June 9, 1986, pp. 46-69

New York Times, various editions

Newell, Nancy Peabody, and Newell Richard S., The Struggle for Afghanistan, Ithaca, N.Y., Cornell University Press, 1981

Niblock, Tim, ed., State, Society, and the Economy in Saudi Arabia, London, Croom Helm, 1982

---------, Social and Economic Development in Arab Gulf States, London, Croom Helm, 1980

Nimatallah, Yusuf, "Arab Banking and Investment in the U.S.", IMF, February 22, 1985

Nimir, S.A., and M. Palmer, "Bureaucracy and Development in Saudi Arabia: A Behavioral Analysis," Public Administration and Development, April-June 1982

Bibliography

Novik, Nimrod, Encounter With Reality: Reagan and the Middle East, Boulder, Colo., Westview Press, 1985
Noyes, James H., The Clouded Lens, Stanford, Calif., Hoover Institution, 1982
O'Ballance, Edgar, "The Iran-Iraq War," Marine Corps Gazette, February 1982, pp. 44-49
Ochsenwald, William, "Saudi Arabia and the Islamic Revival," International Journal of Middle East Studies 13, no. 3, August 1981, pp. 271-286
Odell, Peter R., and Rosing, Kenneth E., The Future of Oil: A Simulation Study, London, Nichols, 1980
O'Dwyer-Russel, Simon, "Beyond the Falklands-The Role of Britain's Out of Area Joint Forces", Jane's Defense Weekly, 11 January, 1986, pp. 26-27
OECD/IEA, Oil and Gas Statistics, 1985, No. 4, Paris, 1986
The Oil and Gas Journal, "Worldwide Report", December 31, 1984
Olson, William J., "The Iran-Iraq War and the Future of the Persian Gulf", Military Review, LXIV, 2, March 1984, pp. 17-29
Oman and Its Renaissance, London, Stacey International, 1980
Oman: A Practical Guide, London, MEED, 1982
Oman, Sultanate of, Oman in Ten Years, Muscat, Ministry of Information, 1980
---------, Second Five Year Plan, 1981-85, Muscat Development Council, 1981
Organization of Petroleum Exporting Countries, Annual Report, Vienna, various years
Osbourne, Christine, The Gulf States and Oman, London, Croom Helm, 1977
Pahlavi, Mohammed Reza, The Shah's Story, London, Michael Joseph, 1980
Paul, Jim, "Insurrection at Mecca", MERIP Reports, no., 86, October 1980
Perlmutter, Amos, Handel, Michael, and Bar-Joseph, Uri, Two Minutes Over Baghdad, London, Corgi, 1982
Perry, Charles, The West, Japan, and Cape Route Imports: The Oil and Non Fuel Mineral Trades, Cambridge, Mass., Institute for Foreign Policy Analysis, 1982
Peterson, J. E., "Defending Arabia: Evolution of Responsibility", Orbis, XXVIII, 2, Fall 1984, pp. 465-488
---------, Oman in the Twentieth Century: Political Foundations of an Emerging State, London, Croom Helm, 1978
---------, Yemen: The Search for a Modern State, Baltimore, John Hopkins University Press, 1982
Petroleum Intelligence Weekly, New York

Bibliography

Pierre, Andrew J., "Beyond the 'Plane Package': Arms and Politics in the Middle East," International Security 3, no. 1, Summer 1978, pp. 148-161

---------, The Global Politics of Arms sales, Princeton, N.J., Princeton University Press, 1982

Pipes, Daniel, "Increasing Security in the Persian Gulf", Orbis, 26, Spring 1982

Plascov, Avi, Security in the Persian Gulf: Modernization, Political Development and Stability, Aldershot, Gower, 1982

Platt's Oil Price Handbook, New York

Poullada, Leon B., "Afghanistan and the United States, The Crucial Years", Middle East Journal, Spring 1981, pp. 178-190

Pradas, Col. Alfred B., Trilateral Military Aid in the Middle East: The Yemen Program, Washington, D.C., National Defense University, 1979

Pry, Peter, Israel's Nuclear Arsenal, Boulder, Colo., Westview Press, 1984

Quandt, William B., "The Crisis in the Gulf: Policy Options and Regional Implications", American-Arab Affairs, 9, Summer 1984, pp. 1-7

---------, "Riyadh between the Superpowers", Foreign Policy, no. 44, Fall 1981

---------, Saudi Arabia in the 1980s: Foreign Policy, Security and Oil, Washington, D.C., Brookings Institution, 1982

---------, Saudi Arabia's Oil Policy: A Staff Paper, Washington, D.C., Brookings Institution, 1982

Ra'anan, Uri, The USSR Arms The Third World, Cambridge, Mass., M.I.T. Press, 1969

Randol, William L., "Petroleum Monitor", First Boston Corporation

Ransom, David M., Lt. Colonel Lawrence J. MacDonald, and W. Nathaniel Howell, "Atlantic Cooperation for Persian Gulf Security", Essays on Strategy, Washington, D.C., National Defense University, 1986

Record, Jeffrey, The Rapid Deployment Force, Cambridge, Mass., Institute for Foreign Policy Analysis, 1981

Roberts, Hugh, An Urban Profile of the Middle East, London, Croom Helm, 1979

Ross, Dennis, "Considering Soviet Threats to the Persian Gulf", International Security 6, no. 2, Fall 1981

---------, Soviet Views Toward the Gulf War," Orbis, XVIII, 3, Fall 1984, pp. 437-446

Rouleau, Eric, "Khomeini's Iran", Foreign Affairs, Fall 1980, pp. 1-20

---------, "The War and the Struggle for the State", MERIP Reports, no. 98, July-August 1981, pp. 3-8

Rowen, Hobart, "Reassesing Saudi Arabia's Economic Viability", Washington Post, July 20, 1986

Bibliography

Royal United Services Institute/Brassey's, International Weapons Development, 4th ed., London, Brassey's, 1981

Rubin, Barry, Paved with Good Intentions, New York, Oxford University Press, 1980

Rubinstein, Alven Z., "Afghanistan: Embraced By the Bear," Orbis 26, no. 1, Spring 1982, pp. 135-153

---------, The Great Game: Rivalry in the Persian Gulf and South Asia, New York, Praeger, 1983

---------, "The Last Years of Peaceful Co-Existence: Soviet-Afghan Relations 1963-1978", Middle East Journal, 36, no. 2, Spring 1982, pp. 165-183

---------, Soviet Policy Towards Turkey, Iran, and Afghanistan: The Dynamics of Influence, New York, Praeger Publishers, 1982

Russi, Pierre, Iraq, the Land of the New River, Paris, Les Editions, J.A., 1980

Rustow, Dankwart, Oil and Turmoil: America Faces OPEC and the Middle East, New York, Norton, 1982

Ruszkiewicz, Lt. Col. John J., "A Case Study in the Yemen Arab Republic", Armed Forces Journal, September 1980, pp. 62-72

Sabah-Al, Y.S.F., The Oil Economy of Kuwait, Boston, Keegan Paul, 1980

Sabini, John, Armies in the Sand: The Struggle for Mecca and Medina, New York, W. W. Norton, 1981

Safran, Nadav, Saudi Arabia: The Ceaseless Quest for Security, Cambridge, Mass. and London, Belknap Press of Harvard University Press, 1985

Saikal, Amin, The Rise and Fall of the Shah, Princeton, N.J., Princeton University Press, 1980

Salameh, Ghassane, "Checkmate in the Gulf War", MERIP Reports, XIV, 6/7, July-September 1984, pp. 15-21

al-Salem, Faisal, "The United States and the Gulf: What Do the Arabs Want?", Journal of South Asian and Middle Eastern Studies, 6, Fall 1982

Saudi Arabia, Kingdom of

---------, Annual Report of the Saudi Fund for Development, 1984-1985, Saudi Arabia, 1985

---------, The Kingdom of Saudi Arabia: Relief Efforts, Ministry of Finance and National Economy, Saudi Arabia, 1985

---------, Ministry of Finance and National Economy, Central Department of Statistics, Population Census, 14 Vols., Dammam, 1977

---------, Ministry of Finance and National Economy, Statistical Yearbook, annual, Jidda, various years

---------, Ministry of Planning, Second Development Plan, 1975-1980, Springfield, Va., U.S. Department of Commerce, Bureau of International Commerce, 1975

Bibliography

---------, Saudi Arabia, Foreign Trade Statistics, 1984 AD
---------, Saudi Arabian Monetary Agency, Research and Statistics Department, Statistical Summary, Riyadh, various years
---------, "Soviet Air Force in Afghanistan", Jane's Defense Weekly, July 7, 1984, pp. 1104-1105
---------, Third Development Plan, 1980-85, Riyadh, Ministry of Planning Press, 1980
Sciolino, Paulo, "Iran's Durable Revolution," Foreign Affairs, Spring 1983, pp. 893-920
Schmid, Alex P., Soviet Military Interventions Since 1945, New Brunswick, N.J., Transaction, Inc., 1985
Schmitt, Richard B., "U.S. Dependence on Oil, Gas Imports May Grow", Wall Street Journal, April 23, 1985
Schrage, Daniel P., "Air Warfare: Helicopters and the Battlefield", Journal of Defense and Diplomacy, Vol. 3, No. 5, pp. 17-20
Schultz, James B., "New Strategies and Soviet Threats Spark EW Responses", Defense Electronics, February, 1985, pp. 17-21
Sella, Amon, Soviet Political and Military Conduct in the Middle East, London, Macmillan, 1981
Senger, F.M. von, and Etterlin, Tanks of the World 1983, Anapolis, Md., Nautical & Aviation Publishing Co., 1983
Shamir, Yitzhak, "Israel's Role in a Changing Middle East," Foreign Affairs, Spring 1982, pp. 789-802
Shaw, John, "Saudi Arabia Comes of Age," Washington Quarterly, Spring 1982
Shaw, John A., and David E. Long, Saudi Arabian Modernization, Washington Papers 89, New York, Praeger, 1982
Sick, Gary G., All Fall Down: America's Tragic Encounter with Iran, New York, Random House, 1985
---------, Alvin A. Rubinstein, ed., The Great Game: Rivalry in the Persian Gulf and South Asia, New York, Praeger, 1983
SIPRI, World Armaments and Disarmaments: SIPRI Yearbook 1985, London, Taylor & Francis, 1985
Snyder, Jed C., Samuel F. Wells, Jr.,. eds., Limiting Nuclear Proliferation, Cambridge, Mass., Ballinger Publishing Co., 1985
"Special Report, Middle East Aerospace: Saudi Arabia," Aviation Week and Space Technology, May 23, 1983
Staudenmaier, William O., "Military Policy and Strategy in the Gulf War," Parameters: The Journal of the Army War College, 12 (June 1982)
Stauffer, Thomas R., U.S. Aid to Israel: The Vital Link, Middle East Problem Paper no. 24, Washington, D.C., Middle East Institute, 1983
Stempel, John D. Inside the Iranian Revolution, Bloomington, Indiana University Press, 1981

## Bibliography

Stewart, Richard A. "Soviet Military Intervention in Iran, 1920-46," Parameters, Journal of the U.S. Army War College 11, no. 4 (1981), 24-34

Stobach, Robert, and Yergin, Daniel, eds., Energy Future, New York, Random House, 1979

Stockholm International Peace Research Institute, Tactical Nuclear Weapons: European Perspectives, New York, Crane, Russak & Co., 1978

---------, World Armaments and Disarmament: SIPRI Yearbook, various years (computer print out for 1982), London, Taylor E. Francis, Ltd.

Stookey, Robert W, The Arabian Peninsula: Zone of Ferment, Stanford, Hoover Institution, 1984

---------, South Yemen: A Marxist Republic in Arabia, Boulder, Colo., Westview Press, 1982

Sullivan, William H., "Iran: The Road Not Taken," Foreign Policy, no. 40 (Fall 1980), 175-187

---------, Mission to Iran, London, W. W. Norton, 1981

---------, "A Survey of Saudi Arabia," Economist, February 13, 1982

Sweetman, Bill, "New Soviet Combat Aircraft", International Defense Review, 1/1984, pp. 35-38

Szuprowicz, Bohdan O., How to Avoid Strategic Materials Shortages, New York, John Wiley, 1981

Tahir-Kheli, Sharin, and Shaheen Ayubi, The Iran-Iraq War: New Weapons, Old Conflicts, New York, Praeger Publishers, 1983

Tahir-Kheli, Sharin, and Staudenmaier, William O., "The Saudi-Pakistani Military Relationship: Implications for U.S. Policy," Orbis, Spring 1982, pp. 155-171

Taylor, Alan, The Arab Balance of Power, Syracuse, N.Y., Syracuse University Press, 1982

Thompson, W. Scott, "The Persian Gulf and the Correlation of Forces," International Security, Summer 1982, pp. 157-180

Tillman, Seth, The United States in the Middle East, Bloomington, Indiana University Press, 1982

Truver, Dr. Scott C., "Mines of August: An International Whodunit", Proceedings of the U.S. Naval Institute, May 1985, Volume III/5/987, pp. 94-118

Turner, Louis, and Bedore, James M., Middle East Industrialization: A Study of Saudi and Iranian Downstream Investments, London, Saxon House, 1979

United Arab Emirates, Ministry of Information and Culture, A Record of Achievement, 1979-1981, Abu Dhabi, 1981

U.S. Arms Control and Disarmament Agency, World Military Expenditures and Arms Transfers, various editions, Wahington, D.C., 1980

Bibliography

U.S. Central Intelligence Agency, <u>Economic and Energy Indicators</u>, DOI, GIEEI, Wahington, D.C., Government Printing Office, various years
---------, <u>Handbook of Economic Statistics</u>, various editions
---------, <u>International Energy Situation: Outlook to 1985</u>, 041-015-00084-5, Washington, D.C., Government Printing Office, 1977
---------, <u>International Energy Statistical Review</u>, NFAC, GI-IESR, Washington, D.C., Government Printing Office, various years
---------, <u>USSR Energy Atlas</u>, Washington, CIA, 1985
---------, <u>World Factbook</u>, Washington, D.C., Government Printing Office, various years
U.S. Congress, House of Representatives, Committee on Appropriations, <u>Foreign Assistance and Related Programs Appropriations for 1982. Part 7: Proposed Airborne Warning and Control Systems (AWACS), F-15 Enhancement Equipment, and Sidewinder AIM 9L Missiles Sales to Saudi Arabia</u>, 97th Cong., 1st Session, Hearings
U.S. Congress, House of Representatives, Committee on Foreign Affairs, <u>Activities of the U.S. Corps of Engineers in Saudi Arabia</u>, 96th Cong., 1st Sess., 1979
---------, <u>Proposed Arms Sales for Countries in the Middle East</u>, 96th Cong., 1st Sess., 1979
---------, <u>Proposed Arms Transfers to the Yemen Arab Republic</u>, 96th Cong., 1st Sess., 1979
---------, <u>Saudi Arabia and the United States</u>, Congressional Research Service Report, 97th Cong., 1st sess., 1981
---------, <u>Saudi Arabia and the United States: The New Context in an Evolving 'Special Relationship,'</u> No. 81-494 0, Washington, D.C., Government Printing Office, 1981
---------, <u>U.S. Interests in, and Policies Toward, the Persian Gulf, 1980</u>, No. 68-1840, Washington, D.C., Congressional Printing Office, 1980
---------, <u>U.S. Security Interests in the Persian Gulf</u>, No. 73-354-0, Washington, D.C., Government Printing Office, 1981
U.S. Congress, House of Representatives, Committee on Foreign Affairs and Joint Economic Committee, <u>U.S. Policy Toward the Persian Gulf</u>, 97th Cong., 1st sess., 1975
U.S. Congress, Senate, Committee on Armed Services, <u>Military and Technical Implications of the Proposed Sale of Air Defense Enhancements to Saudi Arabia. Report of the Hearings on the Military and Technical Implications of the Proposed Sale of Air Defense Enhancements to Saudi Arabia, Based Upon Hearings Held before the Committee in Accordance With Its Responsibilities under Rule XXV (C) of the Standing Rules of the Senate</u>, 97th Cong., 1st Session

Bibliography

U.S. Congress, Senate, Committee on Energy and Natural Resources, Geopolitics of Oil, No. 96-119, Washington, D.C., Government Printing Office, 1980

U.S. Congress, Senate, Committee on Foreign Relations, Arms Sales Package to Saudi Arabia--Part 2, 97th Cong., 1st Sess., 1981

---------, Fiscal Year 1980 International Security Assistance Authorization: State Department Briefing on the Situation in Yemen, 96th Cong., 1st Sess., 1979

---------, The Future of Saudi Arabian Oil Production, Staff Report, 96th Cong., 1st Sess., 1979

---------, Persian Gulf Situation, 97th Cong., 1st Session., 1981

---------, The Proposed AWACS/F-15 Enhancement Sale to Saudi Arabia, 97th Cong., 1st Session, Staff Report, 1981

---------, Saudi Arabia, A Report by Senator Mike Mansfield, 94th Congress, 1st Session, October 1975

---------, U.S. Arms Sales Policy, 94th Cong., 2nd Sess., 1976

---------, War in the Gulf, 98th Cong., 2nd Session, Staff Report, 1984

U.S. Defense Security Assistance Agency, Foreign Military Sales, Foreign Military Construction Sales and Military Assistance Facts, Washington, D.C., Government Printing Office, various years

U.S. Department of Defense, Soviet Military Power, Washington, D.C., Government Printing Office, various years

---------, Foreign Military Sales, Foreign Military Construction Sales and Military Assistance Facts, September 1984

---------, Saudi Arms Sale Questions and Answers, February 24, 1986

U.S. Department of Energy, Secretary of Energy Annual Report to the Congress, DOE-S-0010(84), September, 1984

---------, Energy Projections to the Year 2000, DOE/PE-0029/2, October, 1983

---------, Annual Reports to Congress, Washington, D.C., Government Printing Office, various editions

---------, Petroleum Supply Monthly, various editions

---------, World Energy Outlook Through 2000, April, 1985

U.S. Energy Information Administration, International Energy Annual Washington, D.C., DOE/EIA-02 (84)

---------, Impacts of World Oil Market Shocks on the U.S. Economy, DOE/EIA-0411, July, 1983

---------, Monthly Energy Review, Washington, D.C., Government Printing Office, various editions

---------, International Energy Annual, Washington, D.C., Government Printing Office, various editions

U.S. Department of Energy, International Affairs, International Energy Indicators, DoE/IA-0010, Washington, D.C., Government Printing Office, various years

Bibliography

U.S. Department of State, Bureau of Public Affairs, Afghanistan: Three Years of Occupation, Special Report no. 106, Washington, D.C., December 1982

U.S. General Accounting Office, Perspectives on Military Sales to Saudi Arabia, Report to Congress, October 2, 1977

U.S. Library of Congress, Congressional Research Service, Foreign Affairs and National Defense Division, Saudi Arabia and the United States: The New Context in an Evolving "Special Relationship", Report prepared for the Subcommittee on Europe and the Middle East, Committee on Foreign Affairs, U.S. House of Representatives, 1981

--------, Western Vulnerability to a Disruption of Persian Gulf Oil Supplies: U.S. Interests and Options, 1983

U.S. News and World Report, various editions

Van Creveld, Martin, Military Lessons of the Yom Kippur War: Historical Perspectives, Washington Paper no. 24, Beverly Hills, Calif., Sage Publications, 1975

Van Dam, Nikolaos, The Struggle for Power in Syria, London, Croom Helm, 1981

Van Hollen, Christopher, "Don't Engulf the Gulf," Foreign Affairs, Summer 1981, pp. 1064-1078

Volman, Daniel, "Commanding the Center," MERIP Reports, XIV, 6/7 (July-September 1984), pp. 49-50

von Pikva, Otto, Armies of the Middle East, New York, Mayflower Books, 1979

Yegnes, Tamar, "Saudi Arabia and the Peace Process," Jerusalem Quarterly, no. 18 (Winter 1981)

Vertzburger, Yaacov, "Afghanistan in China's Policy," Problems of Communism, May-June 1982, pp. 1-23

Wall Street Journal, various editions

War Data, Special editions of the "Born in Battle" series, Jerusalem, Eshel-Dramit

Washington Post, various editions

Washington Times, various editions

Weinbaum, Marvin G., Food Development, and Politics in the Middle East, Boulder, Colo., Westview Press, 1982

Weissman, Steve, and Herbert Krosney, The Islamic Bomb, New York, Times Books, 1981

Wells, Donald A., Saudi Arabian Development Strategy, Washington, D.C., American Enterprise Institute, 1976

Wenger, Martha, "The Central Command: Getting to the War on Time," MERIP Reports, XIV, 9 (Fall 1984), pp. 456-464

Whelan, John, ed., Saudi Arabia, London, MEED, 1981

Bibliography

White, B.T., <u>Wheeled Armoured Fighting Vehicles In Service</u>, Poole, Dorset, Blandford Press, 1983

Wiley, Marshall W., "American Security Concerns in the Gulf," <u>Orbis</u>, XXVIII, 3 (Fall 1984), pp. 456-464

Wittam, George H., "Political and Military Background to France's Intervention Capability," National Institute for Public Policy, McLean, Va., June 1982

Witton, Peter, <u>UAE--10th Anniversary</u>, London, MEED, 1981

Wohlstetter, Albert, "Meeting the Threat in the Persian Gulf," <u>Survey</u>, XXV, 2 (Spring 1980), pp. 128-188

Wolfe, Ronald G., ed., <u>The United States, Arabia, and the Gulf</u>, Washington D.C., Georgetown University Center for Contemporary Arab Studies, 1980

World of Information, <u>Middle East Review</u>, London, various years

World Industry Information Service, <u>Energy Decade: A Statistical and Graphic Chronicle</u>, San Diego, Calif., 1982

Yodfat, Aryeh Y., <u>The Soviet Union and the Arabian Peninsula: Soviet Policy towards the Persian Gulf and Arabia</u>, New York, St. Martin's, 1983

Zahlan, Rosemarie Said, <u>The Creation of Qatar</u>, London, Croom Helm, 1979

Zelniker, Shimshon, <u>The Superpowers and the Horn of Africa</u>, Center for Strategic Studies, Tel Aviv University, Paper No. 18, September 1982

# INDEX

A-4, 115, 228
A-4KU, 115, 228
A-6, 89
A-7, 88, 119, 120
A-10, 86, 88, 89,209
Anti-Aircraft-General, 86-90, 92, 101, 105, 136, 148, 155, 158, 178, 203
AA-10, 88
AA-7, 88
AA-8, 86, 88
AA-9, 90
AA-X-P2, 86
AA-X10, 86
Abdullah, Crown Prince, 110, 134, 140, 144, 156, 235
Abqaiq, 172-174, 181
Abrahms (See M-1)
Abu Dhabi (Also see UAE), 25, 35, 46, 50, 103, 106, 120, 121, 126, 182
Acrid, 90
Air Defense Center (ADC), 179, 188
Aden, 104, 115, 119
ADIZ, 182
ADV (Tornado variant), 25, 26, 28, 38, 44, 45, 74, 78, 84-90, 93, 95, 97-99, 102, 104, 106, 107, 110, 112, 116, 118, 120, 123-127, 129, 134-142, 145-147, 149, 150, 153, 155, 159-161, 163-165, 168, 170, 172, 177, 181, 183, 184, 186-188, 190, 191, 194, 217, 228, 253, 262
advisors (foreign)--general, 25, 26, 74, 93, 95, 97, 98, 104, 106, 107, 110, 112, 118, 120, 134-142, 145, 149, 153, 155, 161, 239

AEW, 246-247
Afghanistan, 12, 14, 20, 28, 40, 42, 74, 77, 80, 89, 91, 93, 94, 98, 123, 126
Africa, 13, 35, 38-40, 42, 46-50, 77, 80-82, 95, 98, 108, 109, 124-126, 264
Armored fighting vehicles (AFV), 27, 82, 107, 143-145, 148, 155
AGM-45, 246
AGM-65A, 206
AGM-65D, 205-206
AGM-84A, 204
agriculture, 105, 118
AH-64, 87, 153
AIM-7, 163, 180, 182, 187, 188, 200, 107, 253, 257
AIM-7E, 253
AIM-7F, 163, 180, 187, 188, 253
AIM-7M, 257
AIM-9F3, 180
AIM-9J, 88, 187
AIM-9L, 15, 16, 18, 88, 163, 180, 187, 198, 202, 218, 225, 228, 247, 251
AIM -9L/P, 197, 223
AIM-9M, 88, 180, 207, 257
AIM-9P, 163
AIM-9P3, 187, 218
AIM-9P4, 15, 18
Ain Dar, 173
Air Defense Enhancement Package, 179-187
air-to-air combat, 15, 18, 86-88, 90, 163, 165, 180, 187, 194

# Index

air-to-ship, 16, 18, 102
air-to-surface, 21, 86, 87, 92, 102, 158, 163, 165, 171
airborne forces, 16, 51-60, 86, 88, 92, 100, 143, 148, 172, 182-184, 209
airlift, 53-55, 57-60, 61, 64-65, 95, 141, 147, 192
airpower, 16, 23, 113, 192
airspace, 177, 181, 182, 184
Al-Anad, 105
Al Kharg, 174
Al Khasab, 69
Al Khobar, 174
al-Ahmed, 116
Al-Sabah family, 117
Al-Thani family, 119
al-Thaqib, 189, 190
ALAT, 73, 119, 160, 263
Alawite, 110
Algeria, 30, 34, 35, 76, 77, 80, 97, 98
Algosaibi, Dr. Ghazi, 235
Ali Antar, 104
Ali Nasr Mohammed, 103-105
alienation, 94
Alif, 105, 114, 115, 119, 126
ALINDIEN, 53-55
Aliz, 28, 39, 40, 53, 117, 119, 121, 156, 172, 190
Alligator-class, 92
Alouette, 27, 53
Alphajet, 119, 120, 228
ALQ-101, 246
ALQ-119, 246
ALQ-131, 246
ALQ-99, 246
ALR-45, 246
ALR-56, 200, 246
ALR-67, 200, 246
ALR-73, 200, 246
alternative fuels, 12
AML-90, 26
Amman, 45
ammunition--general, 50, 152, 159, 243
amphibious, 21, 53-60, 111, 146, 171, 172
AMRAAM, 200, 207, 253, 257

AMX--general, 26, 27, 86, 119, 120, 144, 148, 149, 151
AMX-10, 27, 52, 148
AMX-13, 55
AMX-30, 26, 27, 119, 120, 144, 148, 149, 228, 259
AMX-30SA, 148
AMX-40, 86, 151, 259
anchorages, 93, 104
Angola, 35, 98
anti-radiation, 17, 86, 179, 246
anti-ship, 17, 87, 92
anti-tank, 86, 87, 143, 148, 155
APCs (armored personnel carriers), 27, 82, 96, 107, 111, 143, 148, 155
APG-63, 90, 206
APG-64, 224
APG-70, 201, 206, 224, 255, 257
APQ-159, 224
APY-2, 250-251
Arab-Israeli issues--general, 14, 24-27, 42-49, 78, 144, 150, 166-168, 185, 191, 214-216, 240-261, 265
Arab-Israeli peace settlement, 14, 24, 42-49, 210, 259-260, 265-267
ARAMCO, 46, 50, 175, 176, 216
armor--general, 23, 26, 27, 40, 41, 85, 86, 96, 100, 102, 104, 106, 107, 112, 117, 120, 133, 140-144, 147-151, 153, 155, 171, 210, 241, 262
arms exports--general, 74-97, 129
arms imports--general, 16, 20 74-97, 129, 152, 165
arms sales--general, 19, 21, 26, 50, 74-97, 142, 262-265
artillery, 26, 27, 40, 82, 96, 100, 111, 113, 120, 143-145, 148, 152
AS-4, 87
AS-6, 87, 163
AS-7, 87
Aseb, 107
Asia, 13, 14, 17, 35, 39, 46, 50, 79, 81, 82, 84, 85, 96, 118, 237, 261, 264, 265
Asia-Pacific, 35
Aside, 171
Asir, 78

# Index

Askargh, 91
ASPJ, 257
Assad, 42, 103, 110, 119
assassination, 24, 112, 113, 116, 117, 119
ASTROS, 86, 142, 148
ASW, 87, 92
AT-6, 86
AT-7, 86
AT-8, 86
Atlantic Causeway, 58
Atlantic Conveyor, 58
Athens, 179
Australia, 35
Austria, 32
AV-8A, 62
AV-8B, 62
avionics--general, 88, 90, 164, 165, 180, 181
AWACS--general (Also see E-3A), 16, 18, 79, 86, 90, 99, 136, 138, 146, 159, 161, 163, 166-168, 180, 183-191, 193, 194, 196, 201, 217, 219, 247, 250-253, 258
Azores, 64
B-26, 26
B-52, 66. 69
B-707, 246
Baath, 101, 236-237
Bab el-Mandeb, 103-106, 108-109
BAC-167, 17, 21, 26, 117, 146, 163, 164, 220, 241
Backfire, 249
Bagdhad, 48-50, 182
Baghram, 91
Bahrain, 13, 32, 35, 36, 40, 41, 46, 50, 69, 76, 77, 80, 99, 113-115, 119, 122, 126, 175, 182, 227-229 262
--military forces and internal security, 114-117
Prince Bandar bin Sultan, 213-215
BAPCO, 114
Bar-Ilan, 48-50
Barentu, 107
Basil, Frank E., 136, 189
Batman, 68
battle-management (see $C^3I$)

BDM, 136, 138, 189
Beirut, 54
Belgium, 32
Benin, 98
Berbera, 69
Berri, 171-174
berths, 174-176
Bisseau, 98
Blackhawk (UH-60), 16, 144, 153, 197, 198, 204
blackmail, 116
Blindfire, 229
Blowpipe, 60
BM-24, 86
BM-25, 86
Boeing Corporation, 136, 138, 142, 189, 195
Boeing Consortium, 189-191
Bold Gannet, 58
border issues, 14, 16, 19, 22, 23, 25, 26, 43, 45, 74, 91, 105, 109, 113, 119, 122, 127, 128, 144, 153, 156, 157, 168, 169, 182-186
BP, 30, 105, 114, 174, 176, 216
Britain--general (Also see U.K.), 15, 17, 20, 21, 23, 25-27, 35, 37, 82, 114, 118, 127, 135, 137, 138, 142, 143, 144, 151, 153, 155, 157, 165, 177, 192, 194, 262-264
--role in Tornado sale, 214-216, 220, 252-258
--role of advisors, 17, 25-28, 133-141, 161-169, 214-216, 220, 252-258, 263-264
British Aerospace, 17, 138, 228, 244
Brunei, 35
Buccaneer, 61
budget deficits, 31
Buraimi Oasis, 25
Burundi, 98
Bushihr, 181
Bussert, James, 123, 126
BVR (beyond visual range), 146, 207, 221, 224,
C-123, 26
C-130, 27, 61, 113, 136, 138, 141, 146, 161, 163, 246

# Index

C-130H, 146, 163, 246
C-141, 53-55, 61-66, 68
C-160, 53-54
C-17, 61-66, 68
C-212, 146, 163, 247
C-5, 53-,54, 68, 93
$C^3/C^3I$/BM, 27, 54, 64, 66, 78, 87, 99, 102, 116, 137-139, 141-143, 146, 147, 152, 161, 164, 166-168, 171, 176, 184, 188-190, 193, 195, 208, 228, 252, 263, 264
caches (arms), 50, 114
Cadillac Gage, 139
Cairo, 68
Camp David, 19, 42-44, 266
Canada, 32, 35, 36, 47, 50
Candid, 187
Carlson al-Saudia, 236
carrier forces--general, 12, 21-23, 26, 27, 53-56, 57, 62-65, 92, 93, 104, 144, 192, 209
Carter, Jimmy, 44, 169, 181, 191
Carter Administration, 169, 181, 191
Catto, Henry, 150
causeway (Bahrain to Saudi Arabia), 114
CBW, 87
CC-2, 250
Central Region, 54
CFM-56, 194
Chad, 54, 77, 80, 109
Challenger tank, 259,
Charybdis, 57
Chieftain, 115, 117, 149
China, 35, 46, 50
Chinook, 61, 153
Chirze, 50
cities--general (Also see urbanization), 31, 33, 36, 46, 47, 50, 99, 102, 106, 107, 128, 130, 153, 158, 171, 174-177, 178, 181, 182, 184, 191
Clemenceau, 22, 53
coal, 12, 37
COG, 42-45, 182, 190, 263
Colbert, 53
commandos, 57, 60, 155

communications, 26, 27, 86, 97, 104, 106, 129, 143, 151, 155, 159, 166-168, 186, 189, 190, 194, 195, 261
Communist, 35, 41, 46, 50, 78, 79, 81-84, 129
computer issues, 32, 77, 109, 136, 159, 165, 173, 186, 190, 194
Condor, 93
conformal fuel tanks, 163-165, 170, 180, 181, 183, 187, 205, 257
Congo, 98
Conin, 123, 126
CONOCO, 47, 50
Conscription, 111, 134, 148, 155, 158, 163
Conservative Gulf States (Also see GCC), 36, 73, 74, 78, 113, 121, 177, 178, 186, 191, 192
construction, 85, 114, 115, 129-131, 136, 137, 139, 142, 157, 178, 189, 192, 264
contingency bases, 14, 22
contractor issues, 38, 138, 149, 152, 161, 180, 189
coproduction, 85, 88, 144
core area, 171-172
Corps of Engineers, 26, 27, 128-130, 136, 137, 139
corvettes, 87, 100-102, 104, 111, 158
Cote d'Azur, 215
counter-insurgency, 120
coup d'etat, 97, 99, 103, 105, 109, 112, 114, 117, 119, 134, 142, 234-239
CPAS, 98
Cranston, Alan, 211-214, 217-218
Creasy, Sir Timothy, 126
Crotale, 56, 152, 158, 183, 228
crude oil, 33, 45-47, 50, 174, 175, 181
cruisers, 107
Crusader, 53
Cryano, 224
cryptography, 194
CSF, Thomson, 224, 229
Cuba, 98
Cyprus, 51, 60
Dahlak, 93, 107, 229
Dammam, 139, 157, 158, 171, 173

294

# Index

Damour, 50
DC-8, 56
debates (See U.S. Congress), 15, 16, 18, 25, 150, 151, 188, 264
DEFA, 223 264, 265
defense budget, 132
demographic, 126, 133
Denmark, 32
deportations, 116, 117
depot-level maintenance, 186, 194
desalinization, 158, 171
destabilizing, 142, 191, 192
destroyers, 93, 100, 101
Dhahran, 25, 66-67, 70, 103, 137, 139, 147, 161, 163, 164, 170, 173, 174, 176, 178-180, 182, 184, 187
Dharhan-Juaymah, 183
Dhofar rebellion, 41
Dibah, 242
Diego Garcia, 22, 60, 69, 192
dispenser (munitions), 86, 165
dispersal, 16, 103, 149, 153, 163, 170, 174, 178
diversification, 114, 149
Djibouti, 55, 140
docks, 92, 93, 107, 138
dog-fighting, 187
Doha, 119
Dragon, 148, 163, 171
drydock, 93
dual capability, 21, 88, 161-168, 205-207, 208-210, 259
Dubai, 35, 46, 50, 120, 121, 126
Dublin, 69
ducting (radar), 107, 164, 172, 183
Duquesne, 53
Durandal, 86
E-2C, 62, 86, 87, 184-186, 194, 248, 251
E-3A, 16, 18, 66, 74, 86, 88, 99, 137, 145, 146, 159, 161, 163, 176, 180, 181, 183-188, 190, 192-195, 201, 203, 217, 219, 247-249, 251-252
E-3X, 257
E-6, 195
EA-6B, 62
Eagle 17, 166-168

East German, 85
Eastern Province, 152, 155, 156, 173, 183, 203
ECM/ECCM/ESSM, 61, 88, 90, 163, 165, 186-188, 193, 207, 221, 224, 244-248, 249, 258,
economic development, 105, 108, 121
Ecuador, 30, 34
education, 97, 131, 259
EEC (European Economic Community), 32, 38, 116
effectiveness issues, 115, 155, 179, 190
Egypt, 14, 18, 23, 25, 26, 35, 42, 43, 64-65, 58, 70, 73, 75-77, 80, 109, 111, 151, 192, 264, 266
Eilyahu, 48-50
elections (U.S.)--impact on relations with Saudi Arabia, 18, 108, 116, 117, 169, 184
ELINT, 90 184, 186, 187
ELF-1, 136
Emirates (see UAE), 13, 120, 121
encryption, 188
Equatorial Guinea, 98
equipment diversification (see diversification)
ERAM, 86
Eritrean rebels, 107
Ernest, 123, 126
Erzurum, 68
ESM/ESSM (Also see ECM), 46, 47, 50, 52, 54, 86, 92, 246-250, 258
espionage, 18
Etendard, 53, 54, 100
Ethiopia, 20, 73-78, 80, 88, 89, 93, 95, 98, 107-109, 112, 124-126, 160, 229
--military forces, 107-108
ethnic, 126, 156
Eurofighter, 259
Europe--general, 12, 15-17, 19, 21, 24, 30, 32, 33, 35-39, 45-47, 50, 78, 81-85, 96, 97, 99, 102, 112, 134, 137, 141, 146, 151, 152, 155, 178, 185, 29-240, 261-263, 265, 266
European Economic Community (see EEC)

# Index

Exocet, 56 87, 100, 101, 115, 118-120
expatriate, 41, 106, 114, 115, 117, 119-121
expatriates, 114, 117
experts, 12, 78, 89, 91, 94, 105, 132-134, 151
extradition, 113
extremism, 24, 112, 117, 259
Eytan, 123-126, 166-168
F-4, 62, 87, 89, 99, 100, 120, 181, 183, 193, 209
F-4D, 61, 100, 181, 209
F-4E, 100
F-4J, 89
F-5--general, 21, 22, 26, 27, 66, 87, 100, 113, 114, 137, 138, 145, 146, 161-164, 170, 181, 184, 196, 202, 215-217,222-228, 241, 252-255
F-5B, 146, 163, 228, 241
F-5E/E-II, 21, 22, 27, 66, 100, 114, 145, 146, 161-164, 181, 222-224, 225, 241, 244, 249, 252-255, 258
F-5F, 66, 146, 163, 164, 228, 241, 253-255
F-8E, 54, 56
F-14, 62 100, 181, 188, 194
F-15--general, 15-22, 27, 66, 68-69, 74, 79, 86, 87, 90, 91, 99, 101, 102, 113, 137, 138, 145, 146, 152, 162-170, 180-182, 187, 188, 192-194, 196-203, 205-210, 213, 215-217, 221,-225, 228-230, 243-244, 249, 251,259, 264
F-15C/D, 15, 16, 18, 20-22, 64-66, 74, 87, 90, 91, 102, 146, 162-165, 181, 194, 196-203, 205-209, 217, 221-224, 243, 247
F-15E, 86, 101, 102, 201, 206-207, 215, 223-224, 230, 243, 251-259
F-16, 61, 86, 88, 90, 117, 119, 141, 255, 259
F-18, 62, 188
F-20A, 86, 253, 258-259
F. 53 (See Lightning), 26, 163
F-86, 26
F-111, 89, 164, 209
Fahd, King, 16, 17, 44, 157

Fahd Peace Plan, 44-45
Faisal, King, 26, 137
Falklands, 57, 216
Faquih, 48-50
FAR (Forces d'Action Rapide), 52-55
Farah, 91
Fasht-e-Dibal (reef), 115, 119
Fast Kit, 180
Faw, 18, 99, 115, 116, 218
FB-59, 100
Fearless, 58
Federal Republic of Germany (see FRG)
Fencer, 88, 90, 123, 126
Ferranti, 163, 183
Fez, 45
FGA-76, 120
FGA-78, 119
Finland, 32
Firefly III, 201
Fitter, 88
Flanker, 88
Flavin, 46, 50
FLIR, 106
Flogger, 88
FMS (Foreign Military Sales)--general, 80-85, 96, 127-131, 128-130, 135, 136, 141, 264
Foch, 53
foreign advisors (Also see advisors), 51-60, 133-140, 214-216, 220, 251-252, 263-265
foreign labor, 44 114, 116, 120, 121, 142
Foreign Legion, 53-56
Fox, 60
Foxfire, 90
Foxhound, 88
FPS-117, 190
FR-10, 100
France--general, 12, 15, 17, 21-23, 26, 27, 32, 33, 37, 39, 70, 84-87, 96, 102, 119, 129, 131, 133, 135, 137-139, 140-143, 149, 151, 153, 157-161, 189, 192, 262-264
--role as advisor, 147-160
--effort to sell Mirage 2000, 214-216, 227

# Index

--power projection capability, 51-56
--support of Saudi Arabia, 142-160
FRG, 32, 80, 84, 96, 129, 153, 189, 262
frigates, 21, 87, 93, 100-102, 107, 111, 145, 158-161
FROG-7, 104
Frogfoot, 89
Fulcrum, 88
fundamentalism, 24, 117, 239
FV-432, 60
Gabon, 30, 34
Gabriel, 87
Gaeta, 61
Gah, 91
Gammon, 89
gas oil separators (GOSP), 172, 173, 177
Gaza Strip, 43, 44, 266
Gazelle, 60
GBU-15, 221
GCC (Gulf Cooperation Council), 13, 16, 19-20, 22, 23, 36, 38-41, 48-50, 70, 73, 77, 78, 80, 85, 99, 102, 103, 106, 110, 112-115, 117, 118, 120-122, 126, 141, 143, 147, 161, 169, 170, 177, 199, 203-205, 210, 227-229, 239, 240, 261-264, 266
Gecko, 89
General Dynamics (Also see F-16), 151
General Operating Center, (GOC), 106, 188
Georgetown, 48-50
geothermal energy, 12
Ghawar, 171, 173, 174
Ghazlan, 173
Glamorgan, 56
Glasgow, 56
GLCM, 61
GNP 12, 39, 48-50, 128
Goalkeeper, 58
Golan Heights, 241-242, 266
Grand Mosque, 54, 236
Greece, 32, 61, 64
guerrillas, 190
Guinea, 98

Gulf (Perisan or Arab)--general, 12-16, 19-25, 27-29, 31-37, 40, 41, 44-50, 63, 67-69, 73-75, 77-80, 82, 84, 85, 88, 89, 91-95, 98, 99, 101-103, 107, 110, 112, 113, 115, 117, 119, 121, 122, 124-127, 130, 140, 141, 145, 147, 149, 151, 157, 158, 164, 166-171, 175-179, 181-188, 190-193, 226-230, 234, 238-244, 247, 249, 251 261-266
Gulf Cooperation Council (Also see GCC), 13, 14, 16, 19, 20, 22, 23
Gulf of Oman, 192
Gurayat, 243
Gurkha, 57
Habib, Ambassdor Philip, 42
Hafr al-Batin, 23, 67, 70, 103, 112, 144, 147-148, 153, 163, 170, 242, 243, 259
Hail 123, 126, 147
Hakkair, 50
Halloran, Richard, 150
Haman, 126
Haradh, 173
HARM, 206, 257
Harpoon, 16, 18, 27, 87, 101, 145, 158, 159, 163, 200, 204-205, 218
Harrier, 21, 57, 60
Hashemite, 26
Have Quick, 194, 250
Hawar island, 115, 171, 173, 174
Hawk surface-to-air missiles, 15, 17, 26, 27, 84, 86, 114-116, 119, 120, 137-139, 143, 144, 146, 148, 152, 153, 163, 166-168, 178, 183, 184, 186, 188, 190, 203, 228, 243, 252
Hawk trainer/fighter, 15, 17, 120-121, 216, 221, 225, 228,
Hawkeye (see E-2C)
heliborne, 16, 171, 197
helicopters--general, 16, 27, 52, 53, 58, 83, 86, 87, 91, 96, 100, 101, 107, 111, 115, 120, 123, 126, 144, 145, 147, 152, 153, 155, 158-160, 163, 168, 190
helipads, 107
Heller, 123-126, 166-168

297

# Index

Hellfire, 86
Herat, 91
Hermes, 8
Hernu, Charles, 160, 215-216
Heseltine, Michael, 214
Hezbollahi, 100
Highlark, 89, 90
Hormuz, Straits of, 22, 33, 56, 118, 175
Horn of Africa, 40, 95, 124-126
HOT, 86, 113, 148, 183
House of Representatives (See U.S. Congress)
hovercraft, 27, 100, 101, 115, 146, 155, 158
HUD, 90, 201
Hunter, 26, 100, 117, 119, 120
Hussein, King of Jordan, 42, 45, 266
IBM, 250
Ibrahim, Khalid bin Abdul Aziz, 215
IDS (variant of Tornado), 17, 21, 43, 99, 132, 169, 171, 174-177, 185, 186, 193-195, 205, 253-254
IEA, 47, 50
IFCCS-1, 201
IFF (indentification of friend and foe), 25, 39, 45, 91, 98, 109, 120, 122, 134, 138, 142, 149, 151, 152, 159, 161, 170, 172, 173, 181, 189, 190, 194, 195, 204, 207, 249, 251, 258
IL-28, 104
IL-38, 93, 104, 107
Il-76, 86, 88, 187
IMF, 39, 40, 47-50
immigrants, 117
IMowhawk, 86
Improved Hawk (see Hawk), 148, 152, 166-168
India, 35, 77, 80, 85, 88, 93, 98, 104, 118, 119, 123, 126, 159, 264
Indian Ocean, 50, 53, 55, 56, 60, 93, 104, 118, 159, 264
Indonesia, 30, 34, 35, 47, 50
infiltration, 97, 116
infrastructure, 26, 27, 101, 118, 127, 128, 130-132, 189

instability (Also see stability, internal stability, and internal security), 13, 20, 109, 112, 117, 121
intercept, 89, 101, 111, 177, 181-183, 185, 187, 194, 195
interdependence, 137, 262
internal security, 27, 28, 44, 97, 104, 112-114, 116, 120, 121, 133, 134, 140, 145, 153, 155, 156, 234-239 261, 262
internal stability, 43, 116, 117, 120, 234-239
interoperability, 22, 112, 144, 147, 153, 190, 194, 221, 263, 264
Intrepid, 58
Invincible, 57
Iran, 12-16, 18-20, 22-24, 27, 28, 30, 32, 35, 36, 42, 43, 47, 50, 73-78, 80, 84, 93-95, 98-102, 108, 110, 112-122, 127, 133, 142, 144, 160, 168-170, 174, 177, 178, 181, 183, 191-193, 203, 205, 208, 210, 237, 246, 259, 261, 263, 264
Iran-Iraq, 12-14, 19, 20, 28, 30, 36, 42, 57, 73, 74, 77, 94, 99, 101, 102, 110, 119, 121, 144, 169, 181, 192, 229
Iraq, 12-14, 16, 19, 20, 22, 23, 26-28, 30, 32, 35, 36, 42, 47-51, 70, 73, 74, 76-80, 84, 88, 94, 97-102, 110, 112, 113, 115-117, 119-123, 126, 127, 132, 133, 139, 144, 160, 168-171, 174, 176, 177, 179, 181, 191, 192, 216, 218, 238, 239, 243, 246, 261-263
Ireland, 22, 32, 192
Islamic--general, 39, 41-44, 112, 114, 116, 117, 262
Ismail, former President of Yemen, 103
Israel--general, 14-16, 18-21, 24-28, 35, 41-45, 48-50, 64, 66, 74-78, 80, 83-85, 110-112, 137, 141, 144, 147, 150-152, 164, 166-171, 176, 178, 179, 184-186, 190, 191, 193, 197, 199, 201, 203, 211, 213, 214, 218, 226-229, 240-260, 261, 263-266
--Saudi threat to, 226-227, 240-260

298

# Index

Italy, 17, 32, 33, 37, 82, 84, 96, 101, 102, 129
ITOW, 86, 145
J-233, 86
Jaber, 116
Jacobs, 123, 126
Jafura, 172
Jaguar, 61, 117, 228
Jalalabad, 91
jamming, 123, 126, 185, 186
Japan, 32, 36, 39
Jerusalem, 44, 166-168
Jewish-American (See lobbying activities)
Jiddah, 67, 139, 157-159, 163, 170, 171
Joint Ministerial Committee, 105
Joint Tactical Information Distribution ( see JTIDS)
Jordan, 14, 18, 42, 43, 48-50, 74, 76-78, 80, 89, 109-111, 120, 141, 151, 170, 171, 176, 185, 213, 227, 241, 244, 246, 264, 266
JP-233, 17
JTACM, 207
JTIDS, 185, 186, 193, 194
Juaymah, 171, 174, 175, 181, 183, 200, 201, 250, 257
Jubail, 139, 157-159, 171, 174
Kabul, 91
Kanovsky, 48-50
Kar, 91, 242
KC-10, 137
KC-130, 146, 163
KC-135, 137
KC-707, 180
KE-3A, 180
Kenya, 69 109, 192
Khaimah, Ras al, 46, 50
Khalid, King, 149, 153
Khalid bin Abdul Aziz al-Ibrahim, 215
Khalifa family, 114, 115, 119
Khamis Mushayt, 103, 107, 140, 141, 144, 147, 148, 153, 161, 163, 164, 170, 178-180, 184
Kharg island, 174
Khasab, 69

Khobar, 174
Khomeini, 94, 99
Khurais, 173
Khursaniyah, 173
King Abd al-Aziz Air Force Base, 136
King Abd al-Aziz Brigade, 156
King Faisal Air Academy, 126
King Khalid City, 242
Korea, 85, 97, 105, 140
Kurds, 50
Kuwait--general, 13, 22, 23, 30, 32, 35, 36, 39-41, 46, 48-50, 56, 76, 77, 80, 94, 98, 99, 103, 109, 110, 113, 115-117, 120, 122, 126, 168, 177, 228, 229, 247, 262
--military forces and internal security, 115-117
Lajes, 68
Lambda, Project, 87, 228
LANTIRN, 206, 207, 254, 257,
Lark, 88-90
Lashkar Gah, 91
Latin America, 81, 82, 84, 132, 136, 156
Lavi, 46, 50, 86, 251, 258
Lawson, Nigel, 216
LCM, 56, 60, 158, 159
LCVP, 60, 158
Leander, 57
Lebanon, 14, 24, 42, 43, 45, 50, 54, 555, 75-77, 80, 112, 151, 176, 251
Leopard, 144, 151
Levant, 77, 78, 80, 126, 166-168, 177
Liberia, 68
Libya, 23, 30, 35, 50, 75-78, 80, 88, 97, 98, 108, 109, 112, 119, 212, 237, 247,
--threat, 112
Lightning (See F.53), 21, 26, 27, 137, 138, 146, 163, 164
Litton, 136, 224, 228
Liwa, 156
lobbying 16, 18, 83, 264 (Also see U.S. Congress).
logistics, 107, 118, 128, 138, 146, 149, 158, 159, 180, 189
London, 47, 50, 126, 179

# Index

LPD, 58
LPG, 174, 175
LSL, 58
LST, 56, 92
Lugar, Senator Richard, 213
Lupo, 87, 101, 102
Lurssen, 115, 158
Lynx, 60
M-1, 27, 50, 86, 144, 148-152, 155, 166-168, 259
M-8, 26, 158
M-6, 16, 26, 27, 117, 144, 148, 149, 158, 159, 163, 166-168
M-16, 50, 148
M-24, 26, 86
M-41, 26
M-47, 26
M-60/M-60A1, 16, 27, 117, 144, 148, 149, 166-168
M-113, 27, 148
MAB, 44, 61-67
Maddalena, 61
MAF, 61-67
Mahe, 93
maintenance, 46, 50, 85, 106, 119, 120, 129, 132, 137-140, 150, 159, 180, 184, 186, 189
Majlis, Majlis as Shura, 99, 235
Makinda, 54 124-126
Makkah, 54, 156, 171, 184
Malagasy, 98
Malaysia, 35
Mali, 42, 44, 76, 77, 80, 95, 98, 107, 109, 192
manning levels, 101, 105, 133, 134, 148, 155, 156, 158, 163, 180
manpower issues, 26, 40, 41, 46, 50, 74, 100, 102, 109, 111, 115, 117, 119, 127, 128, 133, 134, 142, 143, 146, 149, 153, 154, 156, 157, 159, 161, 168, 176, 262
Marine amphibious brigade (See MAB)
Marine amphibious division, 61-67
Marines--general, 52-53, 57-58, 60
Marine Corps (U.S.), 61-62, 65, 83, 87, 92, 93, 96, 104, 209 107, 111
Marrib-Jawf, 105

Marxism, 94, 236
Masira, 69
MAU, 50, 77, 80, 136
Mauritania, 77, 80
Maverick, 21, 146, 163, 164, 205, 241
Mayotte, 55
Mazer-E-Sharif, 91
MB-236KD, 120
MBB, 211
McFarlane, William C., 211, 213
MCV-80, 60
mechanized forces, 23, 27, 100, 117, 134, 140, 143, 145, 147, 148, 155, 156, 159
Mediterranean, 55, 61, 68, 192
Mephistos, 52
MER-10, 205-206
MER-200, 21, 165, 257
Merkava 86, 149
Mexico, 30, 34-36, 46, 47, 50
Mi-8, 92
Mi-24, 87, 91, 107
Mi-26, 107
Mi-28, 107
Mica, 86, 94, 142
MiG fighters--general, 36, 78, 79, 85-92, 99-102, 104, 107, 110, 113, 115, 117, 123-126, 139, 151, 156, 173, 175, 177, 179, 181, 184, 209
MiG-15, 89
MiG-19, 101
MiG-21, 78, 87, 91, 92, 101, 104, 107, 184, 209, 249
MiG-23, 79, 87-91, 101, 104, 107, 110, 247
MiG-25, 86, 90, 91, 101, 247
MiG-27, 90, 209
MiG-29, 78, 85, 86, 88, 90, 91, 102, 110, 123-126, 181
MiG-31, 88, 90
Mikhail, 123, 126
Milan, 52, 171
military advisors (Also see advisors), 98, 112, 134, 142
military balance, 41, 76, 92, 101, 109, 111, 123-126, 166-168

Index

military build-up, 14, 24, 28, 73-75, 111, 112, 141
Milti-Stage Improvement Program (See MSIP)
MIM-23B, 114
mine warfare, 15, 21, 27, 56, 63, 73, 81, 86, 113, 122, 126, 140, 145, 151, 154, 159, 178,
minesweepers, 27, 140, 158, 159
Ministry of Defense, 48-50, 102, 115, 126, 134, 145, 155-157
Ministry of Interior, 134, 156
minorities, 75, 94, 110, 121
Mirage fighters--general, 54, 56, 86, 87, 101, 102, 115, 119, 120, 145, 214-215, 223-224, 228, 230, 241, 253-255
Mirage F-1, 15-22, 27, 74, 79, 86-91, 99-102, 113, 115, 117, 119, 136-138, 140, 141, 145, 146, 152, 158, 162-170, 180-182, 187, 188, 192-194, 196, 264
--BQ, 101
--C/CK, 115, 119, 221-224
--E/EQ, 101, 119
Mirgage IV, 54
Mirage 2000, 54, 57, 145, 158, 214, 215, 223-224, 228, 230, 244, 253-255
Mishari, Prince Ibin Saud bin Abdul Aziz, 237
Mistral, 55
Mitterand, Francois, 160, 214-216
MM-40, 115
modernization, 26-28, 41, 104, 115, 118, 121, 127-131, 133, 137-139, 141-149, 152, 154, 157, 160, 161, 165, 168, 169, 171, 176, 177, 180, 192, 193
Mogadishu, 69
Mohammed Al-Saud Brigade, 155, 156
Moi, 69, 75, 99, 101
Mombassa, 69
Monrovia, 68
Morocco, 45, 64, 68, 76, 77, 80, 98, 120
mountain, 42, 100, 178, 179, 184

Mozambique, 98
MRL, 86, 111, 148, 258
MRLS, 258
MSIP, 20, 21, 90, 101, 102, 165, 197-198, 200, 202, 206, 208, 251-252, 255, 258,
Muhammad, Ali Nasr, 104
munitions, 17, 21-23, 86, 88-90, 95, 102, 127, 142, 146, 163-165, 168, 178, 179, 181, 183, 188, 191-193
Murphy, Richard, 211
Musandem Peninsula, 69
Mutair tribe, 156
MW-1, 221
NADGE, 87
Naif, 156
Naseeb, 126
Nasr, 103-105
Nasser, 28, 41, 236-237
National Guard, (Also see Saudi National Guard), 22, 26, 27, 41, 74, 127, 133, 134, 139, 144, 147, 150, 153-156, 166-168, 190
Nationalist Movement, 236
native manpower and citizenship, 12, 33, 37, 94, 98, 105, 112, 114, 116, 119, 133, 175, 176, 178, 192
NATO, 14, 21, 28, 54, 62, 63, 78, 81, 84-87, 90, 161, 178, 185, 186, 193
natural gas, 173-175, 181
naval issues--general, 16, 19, 23, 27, 78, 87, 92, 93, 95, 99, 102-104, 107, 114-116, 119, 120, 122, 124-126, 135, 137, 139, 140, 142, 146, 157-161, 165, 169, 192, 262, 264
Navasseur, 68
naval forces, 15, 27, 28, 40, 53-66, 69 78, 92, 93, 100, 101, 107, 111, 114, 115, 118-120, 122, 127, 137, 139, 140, 145-147, 154, 157-161, 190, 192, 194, 195, 263
NCOs, 118, 147
Netherlands, 32, 37
Neutral Zone, 35, 36, 177
New York Times, 150
Nigeria 30, 34, 35, 47, 50, 98
Nimatallah, 48-50

# Index

Nimeiri, 108
Nimrod, 61, 248
Nizwa, 25
NORAD, 190
North Korea, 97
North Yemen, Also see YAR, 41, 42, 76, 77, 95, 97, 98, 104-106, 109
--internal security and military forces, 103-107
Northrop (Also see F-20), 138
Norway, 32, 35
"notch", 242-244, 251
nuclear power, 12
Nuhayyan, 121
OAPEC, 48-50
OECD, 31-33, 37, 39, 47, 50, 81
Oerlikon, 183
OF-40, 120
officer readiness and capability, 22, 88, 90, 117-119, 137
offset, 1988-191
offshore 33, 114, 171, 172, 175, 177, 181
oil--general, 12-14, 16, 20, 23-25, 27-40, 42, 45-50, 74, 75, 78, 79, 92, 94, 99, 101, 102, 105, 106, 108, 114-116, 118-123, 126, 131, 132, 134, 142, 143, 148-150, 152, 155, 156, 160, 168-178, 181, 182, 184, 190-192
oil embargo, 12, 27, 28
oil exploration, 34, 46, 50, 106
oil facilities, 23, 116, 152, 168-174, 177, 178, 184, 252
oil glut, 12, 13, 29, 36, 46, 47, 50, 102
oil prices, 14, 24
oil reserves and revenues, 12, 13, 23, 31, 33, 35, 36, 46, 50, 94, 118, 122
oil-loading, 169, 172, 174
Ojjeh, Akram, 215
Oman--general, 13, 14, 22, 23, 25, 35, 36, 40, 41, 46, 50, 76-78, 80, 103, 104, 113, 117-119, 122, 126, 129, 159, 177, 192, 208, 228-229, 262, 263

--military forces and interal security, 117-119
--Omanization 118
OPEC, 28, 30, 31, 34, 36-39, 46, 48-50, 81, 102, 132
Osama, 48-50
Osirak, 179
Otaiba tribe, 156
out of area forces, 50-73
over-the-horizon reinforcements (Also see out of area and USCENTCOM), 15, 22, 191, 192, 220, 240 262, 263
overflights, Israeli of Saudi Arabia, 20, 242-243
P-3F, 100
Pacific, 35, 104, 136
PAH-2, 87
Pakistan--general, 42, 77, 80, 94, 115, 119, 120, 133, 140, 141, 143, 144, 155, 157, 192, 242
--training and support of Saudi Arabia, 132, 139-141, 242
Pakistani training "brigade", 139-141, 242
Palestinian 14, 24-25, 41-45, 50, 117, 237
Panavia (Also see ADV, ISD, and Tornado), 17
Panhard, 26, 52, 55, 148
paramilitary forces, 104, 107, 133, 154
paratroops, 51-52, 55, 57, 60, 141, 143, 148
Paris, 47, 50, 129, 176
Patriot, 86, 258
Paveway, 86
PC-9 (Also see Pilatus), 17, 163, 216, 228
PDRY (Also see South Yemen, 20, 23, 26, 42, 73, 78, 80, 93, 95, 103-106, 108, 112, 119, 144
--military forces, 103-106
--internal stability, 103-106
peace issues, 41-45, 84, 85, 87, 101, 137-139, 142, 143, 146, 150-152, 181, 182, 188-190, 193, 195, 265, 266

# Index

Peace Hawk, 138, 188
Peace Sentinel, 137
peace settlement, 14, 16, 24, 43, 45, 84, 255, 265, 266
Peace Shield, 87, 137, 139, 142, 143, 146, 152, 188-190, 193, 195
Peace Sun, 138
petroleum (Also see oil), 30, 32, 33, 36, 46, 47, 50, 123, 126, 172-175
Petroline, 176, 177
PFLOAG, 114
Phoenix, 86
Pilatus (Also see PC-9), 17, 163, 216
pilgrims, 108
pilots, 26, 88, 117, 182
PLO, 26, 28, 33, 34, 42, 43, 45, 46, 50, 73, 74, 85, 89-91, 93, 95, 103, 106, 107, 114, 115, 119, 120, 122, 123, 126, 140, 141, 143-147, 149, 152-154, 157, 159, 163, 164, 168, 170, 175, 178-181, 183, 184, 186, 187, 192, 212-213 262, 263, 266
PLSS, 257
Poindexter, Admiral John A., 219
police, 97, 104
politicization, 117-119, 121, 145
population, 13, 43, 94, 114, 116-121, 133, 134, 168-171, 174
Portugal 32, 68
post-Assad 110
power projection--general, 12, 15, 19, 21-23, 50-74, 191,-193, 210-214, 220-214, 262, 263
--overall capabilities of West, 21-24, 62-74, 191-193, 263
--British capabilities, 56-60
--French capabilities, 51-55
--Turkish capabilities, 50-51
--U.S. capabilities, 21-25, 50-51, 61-73, 191-192, 239-240, 263
PRC (People's Republic of China) 34, 46, 50, 80, 82, 97, 99, 129
prepositioning, 63 140, 143, 148, 150-151
President Carter (Also see Carter, Jimmy), 44, 169

President Reagan, (Also see Reagan) 16, 18, 45, 150, 151
pro-Israel (Also see lobbying), 18, 83, 264
Python, 86
Qabus, Sultan, 25, 119
Qaddafi, Moammar, 43
Qaisumah, 176
Qandahar, 91
Qatar--general, 13, 30, 32, 35, 36, 40, 41, 46, 50, 76, 77, 80, 99, 113, 115, 119, 120, 122, 177, 262
--military forces and internal security, 119-120
Qatari, 115, 119
Qatif, 157, 158, 173
Quarayyah, 173
R-27, 89
R-31, 90
Rabin, Yitzhak, 211
Racal, 155
radar, 56, 86, 88-91, 137, 152, 159, 163, 165, 172, 178-180, 182-190, 200, 205-207, 223-224, 228, 246, 249, 255, 257
radical movements and trends, 14, 16, 17, 19, 23, 24, 28, 37, 41-43, 45, 74, 75, 78, 93-95, 101, 104, 105, 108-110, 112, 113, 116, 119, 121, 122, 137, 142, 186, 261, 263, 264
radicalism, 24, 41, 43, 75, 104, 110, 119, 121, 238, 240
Rafha, 242
Raphael, 124-126
Rapid Action Force (See FAR)
Rapier, 51, 59, 60, 228
Ras Banas, 68
Ras Tanura, 157, 158, 171-175, 181-183
Rashid, Sheikl, 121
Raytheon, 136, 166-168
Reagan--general, 16-18, 45, 150, 151, 169
rebel, 25, 41, 107, 118
reconnaissance, 56, 73, 86, 93, 101, 111 118, 146, 163

303

# Index

Red Sea, 14, 16, 19, 20, 22, 23, 29, 73, 77, 78, 80, 88, 90, 93, 103, 104, 107-109, 112, 122, 126, 127, 145, 147, 157, 164, 170, 174, 176, 177, 182, 186, 190, 203, 205-206, 208, 226, 229, 242, 244, 261, 263
Redeye, 51, 148
refineries, 29, 114, 174-176
refueling, 88, 103, 146, 164, 165, 170, 185, 187, 190, 192-194
religious issues, 13, 24, 41, 44, 75, 99, 101, 109, 114, 121, 126
remittances, 104, 105
Reunion, 53
RF-4E, 100
RF-5E, 146, 163
Riyadh, 67 103, 137, 147, 148, 155, 156, 158, 159, 163, 170, 171, 184, 188, 190
Rota, 88, 152, 158, 183
Royal Family (Saudi), 215, 235-238, 239
RPG-9, 171
RPVs, 86
RSAF (Also see Saudi Air Force), 163, 180, 182, 194
Ruwaihi, Major General Naseeb bin Haman Bin Sultan, 126
Rwanda, 98
RWR, 200
SA-3, 89, 158
SA-5, 89, 110
SA-6, 89
SA-8, 89, 123-126
SA-9, 88, 89
SA-10, 86, 89
SA-11, 89, 123-126
SA-12, 86, 89
SA-13, 89, 110, 123-126
SA-14, 86, 123-126
Saar, 87
al-Sabah familiy, 116, 117
al-Sabah, Shiek Jabar al-Ahmed, 116
sabotage, 172, 173, 176
SACEUR, 54
SACLANT, 54
Sadada, 242

Sadat, Anwar, 43
Safaniya, 171
Saffron, 126
Sagaie, 52
Said, Wafiq, 215
Saleh, 105, 106
SAMA, 46, 48-50
Sanaa, 105
sandstorms, 172
Sao Tome, 98
SARH, 88
Saudi Amoudi Group, 189
Saudi Arabia--general, 13-33, 35-50, 52-69 73-80, 85, 87, 90, 93-95, 97-99, 101-116, 119-122, 126-196, 261-266
--aid and capital, 29-40
--Air Defense Corps 139, 143, 147-152, 166-168, 203, 252
--Air Defense Enhancement Package, 179-185, 188, 191-196
--Air Force, 16-17, 19-22, 27, 41, 62-70, 73, 79, 87, 99, 103, 137, 138, 145-152, 161--171, 176, 177, 181, 183, 193, 194, 196-224, 239-261
--Army, 16, 138, 140, 144, 147-153, 184, 189, 190
--defense expenditures, 126-132
--F-15 package, 196-207
--Jordanian relations, 136-140
--military industry and offsets, 141-142
--military manpower, 132-133
--military modernization, 147-152
--National Guard, 26-27, 41, 43, 74, 100, 116, 120, 127, 128, 133, 134, 139, 140, 143-145, 147, 148, 150, 153-158, 166-168, 177, 190
--Naval Expansion Plan (SNEP) 138-139, 159-160
--Navy, 27, 41 139, 157-161, 190
--oil, 29-36
--stability, 234-240
--threat to Israel, 226-227, 240-258
--vulnerability, 169-179, 220, 234-239, 241-260
Saudi Communist Party, 236
Saudiization, 138, 189

304

# Index

Sawari (Mast) I & II, 133-141, 157-160
SCADA, 173
SCC, 178
Schmitt, Helmut, 47, 50
Schrage, 123, 126
Scud, 104, 112
SCUD-B, 104
SDRs, 39, 40
Sea Cat, 60
Sea Dart, 60
Sea Eagle, 221
Sea King, 57-58
sealift--see strategic lift
secure communications, 86, 185, 194-195
Seeb, 69, 126
Seek Igloo, 190, 228
Seek Talk, 193, 250
Senate Foreign Relations Committee (Also see U.S. Congress), 211, 213
Serden Band, 91 91
Seychelles, 69, 93
SH-3, 163
Shah of Iran, 12, 14, 28, 30, 78, 99, 101, 139, 142, 143, 148, 152, 168, 169, 177, 181, 183, 188-190
Shahine, 139, 143, 148, 152, 183, 188-190, 203, 228, 252
shamal, 172
Sharjah, 35, 46, 50, 119, 121
Sharurah, 69 103, 107, 140, 144, 147, 148, 151, 153, 163, 170, 183, 184
Shedgum, 174, 176
Sheik Jaber al-ahmed Al Sabah (see Sabah)
Shell, 216
shelter facilities, 130, 147, 161, 178
Shemuel, 48-50
Shi'ite, 24, 75, 99, 114, 117, 119-121, 239
Shindand, 91
shipping, 50, 99, 122, 176, 263
Shiraz, 181
Shobokshi, Ali and Fahd, 236
Shuaib Al Batin, 113
Shuf, 42, 105

Sidon, 176
Sierra Leone, 98
SIGINT (See ELINT/ECM/ESM)
Sigonella, 61
Sinai, 43, 44
Singapore, 85
Sixth Fleet, 61-67
Skua, 87
Skyflash, 17
Skyguard, 120
SLEP (Service Life Extension Program), 58
Slimane, 68
Socialist Labor Party, 236
Socotra, 104
software issues, 165, 180, 186, 187, 189, 193-195
Somalia, 42, 76, 77, 80, 95, 107, 109, 192
Souk al-Manakh, 117
South Korea, 85, 105, 140
South Yemen (Also see PDRY), 15, 26, 41, 76, 77, 93, 95, 98, 103-105, 109, 118, 119, 160, 183, 184
Southern Gulf, 13-15, 23, 73, 84, 99, 102, 177, 193, 262, 265
Southwest Asia, 14, 17, 63, 79, 81, 85, 118, 229, 261, 264, 265
Soviet--general (Also see USSR), 12-14, 20, 28, 37, 41, 42, 44, 74, 78, 79, 81-95, 97, 98, 101, 102, 104, 106-108, 110-112, 116, 123-126, 149, 150, 181, 184, 187, 261, 262, 264
--advisors, 95-98
--arms sales, 74-84, 85-91, 95-97
--backed movements, 41, 93, 150
--military capability, 91-95, 209
--YAR relations, 106
Soviet bloc, 13, 20, 74, 97, 98, 104, 264
Spain, 32, 64, 69
Sparrow ( Aslo see AIM-7), 165, 182, 187
SPM, 175
SS-11, 148
SS-21, 85, 110

305

# Index

SS-22, 87
SS-23, 87, 123-126
standardization, 22, 112, 144, 147, 150, 151, 263, 264
Stinger, 15, 18, 86, 116, 139, 141, 148, 152, 203-204, 228, 258
Stinger-POST, 86, 204, 248
Straits of Hormuz 22, 33, 118
strategic axis, 171
strategic lift, 53, 61, 63, 65-66
Strikemasters (Also see BAC-167), 17, 26, 117
STUFT (Ships Taken Up From Trade), 58
Styx, 101
Su-7, 89, 100
Su-17, 91
Su-20, 100, 101, 104, 184
Su-22, 88, 89
Su-24, 88-90, 123, 126, 181
Su-25, 89, 91
Su-27, 86, 88, 90, 91, 181
SU AWACS, 86
submarine, 83, 87, 92, 93, 96, 104, 107, 111, 159, 160
submunitions, 86, 146, 258
subversion, 105, 112, 113
Sudairi family, 234-238
Sudan, 20, 42, 74-78, 80, 95, 98, 107-109, 112
Suez Canal, 68 109
Sukhoi (Also see Su), 89
Sultan, Prince Abdul Aziz, 25, 118, 119, 121, 126, 151, 160
Summan, 178
Sunni, 110, 114, 117
Super Etendard, 53-55
surface-to-air weapons--general, 15, 18, 26, 52, 59, 60, 82, 86, 96, 110, 116, 139, 141, 148, 158, 177, 178, 183, 188, 190
surface-to-surface weapons--general, 87, 158, 159
surveillance (Also see reconnaissance), 113, 114, 159, 160, 163, 179, 184, 189, 190
survivability, 27, 106, 124-126, 179

SUU-65, 86
Suwaihan, 120
Sweden, 32, 228
Switzerland, 17, 32, 216, 228
synthetic fuels, 33, 37
Syria--general, 14, 19, 24, 35, 39, 42, 43, 45, 48-52, 74-80, 85, 88, 89, 97, 98, 108-112, 116, 123-126, 132, 133, 141, 144, 151, 164, 168, 170, 171, 176, 213, 226, 238, 241, 243, 247, 251, 260, 264, 266
--threat to Saudi Arabia, 110
T-33A, 26
T-55, 107, 163
T-62, 106, 149
T-67, 115
T-72, 120, 259
T-79, 119
T-80, 86, 258
T-shaped jetty, 174
TA-4KU, 115
Tabuk, 21, 67, 103, 107, 133, 140, 141, 144, 147, 148, 153, 163, 164, 170, 176, 178, 225, 242-244, 251-253, 259
TACAN, 201
TADIL, 188, 194
Tadiran, 246
Taif, 67, 147, 163, 164, 170, 171, 179, 180
Taiwan, 85
"taking sides", 16, 17, 19, 265
Tamari, 123-126, 166-168
tangential fuel tanks, 21, 165, 257
tankers, 27, 87, 102, 124-126, 146, 163, 164, 174-177, 180, 193
Tanura-Juaymah-Dharhan, 183
Tanzania, 98
Tapline pipeline, 175, 176
target and targeting, 43, 45, 46, 50, 73, 75, 86, 89, 90, 102, 103, 116, ·146, 163, 171-178, 182-185, 193
Tarut Bay, 174
Tawila, 120
technicians and technocrats, 98, 106, 110, 112, 117, 118, 121, 127, 133, 134, 137, 147, 185

# Index

technology transfer, 17, 85-87, 185-187, 257, 258
Tehran, 182
Tel Aviv, 123-126, 166-168
telecommunications, 143, 189, 193
temperature, 149, 172, 183
terrain, 90, 107, 171, 172, 178, 184, 185
terrorism, 18, 24, 41. 50, 113, 116, 134, 145, 154-156, 171, 190, 205 262
TEWS, 200, 206
TF-70, 192
TF33-PW-100A, 194
al-Thani family, 119-221
Thaqib, 189, 190
Thatcher, Marget, 213, 214-217
Thomson, CSF, 228-229
threats and threat capabilities, 13-17, 19, 20, 22-24, 28, 40, 43, 73-75, 78, 79, 87-95, 98, 99, 101-106, 108-110, 112, 113, 115-118, 120, 122-127, 132, 133, 141, 144, 154, 157, 164, 168-170, 175, 180-183, 185, 191-193, 261-265
Thumrait, 118
Tornado (Also see ADV and IDS), 15, 17, 19, 21, 74, 79, 82, 85-87, 90, 91, 117, 118, 137, 146, 162-165, 170, 181, 190, 191, 194, 195, 205, 213-217, 221-229, 244,-253, 255, 258, 260
TR-155, 52
training, 17, 21, 22, 27, 40, 104, 107, 115, 117-119, 127-128, 130, 131, 133, 135-141, 144, 145, 147, 149, 150, 152, 153, 155, 159-161, 163, 164, 170, 180, 186, 189, 192, 195
Transall (see C-160)
Transcaucasus, 92
Transpeninsular pipeline, 174
transponders, 190, 194
tribal issues, 106, 154-156, 155, 156
Tripartite Alliance, 108
Trucial States, 25
Tu-22, 100, 209
Tu-26, 209
Tu-95, 209
Tunisia, 76, 77, 80
Turkestan, 92
Turkey--general, 14, 21-23, 32, 61, 63-64, 68-70, 76-78, 80, 144, 192, 206
--role in power projection, 50-51, 61, 63-64, 68-70, 208
Turki, Pince, 133, 141, 144
Tyumen, 94
U.K.--general (Also see Britain), 32, 82, 84, 96, 103, 119, 129, 139, 164
U.S. (United States), 12, 14-28, 30, 32, 33, 35-50, 73, 75, 77, 81-85, 89, 90, 93, 95-97, 99, 102, 106, 108, 116-120, 122, 123, 126-153, 157-161, 163-165, 169, 177, 179-181, 184-195, 261-266
--advisory activities, 25-29, 133-142, 169-178, 193-200
--basing problems and issues, 21-22, 62-74, 191-193, 239-240, 263
--impact of domestic politics on Middle East policy, 15-19, 193-198, 210-213, 217-220, 225-226, 261-263
--power projection capabilities, 21-25, 61-73, 191-192, 239-240, 263
--relations with Saudi Arabia, 15-28, 169-187, 193-200, 207-213, 217-233, 239-252, 261-267
--restrictions on technology, 255-259
U.S. Air Force, 20, 137, 169, 179, 180, 184-186, 188-190, 192-194
U.S. Central Command (see USCENTCOM)
U.S. Congress, 15-18, 47, 50, 83, 84, 96, 123, 126, 150, 166-168, 188, 196-197, 201, 210-214, 217, 220, 226-230, 263-265
U.S. Corps of Engineers, 26-27, 128-130, 136-137, 139
U.S. Department of Commerce, 38, 45, 47, 50
U.S. Department of Defense, 50, 62, 98, 123-126, 131, 180, 196, 212, 264
U.S. Department of Energy, 33, 36, 46, 47, 50, 87, 93, 94, 99, 104-106, 108, 112, 114, 116, 119, 120, 122, 132,

## Index

138-140, 142, 156, 157, 164-168, 170, 177, 182, 261, 265
U.S. Department of State, 196, 212
U.S. General Accounitng Office, 218
UAE (United Arab Emitrates), 30, 32, 35, 36, 40, 41, 46, 50, 76, 77, 80, 103, 113, 117, 120-122, 168, 229, 262
--armed forces and internal security, 120-121
Uganda, 109
UH-60 (Also see Blackhawk), 16
UNFICYP, 60
UNIFIL, 55
United Arab Emirates (See UAE)
United Kingdom (see Britain and U.K.)
UR-416, 51
urbanization, 156, 171, 177
USCENTCOM, 12, 22, 23, 28, 53, 61-64, 67-71, 93, 113, 122, 132, 137, 144, 149-151, 153, 157, 161, 190, 208, 227, 229-230, 262-264
USGS (U.S. Geological Service), 33, 46, 50
USSR--general (Also see Soviet), 13, 19, 22, 33, 35, 41-43, 46, 50, 74, 75, 78, 80, 82, 84, 85, 90, 93-97, 101, 102, 104-107, 109, 110, 112, 119, 121-123, 126, 129, 137, 203-204, 208-209, 229, 263
Uthmaniyah, 174
V-150, 144, 145, 155
VAB, 102, 185, 192
VC-10, 61
Venezuela, 30, 35, 36, 47, 50
Vietnam, 82, 97
Vinnel Corporation, 27, 136, 140
vulnerabilities--general, 28, 36, 42, 85, 109, 112-113, 121, 168, 171, 175-177, 179, 184, 186, 192-193, 265
Wadiah, 26
Walsh, Robin, 126
Waribah, 116
Warsaw Pact, 28, 78, 81, 84, 85, 89, 90, 110, 185
Washington, 46-50, 80, 84, 122-126, 128, 129, 131, 166-168, 196

Washington Post, 219
water-injection, 172
Watts, Lt. General Jon, 125
weather, 88, 90, 172
Weinberger, Caspar W. 211-214
Wessex, 58
West Germany (Also see FRG), 33, 37, 82, 151
Westinghouse, 136, 189
Westland, 58-60
Yanbu, 157, 158, 171, 174-177
YAR (Also see North Yemen), 20, 73, 80, 95, 103-106, 114
--armed forces and internal stability, 103-107
Yemens--general, 15, 16, 20, 26, 41, 42, 74-78, 89, 93, 95, 97, 98, 103-107, 109, 118, 119, 133, 160, 170, 171, 183, 184, 190
Yominco, 105
youth issues, 114, 117, 119, 121
Zaire, 109
Zambia, 98
Zayid, Shiek bin Sultan al Nuhayyan, 121
ZSU-23-4, 89